One,
Catholic,
and
Apostolic

One, Catholic, and Apostolic

SAMUEL SEABURY AND THE EARLY EPISCOPAL CHURCH

PAUL VICTOR MARSHALL

CHURCH PUBLISHING
New York

Cataloging-in-Publication Data for this title is available from
the Library of Congress.

ISBN 0-89869-424-8 (cloth)
ISBN 0-89869-447-7 (paper)

Church Publishing Incorporated
445 Fifth Avenue
New York, NY 10016
www.churchpublishing.org

5 4 3 2 1

In Memoriam
Ronald Frederick Marshall
1950–1995

nunc tamen interea haec prisco quae more parentum
tradita sunt tristi munera ad inferas
accipe fraterno multum manantia fletu
atque in perpetuum frater ave atque vale.

CONTENTS

Appendix (on CD-ROM)

PREFACE

My assumption when planning a companion volume to *Anglican Liturgy in America: Prayer Book Parallels* was that attention would need to center on what were at the time the relatively uncharted waters of the 1892 and 1928 prayer book revisions. From there, the projected work would have gone on to a summary and interpretation of the mass of material related to the Episcopal Church's most complicated revision process, that of 1979. A further assumption was that because the 1789 revision and its creators had been the subject of a number of studies, the task regarding that revision would be one of simple summarization.

All of these assumptions proved to be essentially wrong. Much of the news was good, however. In the first place, Lesley Northup has published her study of the 1892 revision. There she situates the revision process in its historical and theological context, and also explains the revision process itself as a cultural phenomenon. In the second place, the 1979 book has received a good deal of attention. Its eucharistic rite is the central focus of Thaddäus Schnitker's *The Church's Worship*. The initiatory rites and their complicated development have been given careful attention by Ruth A. Meyers. Finally, the 1979 revision process itself is examined in Michael Moriarty's work.[1]

Two surprises of a different kind have had a part in reshaping my plans. The first was that in comparing the findings of some contemporary writers on the first American prayer book revisions against the source documents, I came to conclusions that were sometimes quite different from theirs. Thus what was anticipated to be the smallest section of a book of very modest length has become a volume of its own. The second surprise regarded the 1928 book, which turned out to have been planned as an

---

1. Lesley A. Northup, *The 1892 Book of Common Prayer* (Lewiston, N.Y.: E. Mellen Press, 1993); Thaddäus Schnitker, *The Church's Worship: The 1979 American Book of Common Prayer in a Historical Perspective* (New York: Peter Lang, 1989); Ruth Meyers, *Re-Visioning Baptism in the Episcopal Church* (New York: Church Publishing Incorporated, 1997); Michael Moriarty, *The Liturgical Revolution* (New York: Church Publishing Incorporated, 1997).

astonishingly radical revision through much of the process. The deliberate destruction of most of the committee records of the 1928 revision leaves us with tantalizing questions as to how such a conservative revision finally came to be when the various *Reports* of the revisers promised an advanced liturgy.

The consequence of these discoveries is that a separate work needs to be devoted to Bishop Seabury and the liturgical and constitutional crises of 1784 through 1790, and that the other revisions receive treatment later. This brought a final surprise: There emerged a great deal to admire about an unpopular person whose politics and liturgical theology many have portrayed as unhelpful, eccentric, or dangerous. Seabury's piety is not compartmentalized; it combines with his integrity, learning, gentle persistence, and total commitment to his office in a way that commands respect. Bishop White could not, it sometimes seems, write a simple declarative sentence, and White sometimes seems to have no unqualified thoughts, no way of expressing himself without multiple circumlocutions. Seabury's prose is direct and powerful. Of our characters here, only the elder William Smith makes equally interesting reading. His florid prose is very different from Seabury's, but the poet in him serves his point rather than distracting from it.

The convention in referring to American prayer books has generally been to use the date of their adoption by General Convention; thus we speak of the 1892, 1928, and 1979 prayer books, regardless of the year of actual publication or the official date of use. For consistency's sake, I refer to the first two books, 1785 and 1789, according to the year of their adoption by General Convention as well, rather than by the year of their publication. The reader may find them referred to as 1786 or 1790, respectively, in some other studies, particularly as the former work was still being created in 1786, months after its adoption in principle at the 1785 convention. Following well-established custom, the 1785 book is usually referred to as "the Proposed Book."

In the eighteenth century the orthography of the English language had not yet achieved the rigidity we know today. Rather than distract the reader, I have corrected or conformed many variant spellings without comment or annoying overuse of *sic,* and have spelled out idiosyncratic or obsolete abbreviations in the manuscripts. This is precisely what would have happened had those manuscripts found their way to a printer in their own time. Where spellings of surnames vary, I have followed the spelling usually employed by the person referred to. I have indulged myself in the (strictly speaking) anachronistic use of the term "Anglican" for the sake of brevity and variety, and have occasionally had to use the unfortunate terms "Churchman" and "Churchmen" when the context required it. Bishop William White followed what was then the already-obsolete practice of writing a *y* (for the thorn) to express the initial *th* sound ("ye" for "the," "yat" for "that," etc.), and most of these have been modernized as well. When necessary for clarity, spelling and punctuation have been modernized in quoting prayer books prior to that of 1662. Whenever possible, I cite published texts of correspondence and manuscripts, as the reader is more likely to have access to these sources, and because the readers will quickly detect in lengthy quotations an encouragement to encounter these proto-Episcopalians directly. Manuscripts critical to the determination of disputed points are cited to their archival source, as well as their published sources, if any. Some of the most critical for the case to be made here are reproduced in the appendices.

Over the last three centuries, formal liturgical studies have been primarily concerned with the evolution of texts, for good reason. On that foundation scholars have been able to ask more complex questions. The present work is undertaken in the belief that circumstances and processes count as much as texts in understanding the development of Christian liturgy, and that consideration of these factors is a basic and essential task in historical treatments of the liturgy.[2] Certainly texts outlive the circumstances of their origin. This is both their strength and their limitation. They provide a snapshot of what the church expressed at given moments. Unless one appreciates both the chaos from which they arose and their ever-evolving function as they live on, any understanding of them remains solipsistic or quaintly antiquarian.

To illustrate this point, we can move away from liturgy to consider what may fairly be called one of Anglicanism's most sacred cows, the patristic era. It should be clear to us that the behavior of saints, doctors, and councils was as complex as that of any modern figures, no matter how strong might be the temptation to imagine the ancients working away quietly under the direct guidance of the Holy Spirit with no other concerns. For instance, in considering his efforts against Nestorianism, one

---

2. A compelling statement of a similar position is that of Lesley A. Northup, "Public Response and Nineteenth-Century Prayer Book Revision," *Anglican and Episcopal History* 64 (June 1995): 173f.

can only admire Cyril of Alexandria's precise writing, careful thought, accuracy, and skillful reasoning. It would be tempting to assume that his writings, prayers, and pious example were his only tools for advancing his cause, and that the Council of Ephesus (431) stands as a monument to his brilliant defense of orthodox Christology and the status of the Virgin as *Theotokos.*

Things begin to look a bit different when one discovers Cyril's love of intense logomachy against everyone holding views contrary to his. Even less attractive is his possible complicity in the murder of the philosopher Hypatia, who in any event certainly was killed by Cyril's followers.[3] Things look very different indeed when one reads the list of bribes Cyril sent to members of the imperial court and to their servants about the time of the council, "to persuade him that he should think in our favor," or to "persuade Scholasticius that he desist from friendships with our adversaries," and so on through the list of thirteen hefty *eulogiae.* Letter 96 details bribes amounting to one-third of a ton of gold (about nine hundred of his twelve-ounce *libra*), along with much furniture, assorted dry goods, household implements, and twenty ostriches.[4] Certainly there is no point in anyone's becoming scandalized over what may have been quite routine fifth-century corruption, and nothing can diminish Cyril's magnificent talent, but the tale is rehearsed here because it reminds us to be less romantic about the past, and more aware of the many influences that are brought to bear on even the highest of assizes.

This is not to say that the council's decision should be jettisoned because the context in which its decisions arose was very complex and sometimes unethical. I have cited this somewhat lurid case to underscore the variety of ingredients and actions that underlie decisions taken in any group. From the historian's point of view, this is part of getting to the bottom of things. For the rest of us, it is a reminder not to assume that texts or resolutions simply and gently dropped from heaven. We have always to deal with artifacts.

---

3. Hypatia's story is also quite complicated. See Maria Dzielska, *Hypatia of Alexandria* (Cambridge: Harvard University Press, 1995).

4. Cyril of Alexandria, Letter 96, John I. McEnerney, trans., *The Fathers of the Church: St. Cyril of Alexandria, Letters* (Washington, D.C.: Catholic University of America, 1987), 2:151–53. It is possible that the "ostriches" were a kind of furniture. Two hundred of the nine hundred pounds were for a bribe that Cyril orders to be delivered only after the recipient performed, suggesting that the court was characterized by more than one level of corruption.

The present case is no different. Certainly more than one motive was behind the reaction of some southern clergy to Bishop Seabury's consecration and liturgical ideas, and our endeavor is to understand how the deeds springing from those motives had effect on the constitution and liturgical life of the early Episcopal Church. Similar questions naturally arise with each successive prayer book revision. Every prayer book of the American Church is the product of compromise and forbearance.

Thanks are due to many people for their help with this book. First must come acknowledgment of the contribution of Fr. Kenneth W. Cameron, who for decades collected and published essential documents, indices, and calendars of documents in that amazing periodical of his founding, *The Historiographer,* and in the collections he published through his private press, Transcendental Books. When one considers that his work was done before the age of computers or scanners, gratitude is supplemented by no small measure of awe.[5]

I have also been assisted by generous staff members of the Archives of the Episcopal Church, the Archives of the Diocese of Connecticut, and the libraries of The General Theological Seminary, The Episcopal Divinity School, and Yale University. I was assisted by the insight and advice of colleagues and mentors, especially Professors Robert Henery of Nashotah House, Bruce Mullin of General Seminary, and James Turrell of The University of the South. I am also indebted to Fr. Howard Stringfellow, Canon Robert Carroon, Canon Jane Teter, and the eminent historiographer of the Episcopal Church Canon J. Robert Wright.

Some of the early work on this project was completed with the deeply appreciated assistance of grants from the Association of Theological Schools and the Board for Theological Education of the Episcopal Church.

This volume has been delayed by two very tragic events in my family and by an extraordinary — almost Dickensian — number of smaller difficulties. Just when every path seemed clear, additional years of delay resulted from my own transition from professor to diocesan bishop,

---

5. Cameron's corpus includes among its Seabury-related titles *Early Anglicanism in Connecticut* (1962), *The Anglican Episcopate in Connecticut 1784–1899* (1970), *The Church of England in Pre-Revolutionary Connecticut* (1976), *The Papers of Loyalist Samuel Peters* (1978), *Samuel Seabury's Ungathered Imprints* (1978), *Samuel Seabury among His Contemporaries* (1980), *The Episcopal Church in Connecticut and New England* (1981), *The Ethos of Anglicanism in Colonial New England and New York* (1981), *Seabury Traditions* in two volumes (1983), *Colonial Anglicanism in New England* (1984), *The Correspondence of Samuel Parker* (1984), *Connecticut's First Diocesan* (1985), and *Anglican Experience in Revolutionary Connecticut* (1987).

where if nothing else, I formed an appreciation for the steep learning curve that faced Seabury and White in their early episcopates. I thus am doubly grateful for the support and encouragement given me by friends and former colleagues, and for the catalytic action of a seminary professor who told one of my postulants that Seabury was so coarse and offensive a man that a refined and virtuous Samuel Provoost could not subject himself to meet him, much less have conversation with him.

                                                                       +PM

Bethlehem of Pennsylvania
November 14, 2002

KEY TO ABBREVIATIONS
IN THE NOTES

Anglican Episcopate
> Kenneth Walter Cameron, ed. *The Anglican Episcopate in Connecticut (1784–1899).* Hartford, Conn.: Transcendental Books, 1970.

Anglican Experience
> Kenneth Walter Cameron, ed. *Anglican Experience in Revolutionary Connecticut and Areas Adjacent.* Hartford, Conn.: Transcendental Books, 1987.

Beardsley
> E. Edwards Beardsley. *Life and Correspondence of the Right Reverend Samuel Seabury, D.D., First Bishop of Connecticut, and of the Episcopal Church in the United States of America.* Boston: Houghton, Mifflin, 1881.

Berens
> John F. Berens. " 'A God of Order and Not of Confusion': The American Loyalists and Divine Providence, 1774–1783." *Historical Magazine of the Protestant Episcopal Church* 47 (1978): 197–219.

Brett
> Thomas Brett. *A Collection of the Principal Liturgies, Used by the Christian Church ... With a Dissertation upon them ...* London, 1720.

BrettDis
> "Dissertation" in Brett, *Collection.*

Bridenbaugh
> Carl Bridenbaugh. *Mitre and Sceptre: Transatlantic Faiths, Ideas, Personalities, and Politics.* New York: Oxford University Press, 1962.

Buxbaum
> Melvin H. Buxbaum. "Benjamin Franklin and William Smith, Their School and Their Dispute." *Historical Magazine of the Protestant Episcopal Church* 39 (1970): 361–82.

Buxton
> Richard F. Buxton. *Eucharist and Institution Narrative: A Study in the Roman and Anglican Traditions of the Consecration of the Eucharist from the Eighth to the Twentieth Centuries.* Alcuin Club Collections 58. Great Wakering, U.K.: Mayhew-McCrimmon, 1976.

Calcote
> A. Dean Calcote. "The Proposed Prayer Book of 1785." *Historical Magazine of the Protestant Episcopal Church* 46 (1977): 275–95.

Case   William White. *The Case of the Episcopal Church in the United
                   States Considered* (1782). Edited with introduction and appendices
                   by Richard G. Salomon. *Historical Magazine of the Protestant
                   Episcopal Church* 22 (1953): 435–506.

Chorley1   E. Clowes Chorley. *The New American Prayer Book*. New York:
                   Macmillan, 1930.

Chorley2   E. Clowes Chorley. "Samuel Provoost, First Bishop of New York."
                   Historical Magazine of the Protestant Episcopal Church 2, no. 2
                   (June 1933): 1–25.

Copy   William White. " 'Copy of a Letter to Bishop Hobart, Sept. 1, 1819:
                   Relating at His Request, the Incidents of the Early Part of My Life,'
                   Together with Twenty-One 'Notes Connected with My Letter Bp.
                   Hobart,' Added 'Dec. 21, 1830.' " Edited with introduction and
                   notes by Walter H. Stowe. *Historical Magazine of the Protestant
                   Episcopal Church* 22 (1953): 380–434.

Cross   Arthur L. Cross. *The Anglican Episcopate and the American
                   Colonies*. New York and London: Longmans, Green, 1902.

CtFirst   Kenneth Walter Cameron. *Connecticut's First Diocesan*. Hartford,
                   Conn.: Transcendental Books, 1985.

Davies   Horton Davies. *The Worship of the American Puritans, 1629–1730*.
                   New York: Peter Lang, 1990.

DeMille   George E. DeMille. "One-Man Seminary." *Historical Magazine of
                   the Protestant Episcopal Church* 37 (1969): 373–79.

Dibblee   "Letters of the Reverend Doctor Ebenezer Dibblee, of Stamford, to
                   the Reverend Doctor Samuel Peters, Loyalist Refugee in London,
                   1784–1793." *Historical Magazine of the Protestant Episcopal
                   Church* 1, no. 1 (March 1932): 51–85.

Dugmore   C. W. Dugmore. *Eucharistic Doctrine in England from Hooker to
                   Waterland*. London: SPCK, 1942.

Echlin   Edward P. Echlin. *The Anglican Eucharist in Ecumenical Perspective*.
                   New York: Seabury, 1968.

Grisbrooke   W. Jardine Grisbrooke. *Anglican Liturgies of the Seventeenth and
                   Eighteenth Centuries*. London: SPCK, 1958.

Hart   Reprint of *Bishop Seabury's Communion Office* with annotations
                   by Samuel Hart. New York: T. Whittaker, 1874.

Hatchett1   Marion J. Hatchett. "The Making of the First American Prayer
                   Book." Th.D. thesis, General Theological Seminary (New York),
                   1972.

Hatchett2   Marion J. Hatchett. *The Making of the First American Book of
                   Common Prayer, 1776–1789*. New York: Seabury, 1982.

Hawks & Perry
    Francis L. Hawks and William Stevens Perry. *Documentary History of the Protestant Episcopal Church in the United States of America. Connecticut.* 2 vols. New York: J. Pott, 1863, 1864.

Hill
    Harvey Hill. "Worship in the Ecclesiology of William White." *Anglican and Episcopal History* 62, no. 3 (September 1993): 317–42.

HMPEC
    Historical Magazine of the Protestant Episcopal Church, now *Anglican and Episcopal History.*

Hogue
    William Hogue. "The Religious Conspiracy Theory of the American Revolution: Anglican Motive." *Church History* 45, no. 3 (September 1976): 277–92.

Holmes
    David L. Holmes. "The Episcopal Church and the American Revolution." *Historical Magazine of the Protestant Episcopal Church* 47 (1978): 261–91.

Jarvis1
    Kenneth Walter Cameron, ed. *Abraham Jarvis, Connecticut's Second Episcopal Bishop: Materials for a Biography.* Hartford, Conn.: Transcendental Books, 1983.

Jarvis2
    Samuel Farmar Jarvis. "Memoir of Bishop Jarvis." *The Evergreen* 3, no. 4 (April 1846): 97–99; no. 5 (May 1846): 147–53; no. 6 (June 1846): 173–79. Reprinted in Kenneth Walter Cameron. *The Anglican Episcopate in Connecticut (1784–1899).* Hartford, Conn.: Transcendental Books, 1970.

Johnson
    John Johnson. *The Unbloody Sacrifice, and Altar Unvailed and Supported.* 2nd ed. London, 1724.

Journals
    Journals of the General Conventions of the Protestant Episcopal Church in the United States of America, from the Year 1784, to the Year 1814. Philadelphia: John Bieren, 1817.

L&C Smith
    Horace Wemyss Smith. *Life and Correspondence of the Rev. William Smith.* 2 vols. Philadelphia, 1880.

Lathbury
    Thomas Lathbury. *A History of the Nonjurors: The Controversies and Writings; With Remarks on Some of the Rubrics in the Book of Common Prayer.* London, 1845.

Mampoteng
    Charles Mampoteng. "The New England Clergy in the American Revolution." *Historical Magazine of the Protestant Episcopal Church* 9 (1940): 267–303.

Memoir
    William Jones Seabury. *Memoir of Bishop Seabury.* New York: Edwin S. Gorham, 1908.

Middleton
    Arthur Pierce Middleton. "Prayer Book Revision Explained: Sermons on the Liturgy by Joseph Bend, Rector of St. Paul's,

Baltimore, 1791–1812." *Anglican and Episcopal History* 60 (March 1991): 57–74.

O'Neil   Maud O'Neil. "A Struggle for Religious Liberty: An Analysis of the Work of the S.P.G. in Connecticut." *Historical Magazine of the Protestant Episcopal Church* 20 (June 1951): 173–89.

Overton   J. H. Overton. *The Nonjurors: Their Lives, Principles, and Writings.* London: Smith, Elder & Co., 1902.

Parallels   Paul V. Marshall. *Prayer Book Parallels.* 2 vols. New York: Church Publishing Incorporated, 1989, 1990.

Parker   Kenneth Walter Cameron, ed. *The Correspondence of Samuel Parker: Colonial Anglican Clergyman at Boston, Second Bishop of Massachusetts and Supporter of Samuel Seabury of Connecticut (1744–1804); His Correspondence Calendared, Summarized Interpreted and Indexed.* Hartford, Conn.: Transcendental Books, 1984.

Peaston   A. Elliott Peaston. *The Prayer Book Reform Movement in the XVIIIth Century.* Oxford: Blackwell, 1940.

Perry   William Stevens Perry. *Journals of the General Convention of the Protestant Episcopal Church in the United States of America.* Vol. 3: *Historical Notes and Documents Illustrating the Organization of the Protestant Episcopal Church in the United States of America.* Claremont, N.H.: Claremont Manufacturing Company, 1874.

Peters1   Kenneth Walter Cameron, ed. *The Papers of Loyalist Samuel Peters.* Hartford, Conn.: Transcendental Press, 1978.

Peters2   Kenneth Walter Cameron, ed. *The Correspondence of Loyalist Samuel Peters: An Inventory of Additions.* Hartford, Conn.: Transcendental Books, 1985.

Porter1   Harry Boone Porter. *Samuel Seabury: Bishop in a New Nation.* New York: National Council of the Protestant Episcopal Church in the United States of America, 1962.

Porter2   H. Boone Porter. "Toward an Unofficial History of Episcopal Worship." In Malcom C. Burson, ed., *Worship Points the Way.* New York: Seabury, 1981.

Remarks   *Remarks on the Proceeding of the Episcopal Conventions for Forming an American Constitution.* By a Layman. Boston, 1786.

Rowthorn   Anne W. Rowthorn. *Samuel Seabury: A Bicentennial Biography.* New York: Seabury Press, 1983.

SAC   Kenneth Walter Cameron. *Samuel Seabury among His Contemporaries.* Hartford, Conn.: Transcendental Books, 1980.

Skinner   John Skinner. *Annals of the Scottish Episcopacy, from the Year 1788 to the Year 1816, Inclusive; Being the Period during Which the Late Right Rev. John Skinner, of Aberdeen, Held the Office of Senior Bishop and Primus: of Whom a Biographical Memoir Is Prefixed.* Edinburgh, 1818.

Sprague   William Buell Sprague. *Annals of the American Pulpit.* Vol. 5: *Episcopalian.* New York: R. Carter and Brothers, 1859.

Spurr   John Spurr. *The Restoration Church of England 1646–1689.* New Haven: Yale University Press, 1991.

SSA   *The Address of the Episcopal Clergy of Connecticut, to the Right Reverend Bishop Seabury, with the Bishop's Answer and, a Sermon, Before the Convention at Middletown, August 3d, 1785. . . . Also Bishop Seabury's First Charge, to the Clergy of his Diocess [sic], Delivered at Middletown, August 4th, 1785. With a List of the Succession of Scot's Bishops, from the Revolution 1688, to the Present Time.* New Haven, Conn.: Thomas and Samuel Green, 1785. The Charge is separately paginated.

SSB   *Bishop Seabury's Second Charge, to the Clergy of his Diocess [sic], Delivered at Derby, in the State of Connecticut, On the 22d of September, 1786.* Published at the earnest desire of the Convocation. New Haven, 1786.

SSC   *An Earnest Persuasive to Frequent Communion; Addressed to those Professors of the Church of England, in Connecticut, Who Neglect That Holy Ordinance.* By the Right Reverend Father in God, Samuel, Their Diocesan Bishop. New Haven, 1789.

SSE   *Discourses on Several Subjects. By Samuel Seabury, D.D., Bishop of Connecticut and Rhode-Island.* Vol. 1. New York, 1793. Discourse VI. "Of The Holy Eucharist," 163–84.

SSECR   Kenneth Walter Cameron, ed. *Samuel Seabury, 1729–1796: His Election, Consecration and Reception. The Documentary History of Francis L. Hawks and William Stevens Perry.* Reedited with an Index. Hartford, Conn.: Transcendental Books, 1978.

ST1, ST2   Kenneth Walter Cameron, ed. *Seabury Traditions: The Reconstructed Journal of Connecticut's First Diocesan.* 2 vols. Hartford, Conn.: Transcendental Books, 1983.

Steiner1   Bruce E. Steiner. "Anglican Officeholding in Pre-Revolutionary Connecticut: The Parameters of New England Community." *William and Mary Quarterly,* 3rd Series, 31, no. 3 (July 1974): 369–74.

Steiner2   Bruce E. Steiner. *Samuel Seabury 1729–1796: A Study in the High Church Tradition.* Athens: Ohio University Press, 1971.

Stowe   Walter H. Stowe. "William White: Ecclesiastical Statesman."
                 Historical Magazine of the Protestant Episcopal Church 22 (1953):
                 372–79.

SUI   *Samuel Seabury's Ungathered Imprints: Historical Perspectives of
                 the Early National Years.* Ed. Kenneth Walter Cameron. Hartford,
                 Conn.: Transcendental Books, 1978.

Sydnor   William Sydnor. *The Story of the Real Prayer Book, 1549–1979.*
                 Rev. ed. Wilton, Conn.: Morehouse Publishing, 1989.

Temple   *The Common Sense Theology of Bishop White.* With an introductory
                 survey of his theological position by Sydney Absalom Temple. New
                 York: King's Crown, 1946.

Thoms   Herbert Thoms. *Samuel Seabury: Priest and Physician.* Hamden,
                 Conn.: Shoestring Press, 1963.

Weaver   Glenn Weaver. "Anglican-Congregationalist Tensions in Pre-
                 Revolutionary Connecticut." *Historical Magazine of the Protestant
                 Episcopal Church* 26 (1957): 269–85.

Weil   Louis Weil. "Worship and Sacraments in the Teaching of Samuel
                 Johnson of Connecticut: A Study of the Sources and Development of
                 the High Church Tradition in America, 1722–1789." Th.D. thesis,
                 Institute Catholique de Paris, 1972.

White1   William White. *Memoirs of the Protestant Episcopal Church in the
                 United States of America by the Right Rev. William White, D.D.*
                 New York: E. P. Dutton & Company, 1880.

White2   William White. *Lectures on the Catechism . . . and Dissertations on
                 Select Subjects in the Lectures.* Philadelphia, 1813.

Wilson   Bird Wilson. *Memoir of the Life of the Right Reverend William
                 White, D.D., Bishop of the Protestant Episcopal Church in the State
                 of Pennsylvania.* Philadelphia: James Kay, 1839.

Winter   Robert M. Winter. "American Churches and the Holy Communion:
                 A Comparative Study in Sacramental Theology, Practice, and Piety
                 in the Episcopal, Presbyterian, Methodist, and German Reformed
                 Traditions, 1607–1875." Ph.D. dissertation, Union Theological
                 Seminary in Virginia, 1988.

Wood   Gordon S. Wood. *The Radicalism of the American Revolution.* New
                 York: Alfred A. Knopf, 1992.

Chapter One

SAMUEL SEABURY
AMONG THE REVISIONISTS

Even God cannot change the past.
—Agathon

It has been said that though God cannot alter the past, historians can; it is perhaps because they can be useful to Him in this respect that He tolerates their existence.
—Samuel Butler

This chapter summarizes the argument of this book, with the student particularly in mind. Its general assertions are documented and examined in detail in the chapters that follow.

The Calendar of the Episcopal Church's 1979 Book of Common Prayer includes a commemoration of William White, the first bishop to serve Pennsylvania and the third to preside over the House of Bishops. Notwithstanding these facts, the American Church's first bishop and the first to preside over his peers is not commemorated in its prayer book in his own right. Instead, on November 14 the Calendar provides a commemoration of "The Consecration of Samuel Seabury."[1] On the one hand, commemoration of Seabury's consecration is an acknowledgment that without his bravely taking the highly controversial step of obtaining his episcopal or-

---

1. The Collect for the Day comes as close to a slight as one can imagine in a liturgical text: "We give you thanks, O Lord our God, for your goodness in bestowing upon this Church the gift of the episcopate, which we celebrate in this remembrance of the consecration of Samuel Seabury; and we pray that, joined together in unity with our bishops, and nourished by your holy Sacraments, we may proclaim the Gospel of redemption with apostolic zeal; through Jesus Christ our Lord, who lives and reigns with you and the Holy Spirit, one God, now and for ever. *Amen.*" Compare the collect for William White: "Lord, in a time of turmoil and confusion you raised up your servant William White, and endowed him with wisdom, patience, and a reconciling temper, that he might lead your Church into ways of stability and peace: Hear our prayer, and give us wise and faithful leaders, that through their ministry your people may be blessed and your will be done; through Jesus Christ our Lord, who lives and reigns with you and the Holy Spirit, one God, for ever and ever. *Amen.*"

ders from Nonjurors in Scotland, England's Whig government would never have permitted the transmission of the English episcopate to Pennsylvania, New York, and Virginia. At the same time, however, the decision to commemorate the event rather than to grant a place in the calendar to Seabury himself reflects two other aspects of Seabury's fate in history. The first is that Seabury took some minority positions in politics and theology and held some beliefs that are not easily reduced to slogans, paying the price of becoming a controversial figure. Contempt, even hatred, is not too strong a word for the response he evoked from some figures in American religious circles. The second is that the 1979 Calendar was drawn up at a time when Seabury's personal integrity and effectiveness as a church leader had been to some extent minimized, if not discounted, by two important studies in American liturgy and church history. These studies were in turn followed by authors of several popular books. The effect of all this has been that like members of the modern caste of celebrities, who are sometimes derided as being famous for being well-known, Seabury appears to have been reduced by circumstances to being the bishop famous for having been consecrated. Ironically, while in the 1979 prayer book the Episcopal Church teaches for the first time that the Holy Eucharist is the principal act of worship on Sundays and Holy Days, Seabury alone of its first bishops was consistently teaching about the sacrament in exactly that way almost two centuries earlier.

Scholars of other generations saw Seabury differently than did the 1979 revisers. William Sprague's nine-volume *Annals of the American Pulpit* (1859) devotes its fifth volume to Episcopalians. Sprague's method was to consult printed materials about his subjects and also to correspond with those who might retain memories of them. Sprague's work carried no brief for Anglicanism of any stripe, and his reporting is always generous to his subjects. Nonetheless Seabury stands out in Sprague's reports of the Episcopal Church's first bishops, especially as preacher, pastor, and writer. In fact, Seabury seems to be the only one of the early bishops to be recalled by Sprague's correspondents as at all a good preacher and regular parochial visitor, one who embraced the *work* as well as the *station* of bishop. Eben E. Beardsley's *Life and Correspondence of the Right Reverend Samuel Seabury* (1881) became the standard account of Seabury's person and work for the best part of a century. Beardsley, staying very close to the documents, told the story of Seabury's life in a way that wove together the theological, ecclesial, and liturgical issues of the early Episcopal Church. In his account, Seabury is portrayed as one of the most significant conservatives in the Episcopal Church's early days, a champion of Trinitarian orthodoxy and catholic liturgy, as well as a tireless pastor and physician to the poor. Although there is a hagiographic bent to Beardsley's general tone and occasional reflections that do not appeal to the iconoclastic tastes of the present day, he did not go beyond his evidence.[2] William Stevens Perry, who was to become bishop of Iowa, was an indefatigable collector of manuscripts. In several large volumes he laid out the trail of documents that all students of the early history of Anglicanism in America still must follow.[3] The narrative by which Perry connects the documents, together with Beardsley's account, was to become the story of Seabury as usually told. The work of Beardsley and Perry emphasize the consecration, the struggle for American acceptance of Scottish orders, and the development of the 1789 prayer book, all within the context of the birth of the Episcopal Church. Discernible in their accounts is the evidence of Seabury's influence on the essentially conservative revision of the constitution of the new church, giving it bicameral government and making it more episcopal, particularly with regard to its legislative and judicial processes.

The last scholar to communicate the conventional account (what Marion Hatchett was later to call "the Myth of Origins"[4]), before the shift in interpretation began, was the late H. Boone Porter. After writing of Seabury's early years and the state of Anglicanism in America after the Revolution, Porter recounts Seabury's election in 1783, his failure to obtain consecration in England, and his success with the Nonjuring bishops of Scotland in 1784. Porter summarizes the "Concordat" that contained

---

2. Connecticut maintains a devotion to Seabury that White and Provoost do not enjoy in Pennsylvania and New York. While none of his modern successors have presumed to wear it, Seabury's mitre has often been set out prominently at their consecrations or seating as diocesan. This relic, certainly the first mitre to be seen in American Episcopal churches, or any other American church, for that matter, achieved a significance of its own, as witness the near-doggerel ballad "First Mitre of the West," reprinted from A. Cleveland Coxe's *Christian Ballads* by John N. Norton in his popular biography, *The Life of the Rt. Rev. Samuel Seabury, D.D.* (New York, 1860), 70f. (The ballad is reproduced in Appendix C-7.) New Haven children were evidently being taught Seabury piety, as Norton's book was "published through the offerings of the Sunday School of St. Paul's Church [now St. Paul and St. James], New Haven, Conn." Seabury's daughter made a copy of his mitre for Thomas John Claggett, first bishop of Maryland. See Kenneth Walter Cameron's "Two Bishops and Their Mitres," *The Historiographer* 122 (December 1982): 43–47. In another book of poetry, *Seabury in Memoriam*, ed. John H. Morgan (Notre Dame, Ind.: Parish Life Institute, 1983), 64, one finds "That Mitre," by Chris Hassel.

3. See Hawks & Perry and Perry in the Key.

4. Hatchett2, 1.

the agreement between Seabury and the Scots, and sums up the previously normative view of succeeding events:

> Early in August [1785] the clergy of Connecticut assembled in Middletown to receive formally their Bishop. The latter ordained four men as deacons, delivered his first charge to his clergy, and officially convened them as an organized body. The concordat with the Scottish Church was gladly accepted....
>
> The Church in America also had other needs which Bishop Seabury sought to fill. One of these was in its liturgy. The worship of God and administration of the sacraments had always been of great concern to him, and his acquaintance with the Scottish Liturgy made him strongly aware of certain inadequacies in the English Book of Common Prayer which had hitherto been used by Anglicans in America. He viewed the Diocese of Connecticut as an independent branch of the Catholic Church, and he deemed it his duty and his privilege to supply his jurisdiction with a liturgy framed according to the best scholarship and knowledge of the time. This the Scottish Liturgy certainly was, and he gladly lived up to his pledge with the Scottish bishops. Seabury's adaptation of the Scottish liturgy was published in New London in 1786. It may also be added that Seabury strongly encouraged more frequent celebrations of the Holy Eucharist as the chief and proper service for every Lord's Day.
>
> [After Connecticut and Massachusetts joined the national Church in 1789,] the new union bore immediate fruit in a successful revision of the Prayer Book. Regarding the chief service of the Church, the Holy Communion, the Convention took surprisingly creative action. A new service was compiled, based on the ancient liturgical principles represented in the Scottish Liturgy. Thanks to Seabury, we thus acquired our distinctive American Liturgy, of which our Church has remained justly proud. Its example has subsequently encouraged improvement and enrichment of the liturgies of several other parts of the Anglican Communion.[5]

Here began the slippery slope for Seabury's reputation.[6] Shortly after Porter's work was published, there appeared Carl Bridenbaugh's unremit-

---

5. Porter1, 13–19.

6. The following pages provide a summary of the problems addressed in this study. The scholar looking for precise citations and analysis is asked to be patient through the remainder of this introductory chapter.

tingly partisan *Mitre and Scepter.* Having done much of his work during the period of "Americanism" in the 1940s and 1950s, and writing at the time of the Cuban missile crisis, Bridenbaugh saw all of New England Anglicanism as a kind of totalitarian conspiracy against authentic American values of freedom, equality, and democracy. Seabury and many New England and New York clergy of the Church of England had been loyalists during the Revolution. That well-known fact had generally been seen as a difference of opinion, honestly held for political or theological reasons. Bridenbaugh's theory is that Colonial Anglicans in New England were extraordinarily cynical conspirators, devoid of political or theological integrity. He portrays them as using what he terms "religious double-talk,"[7] to disguise their ambition to build an alternative *imperium* within the bounds of the Puritan theonomic democracies already firmly in place. He finds the plans for an American episcopate a particularly egregious example of Anglican deceit.

Later in the 1960s came Bruce E. Steiner's doctoral study of Seabury himself, published in 1971, certainly still the single book every student of Seabury and the early Episcopal Church must inwardly digest.[8] Steiner advanced knowledge of Seabury in a number of ways, particularly by his analysis of Seabury's involvement in the American Revolution, and through his insights into the politics of the early Episcopal Church. Steiner examines Seabury's relationship to other High Church leaders and his involvement in the efforts to obtain the episcopate in the 1760s and 1770s. He also analyzes carefully the presbyter Seabury as a thinker and writer. His portrayal of Seabury as a person is balanced enough for those modern readers who do not quite believe a biography unless something unattractive is revealed. Seabury's later theological writings also receive treatment in Steiner's work to an extent not previously seen, although a thorough study is still to be produced.

Coming to liturgical matters, Steiner made a jump that would fuel subsequent fires. No detailed record remains of the (nonpolitical) liturgical changes proposed at the convocation of Connecticut clergy at Middletown in August 1785; there may never have been one. Basing his conclusions on the by no means disinterested claims of Samuel Parker, an undocumented reconstruction of E. C. Chorley's, and on a single line in a letter of

---

7. Bridenbaugh, xiii.
8. Steiner2. Specific references to Steiner's and Hatchett's work are not given in this introduction, but are found in the chapters that examine the issues in question.

William Smith's (the existence of which cannot be verified), Steiner concluded that Seabury had endorsed somewhat radical liturgical revisions at Middletown, particularly regarding the creeds and baptismal service, and that these were adopted with little change at a Boston convention that fall. Steiner acknowledged the tentative nature of the Middletown discussion, but his conclusions set the stage for subsequent claims that Seabury had been an advocate of radical change, only to alter his position for reasons of cowardice and expediency.

Steiner, who is not a liturgist or theologian, perhaps pardonably reduced questions of eucharistic theology to questions of eucharistic presence, and with the question so limited, could posit with some ease a pan-Protestant "New England consensus" on the sacrament. If there was such a consensus, it would of necessity be framed in terms of what the sacrament is *not*. He believed that Seabury (and many other Anglicans, including Seabury's teacher, Samuel Johnson) subscribed to this consensus, and he believed that Seabury did not part from it until well after he came into relationship with his Scottish consecrators. This observation would provide support for the view that Seabury understood neither the Scots' liturgy nor their theology when he undertook to study them at his consecration, and that his liturgical conservatism was a stance taken later for reasons having little or nothing to do with theology.

Finally, and certainly because he lived with every scrap of text he could find about Seabury, perhaps to keep his narrative flowing and to give it a bit more human interest, Steiner goes a bit beyond the evidence in that he harmlessly assigns emotional states (e.g., so-and-so "resented" something or was "enraged") and ideas to characters where the evidence does not require or even support the inference. One is often inclined to agree with him, particularly regarding the extent to which Samuel Parker, like the overly helpful Uzzah of old, was attempting to manipulate Seabury and White into union. The problem arises when those who have uncritically relied on Steiner's research have not distinguished his data from his interpretation, and assumed that all the characters' motivations and intentions were capable of precise two-dimensional description.

Because a principal thesis of this study is that an alternative reading of Seabury, Smith, and Parker can be provided to that supplied by Marion Hatchett and those who have followed him, it is important to point out the very great value of Hatchett's work on the first prayer book.[9] He has

---

9. Hatchett2. Based on Hatchett1.

cataloged and sorted in great detail many of the eighteenth-century proposals for liturgical revision. Morgan Dix, whose treatment of historical
data was often casual or highly selective, once observed that the Proposed
Book of 1785 vanished "like a bad dream." Hatchett successfully demonstrates that, to the contrary, it had definite influence on its 1789 successor.
Hatchett further establishes that, compared with many proposals for revision along what he considers progressive lines (some of them quite radical),
the Proposed Book was a balanced and somewhat conservative revision.
Hatchett also shows how the 1789 book was not as uniformly conservative a revision as is sometimes thought. Hatchett has digested the evolution
of the lectionary and Psalter through the various revisions and proposals
for revision, explains the development of the Hymnal, and introduces his
readers to the work of minor figures previously unnoticed in accounts of
the first two American revisions. Furthermore, Hatchett's views have been
followed by virtually every writer on the subject. This book is then to
be understood in part as a respectful but defined minority comment on a
subplot of Hatchett's account.

However, as Hatchett reconstructs the 1784 consecration, he seems to
extend some of Steiner's theories (and asides) beyond the point that the
data can support. As Hatchett reports it, Seabury had no idea of what he
was committing himself to liturgically, and actually hid from his clergy in
Connecticut the agreement with the Scots bishops. He finds Seabury to
have purposely misrepresented the events of the convocation and to have
deliberately distorted American interest in liturgical revision when reporting to the Scots after the convocation. Popular writers have then each
intensified the bad news, as though playing the parlor game of telephone,
with Seabury's reputation suffering more damage at each iteration of the
message.

As to the 1785 Middletown convocation itself, Hatchett believes that
we can reconstruct its liturgical proposals with some precision, and is
convinced that most of the suggested changes came from Seabury himself.
He finds Seabury to have cravenly abandoned "his" proposals when they
were found to be unpopular in Connecticut. In Hatchett's view, the Boston
convention adopted the Middletown suggestions in part because they were
Seabury's; Hatchett believes that Seabury created chaos by a change of
position. William Smith is said to have been moved to a more radical
stance on revision by the Middletown-Boston proposals, with the result
that the Proposed Book was designed to accommodate a supposed New
England radicalism, despite what Hatchett acknowledges to be the absence

of even one verbal parallel between the Boston revisions and the Proposed Book. Seabury is said to have embarrassed Parker by his criticism of the Proposed Book, criticism that Hatchett says was motivated by a continuing need to rehabilitate himself with those people in Connecticut who were still upset by the Middletown proposals.

As far as Seabury's own liturgical work is concerned, Hatchett believes the bishop's 1786 Communion Office was ignored, even resisted, by the Connecticut clergy. He characterizes as "radical" the collects in his liturgical notebook that were included in the 1789 prayer book and observes that the notebook includes abbreviated versions of traditional daily office canticles. It is not noted that while the Venite is shortened, there is also printed Cantate Domino and most singularly the Magnificat, which had been deleted from 1789 and was not restored until more than a century later. In the office book he published, Seabury would restore the Athanasian Creed as well. The complaint that this book also edits the Benedictus is a slip; that canticle does not appear in Seabury's notebook at all, but is mutilated in the 1789 book.

In Beardsley's biography of Seabury there is unfortunately introduced the issue of "credit" for the adoption of the Scottish eucharistic prayer in 1789. Beardsley generously allotted a measure of "credit" to William Smith, who reportedly read the prayer in the House of Deputies to quell opposition to it. Beardsley did not note that Smith was acting at the request of the bishops, nor did he consider the fact that Smith had written to the younger William Smith as well as Samuel Parker attacking the use of that very prayer. Hatchett takes the "credit" issue beyond this and concludes that "American Episcopalians probably owe more of a debt to William White, Samuel Parker, two men both named William Smith, and others whose names are unknown, than to Samuel Seabury" for the adoption of the prayer, as these people were "already inclined in that direction."[10]

The 1789 book as printed in 1790 varied from what Seabury agreed to in Philadelphia. Hatchett construes Seabury's objection to the editorial alteration, changing the very carefully negotiated rubric permitting and explaining the substitution for "he descended into hell" in the Apostles' Creed as a cynical attempt to leave an opening to reject the prayer book of 1789 if it proved unpopular in Connecticut.

In general, Hatchett portrays Seabury as not interested in or cooperating in efforts for unity in the early Episcopal Church, and does not report what

---

10. Hatchett2, 3.

it was that "northern" churches were seeking as conditions for union. Hatchett accepts the allegations of his enemies that Seabury interfered with churches in other states, and claims that Seabury alienated people by signing letters as "Bishop of All America." Seabury is said by him to have had "little respect" for Anglicans who supported the American Revolution.

While the points just listed, and others, must be dealt with below in detail, there are several overarching issues to be named here in a general way. The first is balance in using evidence. Both the revisionists and the older, more hagiographic writers treat the issues and the individuals involved in them monochromatically and monodimensionally. Although Seabury's character and veracity are repeatedly questioned in Hatchett's work (and he does not report a single occasion of Seabury acting honorably), he does not discuss Samuel Parker's vacillations and the elder William Smith's ambition and machinations in the formative years of the church. This is despite the contradictions in their writings and the elder Smith's unique status as the only priest whose integrity genial Bishop White ever questioned publicly.[11] The evidence of his own pen shows that William White did not understand the issues involved in the adoption of the Scottish prayer or retention of sacerdotal vocabulary until the early nineteenth century, and even then he maintained something very like a state of denial about it. In general, the complex motivations and theologies of the people with whom Seabury had to deal are ignored in modern reconstructions.

Problems arise in that, as it is interpreted by the revisionists, *Seabury's behavior during his involvement with American prayer book reform is entirely inconsistent with what we know of him before and after his liturgical involvement from 1785 to 1789.* As we shall see, Seabury was noted as a straightforward, if not blunt, speaker and preacher long before his consecration to the episcopate. He was outspoken in his opposition to the rebellion against the Crown, survived kidnapping and imprisonment at the hands of a terrorist band from New Haven, and continued to serve the doomed loyalist cause at no small personal cost. It was after the war, as he was managing the evacuation of loyalists to Nova Scotia, an evacuation that he himself planned to join after getting the other refugees safely away,

---

11. Privately he exhibited the same hesitation to criticize. Regarding two great clerical eccentrics, Jacob Duché and Samuel Peters, White wrote, "Although I shall always remember those two gentlemen with respect and affection, on account of their merits and of their kindness to me; yet there was in each of them a singularity of religious character, which lessened the profit of intercourse with them." Wilson, 27.

that he learned of and accepted his election as bishop of Connecticut. He chose the much more difficult task of staying behind and serving, whereas White and Provoost caused themselves to be elected — or at the least "co-operated fully with the search process." The Connecticut government had been especially hostile to loyal members of the Church of England during the Revolution; its treatment of persons even suspected of loyalist sympathies through generalized terrorism, at least one death camp, and ex post facto laws remain blemishes on its escutcheon. The years following the war saw the state only slowly adopting the spirit of the new nation, but this tardiness cannot be attributed to Anglican presence. Connecticut was to avoid adopting a constitution until 1818, and for more than a decade after that maintained a Congregational religious establishment. Seabury's entire episcopate was exercised under disabilities (official and otherwise) unlike anything that may have inconvenienced others of the first American bishops. The suggestion that a man who persevered under such circumstances should be described as panicky, toadying, and dissembling in the considerably less life-threatening issue of liturgical reform invites careful examination at the very least. Seabury's advice to a young priest in 1788 was a heartfelt expression of his own life's pattern: "A steady course of proper conduct, without servility or negligence, will recommend you."

In addition to the damage done to Seabury's reputation by revisionist historians, we must note a place where abuse of his name is a traditional part of a subculture. The curious are directed to *The Episcopal Recorder* in this regard, where the story is repeated many times in the 1800s. There we see that writers from the Reformed Episcopal Church frequently have not told its story in terms of differences of opinion honestly held, but with the blaming, repudiative, and highly judgmental language of the religious ghetto. The history of this polemic seems to have been an early determination that attacking the person will bolster an argument. Many REC authors have written of Seabury as though he had injured them personally. Throughout their history, they have told of Seabury not as someone with whom they disagree, but as evil, untruthful, and stupid. Their story oddly continues to recite that Seabury, despite being a worthless, dissembling, and stupid fellow, managed to foist a heretical eucharistic liturgy on the entire Episcopal Church and single-handedly pollute its prayer book with the word "priest." Naturally, they restrict High Church sentiment to Connecticut, with an occasional nod to New York. We will come to an answer given these attacks by William Stevens Perry.

While *The Episcopal Recorder* reiterated these charges for decades, we must not assign its sentiments to the nineteenth century alone. As late as 1994 a normally judicious historian from the REC unconsciously abandoned scholarly objectivity when Seabury appeared in a secondary role in his work.[12] The bibliography and notes in Allen Guelzo's book reveal that he did not feel obliged to acquire a firsthand knowledge of Seabury, and the only Seabury work cited is a single sermon that is taken out of context and incorrectly reported as to its audience and its place in the religious debates of the time. Guelzo has the simplest facts wrong as to Seabury's personal history, residence, election, consecration, and participation in the life of the early Episcopal Church. Guelzo reports Seabury as an unwanted pest at Lambeth Palace when there is ample data that could have been consulted about the ecclesiastical and civil politics of England at that time. Guelzo is unaware that George Berkeley Jr. had long before paved the way with the Scots, and that Seabury did not turn up as a surprise on Skinner's doorstep — in fact, the Scottish bishops wondered aloud why he was so late in appearing. Guelzo has the relationship of the Connecticut clergy to White's *Case of the Episcopal Churches Considered* wrong and misreports who approached whom in the quest for unity in the early Episcopal Church. In a curious expression of gratuitous spite, he reports the Seabury ordination of Joseph Pilmore as though this were done carelessly and unaware of the man's evangelical commitments, leanings that Guelzo believes to have made him a success despite his Connecticut ordination. Nothing could be further from the truth: Seabury made it clear from the first that he would provide ordination for candidates from all of the states, regardless of churchmanship, until they had their own bishops. Furthermore, Seabury's ordination record book lists Pilmore's lay and clerical recommenders, which include no less a man than Seabury's steadfast admirer, the Rev. Charles Wesley! In another place, Guelzo gives to William White the rôle actually taken by William Smith in making the 1785 Proposed Book. There is more, but these examples are typical.[13]

The Reformed Episcopal Church continued to call the Proposed Book "Bishop White's Prayer Book," an appellation more touching than informative. They did this despite the actual number of contributors and White's written confession that the project was a blunder on more than

---

12. Allen C. Guelzo, *For the Union of Evangelical Christendom: The Irony of the Reformed Episcopalians* (University Park: Pennsylvania State University Press, 1994).

13. Ibid., 24, 28–32, 36, 44, 45, 258.

one score and that in any case he did not approve of all of the book's contents. Guelzo insists that the only objection to the Proposed Book was the incoherent "muttering of Seabury," when Seabury was less opposed to the book than some clergy and laity south of Pennsylvania, and certainly never made the issue personal with Smith and White, as did Maryland's first bishop, Thomas Claggett. The English bishops had some critical observations to make on the 1785 proposal as well, but this fact is not attended to. Guelzo tells us that Seabury was of very limited intelligence and "clumsy," and so on. In short, Guelzo repeats the party line of his then coreligionists without inquiry into the evidence. I believe that he does this in all innocence, just as most writers would not necessarily go to the library if they needed to refer to Hitler, the "Pilgrims," or Elvis Presley within a larger tale — in our culture there is a fund of information, accurate or not, that all share. "Everybody knows" certain things. That is, what seems to make an otherwise respected historian go astray here is that at this point he is not reporting on a historical inquiry, but semiautomatically reciting a Haggadah learned in formative years. It is a tale of deliverance in which Seabury is cast as First Villain, Bishop Hobart as Pharaoh, and Bishop Cummins as Moses.

Nobody is neutral about Seabury, but a bimodal response is always a kind of applause. Of more concern to us than years of calumny from the Reformed Episcopalians is that in general, among people who are actually practicing history, the revisionist view treats liturgical reform with very little reference to the ecclesial and political situation in which it took place. The American prayer book's origins and development are best understood organically, as a part of the new church's struggles to understand itself, to heal its wounds, and to find its mission. It is with an attempt to interpret that context that our own reconstruction will begin.

An Alternate View

A person who takes a principled stand in a calm manner can and should expect just doing so to bring out all the anxiety in the environment, often in the form of hostility. In other words, resistance or sabotage is to be expected by those whose ideas disrupt business as usual. It is the fact of Seabury's principles, not his alleged personal failings, that brings him trouble in the new church. On a higher level, in the context of what Bruce Steiner calls the "non-theological Anglicanism" of Pennsylvania and points south, the Connecticut church as a whole suffered because the clergy and its leadership had principles and stuck by them when the pressure was to go along with half measures. It was the Connecticut clergy, not either of their bishops-elect, who responded in detail to White's temporizing *The Case of the Episcopal Churches Considered.*

That aside, an assessment of the place of Anglicanism in the New England states yields a picture very different from that drawn by Bridenbaugh. He, after all, relies heavily on the sometimes hysterical writings of implacable ideologues in New England and on the aspirations of Establishment dreamers in England, while ignoring the evidence of the missionaries and, more important, that of their parishioners. Despite his claims, it will be seen that New England Anglicans were far from being the local gentry; in addition, they thought that they were practicing religion, not fifth-column politics. At least until the outbreak of hostilities in 1775–76, it can be shown that ordinary people, and even the colonial government, did not share the conspiracy theory cherished by Seabury's Yale classmate (and future college president) Ezra Stiles, and others whom Bridenbaugh quotes. In fact, Connecticut people were increasingly finding ways for Anglicans and Congregationalists to share power, to the considerable chagrin of religious polemicists, especially Stiles.

As to politics, the situation is mutivalenced, even ironic. While it does seem to be true that High Church Anglicans were more likely to be Loyalists than Low Church people were, the situation is not that simple. Thus it is important to note that while Seabury will be seen to have opposed the Revolution, he also thought there was a good deal wrong with the relationship between England and the colonies, and he advocated a commonwealth relationship with England much like the one Canada was later to enter. Conversely, William White, a chaplain to revolutionary forces and to the Continental Congress, later wrote that he himself never advocated revolution, and still would not have favored taking up arms, even for "the great blessing of Independence," as the Proposed Book put it.

Distinctions of churchmanship and politics did indeed, as the revisionists insist, mar the organization of the Episcopal Church following the Treaty of Paris. What needs to be added to their assessment is the fact that the evidence indicates that it was the victorious rebels who held the grudges, as witness Samuel Provoost's obsession with Seabury and his expressed pleasure that Seabury's life was in jeopardy. That obsession at one point threatened to keep New York out of the ecclesiastical union of 1789. On the other hand, Loyalists either fled the country or proceeded at once to adapt their worship to the new situation. Thus Seabury's first official act was the promulgation of an injunction adapting the liturgy to new political realities.

The philosophical chasm between the High Church clergy, most of whom were former missionaries of the Society for the Propagation of the Gospel (SPG), and many of those of the "southern states" (an expression of the time, usually indicating everything on the map south of Connecticut) was deep. White is candid about his intellectual debt to Locke, and the "rights of man" pervade the ecclesiology expressed in *The Case of the Episcopal Churches Considered* as well as his later writings. Seabury essentially maintained that the church as a divine institution could not look to current political theories in understanding its charter, and he comments pointedly on the rapidly growing importance of power rather than responsibility as the central thought in American civil and religious life. North and South were further divided. New England was primarily served by SPG missionaries (who served other places as well, of course), most of whom were themselves converts or the sons of converts from Congregationalism. They lived on very modest stipends and were highly conservative in matters of doctrine and practice. Many southern clergy enjoyed different circumstances. In places they were state appointees, some living quite well. Many were descended from or were themselves members of the puritan or evangelical wings of the Church of England. Divided by politics, theology, liturgical style, and economic background, the young church was not necessarily a good prospect for unification, let alone unity, and it is commonplace among writers to marvel at the union accomplished in 1789.

The matter of economics is not unimportant. Seabury lived in an age when social distinctions were keenly felt, to a degree unimaginable today, as Gordon Wood has demonstrated.[14] Seabury, like most SPG clergy, depended on his work for his livelihood. "Gentlemen," as his age understood the term, did not depend on their earnings for their livelihood, although they certainly may have chosen to follow professions. Although educated clergy were given honorary status as gentry, it was by virtue of their education rather than their cloth, and Wood shows that economic distinctions were never forgotten. This served to isolate Seabury further. Of the principal figures in our account, Seabury alone did not have independent means. Samuel Parker was the son of a prosperous attorney; the elder William Smith had made a fortune in land speculation; William White and Samuel

---

14. *The Radicalism of the American Revolution* (New York: Alfred A. Knopf, 1992).

Provoost inherited wealth.[15] Seabury worked his passage to Britain for his consecration; Virginia's first bishop-elect decided that he could not make the trip because of his poverty and resigned. Patricians White and Provoost went for consecration at their own expense (Trinity Church also gave Provoost a £180 expense account for the trip, more than three times Seabury's old SPG salary), and Provoost was to some degree lionized by English society.[16] White's rejection of Scandinavian or Scottish bishops as a source of orders in the *Case,* because of their perceived oddity and foreignness, today reads like a simple case of xenophobia, if not snobbery.

Unlike his southern counterparts, Seabury had not sought his office, and was in fact but the second choice of the Connecticut clergy. Consistent with his conception of a ministry that was essentially dutiful and "useful," he threw himself into his task without reservation. It will be seen that Seabury made overtures to the South regarding union, and felt rebuffed that these went largely ignored. Nonetheless, by insisting on recognition of his orders and upon what he believed were apostolic principles of government, and by advancing the catholic cause in liturgy, Seabury affected the shape of the eventual union dramatically.

In the matter of his consecration, we shall see that Seabury did indeed know what he was promising, which was to study the Scots liturgy, and if he approved of it, to advocate "gently" for its use. This promise was kept with exactitude. Correspondence from Connecticut clergy to the Scots demonstrates that despite modern claims to the contrary, Seabury had put them fully in the picture regarding his commitments to his Celtic consecrators.

"Read his journal, the record of his travels from place to place in his Diocese, of his work among and for his people, done in the consciousness of the ever-present power of God, and you shall find limned there the portrait of a true Bishop, of a 'simple, grand, conciliatory, uncompromising

---

15. Visitors to Philadelphia who take the Park Service tour of the old city are shown the house of a prosperous tradesman and a well-to-do professional, and then as an example of the homes of the rich, they are shown White's house.

16. The effect of wealthy clerics on the life of the Episcopal Church requires another study. For instance, and it is difficult not to multiply examples excessively, family wealth made some of the projects of Wm. A. Muhlenberg possible, to the benefit of many, and yet he almost always acted in independence of the church, especially when he thought he was acting in its interests but against its will. A little later, Wm. Reed Huntington was to record with perfect naïveté that it was only late in life that he fully realized that most people did not escape the city heat all summer as he did, and that city churches ought to take this fact into account. E. A. Hoffman used his wealth and position to work his will on The General Theological Seminary in New York in a way that has had pronounced cultural impact on much of the Episcopal Church.

man,' of a man humble as he was honest, a man of faith and conviction."[17]
While Beardsley's mode of expression here is perhaps too pious for our day,
certain aspects of Seabury's character as he draws it are highlighted by the
documents studied below. Seabury was usually cordial and cooperative
toward people whom he knew to oppose him, particularly William Smith
and Samuel Provoost. His reaction to Samuel Parker's stinging accusations
in 1788 is polite, conciliatory — and unyielding on points he considered
essential. Seabury stands out in any day as locating the "collegial" nature
of the episcopate not primarily in a tediously self-referential club of the
purple, but in the bishop's quotidian collegiality with the presbyters of
the diocese. Anyone at all acquainted with the English church of the time
recognizes Seabury's position as truly radical, and it might provoke comment today in some places. While Seabury believed that certain decisions
(liturgical ones chief among them) were ultimately the province of bishops
in synod, he understood bishops to make their decisions with the advice
of "their proctors of the clergy." When it is realized that he followed this
principle consistently, perhaps even rigidly, the actions that so puzzle some
writers make sense.

In reviewing the general background of liturgical revision in the America of the 1780s, the researcher finds the field crowded with reformers
and schools of thought. This stems in part from the perennial nature of
what has been called the "liturgical dilemma" of Anglicanism, the distance between its theology and its liturgy even in the mainstream. Various
circumstances and religious movements in the Church of England raised
other liturgical issues, a fact that complicates the study of American prayer
book origins. Because of the large number of proposals in the air, the temptation exists to lump all those who wanted to trim the prayer book under
the name "Latitudinarians" and classify all those who wanted to enrich
its texts as "liturgical archaeologists," and this temptation has not always proved irresistible. There were in fact people building fairly complex
liturgies on "primitive" models precisely to avoid Trinitarian language
(Whiston), and there were people on the theological right whose liturgically very rich and "antique" work also included eliminating repetitions,
avoiding difficult doctrinal statements, and even replacing the gospel canticles in the daily office (Deacon). It will be important to separate the
"Latitudinarian" suggestions that were entertained in New England and

---

17. William A. Beardsley, "The Episcopate of Bishop Seabury," *HMPEC* 3, no. 3 (September 1934): 224f.

Philadelphia into two groups. First there were those who sought to stream-line and make intelligible (or inoffensive) the liturgical celebration. On the other hand were those who had real leftward doctrinal change in mind. Thus it was one thing to make the sign of the cross optional at baptism, and quite another to remove language of regeneration from the service; one thing to admit parents as sponsors in infant baptism, and another to alter the obligations the sponsors took upon themselves and to eliminate those accepted for the child. We will find that Seabury never criticized revisions made for purposes of clarity or tender consciences, and in one case, the exhortations at Holy Communion, certainly advanced revision. He remained nonetheless highly critical of those revisions that tended, as he put it, to "lower" doctrine. In this regard the opinion was offered a century ago that "perhaps the Church owes him less for what he did, than what he prevented from being done."[18]

In the same way, it is said that virtually everyone, from the Puritans to the Nonjurors, desired or was comfortable with some invocation of the Holy Spirit at the Eucharist, a feature absent in the 1662 service of Holy Communion. We can begin to make distinctions when we recognize that desiring, or acquiescing in, the use of a nonconsecratory invocation did not make one an advocate of the advanced eucharistic theology borne by the liturgy of Nonjuring tradition, particularly that of Scotland. We shall see that men who are said to have advocated the Scottish prayer simply because they wanted or permitted some kind of epiclesis of the Spirit were in fact quite critical of the 1764 Scottish prayer and the theology behind it.

Regarding the fateful meeting at Middletown, I shall argue that three distinct events took place there regarding the liturgy. The first concerns Seabury's Concordat with the Scottish bishops, and it can be demonstrated that not only did the clergy know its contents, but they responded to it as well. The second is Seabury's "Injunction," outlining changes clergy were to make to accommodate the liturgy to the new political reality; this document appears to have been followed or at least paralleled by the Philadelphia revisers of 1785. The third is the liturgical think tank that met at the end of the convocation. Far from meeting at Seabury's instigation, the talks were held at Samuel Parker's suggestion and request, and it can be shown that Parker had been discussing liturgical reform for some time previous to the meeting. It is essential to understand that the committee's proposals were just that, a list of topics for discussion

---

18. Sprague, 152.

at the September clergy conference in New Haven. Whatever the topics listed at Middletown were, within a few days it was clear that Seabury's presbyteral colleagues were not yet ready to make liturgical changes (there were other issues facing the new diocese), and Seabury unambiguously wrote to Parker on two separate occasions that he did not wish him to proceed with the Middletown list in Boston. Parker, who retained the letters, nonetheless went ahead at the Boston convention. Seabury wrote even more directly against revision to the Philadelphia revisers.

Here can be seen the limited utility of focus on liturgy (or any other area) as the sole issue in an inquiry. Our subject was aware of himself as bishop before he considered himself a liturgical reformer, and Seabury was acting in strict accordance with his principles of collegial government, and certainly wished more than three days to pass after his reception as their bishop without his clergy dividing. He wrote that he would address the issue of liturgical reform again when "tempers have cooled." None of the revisionists have noted that this was not an empty promise, and far from toadying to them, Seabury brought the issue before his clergy when he judged that the time was right. In the summer of 1786 his Communion Office was published, and in the spring of 1787 the Bishop of Connecticut appointed a committee for the revision of the rest of the prayer book, prompting one right-winger to half-jest that the Bible would be revised next.

Reconstructing the Middletown proposals in perfect detail is impossible. The documents relied on as a rule give no content, and those that give some tell us very little or state what is impossible. Parker compared the Proposed Book to Middletown without having seen the parts of the Proposed Book that contained the most serious revision, namely, Baptism, Burial, the Articles of Religion, and the Catechism. Both Parker and William Smith tended to promote new revisions by claiming that the changes were just like whatever their correspondent of the moment was doing. Parker gave two accounts of his own liturgical practice, in one case claiming to follow Seabury's instructions, and in the other proud to have defied them. Parker's own view of episcopal authority was highly fluid at best. Any embarrassment Parker may be said to have had over the Middletown/Boston proposals he created for himself.

To reconstruct Middletown, at least in part, we must subtract from the Boston alterations, which Parker admitted went beyond Middletown, those additions he identified as going beyond Middletown, and also those few items on the Boston list to which we know Seabury objected in the

Proposed Book. What emerges is a syllabus of changes that simplify and streamline liturgy without involving doctrine or adopting changes that were at the time hallmarks of heresies then current. There is some slight accommodation to New England's puritan scruples about the sign of the cross at baptism and "with my body I thee worship" in the marriage ceremony (both of which others objected to as well), but by and large the resultant set of proposals can be called mainstream and somewhat cautious.

Again, Parker had not seen most of the Proposed Book, as he complains to White and mentions to Seabury, when he wrote to Seabury that it was largely conformable to Middletown. Seabury's own analysis was different, but he had the advantage of seeing the entire Proposed Book before offering comment to the diocese. In his Charge to the clergy in 1786 and again in a 1789 letter to William White, he never objects to streamlining, eliminating repetitions, and the like, but focuses his criticism narrowly, on the revisions that erode doctrine. He writes to Parker that he does not claim that heresy itself is contained in the book, but that it "lowers" the liturgy in a way that accommodates heterodoxy.

The New England clergy did not ambush the Proposed Book, and Seabury's criticisms were kind when compared to some comments from the South. Despite recent arguments about the popularity of the book, it can be demonstrated to have been thoroughly tried in a few parishes only. White complained that the Philadelphia clergy were the ones who tried it in depth and that they felt somewhat abandoned by their colleagues in other places. Bishop White was later to be quite candid about the book's shortcomings. Furthermore, one scholar argues that most of the church saw the 1785 book as urban elitism and rejected it on that ground.

To understand his work we must realize that Seabury was a participant in Steiner's "New England Consensus" on the Eucharist only as that supposed consensus is focused narrowly on how sacramental presence, if any, was *not* to be defined. This is not very helpful information, however, as no one on the New England field was arguing for either transubstantiation or a Lutheran sense of real presence. Furthermore, when nuance is admitted into court, and when questions other than presence are admitted with it, it is clear that there was no New England consensus on the Eucharist any more than there was or is an Anglican consensus. By adopting a eucharistic prayer containing institution narrative,[19] memorial, oblation,

---

19. The Anglican habit of referring to this passage as the institution *narrative* rather than the *words of institution* immediately sets Anglican thinking about the Eucharist apart from Roman and Lutheran and some protestant thinking. The *narrative* is of something done, which

and invocation of the Spirit, *in that order,* the Nonjurors believed that they were ruling out the doctrine of transubstantiation, and Seabury agreed with that sentiment. By introducing the concept of sacrifice, particularly propitiatory sacrifice, into the discussion, the Nonjurors moved the question far beyond the reaches of any Protestant consensus. Their teaching that Christ was present in "virtue and effect," although not corporeally, was also not what the Congregationalists were teaching. We shall also see that Seabury's edition of the Scottish rite is more sacerdotal than the 1764 original from which he worked. Despite modern writers' worry over Seabury's seeming equation of Cranmer's 1549 English liturgy with that of the Scots, it is arguable that this mode of speaking was, and in some cases still is, a kind of code for a complete eucharistic rite composed in the Cranmerian tradition. Far from being ignorant in these matters, Seabury emerges as a careful editor. The Communion Office has significant variations, all of which reflect a considered theological position, one sometimes at odds with that of his consecrators. We will see in the Communion Office a stricter enforcement of certain controverted "Usages" than is contained in the original. Two items that later generations considered editorial mistakes are in fact rather elegant expressions of Seabury's very high view of the sacerdotal dimension of ordained ministry.

Could Seabury have known of these teachings before he was consecrated? He could indeed, as the teachings found their richest expression in England with John Johnson of Cranbrook, himself no Nonjuror, a generation before Seabury's school days. Johnson's work, as well as that of Dean Hickes, provoked considerable discussion and not a few replies, and no one aware of the Church of England's theological scene could have been ignorant of the theories in question. Seabury's teacher, Samuel Johnson, knew of these works, and it is no surprise, accordingly, that Seabury preaches of the Eucharist not just as sacrifice, but as propitiatory sacrifice, almost thirty years before his consecration by the Scots. For Seabury, studying divinity at Yale, not to know of John Johnson — the hot topic of the preceding generation — would be like a seminarian today not having heard of Barth, Tillich, or Niebuhr. These twentieth-century theologians are not news, but they must still be taken into account.

The notebook that Seabury carried to the 1789 General Convention,[20] with his eucharistic prayer written out in it, is not evidence that the

---

may still be done; the *words* take one, however unwillingly, to the world where the expression *hocus pocus* was born of *hoc est corpus.*

20. *Parallels,* 2:497ff.

Communion Office had failed. Rather, by the dated items that precede it in the book, we can see that the prayer was added to the notebook in 1789, along with other items, probably in preparation for the convention. Later portions of the notebook seem to be a comment on the 1789 prayer book, as alternative epicleses of the Holy Spirit are included in apparent opposition to the 1789 weakening of Seabury's text. It has been observed that the notebook contains abbreviated versions of a morning prayer canticle; it has not been noted that it also contains material eliminated in the 1789 book. This suggests that Seabury was not comfortable with all of the compromises made at Philadelphia to get the Scottish prayer into the liturgy. In 1795 he published an office book: the daily services with important changes from the prayer book version. In the first place, he reinserted the Athanasian Creed, completely left out of the 1785 and 1789 books. Second, the Psalms were reproduced in their entirety, but with revised translation. It will be recalled that the Psalms, with their curses of enemies, were a problem for most Christians of the time. Rather than use the "selection" provided in the 1789 prayer book as a way to avoid offensive passages, Seabury followed a conservative plan of Psalter revision. That method was technically within the rules of Hebrew grammar, but changed the translation of the offensive verbs to the English future tense wherever possible, thus removing much of their sting and allowing the entire Psalter to be used. Thus "smite them, Lord" becomes "the Lord will smite them." In this book, as well as his burial office for children, Seabury may have been aided by the younger William Smith.[21]

The issue of "credit" for the 1789 inclusion of the Scottish prayer is beside the point, but a good deal has been made of it, so it needs comment here and will be addressed in detail below. The elder William Smith not only did not advocate the use of this prayer, he wrote against it. William White insisted into his last years that the prayer does not mean what it says, and claimed to have gone along with it because it was inoffensive; he certainly claimed (and exhibited) no enthusiasm for it. William Smith the younger did use the prayer, and does mention it in a letter to Seabury, and briefly in one to the elder Smith that is mostly on other subjects. It cannot be observed too strongly that the alleged circular letter that it is claimed that he wrote "to an unspecified number" of convention deputies upon firsthand inspection turns out to be a verbatim copy of a passage in

---

21. There is material for a biography of the younger Smith gathered in Kenneth Walter Cameron, ed., *Samuel Seabury among His Contemporaries* (Hartford, Conn.: Transcendental Books, 1980).

the letter to the elder Smith; it is in the *elder* Smith's handwriting and is preserved among *his* papers. Far from being a circular letter, it appears to have been notes for personal use the older man made from the younger's letter. What the revisionists appear to have overlooked is the fact that the one influential person who did understand the chief issue in the Scottish prayer — oblation — did write to White advocating its use. That person was Samuel Parker, deputy from Massachusetts, but he did not propose its use when the House of Deputies set out the eucharistic rite. The prayer was proposed in the House of Bishops, which meant it was proposed by Seabury. The prayer had not been proposed by any of the "unnamed others" in the House of Deputies, where the Holy Communion service originated.[22] No one other than Seabury proposed use of the prayer when the 1789 revision was being undertaken. William Smith the elder, always anxious about his own ambitions, was acting on instructions when he read the prayer to the deputies from the chair.

Whether or not modern writers wish to give Seabury credit for the 1789 book's conservative features, his contemporary detractors certainly did. Benjamin Rush, a signer of the Declaration of Independence, writer of the first American text on psychiatry, and one of the most noted figures of the period (and William Smith's physician), left Bishop White's Christ Church and became a Presbyterian, blaming the liturgical ruin of the Episcopal Church on "superstitions" introduced by Samuel Seabury. In any event, despite any reservations he may have had about it, Seabury was an advocate for use of the 1789 book, dealing gently and effectively with recalcitrant clergy. In the 1792 revision of the ordination rites, he fought a successful campaign, single-handedly, for the retention of sacerdotal language regarding absolution.

After all of these things are considered, the fact seems to be that Seabury was most concerned with the constitution of one Anglican church in America marked by Catholic doctrine and worship. His actions must also be interpreted in the light of his beliefs about how such a church should carry out its apostolic identity. He owes his ecclesiology and sacramental theology first of all to Samuel Johnson. This theology focused his attention on the church and made him concerned for its government, for the apostolically (if not dominically) ordered function of its hierarchy, and for its liturgical life. It is in regard to each of these issues that he and the other

---

22. Seabury would rejoice to know that in the Episcopal Church as presently configured, all liturgical matters must originate in the House of Bishops, and that except in the convention of 2000, this rule has been observed.

former SPG clergy came up against the plans of William White and many of the southern clergy, and in a surprisingly large measure, prevailed. It seems that we can return to the view of Beardsley and Porter in the main, although the reader will find below a more appreciative approach to Seabury's liturgical work than either of those writers or the great Dean Samuel Hart displayed.

This alternative view challenges a great deal of previous scholarship, and the bulk of what follows is devoted to substantiating that alternative view.

– Chapter Two –

ANOTHER WORLD:
THE CONNECTICUT CHURCH

Prerevolutionary Experience

Seabury's differences from principal figures in the postrevolutionary church are pronounced. They are so in part because Anglican experience in New England, particularly in Connecticut, was very little like that of members of the Church of England living in the colonies to the south. Here we are concerned with how the experience of Anglicans in New England differed from that of their southern coreligionists in relationship to the state; we also look at their relationships to their Congregationalist neighbors in religious and social matters. Then we examine the perception of them as "invaders" plotting the overthrow of the Puritan system. We survey the reaction to the requests for a resident episcopate, requests that came most persistently from the SPG clergy in Connecticut and neighboring states. It has been suggested that the threat of episcopacy was a cause of the American Revolution. Is that the case? As these questions overlap, some themes reappear with regularity.

Outside of New England, Anglicans had the upper hand to one degree or another, and Maryland, Virginia, and South Carolina had even transplanted the system of English parish life to the colonial setting.[1] Although political rights granted to dissenters varied among the southern colonies, most Anglicans lived in colonies where there was at least some toleration in matters of worship, and in many of those places they had preeminence. Only in Virginia was the Church of England the sole legally recognized religious body, but even there de facto toleration of other Protestants was of long standing, and was certainly unremarkable by the third quarter of the eighteenth century.[2]

---

1. Holmes, 262.
2. Elizabeth H. Davidson, *The Establishment of the English Church in Continental American Colonies* (Durham, N.C.: Duke University Press, 1936), 87.

If south of Connecticut Anglicans had at least a level playing field, and often enjoyed considerable advantage, the case was quite different in New England, where life was sometimes made quite difficult for "Churchmen," as Congregationalists and Anglicans alike termed those loyal to the English establishment.[3] Non-Congregationalists were to suffer some civil disabilities in Connecticut until 1818, when the federal government forced the Constitution State to adopt a formal constitution in place of the Standing Order.[4] In that year a non-Congregationalist for the first time delivered the election day sermon. By no means unwilling to highlight the radical cleavage between church and state that had taken place, Harry Crosswell of Trinity Church in New Haven used prayers from the Book of Common Prayer and from Seabury's state prayers, and took as his text for the occasion, "Render unto Caesar the things that are Caesar's and to God the things that are God's." Puritan antidisestablishmentarianism died hard, however, and it was only some years later that Connecticut and Massachusetts abandoned state support of Congregationalist churches.

Those days were to come long after Seabury's death, however. The notion that the "Pilgrims" and their successors had a commitment to religious liberty for anyone other than themselves is a myth that seems incapable of dying.[5] Generally speaking, their view of religious liberty for others was "free liberty to keep away from us."[6] Connecticut's laws imposing religious taxation and strictly regulating Sabbath observance were considered extremist by the Congregationalists of other New England colonies.[7] In the matter of maintaining Puritan orthodoxy, New Haven (during its time as a free-standing colony) was somewhat tolerant, however, and would let a Quaker preacher go with a warning after a first offense. A second offense meant branding on the face with an H (for heretic) and imprisonment until the preacher had worked off the cost of expulsion from the colony. The

---

3. "Episcopalians" was also in use well before 1776. The more polemical expression "churchmanship," however, belongs to the next century.

4. See John J. Reardon, "Religious and Other Factors in the Defeat of the 'Standing Order' in Connecticut, 1800–1818," *HMPEC* 30 (June 1961): 93–110.

5. The myth became powerful enough to provide the subject for an entire hymn in Leonard Bacon's, "O God, Beneath Thy Guiding Hand" (1833), where the third stanza reads

> Laws, freedom, truth and faith in God
> Came with those exiles o'er the waves;
> And where their pilgrim feet have trod,
> The God they trusted guards their graves.

6. Nathaniel Ward, quoted in Weaver, 269.

7. O'Neil, 173f.

truly persistent were to have their tongues bored through with red-hot pokers.[8]

Toleration of Anglicanism had been imposed directly by the Crown in Massachusetts. As more and more of its citizens chose to follow non-Congregationalist ways, Connecticut adopted in 1708 an Act of Toleration that excused them from Sabbath attendance in Congregationalist churches, but at first Anglicans were still required to pay the taxes levied to support the Puritan establishment. In the early days of this uneasy peace, a good deal of sniping at Anglicans took place, a favorite assault being the state imposition of days of fasting to coincide with major feasts of the Anglican liturgical calendar, a practice that was still complained of late in the century. It is to be remembered that not even Christmas was observed in Connecticut. Failure to observe the fasts was punished by fines or imprisonment.[9] In a document that lay unfinished at his death, Seabury complained of this practice, adding that he never did observe the fasts that were ordered when they interfered with the fifty days of Easter.[10]

That laypeople loyal to the Church of England would want to come to rigidly theonomic Connecticut was thinkable to Congregationalists, and they did come, from England and from other colonies. That members of their own fold should leave it for the Church of England was not as easy for them to understand and provoked very strong feeling. There is no more striking example of this reaction than that of the sister of Richard Mansfield of Derby: When he went to England for Anglican ordination, she prayed that he might be lost at sea — on the eastward leg of the journey, before suffering the disgrace of episcopal ordination.[11]

That such a charged atmosphere, together with the use of corporal punishment, taxation, and prison in religious matters was not unprecedented in the Anglican mother country is not the point here, nor is our burden the discrediting of the Puritan societies erected in New England. These details are important only in beginning to explain why the New England participants in the formation of the Episcopal Church were usually so

---

8. Weaver, 269, citing *New England Colonial Records*, 239.

9. Weaver, passim, and esp. 280. See also Stephen Nissenbaum, *The Battle for Christmas* (New York: Vintage, 1997).

10. The "Complaint Against the State of Connecticut" was drafted on the back of a letter dated in 1793, so there is a three-year window for its composition. It outlines the many interferences of the state in the financial affairs of the Episcopal Church. After Seabury's death, things got worse, the state throwing up any possible barrier to the establishment of Episcopal institutions of learning. See Kenneth Cameron, *Connecticut's First Diocesan* (Hartford, Conn.: Transcendental Books, 1985), 38.

11. Mampoteng, 285.

much more conservative than their southern counterparts. That explanation begins with the suggestion that those who suffer attack or disabilities because of their religious affiliation would have a conservative attitude toward, and strong allegiance to, their religion's distinguishing principles in part merely to survive. Those distinguishing principles were to be in New England exactly what had been the center of debate in England since Elizabeth's time: episcopacy and liturgy. The debate came to a head in a way that has kept Anglican-Congregationalist tensions in Connecticut alive in many memories.

Yale College had been founded in 1701 and began operation in 1702 to provide the colony with clergy, physicians, and jurists. Together with Harvard it produced most of the clergy working in Connecticut in Seabury's day, Congregationalist or Anglican. In 1722 its rector (president) was Timothy Cutler, who had been brought from Massachusetts to Stratford, Connecticut, because he was one of the best preachers in New England. Connecticut church leaders hoped that his eloquence would counter the attractiveness of Anglicanism to growing numbers of Congregationalist laypeople. At Yale, Cutler and the college tutor, Daniel Browne, read and discussed theology with local clergy, including Samuel Johnson, later president of King's (Columbia) College. Johnson had been studying the Book of Common Prayer since at least 1716, and was using selections from it in his worship services in West Haven. The practices of the other members of the group are not known, but on the "Dark Day," September 12, 1722, Cutler ended his prayers at Yale with a phrase from Psalm 106:48 that signaled his own departure from the passivity of public prayer in Congregationalism: "and let all the people say, Amen." Anglican congregations said their Amens to liturgical prayers aloud; Congregationalist assemblies of the time did not audibly join the minister's prayer. There could have been few clearer signals that Cutler had changed loyalties. On the next day the college trustees met with Cutler, Browne, Johnson, John Hart (East Guilford, now Madison), Samuel Whittelsey (Wallingford), Jared Eliot (Killingworth), and James Wetmore (North Haven). Sometime later the "Yale Apostates" gave in to the relentless pressure to communicate their sentiments in writing:

> Having represented to you the difficulties which we labour under, in relation to our continuance out of the visible communion of an Episcopal Church, and a state of seeming opposition thereto, either as private Christians, or as officers, and so being insisted on by some

of you (after our repeated declinings of it) that we should sum up our case in writing, we do (though with great reluctance, fearing the consequence of it) submit to and comply with it, and signify to you that some of us doubt the validity, and the rest are more persuaded of the invalidity of the Presbyterian ordination, in opposition to the Episcopal; and should be heartily thankful to God and man, if we may receive from them satisfaction therein, and shall be willing to embrace your good councils and instructions in relation to this important affair, as far as God shall direct and dispose us to it.[12]

There was one formal debate after which three of the apostates recanted, but there was not to be any prolonged dialog on the nature of apostolic ministry. The trustees instead voted "to excuse the Rev. Mr. Cutler from all further service as Rector of Yale College."[13] It may be an overstatement to say that "this event shook Congregationalism throughout New England like an earthquake, and filled its friends with terror and apprehension,"[14] but it is not much of one, and ink was to be spilled for decades in the effort to repair the perceived damage. Local confidence in the ecclesiastical structure dropped, particularly as only one member of the New Haven clergy association had not been associated with the defection. Confidence in the fledgling college also diminished. At least one Yale student was warned that, in the wake of the defections, Yale could not be depended on for an orthodox education, and at his father's direction left to study divinity at Harvard. He was Samuel Seabury, the father of our subject. Cambridge was not to prove a safer haven for him, however, for the elder Seabury was soon to follow the Yale Apostates into Anglican orders.

The Apostates, like the many Congregationalists who subsequently experienced conversion to Anglicanism during or after their Yale years, were to be committed to conservative or High Church principles regarding liturgy and episcopacy in the days of the Episcopal Church's formation; those principles were, after all, what they had converted for. Most of them had become missionaries of the conservative Society for the Propagation of the

---

12. Text in Weil, 41f. There never seems to have been a movement to commemorate liturgically "The Conversion of Timothy Cutler, Samuel Johnson, and their Companions," but the effect of their transformation on the next hundred years of Anglican life in the United States is pronounced.

13. Sprague, 51. While Cutler, Browne, and Johnson were in England for ordination, Browne died of smallpox. Johnson was, all in all, a net gain to Yale, as it was he who convinced George Berkeley, future bishop of Cloyne, to endow the college so lavishly.

14. O. E. Winslow, *Jonathan Edwards*, in Weaver, 278.

Gospel in Foreign Parts. The SPG, also founded in 1701, was to follow the British flag around the globe, but its first efforts were in the Americas.[15] Some of the missionaries of the "Venerable Society" gave a good deal of energy to polemical writing, particularly in New England.[16]

A system of resident "commissaries" was begun to provide quasi-episcopal oversight in some of the southern states, but without much success. The New England clergy received direction in a general way from the SPG, and ultimately from the Bishop of London, who had charge of all colonial clergy. Both before 1776 and to the end of the Revolution, SPG missionaries were at the front of the movement for a resident bishop in the new world.[17] The request for a bishop was not just theoretical or sentimental; a vital piece was missing from an articulated body. Besides the obvious inconvenience and mortal danger involved in sailing to England for ordination,[18] lack of immediate episcopal presence or ecclesiastical courts left priests and laypeople in suspended animation upon occasion. Besides the pronounced need for supervision of the clergy, there were thorny pastoral questions to deal with, as the following letter from Jeremiah Leaming to the secretary of the SPG so well illustrates:

> I desire to lay the following before the Lord Bishop of London, and His Grace the Archbishop of Canterbury, and beg you to acquaint me with their determination. The case is this: There was a sailor married a woman, and soon after went to sea, in the last war, [vs. the French] was taken by the enemy and put in prison. Soon after his captain was released, and supposed the sailor to be dying, as he was very sick when he left him. When the captain came home, he reported

---

15. O'Neil provides a general introduction. A great deal of the documentary material is accessible in Kenneth Cameron's collections generally.

16. For example, Jeremiah Leaming (1717–1804), who was to be the first choice of the Connecticut clergy for bishop, was in many ways a stereotype of the adult convert who became an SPG missionary; converted after Yale graduation, he went to England for orders and then served parishes as an SPG missionary. He published *A Defence of the Episcopal Government of the Church* (1766) and *A Second Defence of the Episcopal Government of the Church* (1770), as well as the sermon he preached at the funeral of Samuel Johnson.

17. Abraham Jarvis's last letter to the SPG requesting continued financial support and above all a bishop, but not naming a candidate, was written on May 5, 1783 (after Seabury's acceptance of election), reminding the society that the SPG missionaries did not cause or support the Revolution. [*Jarvis* 25f.]

18. Samuel Seabury wrote to the SPG that "it is evident from experience that not more than 4 out of 5 who have gone from the Northern Colonies have returned; this is an unanswerable argument for the absolute necessity of Bishops in the Colonies. The Poor Church of England in America is the only instance that ever happened of an Episcopal Church without a Bishop and in which no Orders could be obtained without crossing an ocean of 3000 miles in extent." Samuel Seabury to Secretary, SPG, April 17, 1766, Thoms, 33.

the sailor was dead: the wife, supposing she was a widow, married three years after. Six years after she was married, and ten years after the sailor leaving her, she received a letter from him, being the first notice she had of his being alive, though he had been nine years in Jamaica, and neglected to write. Three years after she received this letter, the sailor came here; but he would not live with her, as she had children by the last man, and none by him. It is now four years since he went from hence, and has not been heard of. Now the man and woman who live here, desire to be admitted to the Lord's Supper, and are very worthy people, except the affair above mentioned. I beg the advice of my spiritual rulers, that I may know whether I ought to admit them or not. If you can send it soon, you will greatly oblige.[19]

When they were not caught up in such melodrama, did these missionaries understand themselves to be subversives? They could hardly have done so, for they were never injected into a locale to start a church by wooing members away from the Congregationalist establishment, but were sent in response to a request from an already-gathered congregation of Anglicans. Part of the umbrage taken at their presence comes from the title "missionary." When Anglicans responded to Puritan outrage at the presence of missionaries by pointing out that their mission was to congregations already in place, the reply came that this could not be the case, because only a bigot would have scruples over attending the worship services of the Congregationalists.[20] Many settlers who had come to New England in the 1630s were nonseparatist Puritans, continuing what they considered to be the best parts of England's established religion. The concept, dating back to Increase Mather, that the colonial Puritan establishment continued the Church of England with the objectionable parts left out did not survive to be employed in the eighteenth-century debates, but the idea that it was the true church did, although this claim was also made by American colonists of many other persuasions. Despite this competition, more than once has it been observed that among a wide range of colonial Protestants a rudimentary kind of ecumenical consensus existed, namely, that the Church of England was second best.

Despite its apparent status as second best, Anglican presence grew. It grew in part because it provided an alternative to what some considered to

---

19. Jeremiah Leaming to Secretary, SPG, June 10, 1761; Hawks & Perry, 2:23. There is no record of a reply.

20. Hogue, 286, 288.

bc the excesses of the Great Awakening. Perhaps surprisingly, New England Anglicanism grew during the Revolution, particularly in Connecticut. Charles Inglis attributed this growth to the Connecticut clergy's loyalty and integrity:

> Their adherence to the dictates of conscience by persevering in loyalty and preaching the gospel unadulterated with politics, raised the esteem and respect even of their enemies, whilst the pulpits of dissenters resounded with scarcely anything else than the furious politics of the times, which occasioned disgust in the more serious and thinking. The consequence is that many serious dissenters have actually joined the Church of England.[21]

Almost a century before, however, as Anglican presence had begun to grow in Boston, the Congregationalist establishment tightened its own myth of origins. Cotton Mather uttered what has become the classic statement of this position in 1690, hitting out at bishops, the prayer book, and the surplice:

> We came into the wilderness because we would worship God without episcopacy, that Common Prayer, and those unwarrantable ceremonies, which the land of our Fathers' sepulchers has been defiled with.... Let us not so much as touch the unclean thing, or hide so much as a rag or pin of a Babylonish garment with us.[22]

What was worship without prayer book, bishop, and surplice like? Was there in fact a liturgical or sacramental consensus shared by all New Englanders that would have shaped young Seabury's mind and necessitated his rethinking those subjects entirely when he met his Scottish consecrators?[23]

One point of agreement is perhaps unexpected: Laity in both Anglican and Congregationalist assemblies knew what their service would be like, although the Anglicans knew both structure and text, while the Congregationalists could anticipate structure only. This foreknowledge came from the fact that although the Congregationalist establishment worshiped without a prayer book, there was little liturgical anarchy among his New

---

21. Charles Inglis to SPG, May 20, 1780; Thoms, 21.

22. Weil, 40. One of Mather's more remarkable traits was his habit of recording his private occasional prayers and ejaculations. When he saw Africans, for instance, he prayed that their souls be washed white, and he had a prayer that he customarily used when people walking by took insufficient notice of him. Davies, 147f.

23. The "consensus" theory is Steiner's (Steiner1, 342f.), and will be visited in more detail below in chaps. 5, 6, and 7.

England neighbors in Seabury's youth. That is, the shape of the Congregationalist service was not of the minister's design, but followed the "form
and order"[24] with enough rigidity that William Blacktree is remembered
as complaining that he "had left England to escape the power of the Lord's
Bishops, but found himself in the hands of the Lord's Brethren."[25] New
England produced more than forms of worship: The Ainsworth Psalter
and the Sternhold and Hopkins Psalter had been replaced with one of
America's first important literary works, the *Bay Psalm Book* of 1640.

Predictable form does not make for consensus, when what is contained
in the form differs significantly. Where an Anglican would know the words
of each prayer ahead of time, and could participate in them through that
knowledge, a Congregationalist neighbor had to go wherever the minister's extemporaneous prayer went, and the prayer could cover significant
ground, as extemporaneous prayer was known to go on for more than
two hours.[26] To the Congregationalist used to such a prayer, the collects,
General Thanksgiving, and even the Prayer for the Whole State of Christ's
Church in the prayer book offices must have seemed a sparse and dilettan-
tish stab at praying, while to the Anglicans the minister's prayer in their
neighbors' churches may well have seemed something of a rant or a display
of ego.

For Horton Davies, the fundamental difference between Puritans and
Anglicans can be detected in the refusal of the former to observe a liturgical calendar. He locates this refusal not in a simple disagreement over
whether such observances were superstitious, but in the core issues of
spiritual formation. For him, the refusal to commemorate the past, even
events in the life of Christ, let alone events in the lives of the saints, puts
all the emphasis on present-day sanctification. "Puritans, in their type of
spirituality did not, like Roman Catholics or Anglicans, aim directly at
the imitation of Christ. Rather they recapitulated the story of Everyman
Adam, from temptation and fall, through reconciliation, restoration, and
renewal."[27] Davies believes that basic understanding of the sacraments
themselves was also quite different in the two communities. What they
had in common obscures their difference at first glance, and that common

---

24. Davies, 145.
25. On the extent to which Puritan religion filled the ritual gap created by abandoning the
prayer book with rites of their own creation, and for an appreciation of the extent to which
ritual created social cohesion for them, see E. Brooks Holifield, "Peace, Conflict, and Ritual in
Puritan Congregations," *Journal of Interdisciplinary History* 23, no. 3 (Winter 1993): 551–70.
26. Davies, 17.
27. Ibid., 41.

terminology is the use of the word "covenant." Covenant terminology is used differently with regard to sacramental worship, however. When it came to attendance at the Lord's Supper, Anglicans found in Holy Communion the healing benefits of covenant, and it is arguable that the 1552 rite on which 1662 was based was in fact a structured experience of justification by God's grace. For the Congregationalists, the sacrament is God's seal on the covenant, and also the sign that communicants belong to it and are living its terms.[28] Accordingly, "visible sainthood" was required both for church membership and for admission to Holy Communion.[29] Fear of attendance at the Lord's Supper in an unregenerate state brought terror to many Congregationalists,[30] which had the result of producing a fairly small group of communicants in each congregation. Members of this group often became the identified elite.

Puritan worship had done away with sponsors at baptism; parents brought their own children to the font, relying on the scriptural assurance that "the promise is to you and your children" (Acts 2:39). The precondition for baptism that parents be regenerate led to a crisis: What was to become of the children of parents who could not report an experience of regeneration? Were they to grow up as heathen? The Ministerial Conventions of 1657 and 1662 produced the "Half-Way Covenant," by which parents who were believers, even if not regenerate and communicants, could bring their children to baptism and pass church membership on to them.

Congregationalist discussion of the Lord's Supper came to fall chiefly under three heads. Some held it to be entirely a memorial in the psychological sense, of benefit only if the recipient's attitude were right. Others, led by Solomon Stoddard, believed (as Wesley would) that attendance at the supper was in itself a "converting ordinance," participation in which could help bring about regeneration. A third view implied some mystical presence of Christ, but like the converting ordinance view, it implied no presence of Christ's body or blood.[31]

Davies doubts that there was a general "sacramental renaissance" between 1680 and 1720 among New England Congregationalists. He supports this contention by appeal first to all the literature of the time that

---

28. Ibid., 156.
29. Ibid., 13. See also Edmund Sears, *Visible Saints* (New York: New York University Press, 1963), for an idea of the pervasiveness of this concept in the construction of Puritan society in New England.
30. Davies, 170f.
31. Ibid., 169.

laments poor attendance at the sacrament, and also notes that the "converting ordinance" theory reduced Holy Communion to a sermon. Time was not kind to Stoddard's conversion theory, and his grandson, Jonathan Edwards, was one of the clergy who were to repudiate his views, returning to a strict requirement of regeneration before communion.

Davies's evaluation of the developed Congregationalist eucharistic theology in New England is balanced, and helps to show how different it was from that of Anglicans:

> In the case of the Lord's Supper, the memorial aspect is never forgotten, nor that of deep thanksgiving, which is true eucharist. The aspect of mystery is often overshadowed by excessive pedagogical explanation... but it is never wholly lost. Increasingly, as the seventeenth century ends, the sense of the banquet shared with Christ is dominant, though rarely is there any adumbration of the eschatological banquet in eternity. The sense of the communion of saints is weak.... The renewal of Christian hope in life after death is not strongly stressed in the rite (the Crucifixion overshadows the Resurrection...) nor is there any sense of the sacrifice of the Church as linked with the Sacrifice of Christ.... The Communion never ceased to be a spur to Christian ethics and a stimulus to sanctification.[32]

Converts to Anglicanism cannot be said to have brought much of the Congregationalist view of the sacraments with them. Regarding baptism and church membership, they celebrated a rite rich with the language of divine initiative and sacramental regeneration. Nothing could be clearer than the priest's declaration after the actual baptism, "seeing then that this child is regenerate..." The prayer book view was that God acted in baptism and grafted the newly baptized into the church; membership depended on God's gift rather than individual experience of regeneration. Evangelicals in England and America would increasingly separate baptism from the experience of New Birth, and by the middle of the nineteenth century their emphasis would come to lie upon the subjective experience of regeneration.

More to the point that will become critical for us later in assessing Seabury's eucharistic theology, Anglicans spoke of Holy Communion in very different terms than did other New Englanders. Where their neighbors may have been terrified to receive the sacrament because of uncertainty

---

32. Ibid., 181.

as to their regeneration, the prayer book invited Anglicans to "Draw near with faith, and take this sacrament to your comfort." This invitation was followed by a confession of sins, the absolution, and the recitation of the "Comfortable Words" (scriptural passages of assurance about forgiveness). Then the eucharistic dialog continued, "lift up your hearts." Receiving communion was in part to experience the divine repair of violated relationship. It was precisely for what may be considered the "unregenerate" aspect of each life that the 1552–1662 Anglican communion service was designed.

This contrast in the theology of worship may be seen in the acknowledged leader of the Connecticut clergy, Samuel Johnson. He oversaw the training of so many seeking Anglican orders, including young Samuel Seabury (a schoolmate of Johnson's son), that one historian has termed him a "one-man seminary."[33] There are several studies of Johnson, the most persuasive of which is that of Louis Weil.[34] Weil saw the Connecticut converts in particular as part of the "Arminian threat to Puritan orthodoxy" because they give due place to reason and placed emphasis "upon the importance of the sacraments for the spiritual growth of the believer." In Johnson and in the students he prepared, we can see not only the differences between Anglicans and Puritans writ large, but also the High Church principles that set off the New England clergy from many of their "southern" counterparts.

For Johnson, liturgy itself was part of the process by which people are sanctified, and this emphasis on the process of "nurturing virtue" rather than instantaneous conversion is an important part of what was different about Anglicanism. Besides taking the common Anglican position that knowledge of what will be said in the service aids (or occasions) devotion, Johnson understands the assembly itself to be of theological importance, both in terms of the experience of union, and in engagement of the senses in stirring up and re-creating the heart:

> For not only the eye, as I observed before, but also the ear would affect the heart, and it would not only animate a spirit of devotion towards God, but a spirit of charity towards one another, to find ourselves surrounded with our Christian neighbors and brethren, all

---

33. DeMille.

34. Weil. See also Lloyd F. Dean, *Samuel Johnson (1696–1772)* (Hartford, Conn.: Transcendental Books, 1980); Donald F. M. Gerardi, "Samuel Johnson and the Yale 'Apostasy' of 1722: The Challenge of Anglican Sacramentalism to the New England Way," *HMPEC* 47 (1968): 153–75.

joining together, and according to the pattern of the holy Apostles
(Acts iv.24), lift up our voices with one accord in the prayers and
praises offered up to Almighty God. My neighbor's voice will be so
far from interrupting that it will rather animate my devotion, and
give it the more life and spirit.[35]

Johnson goes on to say that this union with other worshipers tran-
scends the bounds of the local assembly, connecting us with other believers
in other places. Johnson further insisted that the senses were to be used
in worship, and accordingly insisted that aesthetics had a place in con-
siderations of worship. In "The Beauty of Holiness," he argues that the
"perfection in form" of the liturgy is an experience of beauty that brings
us into contact with the Holy, to which we respond in adoration. Because
beauty participates in the Holy, it gives access to the Holy.[36]

In addition to Johnson's development of a liturgical aesthetic, Weil finds
him to have "synthesized Caroline theology," passing on to his students
what may be considered the classic High Church position on worship
and the sacraments. Like most writers of his time, Johnson freely employed the notion of covenant, but he understands the sacraments to
"convey...benefits of Covenant grace," rather than seeing them as signs
of already-accomplished conversion. In terms of the Eucharist, "convey"
implies that faith receives, but does not create, the benefits of communion.[37] In "The Oeconomy of the Redemption of Man by Jesus Christ"
(1727), Johnson sees the Eucharist as renewing and ratifying the covenant,
language which could be bent to the Puritan approach, had he also not
moved on to speak of the growing soul that "partakes of the Body and
Blood" of Christ.[38] For Johnson the Eucharist is a constant commemoration "so that the transaction may be represented on earth while it is
performed in heaven."[39] Here the High Church notion of Christ eternally
presenting his sacrifice to the Father while the church below re-presents
it is unmistakable, and separates Johnson's students from Congregationalists' theories. It also could distinguish them from some Anglicans of the
time, but not many; even for the "central" churchmanship of Waterland,
"commemoration" implies the present link between the earthly Eucharist
and the sacrifice "which our Lord himself commemorates above."

---

35. Samuel Johnson, "The Beauty of Holiness," *Works,* 3:530, in Weil, 70.
36. Weil, 71.
37. Ibid., 123.
38. Ibid., 128f.
39. Ibid., 148.

The Anglicans in Connecticut could be distinguished from many of their southern counterparts by their relationship to the state and by their fairly uniformly High Church views. Their views of the church and its ministry meant that they, along with SPG missionaries in New York and New Jersey, were the principal source of requests to England for a resident episcopate, while southern churches experimented with other means of governance, including commissaries and direct control by the colonial government. Did Anglicans seeking an episcopate for New England imagine themselves as a fifth column, intent on overthrowing egalitarian Puritan democracies and planting government by prince-bishops in their place?

The first response to such a question must be another question: Were New England colonies in fact egalitarian societies? Carl Bridenbaugh thought they were, and thought that Anglicans looked down on the inhabitants of those colonies as "republican boors."[40] Bridenbaugh dismisses *all* Anglican proposals for a "purely spiritual" episcopate as "clerical double-talk" meant to disguise the real intentions of those he repeatedly describes as the "invaders" of New England, whether or not they were born there.[41] Bridenbaugh apparently writes in complete innocence of liturgy and theology, and thus cannot understand what led the Yale Apostates to their position, or evaluate on their own ground the writings of those interested in an American episcopate.

It does not seem, however, that prerevolutionary America was a society that enjoyed any great equality among persons. The burden of Gordon Wood's study is that it is impossible to appreciate the American Revolution if one cannot appreciate the deep chasm that virtually everyone believed to exist between gentry and ordinary folk in the order of things: The Revolution changed not just the government; it changed how people related to each other. The notion that "all men are created equal" was very radical thinking.[42]

Wood's example-in-chief of how far the revolution was to take American society is not the Anglican South, but Congregationalist New England. For New England Congregationalists, as for virtually everyone at the time, society was hierarchical; their society, particularly in its religious

---

40. Bridenbaugh, xiii. The influence of this book remains stronger than its age would indicate.

41. On republican boors, ibid., xii; on Anglicans as invaders, pp. 26, 65f., 69, for just a few examples. In his view, all Congregationalists were sincere and high-minded, while all Anglicans were deceitful and arrogant hypocrites (218, 223, and passim).

42. Wood, 5, 6, 27f.

dimension, was accordingly an example of "pure patriarchal rule."[43] Congregational churches seated their members according to their social place, and both Harvard and Yale clearly ranked students according to the respectability of their families. Inside its own fence, Yale severely punished students who did not show their betters proper respect.[44] "Massachusetts courts debated endlessly over whether or not particular plaintiffs were properly identified as gentlemen."[45] A civil suit could fail if the right form of words was not employed and the alleged wrong not properly spelled out, and New England courts would reject pleadings if the social rank of a disputant was cited imprecisely.[46] Wood rounds out his survey of colonial social attitudes with an exploration of John Adams's contempt for non-gentry, and then exposes Benjamin Franklin's devotion to that foundation of middle-class morality, the "work ethic," as a sham. As soon as Franklin could afford it, at age forty-two, he retired from work to live the life of a gentleman.[47]

The principal basis for social standing was wealth; one was a member of the gentry precisely because there was no need to devote time and energy to earning one's bread. If they practiced a profession, the true gentry did not live off their work, and John Locke himself had observed that "trade is wholly inconsistent with a Gentleman's calling."[48] Certain learned professions, such as the law and medicine, gave the honorary status, if not the means, of a gentleman.[49] In the case of clergy, the accolade was given cautiously, and clergy without private means, or at least a university education, were not counted, and some uneducated clergy could be dismissed as "pettifoggers, charlatans, quacks."[50]

Without the glebes or state support that many of their southern counterparts enjoyed, SPG clergy were at best members of the second tier, the honorary gentry, living on about £50, while young Samuel Provoost was to have a £200 beginning wage as an entry-level assistant at Trinity Church in New York.[51] Many of the SPG clergy kept school to make ends meet; a

---

43. Ibid., 44.
44. Ibid., 20, 21.
45. Ibid., 25.
46. Ibid., 21.
47. Ibid., 31, 38.
48. Ibid., 36f.
49. Ibid., 21f., where we also read, "On the eve of the Revolution the colonists squabbled over the proper seating order at the governors' tables to the point where Joseph Edmunson, the Mowbray herald extraordinary of the English College of Arms, had to be called in to prepare 'rules of Precedency' to lay down the precise social position of the various colonial officials."
50. Ibid., 36f.
51. Chorley2, 3.

smaller number practiced medicine or other professions. Seabury did both while a presbyter and continued in the medical arts as a bishop although he does not seem to have taken any fees during his episcopate. The world they inhabited was not an egalitarian one, and there is room to suspect that at least to some degree the presence of a bishop would provide a threat to the Congregationalist clerical caste, whose social status was already in some ways granted as a sufferance. The often-repeated story of Ezra Stiles's peevish reply, "We are all bishops here, but if there be room for another, he can occupy it" when asked to provide a seat for Seabury at Yale commencement certainly reflects some such feeling at least as much as it does a theology of holy orders.[52] Of course, it also reflects a change of tactics. Before Seabury's arrival as a bishop, Puritans had avoided use of the term "bishop" entirely.

Nor were New England Anglicans the party of the elite in the secular aspects of their society. While the southern Anglicans numbered quite a few wealthy people in their folds, in New England those people tended to be Congregationalists, Presbyterians, or even Quakers. New England Anglicanism's attraction was primarily for the middle ranks and the poor, and their SPG missionaries were truly involved with people of "all sorts and conditions."[53]

But were they perceived as a dangerous fifth column? Another study of statistical data indicates a steady increase in the numbers of Anglicans elected to office in prerevolutionary Connecticut after 1730. Congregationalist voters did not perceive them as a threat, and were increasingly to share political power with Churchmen until the Revolution. The ever-growing body of Anglican officeholders infuriated Ezra Stiles and other ideologues. It had to be particularly galling that in some towns Anglicans were elected to the Assembly in numbers beyond their proportion of the population. They became militia officers and justices of the peace. There seems to have been a ceiling on inclusion, however, as Anglicans were not elected high court judges.

The election of Anglicans in increasing numbers seems to reflect three factors. First, some Anglicans were beginning to enjoy economic success. Second, some political alliances were forged with the Old Lights after the Great Awakening. Finally, and perhaps most important, Anglicans could be elected because most of them were adult converts who had come over

---

52. Beardsley, 237.
53. For the data, see Bruce E. Steiner, "New England Anglicanism: A Genteel Faith?" *William and Mary Quarterly* 28 (1970): 122–35.

in reaction to the Great Awakening, or because of the liturgy, or because of a belief in the necessity for apostolic ministry as Anglicanism understood it. The new Anglicans still had Congregationalist family and friends who were not willing to shun them, despite the urgings of their ministers. As much as Stiles and others tried to stir up popular enmity, people were by and large trying to get along with each other on a daily basis.[54]

Congregationalist objection to the presence of bishops was certainly based on principle. It was also based on practicalities. Sufficiently large numbers of their people had already converted to Anglicanism and accepted its account of the doctrines of the church and of apostolic ministry; the presence of a bishop would only lead to the loss of more people.[55]

Was the possible arrival of a bishop a cause for declaring independence? The theory that the possibility of bishops being sent was a cause of the Revolution goes back to Mellen Chamberlain in 1898, and to the aged John Adams writing to Jedediah Morse in 1815.[56] However, given the fact that John Adams was instrumental in getting bishops for America and that the writers of the Declaration of Independence listed their grievances against the Crown in detail, and nowhere mention religious issues, it is extremely likely that the threat of episcopacy was not a cause of rebellion in their minds.

The proposals of Samuel Johnson and others for a purely ecclesiastical episcopate did not quell fears of temporal lordship, because neither the English bishops nor the Connecticut Congregationalists could entirely imagine bishops with purely "spiritual" powers.[57] Arguably, they could have been able to do so, because there was an American model of a church without civil power already in place in some of the southern colonies. Besides their sitting in Parliament, English bishops performed a number of civil (not secular) functions, including jurisdiction over the probate of wills and the issuing of marriage licenses. In the southern colonies where the church was established, these episcopal functions had been taken over by the governor, or else the legislature substituted alternative officials, and

---

54. Steiner 1.

55. This is Hogue's reasoning, at p. 288. He also notes, p. 282, that "the colonials' fear of Anglicanism was quite simply their apprehension of defections from their own churches should there be acceptance on a wide scale of Anglican arguments denying the spiritual authority of non-Anglican orders... and they accused the Anglicans of being at odds with the English government, not in collusion with it."

56. Cross, 269. As to Adams's help in getting bishops, see chap. 9 below.

57. Weaver, 284.

no provision was made for an ecclesiastical presence in the legislature.[58] When pressed, Ezra Stiles would admit that his fears of episcopacy were really of "futurity" — his imaginings of what it might become.[59] This did not stop him from mounting a propaganda campaign and crying disingenuously, "For us in New England to be harassed with even the moderate Episcopacy, at least to have it imposed on us, whose fathers fled here for asylum, is perfectly cruel."[60] No one had ever suggested that Congregationalists should be subject to the Anglicans' bishop or bishops, but the Congregationalists found allies in some colonial political authorities, some southern Anglicans, the Calvinist clergy, and in the Whig government, sufficient to prevent any bishops being appointed for the American colonies. Thus the SPG clergy in New England, New York, and northeastern New Jersey were virtually alone in their determination to have an American episcopate, but there is no convincing evidence that their neighbors took up arms against the king over the issue. Bridenbaugh sullenly had to admit that after the Revolution, the only religious establishments left in the thirteen states were Congregationalist.[61]

It is also worth noting that after the Revolution, the largely Puritan assemblies of Connecticut and Massachusetts did nothing to prevent Episcopalians from obtaining bishops. Connecticut was actually of some slight assistance to Seabury, writing to England that there was no objection to his consecration.

New England in the Revolution and Its Aftermath

The Connecticut High Churchmen suffered several kinds of shock during the war. They endured some persecution and also found their theology tested. There were economic consequences as well, and they also found themselves at cross purposes with many of their coreligionists to the south. The irony of the situation is that before the Revolution, the principal charge made against Anglicans in New England was that they were at odds with the English government, not in collusion with it.[62]

---

58. Elizabeth Davidson, *The Establishment of the English Church in the Continental American Colonies* (Durham, N.C.: Duke University Press, 1936), 79ff.
59. Bridenbaugh, 228.
60. Mampoteng, 268.
61. Bridenbaugh, 339.
62. Hogue, 282. It must also be admitted that there were still those like Jonathan Mayhew of Boston, who saw a conspiracy between "the surplice" and "the crown."

A simple equating of Anglicans with Tories would be a mistake; not all Tories were Anglican, and not all Anglicans were Tories. David Holmes studied the positions taken by Anglicans of every stripe during the war.[63] His findings help explain the position in which the Connecticut clergy found themselves after the war. In his research, he found only four clergy north of Pennsylvania who supported the Revolution, and two of them were in fact mild Tories. Only Samuel Provoost of New York and Robert Blackwell of New Jersey were active supporters of the Revolution. Samuel Parker and Edward Bass of Massachusetts were "nominal patriots."[64] On the other hand, of the more than one hundred clergy in Virginia, seventy-four were clearly supporters of independence.[65] William Smith the elder, "the intellectual and somewhat vulgar Provost of the College of Philadelphia," with whom we will have a great deal to do below, changed loyalties often enough to be trusted by neither side.[66] Holmes's summary of key findings is memorable:

> Roughly speaking, Anglican clergy were loyalists in direct proportion to the weakness of Anglicanism in their colony, to the degree of their earlier support of an episcopate for the American colonies, to the 'highness' of their churchmanship, to the degree of their support by the S.P.G., and to the numbers of converts and recent immigrants from Britain and Scotland among them. In lesser percentages, Anglican laity tended to be loyalists for the same reasons.
>
> Conversely, with the exception of the clergy of Maryland, Anglican clergy were patriots in rough proportion to the strength of Anglicanism in their colony, to the degree of their earlier coolness towards an American episcopate, to the extent to which they were low or latitudinarian churchmen, and to the degree to which their parishes were self-supporting. In greater percentages, Anglican laity tended to be patriots for the same reasons.
>
> Where the Anglican church was established at the time of the Revolution, both laity and clergy tended to support the position on the war held by the American members of that establishment; where another denomination was established, almost all of the Anglican clergy and a significant number of the laity tended to be anti-establishment

---

63. Holmes.
64. Ibid., 266, 280.
65. Ibid., 267.
66. Ibid., 282.

and to support the position on the war opposite to that taken by the religious establishment. With the exception of the clergy in Maryland and the possible exception of the laity in Connecticut, most Anglicans, like most colonists of all backgrounds, seemed to follow their leaders in the Revolution — the missionaries following the English-based S.P.G., the locally-supported clergy following their patriotic vestries and parishes, and the laity following the public will. Although Anglicanism supplied more loyalists during the Revolution than any other denomination in the colonies, the majority of all Anglicans were patriots.[67]

Holmes's findings, especially his conclusion that the majority of the patriotic clergy seem to have belonged either to the Latitudinarian or to the Low Church schools of churchmanship,[68] are predictive of the early history of the Episcopal Church. Northern, High Church, bishop-seeking, SPG-supported clergy tended to be loyalist and royalist. Southern, locally supported, low-church, bishop-resistant clergy tended to support the Revolution, principles of democracy, and "the rights of man." Looked at from Holmes's point of view, the idea that the existence of so consistently packaged a complex of emotionally charged issues would make ecclesiastical and liturgical union a problem should surprise no one. We will see that old disagreements on the political issue would frequently pollute later discussion of church questions.

Anglican reaction to the war varied greatly. Holmes counts 150 loyalist clergy and 123 who sided with the revolt, numbers being adjusted for those who changed sides, as did William Smith.[69] The Vestry of Christ Church, Philadelphia, met with William White, their rector, on the night of July 4, 1776, and together with him altered the state prayers. This act was probably the first acknowledgment by a public body of the claims of the Declaration of Independence. Later in the war, White would be the only Anglican cleric active in Pennsylvania.[70] Trinity Church, Boston, omitted all reference to the king in its liturgy from July 18, 1776, and its rector, Samuel Parker, was to be the only Anglican cleric active in Boston.[71] Edward Bass, later to be Massachusetts' first bishop, omitted the

---

67. Ibid., 265.
68. Ibid., 278.
69. Ibid., 283.
70. Ibid., 291.
71. Hatchett1, 88.

state prayers at the request of his vestry.[72] In 1777, Massachusetts was to enact legislation forbidding any preaching or prayer that undermined the revolutionary cause.[73] This was, of course, aimed at the prayer book, and the fine, £50, was the customary annual wage of an SPG missionary.

On the other hand, many loyalist clergy shut their churches rather than omit prayers for the king and royal family. Charles Inglis read the state prayers at Trinity, New York, in the presence of George Washington and the Continental Militia.[74] Jonathan Beach of Redding and Newto[w]n swore that he would "pray for the King till the rebels cut out his tongue," and appears to have been shot at during at least one service.[75] (Beach's brother was a general in the Continental Army.) Many of the Connecticut clergy met on July 23–25, 1776, to consider adjustments necessitated by the war. Their conclusion was at first to abandon use of the Book of Common Prayer, rather than alter it. They adopted a substitute form, consisting of singing, scripture, psalms, sermon, "and lastly, Part of the 6th chapter of St. Matthew, ending with the Lord's Prayer, all kneeling. — The Blessing,"[76] all reminiscent of both Morning Prayer and the ante-communion. A few parishes used this form; others closed for a while. Another New England practice was to allow lay readers to lead Morning Prayer, as they were not bound by any ordination oaths, and could alter the service without breaking any promises.[77]

These solutions were not satisfactory, of course. At their meeting on September 14–15, 1779, the clergy wrote to England for permission to use the prayer book liturgy without any state prayers.[78] The reply came, to do whatever they thought "prudent" under the circumstances, provided that they did not insert prayers for the Congress. By the end of the war, Connecticut churches were using the prayer book without prayers that named any political entity.[79] In a curious way, their strategy for survival was not unlike that of the Scottish Nonjurors, who prayed for the sovereign without mentioning any names.

---

72. Sprague, 143.
73. Mampoteng, 270.
74. Holmes, 275.
75. Hatchett1, 89. The Redding church keeps on display in its narthex a lead ball with an explanatory note about its being dug out of the wall behind the pulpit during the Revolution. If pressed, a warden will explain that the ball and its successors have been stolen many times in two centuries, and that a supply of lead balls must be kept on hand in the church as replacements continue to be needed.
76. *Anglican Experience*, 40.
77. Holmes, 271.
78. *Anglican Experience*, 72.
79. O'Neil, 187. Holmes, 272. Hatchett1, 90.

The (perhaps clumsy) subterfuge of having lay readers lead the services because they were not bound by ordination oaths gives us some introduction to the theological state of the loyalist mind. Holmes, with tongue planted firmly in cheek — or at least one hopes so — reminds his readers that there was a time when people took their oaths very seriously, and adds that they thought that breaking their word was a grave offense that could bring divine retribution.[80] The oath in question, that of the king's sovereignty, was taken at ordination to both diaconate and presbyterate, and was unambiguous:

> That the Kings Highness is the only Supreme Governor of this Realm, and of all other His Highnesses Dominions and Countries. And that no foreign Prince, Person, Prelate, State, or Potentate hath, or ought to have any jurisdiction, power, superiority, preeminence of authority Ecclesiastical or Spiritual within this Realm.

Clergy serving overseas further swore to "assist and defend all jurisdictions, privileges, preeminences and authorities granted or belonging to the King's Highness, His Heirs and Successors, or united and annexed to the Imperial Crown of this Realm." Clergy were bound by this oath to be more than neutral: They were bound to take up the king's side, whatever their private opinions. Clearly the way that clergy were to serve the Crown was by their prayers, so the decision to omit them had to have given many a priest second thoughts. Clergy who supported the rebellion again remind us of the crisis that produced the Nonjuror movement; like the vast majority of English clergy who opted to swear allegiance to William and Mary, most of the American priests said that since July 4, 1776, Congress was the de facto ruler, and was the proper object of supportive prayer.[81]

A good deal of the theological shock endured by the loyalist clergy came from the attack that the Revolution unleashed on their idea of divine order. Their position was that the governing order in the world was of divine origin, and was tampered with at great peril.[82] Both sides of the question were bolstered by appeals to theories of providential intervention in American history, and were doing so randomly, Anglicans then having no organization for discussing issues on a continental basis.[83] While clergy who

---

80. Holmes, 269.

81. Ibid., 279.

82. See Berens, 197–219.

83. See Glenn T. Miller, "Fear God and Honour the King: The Failure of Loyalist Civil Theology in the Revolutionary Crisis," *HMPEC* 47 (1978): 221–42.

supported independence saw the war as the working of God's will for that cause, Thomas Bradbury Chandler thought them "hair-brained fanatics" and considered that "the present rebellious disposition of the Colonies" was "intended by Providence as Punishment" for Britain's failure to promote Anglicanism in its overseas possessions.[84] Loyalists, in short, saw the rebellion as civil war, rebellion against the king and against the God who ordered creation. A loyalist sermon of 1777 warned of the results of rebellion:

> How great must be their Crime, how atrocious their Wickedness, who, in Contempt of every Obligation, have excited, and still support and carry on, the present Rebellion against the legal Government of the British Empire to which they belonged! — breaking through all the Bonds of civil Society, effacing the Principles of Morality from among Men, treading under Foot the Dictates of Humanity and the Rights of their Fellow Subjects, subverting the most mild and equitable System of Laws, introducing the most horrid Oppression and Tyranny, and filling the Country with confusion, Rapine, Destruction, Slaughter and Blood! — How happily, how securely, we once lived under the mild Government of *Great-Britain* you all know. How we have been oppressed and harassed by Congresses, Committees and Banditties [*sic*] of armed Men, none of you can be ignorant. The cruel Effects of their lawless Tyranny many of you yet feel in the Distress of your Families, the Destruction of your Property, the Imprisonment of your Friends, and the Banishment of your Persons from your formerly peaceful and quiet Dwellings — These are the *proper,* the *genuine* Fruits of Rebellion.[85]

Seabury certainly knew what it meant to have been "oppressed and harassed" for his views and actions, although there is no record of his ever uttering a reproachful word concerning his sufferings after the war. This is not to say that those sufferings were unprovoked: Seabury was the author of *Letters of a Westchester Farmer,* witty and well-aimed attacks on the revolutionary establishment. Presaging a good deal of later American thought, Seabury argues, among other things, that the rebellion is good

---

84. Berens, 215. Chandler was later to suggest that the danger of bishops coming to America provoked the Revolution, but there is no evidence for such a theory, which certainly takes Anglicanism more seriously than did many of Chandler's contemporaries.

85. *St. Peter's Exhortation to Fear GOD and Honor the KING, Explained and Inculcated* (New York, 1777), 19.

for the cities, and very bad news for farmers. The letters were answered by Alexander Hamilton, then nineteen years of age; the answers were not very good, but they gained Hamilton a place among the revolutionary elite. On January 5, 1775, the Sons of Liberty, the colonists' most important terrorist organization, staged an elaborate public burning of the Westchester Farmer's work.[86]

It needs to be said in the Farmer's defense that he did not think the relationship of the colonies to the mother country was problem-free. What he proposed instead of bloodshed was a written constitution and something like the commonwealth relationship that Canada now has with Britain. As he would be in the new church, Seabury was in politics an advocate of conservative solutions to freely admitted problems.

On November 22, 1775, the Sons of Liberty invaded New York and kidnapped Seabury from his grammar school in Westchester.[87] Paraded as a captive through New Haven, Seabury was then kept incommunicado for seven weeks. His freedom was obtained early in 1776 by the efforts of Samuel Johnson's son, Seabury's friend William. William's strategy was to galvanize the New York officials. Although the New Yorkers were largely in favor of independence, they objected strongly to having been invaded by a force from Connecticut. Seabury returned to Westchester and enjoyed some peace until the British left Boston. Returning colonial forces went out of their way to trouble him, and threatened to roast the Westchester Farmer alive if they should find him. Seabury fled to Long Island and later became a chaplain and guide in the Loyal American Regiment, for which service he received a small pension after the war.

It is commonly said that friends come and go, but that an enemy is forever. One can begin to understand Seabury's later treatment by the General Convention if one remembers that John Jay and James Duane (later to be mayor of New York) were deputies at the conventions of 1785 and 1789. In 1776 they had also been members of the New York Committee for Safety. In the deliberations of that committee, they were among those voting to send an expedition to find Seabury on Long Island so that he could not give the British further assistance. As their own actions and those of Samuel Provoost demonstrate, they never forgot or forgave Seabury.

---

86. The Seabury-Hamilton logomachy and its aftermath are reported in some detail in Steiner2, 127–54.

87. The story is told at greater length in Mampoteng, 297; Steiner2, 159ff.; and is commented on by Holmes, 275.

While it may be argued that Seabury, as a prominent opponent of revolution, was a fair target for the terrorists, certainly Connecticut's gentle Jeremiah Leaming was not. On the one hand, the Redcoats burned his church and rectory, leaving him with only the clothes on his back. Notwithstanding that loss at the hands of the British, the Sons of Liberty picked him up on a raid and imprisoned him without even a bed from late winter until late summer of 1776, never charging him with any offense. Already in his fifties, Leaming's six months on bare stone left him crippled for life.[88] "Tory hunting" mobs repeated this scene many times. Samuel Peters, admittedly not an attractive personality, barely escaped with his life. Samuel Andrews was imprisoned and his Wallingford church closed. Matthew Graves was pulled from the pulpit by the mob, which then closed his church. James Scovil was a frequent victim of terror raids. Ebenezer Dibblee lived in continual fear of mob violence. By 1781 eight Anglican clergy had been killed in the war.[89]

In Massachusetts, the Rev. William Clark was arrested on mere suspicion of giving directions to fleeing Tories. When arrested, contemporary records tell us, he was "carried to a public house and shut up in a separate room for 3/4 hour to view the picture of Oliver Cromwell."[90] His subsequent fate is less amusing to relate. He was banished but was not actually sent away; instead he was interned in a prison ship, where his health broke.

Like many other colonies, Connecticut passed laws aimed at Tories. The Act of May 1778 confiscated all real and personal property, "as recommended by the Continental Congress, of those who aided, joined, or accepted protection" from the English.[91] The probate judge could, if he thought it warranted, leave something for the survival of the wife and children of the accused, but this was not guaranteed. Another Connecticut statute condemned to the mines anyone who even uttered a loyalist sentiment, and prescribed death for putting such sentiments in writing. Another act denied prisoner-of-war status to those who put themselves under the protection of British troops, and ordered death or thirty lashes plus prison, and in either case, the confiscation of estates.[92]

---

88. Leaming's story may be found in more detail in Mampoteng, Thoms, and *Anglican Experience.*

89. These stories and more are in O'Neil, 185.

90. Mampoteng, 280, quoting Worthingon's *History of Dedham.* The identification of the revolutionary cause with the Roundheads of the previous century was by no means uncommon.

91. *Anglican Experience,* 290.

92. Ibid., 6. Thirty lashes with a cat o' nine tails (=270 lashes) could itself be and often was a death sentence.

In the minds of New England loyalists, there was no greater symbol of their suffering under their rebel neighbors than the Mines of Simsbury, Connecticut, "the mines" to which reference has just been made. A contemporary account is quite sobering:

> Symsbury, with its meadows and surrounding hills, forms beautiful landscape, much like Maidstone in Kent. The township is 20 miles square, and consists of nine parishes, four of which are episcopal. Here are copper mines. In working one many years ago, the miners bored half a mile through a mountain, making large cells forty yards below the surface, which now serve as a prison, by order of the General Assembly, for such offenders as they chuse not to hang. The prisoners are let down on a windlass into this dismal cavern, through an hole, which answers the triple purpose of conveying them food, air, and — light I was going to say light, but it scarcely reaches them. In a few months the prisoners are released by death.... The General Assembly have never allowed any prisoners in the whole Province a Chaplain.[93]

In actuality, the situation appears to have been a bit worse, as the plans show the main shaft to be ordinarily covered by a shack. The only airway constantly open was one and a half inches wide.[94] Other colonies considered the mines the perfect prison for loyalists, and George Washington himself was impressed. Nineteenth-century historian Noah Phelps, whose writing minimizes the horrors of the place, still had to give some details of life in Connecticut's *Niebelheim,* including its slave labor force.[95] The claim that prisoners were not allowed a chaplain must be taken to mean that they were not allowed an Anglican chaplain, for they did receive the comforts of religion from such preachers as Simeon Baxter, writer of *Tyrannicide Proved Lawful.*[96]

---

93. Ibid., 6.

94. The plan is reproduced in ibid., 7.

95. Noah Phelps, *History of Simsbury, Granby, and Canton* (Hartford, Conn.: Case, Tiffany & Burnham, 1845), 120–35. On prisons in general during the Revolution, see Larry G. Bowman, *Captive Americans* (Athens: Ohio University Press, 1976). More on the Simsbury prison mine can be found in Richard H. Phelps, *Newgate of Connecticut and Other Antiquities* (Copper Hill, Conn.: S. D. Viets, 1895) [Richard and Noah Phelps between them produced six works on the subject], and Charles E. Stow, *Simsbury's Part in the War of the American Revolution* (Hartford, Conn.: Lockwood and Brainard, 1896). "Old Newgate," as the mines at Simsbury, later East Granby, were called, is operated as a tourist attraction today.

96. Simeon Baxter, *Tyrannicide Proved Lawful, from the Practice and Writings of Jews, Heathens, and Christians: A Discourse Delivered in the Mines at Symsbury in the Colony of Connecticut, to the Loyalists Confined There* (London, 1782).

It is customary to compare the aftermath of the American Revolution with the "excesses" of the French experience, noting that America saw no Reign of Terror.[97] This is largely but not entirely true. Some states, including Massachusetts, Pennsylvania, and Virginia, passed retaliatory laws against Tories, some banishing them and confiscating their estates, with the result that many fled the country.[98] New York even passed a bill of attainder, to which Bishop Provoost appealed more than once in his campaign against Seabury, whose "life was forfeit," and whom he would apparently have gladly seen dead.

It is difficult to number the refugees, but conservative estimates place the total at eighty thousand, with twenty thousand going to Nova Scotia and Cape Breton.[99] These numbers were hardly insignificant in those days, when the national population was under four million. Losing eighty thousand people was a loss of more than 2 percent of the population. At the time, it was like a city with a population more than 2.5 times that of New York City simply disappearing. Seabury was involved, from the summer of 1782 on, in organizing and dispatching from Manhattan refugees from New York, New Jersey, Connecticut, and Rhode Island. Their destination was Nova Scotia, where the king had given each loyalist two hundred acres of land and where an English bishopric was soon to be erected.[100] Seabury had planned to load the refugees and then take the last ship out himself. The New York clergy, including himself, had written on March 21, 1783, asking for the American episcopate to be located in Nova Scotia.[101] Three days later the Connecticut clergy elected Seabury. It was in April, during his evacuation work, that news of his election reached him in New York.

Suspicion of the Southern Clergy

We have already noted that New England clergy were more likely to have a high view of church, ministry, and sacraments when compared to their southern colleagues. The difference in religion was matched by a difference in politics: There was much more clergy support for independence

---

97. E.g., Wood, 3.

98. Thoms, 83; Mampoteng, 270; *Anglican Experience*, 76.

99. Holmes, 285. Details and correspondence regarding the emigration are in Kenneth Cameron, "Seabury and Migrant Loyalists," in *Anglican Episcopate*, 84ff.

100. *Anglican Experience*, 86.

101. In 1787, Charles Inglis did become the first bishop of what is now the Diocese of Nova Scotia and Prince Edward Island. It may be that the moneys collected for an American episcopate so long before were used for his support.

in the southern colonies than there was in New England. The adversarial relationship to a hostile state church in New England gave Anglicans a different outlook as well. There were grounds for additional suspicion in the not entirely inaccurate perception that the southern colonies harbored immoral or unfit clergy among their many faithful and hard-working priests. For instance, Seabury's predecessor in Westchester, John Milner, had been run out of town for persistent drunkenness and sexual assault on a warden's son, crimes which then as now should have ended his clerical career. What was particularly galling to the SPG clergy was that the man fled to Virginia and became rector of Newport parish in Isle of Wight County.[102]

This view of clergy to the south was by no means confined to New England. Bishop Madison's first charge to his Virginia clergy acknowledges the very bad situation, and calls the clergy to repentance and renewal en masse. Bishop White's nineteenth-century biographer had to admit that "the church had suffered, too, in general estimation, by the bad conduct of many of her clergy in Maryland and Virginia, and the states south of them." He suspected a variety of reasons for the development of this situation, including the sending of unsuitable candidates for ordination and the general leaving of clergy unsupervised.[103] Attempts earlier in the last century to rehabilitate the reputations of the rotten apples among southern clergy had been unsuccessful.[104] The north had its own colorful clergy, of course, but by and large their excesses were such as patrician Samuel Provoost's reputation for extraordinarily lavish entertainment, the elder Smith's drunkenness, and the baronial pretensions of Samuel Peters of Connecticut, who returned to England during the Revolution, just ahead of a lynch mob. There may well have been more serious offenders who remained in office, but our point here is that it was the South that had the *reputation* for employing rogue clergy. The resulting mistrust was keenly felt, and may well have inspired the gratuitous venom that New York printer James Rivington added to his advice to Seabury, "As to the *Southern Bastards* I hope yourself, and every [one] of your Clergy will always

102. Steiner2, 82.

103. Wilson, 94.

104. See David C. Skaggs and Gerald E. Hardagen, "Sinners and Saints: Anglican Clerical Conduct in Colonial Maryland," *HMPEC* 47 (1978): 177–95. The authors review the attempts at rehabilitation and return to the documentary evidence to find that most indictments are merited. Joan Gunderson attempts to moderate this view and place more fault at the door of Maryland clergy, but even if she is right, to a New Englander, Maryland was certainly southern. Joan Gunderson, "The Search for Good Men: Recruiting Ministers in Colonial Virginia," *HMPEC* 48 (1979): 453–64.

keep aloof from them. You can never associate with absurdity & inconsistency."[105] Seabury himself is not known to have engaged in such criticisms. More to our point is the universal agreement that clergy require oversight, *episcope.*

New England clergy viewed the "South" with distrust based on differences of experience, theology, and politics. The first efforts to organize the Episcopal Church on principles much like those guiding the new nation served to widen and deepen the gap between New England and the southern states to something more of the proportions of a chasm.

---

105. James Rivington to Samuel Seabury, July 25, 1785, in Steiner2, 232.

– *Chapter Three* –

THE SEARCH FOR AN AMERICAN ECCLESIOLOGY

Men for whom episcopacy and the concept of apostolic succession had been the rationale of membership in the Church of England were opposing men unaccustomed to giving their church's government much thought. When the crisis of the Revolution forced a consideration of such questions, this latter group had turned naturally to the principles of polity which they vigorously championed in the area of civil government. The deadlock ensuing in 1785 was, therefore, no casual phenomenon, but rather the result of deeply rooted contrasts.

— Bruce Steiner

Let the people think they govern and they will be governed.

— William Penn

Diversity without Inclusivity

The problem of organic union among Anglicans in America was complicated by the absence of unity on most of the topics then in dispute among Christians. We have already seen in Samuel Johnson of Connecticut a deep reverence for the Book of Common Prayer and its sacramental system, an appreciation not shared by all his coreligionists. Outside of Connecticut, limited diversity was a fact of life for late eighteenth-century Anglicans in America and in the mother country. The variety of viewpoints found in the early American church was not in itself anomalous, nor were points of view susceptible to neat sorting by category. John Spurr's study of the Restoration church reminds readers that in the face of acknowledged pluralism, certain supposed theological boundaries are revealed as illusory: "There never had been, nor ever would be, a time when all puritans were Calvinists and all episcopalians were Arminians. Arminianism was available to Restoration Nonconformists, just as Calvinism was to Restoration churchmen."[1] In the same way, it must be noted that while the Book of Common Prayer has had periods of greater and lesser influence in England, in the Restoration period its influence was high. During most of the seventeenth century, energy had gone into books defending the prayer book and the principle of fixed liturgies.[2] That energy was redirected in the Restoration period to commentary on the restored book, from a homiletical and devotional, as well as historical-liturgical, point of view. At the same time, the prominence the restored prayer book enjoyed also heightened scrutiny of it, and from the Restoration period on, interest in prayer book reform grew as well.

All of this being the case, it becomes clear that the multiplicity of ecclesiastical viewpoints and liturgical styles found in the colonies reflected the variety inherent in the English situation, and also reflected the variety of circumstances under which the colonies' proprietors or settlers had come to the New World. On the other hand, some points of similarity can be seen. For instance, in the colonies where the Church of England was established (Maryland, Virginia, the Carolinas, and Georgia), and also in the colonies where it was not, the Westminster *Directory for the Publique Worship of God* seems not to have been much used. Virginia apparently ignored it completely. This latter circumstance is perhaps explained by noting that the majority of the original Virginia clergy were moderate Puritans who had wanted only small alterations, and who had come to America when James I did not significantly move from the position of Elizabeth I in liturgical matters.[3]

Sunday services at the time of the American Revolution have been reconstructed by Marion Hatchett, who noted evidence of small but persistent acts by which uniformity was eroded.[4] He finds a more or less common denominator in the observance of the rubrical Morning Prayer–Litany–Communion (or ante-communion) pattern. There was also underground revision of several kinds taking place. Hatchett notes that the ante-communion was being dropped in the South, except on occasions when the Holy Communion was to follow it. He also reports that "Latitudinarians" on the left and Bishop Seabury on the right all shortened

---

1. Spurr, 314. Spurr goes on to suggest that the real *via media* was to be found not among the Churchmen, but in people such as Richard Baxter, a neo-Arminian.

2. See Paul V. Marshall, *The Voice of a Stranger* (New York: Church Publishing Incorporated, 1993), and Grisbrooke.

3. Winter, 20, 56.

4. Marion Hatchett, "A Sunday Service of 1776 or Thereabouts," *HMPEC* 45 (December 1976): 369–85.

canticles in Morning Prayer.[5] While the use of the gown was widespread, the surplice was not unknown. Tippets, scarves, and hoods were exceptional; their use by Seabury, Claggett, and those of like mind was such an exception.

Marion Hatchett reported in 1976 that the Holy Communion was celebrated in the colonial church more often than was usually thought. Robert Winter's researches confirm and expand that view. Winter finds that, particularly in the cities, sacramental life was relatively rich. While churches in the cities celebrated monthly, in many cities the particular Sunday of the month on which the celebration took place was staggered, so that the Anglican population of a city would have weekly access to the sacrament.[6] Samuel Johnson of Connecticut had encouraged frequent communion, and Bishop Seabury celebrated weekly. A North-South split is seen in the case of music as well. In general, any available instruments were used to accompany hymns, but almost all known church organs of the period were in the north.[7]

More radical revision accompanied ecclesiastical strains and ruptures. The expression of Anglicanism that was gaining ground in the eighteenth century in England and America was the religion of the Evangelicals. Their liturgical style has been characterized as "reminiscent of puritan exceptions" to the prayer book, and they not uncommonly employed supplemental services in free form.[8] The most successful form of Evangelicalism in the Church of England was the Methodist movement. From 1755 on, John Wesley objected to the Athanasian Creed, the Article on Predestination, sponsors at baptism, confirmation in general, absolution in the visitation office, the Ordinal's[9] distinction between presbyters and bishops, the ordination formula accompanying the laying on of hands, and the Sternhold and Hopkins metrical version of the Psalter. In this, he was voicing common complaints, and his objections were like those of both the Puritans and the Latitudinarians.

Wesley's version of the prayer book appeared in 1784. Examining it next to the book of 1662, it becomes clear that Wesley, like Luther, performed liturgical reform by excision and pruning, rather than following Cranmer's road of creating and conflating texts. Because Wesley's revisions

---

5. Ibid., 376. One might add that some Nonjurors shortened it as well, as we shall see.
6. Winter, 84, 88.
7. Ibid., 136f.
8. Hatchett1, 84.
9. This word for a book of ordination rites is unknown outside of Anglicanism.

were like many others, it is not possible to say that he had influence on the American book of 1785. It is more likely that the books shared common ancestors. John's brother Charles did not view his brother's liturgical reforms with equanimity. He saw John lining up with the still-hovering shades of the Long Parliament of 1641:

> Your Liturgy so well-prepar'd
> To E[ngland]'s Church proves your regard,
> Of churches national the best
> By you, and all the world confest:
> (Why should we then bad counsel take
> And for a worse the best forsake?)
> You tell us, with her Book of prayer
> No book is worthy to compare?
> Why change it then for your Edition,
> Deprav'd by many a bold omission?
> We never will renounce our creed,
> Because of Three but One you need,
> No longer the Nicene approve,
> The Athanasian Mound remove,
> And out of your New book have thrown
> God One in Three, & Three in One.
>
> The Articles curtail'd must be,
> To compliment Presbytery:
> The Saints alas & Martyrs are
> All purg'd out of your Calendar,
> Since you for Saints acknowle[d]ge none
> Except the Saints of Forty-one,
> With their fanatical Descendants,
> The noble House of Independents![10]

Charles Wesley goes on to chide brother John for arrogating to himself the dignity of the episcopate by ordaining elders and superintendents, the breach that cut Methodism adrift from the stabilizing factor that the churchmanship of its early leaders supplied. In another place, Charles's disapproval is expressed concisely:

---

10. Charles Wesley, "To the Rev'd [John Wesley]," in S. T. Kimbrough and Oliver A. Beckerlegge, eds., *The Unpublished Poetry of Charles Wesley* (Nashville: Kingswood Books, 1992), 3:97f.

> So easily are Bishops made,
> By man's or woman's whim;
> Wesley his hands on Coke hath laid,
> But — who laid hands on him?[11]

In September 1784 John Wesley issued a kind of pastoral letter to the Methodists in North America. In it, he expressly claimed that the offices of the presbyterate and the episcopate are identical, and expressed his hope that all Church of England members in the new nation would govern themselves through presbyteral succession, free now "simply to follow the Scriptures and the Primitive church." He tells them that he has appointed Coke and Asbury to superintend American Methodists "jointly," and has also ordained some elders. He mentions, almost in passing, that he has put out a liturgy "little differing" from the 1662 prayer book, and wishes it to be used on Sundays, and the litany on Wednesdays and Fridays. At all other occasions of worship, the local leaders are free to make their own arrangements.[12] By the early 1800s Wesley's prayer book services were abandoned and all but forgotten in American Methodism.

There were attempts at repairing the breach between Methodists and the American branch of the Church of England, and discussions were held in Baltimore in the winter of 1784, despite Wesley's "rash act" of the preceding September, at the same time that initial steps for unifying Church of England congregations in this country were getting under way. Coke and Asbury seem to have believed that elders would be willing to accept reordination, and Coke seems to have been prepared as late as 1792 to accept ordination to the episcopate for the good of the movement.[13] Steiner believes that this willingness, even desire, for reordination as a "proper" bishop was Coke's motivating force, and that he never understood the nature of American Methodists, whose real leader was Asbury, whom Coke himself had ordained.[14]

Methodism was far from univocal in its approval of Wesley's moves. Again, Charles Wesley believed his brother's "rash act" had been doubly premature, in that the solution to the Methodists' problem of orders lay

---

11. *Memoir,* 376.
12. John Wesley to "Dr. Coke, Mr. Asbury, and our Brethren in North America," September 10, 1784, *Fac-Similes of Church Documents* (New York, 1880), 46.
13. John Vickers, "Episcopal Overtures to Coke and Asbury During the Christmas Conference, 1784," *Methodist History* 14, no. 3 (1976): 203–12.
14. Steiner2, 313.

in the ordination of Samuel Seabury as bishop for American Anglicans. Wesley wrote to Thomas Bradbury Chandler:

> London, April 28th, 1785
>
> What will become of those poor sheep in the wilderness, the American Methodists? How have they been betrayed into a separation from the Church of England, which their preachers and they no more intended than the Methodists here? Had they had patience a little longer, they would have seen a *real primitive Bishop* in America, duly *consecrated by three Scotch Bishops,* who had *their* consecration from the English Bishops, and are acknowledged by them as the same as themselves. There is therefore, not the least difference betwixt the members of Bishop Seabury's Church and the members of the Church of England.
>
> You know I had the happiness to converse with that truly apostolical man, who esteemed by all that know him as much as by you and me. He told me that he looked upon the Methodists in America as sound members of the Church, and was ready to ordain any of their preachers whom he should find duly qualified. His ordination would indeed be genuine, valid and Episcopal. But what are your poor Methodists now? Only a new sect of Presbyterians. And after my brother's death, which is now so very near, what will be their end? They will lose all their usefulness and importance; they will turn aside to vain janglings; they will settle again upon their lees, and, like other sects of dissenters, come to nothing.[15]

Seabury was not entirely closed to the possibility, but for him, any discussion of reunion without immediate "return" to the church he considered them to have left, he saw as "something like impudence."[16]

Further variety was found in the Unitarian and many varieties of Latitudinarian plans for revision of liturgical books. It can be noted here that New York's first bishop, Samuel Provoost, expressed the core of their sensibilities:

> The doctrine of the Trinity has been a bone of contention since the first ages of Christianity, and will be to the end of the world. It is an abstruse point, upon which great charity is due to different opinions,

---

15. Charles Wesley to Thomas Bradbury Chandler, April 28, 1785, Hawks & Perry, 2:261.
16. Samuel Seabury to William Smith the elder, August 15, 1785, Hawks & Perry, 2:271f.

and the only way of securing *ourselves* from error, is to adhere to Scripture expressions, without turning into definitions.[17]

Competing Solutions to the Problem of Governance

America's religious pluralism remains a fascination for scholars. Peter Doll believes that the changed status of churches in postrevolutionary America not only invigorated American Anglicanism, but also caused England to revise its colonial policies, the better to preserve a single English identity in each colony. Doll's study certainly demonstrates the relationship of the episcopate to colonial policies in general, especially in Canada. The rest of the empire would see colonial bishops as well. Doll's references to the United States come, not surprisingly, primarily from those writers who knew some sort of established Anglicanism in their home colonies.[18] J. C. D. Clark has brilliantly, if not conclusively, mounted the argument that the American Revolution was marked by a competition between denominational forms: Would the new nation operate like Anglicans, Presbyterians, or Congregationalists? His verdict is that the Baptist ethos won.[19]

The formation of the Episcopal Church was also something of a competition; its early years were experiences in an atmosphere of competing theological and liturgical positions. To begin with the more conventional paradigm, but one still novel in that it was without political power, consider the concept of a "purely spiritual" episcopate. A Church of England episcopate free of all secular (and civil) connections had been proposed at least as early as 1641 by Bishop Ussher.[20] The idea was revived as it became increasingly clear in the later 1680s that James II represented both the threat of a Roman Catholic dynasty arising in England and also the threat of reversing the Reformation through the appointment of Roman Catholic bishops. As it became likely that James would be replaced if no solution were found in matters of religion, many clergy and laypeople searched for ways to avoid having to violate their oaths of allegiance, for

---

17. Samuel Provoost to William White, October 10, 1786, ibid., 2:288ff.

18. Peter M. Doll, *Revolution, Religion, and National Identity* (Madison, N.J.: Fairleigh Dickinson University Press, 2000).

19. J. C. D. Clark, *The Language of Liberty 1660–1832: Political Discourse and Social Dynamics in the Anglo-American World* (Cambridge: Cambridge University Press, 1994). Clark also treats helpfully in what the transition from the vocabulary of "liberty" to that of "freedom" means for American self-understanding.

20. Spurr, 26.

the legislative removal of the sovereign was not anticipated in the promises of absolute fealty. The Archbishop of Canterbury proposed legislation that would simply prohibit a Roman Catholic king from appointing bishops, and this proposal was repeated occasionally, but not enacted by Parliament. Others envisioned an English church independent of the state, and were prepared for the relative poverty that such a change would bring: "the more we are cramped in our temporal, the more stress should be laid in the exercise of that spiritual power by which the church subsisted so many ages before Constantine."[21]

Such a notion of a "purely ecclesiastical" episcopate went against both English tradition and recent history. At the Restoration, it had been the king who brought bishops back into the House of Lords, who had sanctioned the Act of Uniformity, and who had commissioned the Savoy Conference. The Church of England had come to depend on the king for its privileged place among religious groups in England's newly pluralistic society. Beyond that, in the daily experience of English subjects and in the memories or imaginations of American colonials, the idea of a purely spiritual episcopate seemed a contradiction, if not an impossibility, as John Spurr has pointed out:

> Contemporary perceptions of the episcopal office were shaped by diverse cultural and social models...the notion of the bishop as a "right reverend father in God" to his flock sat easily with patriarchal assumptions. The Restoration bishop was also a prince of the Church of England, a baron of the realm and a member of the House of Lords, a feudal lord with his own courts and jurisdiction, a courtier and government agent, and in consequence, all too often, a venal and negligent pastor.[22]

When an American episcopate was discussed, many in England asked how the bishop was to be supported in the accustomed style. Gifts and bequests to a fund for the Support of an American Episcopate had reached £2500 by the mid-1700s. At the time of the fund's founding, Canada was wholly French, so one may conclude that "American" here means the thirteen colonies to the south. Letters came from Connecticut as early as the 1720s, seeking a bishop for America, and many petitions to the Bishop of London and to the king have been calendared.[23] There also were,

---

21. Ibid., 147.
22. Ibid., 161.
23. See *Case*, 32.

of course, letters, particularly from the southern colonies, opposing such plans.[24] By 1758 a clergy organization representing New York, New Jersey, and Connecticut had been formed with the primary objective of procuring the episcopate.[25] Some of its members, while working for episcopacy, also worked against the spread of the commissary systems, where the emphasis was always temporal, the exact opposite of a "purely spiritual" episcopate. In 1763 Samuel Seabury, who had been secretary of the group since it began, had the duty of refuting charges brought against them:

> Whereas an anonymous Writer, who styles himself *The American Whig*, in his last Monday's Publication, viz. No. II, hath accused "a certain Convention of the Episcopal Clergy here," of having transmitted "seven petitions, to some of the most respectable personages in England, earnestly soliciting Bishops for America; representing the deplorable condition of an *unmitred Church, &c.* — and not sparing very injurious reflections upon the other denominations, as *seditious Incendiaries, and disaffected to King and government:*" I beg leave to observe, that I have acted as *Secretary* to the Convention, from its first formation, have particularly attended to, and carefully read, every petition that they have transmitted to England, "soliciting Bishops for America," and I do affirm, that the Convention have never made any "injurious reflections upon the other Denominations," by representing them either "as seditious incendiaries," or as "disaffection to the King and government." I do moreover affirm and declare, that this assertion of the *American Whig,* is absolutely, utterly and entirely false and groundless. And I hereby call upon him in this open manner, both as a member of, and as Secretary to the Convention, publicly to produce the authorities upon which he asserted so infamous a falsehood. In this case the most positive proof is insisted on, nor will the respectable Public be put off with a poor, simple, "We are told," which is nothing to the purpose.[26]

The Connecticut clergy, meeting in the fall of 1766, replied to the Bishop of London's observation that the level of rebellion already present in New England did not make it likely that a bishop could be appointed there. A long reply, signed by Samuel Johnson, as president of the Connecticut

---

24. Wm. Stevens Perry, in his *Historical Collections* (1870, et seq.), collected sentiments on both sides of the episcopal question coming from Virginia and other states.

25. *SAC* collects requests from the early 1760s, beginning on p. 74.

26. *Mr. Gaine's Gazette,* Monday, March 23, 1763, repr. in *SAC,* 77.

convention, points out that the church people are loyal, that confirmation and ordination are needed, and then considers the opposition to bishops by Anglicans in other colonies. Johnson and colleagues consider the opposition to bishops the best reason for sending them, although the state of the clergy is also a concern:

> We are sadly sensible, may it please your Lordship, that some of the Colonies are not desirous of Bishops, and we have heard that there are some persons of loose principles, nay, some even of the Clergy of these Colonies, where the Church is established, that (insensible of their miserable condition) are rather averse to them; but this is so far from being reason against it, that it is the strongest reason for sending them Bishops; because they never having had any Ecclesiastical Government or order, (which ought, indeed, to have obtained above 70 years ago) the cause of religion, for want of it, is sunk and sinking to the lowest ebb; while some of the Clergy (as we are credibly informed, but are grieved to say it) do much neglect their duty, and some of them on the Continent, and especially in the Islands, are some of the worst of men: and we fear there are but too many that consider their sacred office in no other light than as a trade or means of getting a livelihood; and many of the laity, of course, consider it as a mere craft, and deplorable ignorance, infidelity and view greatly obtain; so that unless Ecclesiastical Government can so far take place, as that the Clergy may be obliged to do their duty, the very appearance of the Church will in time be lost, and all kinds of sectaries will soon prevail, who are indefatigable in making their best advantage of such a sad state of things. It is, therefore, we humbly conceive, not only highly reasonable, but absolutely necessary, that Bishops be sent to some at least of the Colonies (for we do not expect one here in New England) and we are not willing to despair, but that earnest and persevering endeavors may yet bring it to pass.... [27]

Resistance from outside of Anglican circles was pronounced. Ezra Stiles organized a convention of Presbyterians and Congregationalists in 1766 to oppose an American episcopate. Connecticut Anglicans found the success of groups such as these to be a major challenge to church life in America: "Every blazing enthusiast throughout the British Empire is tolerated in the

---

27. Letter of Connecticut clergy to the Bishop of London, October 8, 1766. Hawks & Perry, 2:100ff.

full enjoyments of every peculiarity of his sect. What have the sons of the Church in America done that they are treated with such neglect?" was their complaint in 1771.[28] Whether they were always aware that it was the Whig government and not the hierarchy that was the real obstacle is not always clear.

At the end of the war, Benjamin Franklin, ambassador in France, advised Americans to get consecration wherever they could, not ruling out the Scandinavian Lutherans or the Moravians.[29] The plan that would eventually succeed, however, came from an Englishman, the Rev. Dr. George Berkeley (son of the munificent bishop of Cloyne), who began in 1782 to suggest to the Scots that they were in the best position to convey the episcopate to an American church.[30] It is not unlikely that Berkeley was himself willing to be drafted as the American bishop, and he suggested Philadelphia as the ideal see city. He argued that a succession from the Scots would be least objectionable to the general American population, as the Scottish episcopalians were not connected to the English crown. The Scots, however, feeling that the level of persecution they already endured was sufficient, preferred to wait until American independence was secured, to avoid the consequences of their appearing to meddle in the war.

In 1783 some American clergy, Seabury among them, renewed the requests to England for an American episcopate, asking now that it be located in Nova Scotia, the place to which they were headed as refugees from the reprisals that the victorious rebels were beginning to inflict.

Another solution, this one public, had been proposed from Berkeley's intended see city, Philadelphia. In August 1782, "despairing of speedy acknowledgment of our independence...and perceiving our ministry gradually approach to annihilation," William White published *The Case of the Episcopal Churches Considered*.[31] In complete contrast to its author's intentions, nothing did more toward propelling the Connecticut clergy to their unilateral decision to send a bishop-elect across the Atlantic for consecration than did the publication of *The Case*. White published anonymously, as did many authors of the period (including William Smith), but there was no real secret about the authorship, and people on both sides of the question knew to send their responses to him. White was

---

28. A letter of 1771, quoted in Lloyd F. Dean, *Samuel Johnson (1696–1772)* (Hartford, Conn.: Transcendental Books, 1980), 22.

29. Perry, 275n.

30. The correspondence is summarized in Hawks & Perry, 2:235ff.

31. Wilson, 81.

thirty-four when *The Case* was published, and by that time he had been a chaplain to the Continental Congress, and was one of the very few clergy still active in Pennsylvania.

It is sometimes said that the reason the democratic governance of the Episcopal Church so much resembles that of our national government is that the two were organized by the same people. This is not true, for the most part. What is the case, however, is that the architects of both the new church and the new republic shared a philosophy. Its chief point was John Locke's view that the will of the people is supreme and alone provides the basis for governmental power, an idea that we shall see Seabury continue to reject in matters ecclesiastical. In contrast, for White democracy is the model of the church; before treating the question of orders and ordination, White sets out his theory that in America the basic unit of the church is the parish, not the diocese.[32] For White, there were two important consequences of this principle. "One natural consequence of this distinction, would be to retain in each church every power that need not be delegated for the good of the whole. Another, will be an equality of the churches; and not, as in England, the subjection of all parish churches to their respective cathedrals."[33]

White also claimed to believe that the new church should follow the governmental principles of the Church of England, but without accepting any foreign jurisdiction "or influence." He took this somewhat unlikely position, he says, because he believed it "would remove that anxiety which at present hangs heavy in the minds of many sincere persons," or induce the next wave of immigrants to form their own Anglican church.[34]

At the same time, White was very conscious of his own Englishness, and was ready to establish a presbyterally based church, even though a valid episcopal succession could be attained elsewhere, as Franklin had advised. White cared very much what the English thought, and later was to write Bishop Hobart that he rejected the idea of non-English succession for fear of English "resentment," but never explains why that was a concern in a country that had just separated itself from England by violence.[35] In *The Case* itself, the excuse given for not approaching the willing Scandinavians or Moravians is not convincing, except as a token of xenophobia. White

---

32. *Case,* chap. 2.
33. Ibid., 453.
34. Ibid., 446.
35. Wilson, 81.

would not even consider requesting orders of them: "the proposal to constitute a frame of government, the execution of which shall depend on the pleasure of persons unknown, differing from us in language, habits, and perhaps even religious principles, has too ludicrous an appearance to deserve consideration."[36] It must have seemed to the Connecticut clergy that White was closing every episcopal door, and doing so quite gratuitously, in order to carry out his plan. This impression must have been doubled when White reissued *The Case* unchanged in 1783, for by then everyone knew that the outcome of the Revolution would be peaceful and fairly cooperative relations with England.

To launch his presbyteral plan, White sets about a historical and theological demolition of the importance of the episcopate — a fact of overwhelming irony, considering his extraordinary (in every sense) tenure as a bishop. He explicitly rejected the idea that episcopacy was essential to the life of the church.[37] For White, as for many others in European Christianity, a bishop was understood to be a priest to whom the power of ordination and confirmation was given, along with certain administrative duties, and certainly this view was present in the Ordinal of the Church of England. Carefully, if eccentrically, White sets up his argument by first defining the "Christian Tradition" as the first three Christian centuries plus the Reformation.[38] He is selective within that small slice, however, and does not deal with those patristic sources that expound the essential nature of the episcopate, but instead observed that in the early church the laity were involved in church government, and that "the bishop was not more than a president."[39] The most he will concede is that the episcopate is a part of apostolic ordering of the church, not part of apostolic doctrine, and concludes that a lack of succession should in no way limit the actions of real believers:

> Now, if the form of church government rest on no other foundation, than ancient and apostolic *practice;* it is humbly submitted to consideration, whether episcopalians will not be thought scarcely deserving the name of christians, should they, rather than consent to a

---

36. *Case,* 458.
37. Hill, 329f.; Temple, 26. White may appear to moderate this position in his 1808 sermon to the General Convention, but the reader is left to judge what his characteristically opaque prose intends to convey. Even in this passage, he declines to take a position on succession as a mark of the "superior order" of clergy.
38. Hill, 318.
39. Temple, 25.

temporary deviation, abandon every ordinance of positive and divine appointment.[40]

White was aware that the sixteenth and seventeenth centuries had given Anglicans other occasions to write about bishops and church government, and about ecclesiastical boundary situations. He sweeps them away with one gesture: "Particular expressions which writers use from zeal for that form they endeavor to establish, are not to be given in proof of their opinion, concerning the conduct suited to extraordinary occasions."[41] As far as he is concerned, there is no light at the end of the tunnel, and Americans should simply proceed without waiting for peace or episcopacy, "founded on the presumption that the worship of God and the instruction and reformation of the people are the principal objects of ecclesiastical discipline; if so, to relinquish them from a scrupulous adherence to episcopacy, is sacrificing the substance to ceremony."[42] The unattainability of orders, of course, was a question White begged, even manipulated, and the Connecticut clergy and other readers were not unreasonably afraid that White was simply determined to carry out his plan regardless of the evidence, which, in fact, he was.

The church that White envisioned was democratic, and not particularly concerned with doctrine: the "president" could admit deacons and priests who would acknowledge scripture as the rule and faith and life, "yet some general sanction may be given to the thirty-nine articles of religion so as to adopt their leading sense." It was White's view that the articles "designedly left room for a considerable latitude of sentiment."[43] The new church was to have no provision for the excommunication of any of its members.

To sum up, much of the burden of *The Case* is that the church could appoint "emergency" bishops, each of whom would also be pastor of a church, not supported by a diocese. The "superior order of clergy" were to be elected by clergy and laity, and were subject to the same group's judgment and sentence of deposition.[44] (This would be a point on which Seabury would be unwilling to compromise.) If some day historic succession were to become available, White was content to allow "conditional reordination." If the title of bishop were offensive, he suggests calling the emergency bishop a president.

---

40. *Case*, 465.
41. Ibid., 468.
42. Ibid., 460.
43. Ibid., 454f.
44. Ibid., 451f.

To the Connecticut clergy, White's argument could receive consideration only if theirs was a boundary situation in which valid succession was truly unavailable — and they did not yield that point in the least. For White, the question was settled as well, and as late as 1830 he believed he had been right in the proposals made in *The Case*.[45]

Interestingly, given White's participation in the far-reaching revision of 1785–86, he maintains in *The Case* that liturgical revision should be kept to an absolute minimum, for the sake of unity and to keep the church recognizable to future immigrants from England.[46]

We will see that White's booklet energized many to get plans for an American church moving. Not everyone was pleased, however. Jacob Duché, White's former rector in Philadelphia, wrote to him that he had acted prematurely. He continued that it was much too early to give up on apostolic succession, observing presciently that impatience was becoming the hallmark of the American personality.[47] Alexander Murray, the SPG missionary to Reading and Mulatton (now Douglassville), Pennsylvania, rebuked White on both practical and theoretical grounds, concluding, "If, then, you plead *necessity* for Presbyterial [*sic*] Ordinations it is a necessity of your own making, which can never justify such an extraordinary step, which will necessarily give rise to new divisions and sects."[48]

We are, however, primarily interested in *The Case* as catalyst to the Connecticut clergy. They took up formal discussion of White's book at a meeting in which they concluded that it was now necessary to act for the preservation of apostolic ministry as they understood it. Lest they be washed away in a presbyterian flood, they elected Jeremiah Leaming their bishop, with Samuel Seabury as alternate choice, should Leaming say *nolo episcopari,* which he did. They minced no words in replying to White: "Really, sir, we think an Episcopal Church without Episcopacy, if it be not a contradiction in terms, would, however, be a new thing under the sun."[49] They found White's motives "purely political," to disguise a presbyterian plan with episcopal-sounding language to win over present Church of England members, and to prevent future immigrants from beginning a new Anglican church.[50] These two points were beyond debate, as

---

45. Copy, 593.
46. *Case,* 455.
47. Jacob Duché to William White, August 11, 1783, Perry, 261. In his younger days, Duché gained some notoriety for strolling the streets of Philadelphia under a parasol.
48. *Case,* 484.
49. Ibid., 479.
50. Ibid., 478.

White had made them himself with regard to conservatism in liturgical reform. The Connecticut priests disagreed with White's reading of theology and history, remarking that

> As far as we can find, it has been the constant opinion of our Church in England and here, that the Episcopal superiority is an ordinance of Christ, and we think that the uniform practice of the whole American church, for near a century, sending their candidates three thousand miles for holy orders, is more a presumptive proof that the Church here are, and ever have been, of this opinion.[51]

In May 1784 they would add, in declining an invitation to the organizing convention in New York, that "the Christian Church is not a mere piece of secular manufacture, indifferently wrought into any shape or mould, as the Political potter fancies." They add that they are working on something, and that if it should succeed, others will know of it.[52] From Boston, the southerners were told that Massachusetts at its September gathering in 1784 wanted unity, but confessed that they "cannot conceive" of union without bishops.[53] Thomas Bradbury Chandler had a pragmatic view, and chided White for proposing a church not governed by bishops but by those who govern bishops.[54]

It is important to remember that the Episcopalian theology recited above is that of the clergy who sent Seabury abroad, not one he imposed on them after his sojourn with the Scots. Their parting shot was to point out that exceptions to episcopal ordination in English history were expressions of toleration only, and were objected to at the time. Unlike White, and here support is given to the idea that the possibility of Seabury's seeking ordination in Scotland or Scandinavia had been discussed beforehand, they are confident that orders can be found:

> Is there any reason to believe, that all the bishops in England, *and in all the other reformed Churches in Europe* are so totally lost to a sense of their duty, and to the real wants of their brethren in the Episcopal Church here, as to refuse to ordain bishops to preside over us, when a proper application shall be made to them for it?[55]

---

51. Ibid., 479.
52. Abraham Jarvis to Jonathan Beach, May 1784, *Jarvis1*, 26.
53. Samuel Parker to William White, September 10, 1784; J. Graves to White and others, September 8, 1784, Perry, 62ff.
54. Thomas Bradbury Chandler to William White, September 2, 1785, Perry, 70ff.
55. *Case*, 480, emphasis added.

It was not long before attempts to organize a church along the congregational and presbyterian lines White suggested began to emerge, although the issue of presbyteral ordination was not addressed. In August 1783, a meeting of Maryland Churchmen chaired by the elder William Smith adopted the "Fundamental Rights" of the church, of which the fourth is of particular interest:

> IV...to revise her Liturgy, Forms of Prayer, and public Worship, in order to adapt the same to the late Revolution and other local Circumstances of America; which it is humbly conceived, may and will be done without any other or farther Departure from the venerable Order and beautiful Forms of Worship of the Church from whence we sprang, that may be found expedient in the Change of our Situation from a Daughter to a Sister-Church.[56]

Abraham Beach had suggested an organizational meeting to White early in 1784.[57] Accordingly, on May 11–12, 1784, a conference was held in New Brunswick, New Jersey. Clergy came from Pennsylvania, New Jersey, and New York, and a few laypeople were in attendance. This was the first church meeting since the Revolution to be composed of church people who had supported both the loyalist and rebel causes, and the meeting was reported as having been peaceful but strained. At this meeting plans were laid for a general gathering of Episcopalians from all the states, with an eye toward union. Benjamin Moore of New York advised them that he and others in New York could not join the plan, as they disapproved of "mixed conventions" (of clergy and laity) and were supporting Connecticut's efforts to obtain a bishop (but apparently did not mention who was the bishop-elect).[58] Moore's letter is important evidence that the attitude of the Connecticut clergy was not theirs alone.

Later that month, Pennsylvania Episcopalians met to work on the structure and principles of a national church. The "Fundamental Rights" of the church in Maryland became the basis for the first draft of the "Fundamental Principles" of the new church. The fourth principle allowed for a three-fold ministry, "exercised according to reasonable laws to be duly made." The only authority for legislation of any kind is to be "a representative body of the clergy and laity" meeting together. The American

---

56. Perry, 22ff.
57. Abraham Beach to William White, January 26, 1784, Perry, 8.
58. Steiner2, 227.

assumption that power flows upward is expressed in the sixth draft principle: "That no powers be delegated to a general ecclesiastical government, except such as cannot conveniently be exercised by the clergy and laity, in their respective congregations."[59] Here White's influence can be detected with no difficulty.

On October 6–7, 1784, a convention was held in New York, with representatives of New York, New Jersey, Delaware, Maryland, and Virginia (Virginia unofficially, because of the laws of that commonwealth). Samuel Parker attended as an observer from Massachusetts and Rhode Island, and advised against forming a church constitution until the question of bishops was settled.[60] Nevertheless, the "Fundamental Principles" adopted in Pennsylvania were revised in a less tendentious way as regards governance:

1st. That there shall be a general convention of the Episcopal Church in the United States of America.

2d. That the Episcopal Church, in each state, send deputies to the convention, consisting of clergy and laity.

3d. That associated congregations, in two or more states, may send deputies jointly.

4th. That the said Church shall maintain the doctrines of the gospel, as now held by the Church of England, and shall adhere to the liturgy of the said Church, as afar as shall be consistent with the American revolution, and the constitutions of the respective states.

5th. That in every state where there shall be a bishop duly consecrated and settled, he shall be considered as a member of the convention *ex officio.*

6th. That the clergy and laity, assembled in convention, shall deliberate in one body, but shall vote separately; and the concurrence of both shall be necessary to give validity to every measure.

7th. That the first meeting of the convention shall be at Philadelphia, the Tuesday before the feast of St. Michael next; to which it is hoped, and earnestly desired, that the Episcopal churches in the several states will send their clerical and lay deputies, duly instructed and authorized to proceed on the necessary business herein proposed for their deliberation.

---

59. Text in Wilson, 99.
60. Steiner2, 230.

Nothing was done here to relieve the fears of those who were troubled by the specter of a mixed convention having authority over priests and bishops, and the right of "deprivation" was long to remain a sore point with the High Churchmen.

The issue of lay participation in church government in general was a problem for many. It was a complicated problem because the English system was not capable of duplication in the new republic. In the matter of electing English bishops, for instance, the sovereign as supreme governor of the church gave a cathedral chapter permission to elect a certain candidate and that candidate alone. The chapter then went through the form of an election, preserving ancient form in an altered setting. In postrevolutionary America there was neither sovereign nor chapter. In the matter of legislation, each province in England met in Convocation, whose legislative acts were reviewed by Parliament. However, Convocation in England had been dissolved in England in 1717, and would not be reconstituted until 1852. In America there were no archbishops, no provinces, no provincial convocations, and little governmental oversight, especially in the north.

The question became: Which bodies will perform these functions in this new, unprecedented situation? Samuel Parker believed that the dean and chapter were replaced in this country by all the parochial clergy of a diocese. White's suggestion, which clearly became the majority view, was that a mixed assembly of clergy and laity would take on all these functions, particularly those of Convocation. White expressed the belief in *The Case* that by having laity in the convention, the role of Parliament was also duplicated. Well before Samuel Seabury was elected bishop, however, Connecticut had established an informal Convocation, and continued to use that name; its members were clergy alone. In the majority view, it was the clergy and people, while in the early Connecticut view (which had sympathizers elsewhere), it was the bishop and, to some extent, Convocation when acting as electors, who replaced the English sovereign as head of the church. Both sides claimed the support of the New Testament and of patristic writers, and each in its way was struggling to find a paradigm that would stand in the place of the English system. There was a third approach. The Scottish church was governed by a college of bishops, and although Seabury occasionally expressed a preference for that view, he recognized that it would not be a possibility in America.[61]

---

61. There is no unanimity in Anglicanism on who elects a bishop and how the election takes place. In some jurisdictions the bishops elect; in others there is a body of electors; in the

In Connecticut it would not be until the twentieth century that laypeople sat on its diocesan Standing Committee. Previous to that, the laity had a good deal to say about the temporal affairs of the diocese, but the Standing Committee of priests alone dealt with spiritual and governance issues. Many of them believed that in this arrangement the English system was most accurately reproduced.

Was there reason for the Connecticut clergy of the 1780s to fear lay control, or was the argument theological only? It seems that there was some practical basis for anxiety. In Virginia and North Carolina the clergy were kept very much under the thumb of vestries.[62] Eventually all glebe lands in Virginia would be expropriated by the legislature.[63] From the beginning, South Carolina's church gave control to laypeople. These facts were not unknown to the North. Northern clergy were by no means interested in a system where they could be deprived of their livings by the perhaps arbitrary decisions of a court not composed of their peers. White's plan called for lay courts to try and to sentence even bishops, so the anxiety had some basis in fact. It was also noticed by promoters of the plan. In letters to Samuel Parker, White twice attempted to downplay the significance of lay participation, once explaining its necessity in terms of the temper of the time alone.[64]

Seabury, Parker, and others would maintain the assault on the Fundamental Principles and early versions of the church's constitution. In his first letter to William Smith the elder, after taking up his duties as bishop, Seabury says that he has no objection at all to laity participating in the election of their bishop. He then takes on the philosophy of the day and its ecclesiastical implications in an eloquent statement of the conservative or High Church position:

> In short, the rights of the Christian Church do not arise from nature or compact, but from the institution of Christ; and we ought not to alter them, but to receive and maintain them, as the holy Apostles left them. The government, sacraments, faith, and doctrines of the church

United States a diocesan convention elects, and so on. No jurisdiction permits the election of a layperson or a deacon to the episcopate, however.

62. Elizabeth H. Davidson, *The Establishment of the English Church in Continental American Colonies* (Durham, N.C.: Duke University Press, 1936), 88.

63. Christ Church in Alexandria kept its glebe lands because at the time of the expropriation, that place was within the bounds of the District of Columbia. Upon its return to Virginia, the parish had to appeal all the way to the Supreme Court to keep its lands.

64. William White to Samuel Parker, fragment, Perry, 59f.; William White to Samuel Parker, June [n.d.], 1785, Perry, 89.

are fixed and settled. We have a right to examine *what they are,* but must take them *as they are.* If we new model the government, why not the sacraments, creeds, and doctrines of the Church? But then it would not be Christ's Church, but *our* Church; and would remain so, call it by what name we please.[65]

Seabury and Parker held to their position until it was to some degree accommodated in the constitution of the united church by provision for a separate House of Bishops with almost the same power to initiate and veto legislation as that enjoyed by the deputies. It would not be until the middle of the next century that provision was made for the trial of bishops by their peers alone. On this, as on every issue of concern in this study, Parker would vacillate. Seabury was quite direct in saying that he wanted union, but wanted it on what he considered apostolic terms.[66] Parker honed the great issue, "A Bishop amenable to Laymen was not, I believe, the Custom of the primitive Church."[67] Although Seabury maintained his position firmly until it was accepted, Parker fudged considerably in a 1789 letter to White, in an effort, it must be admitted, to advance the cause of union.

> This, however, in my mind, is the greatest obstacle to a union with our brethren in Connecticut. It is in vain to dispute which form comes nearest to the primitive practice. *The question is, which is most expedient under our present circumstances.* They are doubtless too rigid in their sentiments, at least for the latitude of America, and must finally be obliged to relax a little. They think, on the other hand, that your Constitution is too democratical for Episcopal government, and especially in permitting the Laity to sit as judges at the trial of a Bishop, and to have a voice in deposing him. [He then quotes Seabury's letter to him about coming to union on even terms.] Here certainly appears a disposition to unity; where, then, is the impediment?[68]

In June 1789, Seabury wrote to White that the Connecticut laity, upon consultation with their bishop, "declined every interference in Church

---

65. Samuel Seabury to William Smith, August 15, 1785, Hawks & Perry, 2:277f.
66. Samuel Seabury to William White, January 18, 1786, ibid., 293.
67. Samuel Parker to William White, September 15, 1786, ibid., 324f.
68. Samuel Parker to William White, January 20, 1789, ibid., 378ff.

government or in the reformation of Liturgies."[69] As this convention was held because Seabury wanted the laity to contribute money to an educational project, it seems unlikely that Seabury would have not attended to or manipulated their requests. An examination of other data led Bruce Steiner to the conclusion that the laity in Connecticut were indeed not eager to sit in church conventions.[70] Connecticut sent lay representatives to the General Convention of 1792.

Seabury on Church and Ministry

Neither politics nor ecclesiology was compartmentalized in Seabury's thinking. Ethicist Frank Kirkpatrick has studied Seabury's writings, including the mass of unpublished sermons, in search of a core belief from which others proceed. As anyone who has glanced at Seabury's writings knows, his favorite sermon topic is charity.[71] Kirkpatrick demonstrates that this is not an accident. Seabury understood the world to be designed by God in such a way that its proper functioning requires individual and corporate self-giving on a constant basis. The mechanisms of church and state were to operate so as to enable caring to happen. In contrast to others who appear in this book, Seabury saw riches as a kind of trap, and insisted that wealth was opportunity to give. He set a pattern for taking little and giving substantially: Seabury died with a net worth of £224, less than the annual salary of most of his colleagues in the American episcopate.

As Seabury understood the world, it was ordered to enable charity within community. He thus sees all hierarchy, in church or state, as established to keep that community aligned with its chief goal and pressing toward it. His belief in the centrality of love led him to reject the atomistic and selfish fruit that he saw the "rights of man" philosophy bearing. No one can say that he is completely wrong on this point, and Kirkpatrick quotes other eighteenth-century notables who say that charity declines in a democracy, although some would disagree with his belief about how completely and explicitly God may be said to have ordered the state in particular.

---

69. Samuel Seabury to William White, June 20, 1789, ibid., 2:328. The sentiment is repeated in a letter to William Smith, August 23, 1789, ibid., 2:332f.

70. Steiner2, 228.

71. Frank G. Kirkpatrick, "Samuel Seabury: Virtue and Christian Community in Late Eighteenth Century America," *Anglican Theological Review* 74, no. 3 (1992): 317–33.

When we understand that Seabury perceived the ordering of the church having the goal of charity in community, we can undertake a preliminary examination of Seabury's own ecclesiology as he expressed it in his first two charges to the clergy and in a lengthy letter to William Smith the elder. Knowing at this point what Seabury's views and commitments were will make the actions for which he is criticized by modern writers understandable: He was following his convictions and keeping his promises.

Because in Seabury's philosophy the church is understood to have been established by God along fixed principles that must be observed if it is to do its job, Seabury cannot agree with those who depart from its charter. There is too much at stake. Thus on August 15, 1785, after his first Convocation with the clergy, Seabury wrote a very long letter to William Smith the elder, commenting on southern plans for the proposed union.[72] After treating other business, Seabury admits that being at a distance from the framers, he has to moderate his reactions, but then writes, "But, my dear Sir, there are some things which, if I do not much misapprehend, are really wrong." His first criticism is that they have made too many rules, allowing themselves little room to maneuver. When he comes to episcopacy, which he believes was divinely established, he points out how they have gone further than Jerome in locating the heart of ordained ministry in the presbyterate, and thus miss the fundamental relationship of presbyters to the bishop whose ministry they share:

2. I think you have too much circumscribed the power of your Bishop. That *the Duty and Office of a Bishop, differs in nothing from that of other Priests, except in the power of Ordination and Confirmation* (pamph. 16,) *and the right of Presidency, &c.* is a position that carries Jerome's opinion to the highest pitch. *Quid facit Episcopus, quod Presbyter non faciat, excepta ordinatione?* But it does not appear that Jerome had the support of the church in this opinion, but rather the contrary.... Whatever share of government Presbyters have in the Church, they have from the Bishop, and must exercise it in conjunction with, or in subordination to him. And though a congregation may have a right — and I am willing to allow it — to choose their minister, as they are to support him and live under his

---

72. Samuel Seabury to William Smith, August 15, 1785, Hawks & Perry, 2:277f. Because of the importance of this letter, I have also reproduced it in Appendix B-1, courtesy of the Archives of the Episcopal Church.

ministry, yet the Bishop's concurrence or license is necessary, because
they are part of his charge; he has care of their souls, and is account-
able for them; and therefore the Minister's authority to take charge
of that congregation, must come through the Bishop.

Seabury then explains that while it is true that presbyters choose their
bishop, bishops from elsewhere come to perform the consecration, demonstrating their own approval as well as the consent of the catholic church,
and implying what he later makes explicit, that only bishops can ordain
bishops. Then Seabury lays down a principle that he followed throughout
his career, one that explains the actions that mystify some writers:

> The Presbyters are the Bishop's council, without whom he ought to
> do nothing but matters of course. The Presbyters have always a check
> upon their Bishop because they can, neither Bishop nor Presbyters,
> do any thing beyond the common course of duty without each other.

Seabury notes that this principle applies to the diocese, where bishop
and priests form an organic whole. He adds that presbyters participated
in ecumenical councils only by special permission, but knows that on occasion they did participate. Seabury then turns to the powers of the laity,
which he explicates with a blunt practicality that reflects his New England
origins:

> The people being the patrons of the Churches in this country, &
> having the means of Bishops' and ministers' support in their hands,
> have sufficient restraint upon them.

When the people have a grievance against a member of the clergy, Seabury would have them apply to the bishop, who will try the offending
cleric in a court of presbyters. He then comes to the great sore point. "If a
Bishop behaves amiss, the neighboring Bishops are his judges — Men that
are not to be trusted with these powers are not fit to be Bishops or Presbyters at all." Later in the letter Seabury expands on this theme pointing
out that no one has greater respect for the laity than he; it is for their sake
that clergy are ordained in the first place. Notwithstanding that truth, he
cannot see them as judges over bishops and priests "because they cannot
take away a character which they cannot confer. . . . Where there is no authority to confer power, there can be none to disannul it." It is not known
whether Smith or White had an answer to this last objection.

Seabury then recounts at length his desire for union, beginning with the observation that he does "not think it necessary that the Church in every State should be just as the Church in Connecticut is." He does insist that bishops have the power of government, not just of ordination and confirmation. He asks that this letter be read to the convention, but there is no indication in the minutes that Smith read it there.

One sentence of Seabury's explains the position he would take in leading his clergy. In his Second Charge (1786),[73] Seabury observes, "We know nothing of God, but what he has been pleased to reveal to us." From that standpoint he observes that "novelty and truth can scarcely come together. For nothing in religion is now true, that was not true seventeen hundred years ago." He is quite prepared to admit that "school divinity" and other disciplines may discover new and better ways of understanding the deposit of faith, but that none of these advances "alter the nature of the Christian Religion." The first point Seabury makes in describing the essence of the faith is "the means of reconciliation with God, through Christ." Then he addresses the matters in contention:

> It is therefore our business to hold the same faith, teach the same doctrines, inculcate the same principles, submit to the same government, recommend the same practice, enforce the same obedience, holiness, and purity, and to administer the same sacraments, that the Apostles and primitive Christians did.[74]

The epistemological and historical problems attendant upon such a claim are stunning, but many of the English battles of the previous century and a half over church and ministry were fought on precisely this ground, with all parties sure that it was possible to discover exactly how a church in a particular designated Golden Age taught the faith and organized its life.

Seabury concludes this section of his charge by urging the clergy not to accommodate "our systems, or our sermons to popular humor or fancy."

---

73. SSB, 9.

74. Ibid., 12. In the next century, incessant reference to the primitive church would begin to cloy, as witness an interchange in *The Importance of Being Earnest:*

DR. CHASUBLE. [With a scholar's shudder.] . . . The precept as well as the practice of the Primitive Church was distinctly against matrimony.

MISS PRISM. [Sententiously.] That is obviously the reason why the Primitive Church has not lasted up to the present day.

We can see Seabury's understanding of doctrine and governance at work in every position he took in subsequent years. The evidence is that he also followed through on his views of a bishop's collegiality with presbyters. He reports taking "the most deliberate pains" in consulting clergy and laity both on issues facing him before the second 1789 convention.[75] This squares with his 1785 letter to Parker, deferring to the wishes of Connecticut people in the matter of liturgical revision.[76]

Seabury was a hard-working bishop, in marked contrast to some others of his day in England and America. He was also a straightforward man, who could observe with regard to confirmation that "it is unreasonable to expect that people should comply with a rite before they are convinced of their obligation to do so."[77] Accordingly, his view of the compleat clergyman was highly pragmatic; his most commonly employed adjective with regard to them is "useful."[78] In his first charge to the clergy, when discussing qualifications for candidates, he makes his point unforgettably:

> By qualifications, I mean not so much literary accomplishments, though these are not to be neglected, as aptitude for the work of the ministry. You must be sensible that a man may have, and deservedly have, an irreproachable moral character, and be endued with pious and devout affections, and a competent share of human learning, and yet, from want of prudence, or from deficiency in temper, or some singularity in disposition, may not be calculated to make a *good* Clergyman; for to be a *good* Clergyman implies, among other things, that a man be a *useful* one. A clergyman who does no *good*, always does *hurt:* There is no medium.[79]

Seabury has an idea of which personal characteristics promise usefulness: "good temper, prudence, diligence, capacity and aptitude to teach," and confesses himself countercultural in emphasizing these gifts. Other pragmatic concerns were "their personal appearance, voice, manner, clearness of expression, and facility of communicating their sentiments," again implying that this is a higher standard than was usually applied. He has no

---

75. Samuel Seabury to William Smith, August 23, 1789, Hawks & Perry, 2:332f.
76. Samuel Seabury to Samuel Parker, November 28, 1785, Hawks & Perry, 2:257f.
77. SSA, c-10.
78. At that time some English clergy were reassessing their call to usefulness in an effort at self-reform. See Donald Spaeth, *The Church in an Age of Danger* (Cambridge: Cambridge University Press, 2000), and Jeremy Gregory, *Restoration, Reformation, and Reform, 1660–1828* (Oxford: Clarendon Press, 2000). Spaeth examines Wilshire, and Gregory the diocese of Canterbury.
79. SSA, c-7.

interest in perpetuating the English custom of sending the less promising sons of wealthy families into the church. He is determined to do as careful a job of discernment at the beginning of the journey towards ordination as he can, for "It is always easier to keep such persons out of the ministry, than to get rid of them when once admitted."[80]

There was a point to this concern for practicality; it was not an abstract passion for good order or an obsessive task-orientation. When Seabury wrote that the clergy exist for the sake of the laity, he meant just that. For Seabury, "hierarchy" was totally a pragmatic concept. Thus clergy were to be useful so that the whole church would grow in holiness. For Seabury, any surrendering to the spirit of the time, letting up on "the obligation of holiness and purity," and minimizing of "the necessity and efficacy of the holy sacraments" was abandonment of the office, a betrayal of "God and our Saviour, [and] the people under our care." Holiness involved integrity, too, and willing desertion of the calling involved betrayal of "our own most solemn vows and promises."[81] The combating of heresy (he names Deism, Socinianism, and Arianism) was a part of the safeguarding of the faith for the faithful. For Seabury, the means of combating heresy ought not contradict the end, holiness. Religious debate conducted uncharitably defiles religion. Thus the arsenal of the holy and useful priest was limited to "sober reason and fair arguments."

Seabury understands baptism as a dynamic link with Christ, and sees the Eucharist as the chief bolster and expression of the people's holiness. Sacraments themselves are as useful as they are holy:

> But as the appointed means of keeping up that spiritual life which we received in our New-birth; and of continuing that interest in the benefits of blessings of Christ's passion and death, which was made over to us, when we became members of his mystical body. They called and esteemed it to be the Christian Sacrifice, commemorative of the great sacrifice of atonement which Christ had made for the sins of the whole world; wherein, under the symbols of bread and the cup, the body and blood of Christ which he offered up, and which were broken and shed upon the cross, are figured forth; and being presented to GOD our heavenly Father, by his Priest here on earth, the merits of Christ for the remission of sins are pleaded by him, and we trust, by our great High Priest himself in heaven: And being

---

80. Ibid., c-8.
81. SSB, 2nd ed.

sanctified by prayer, thanksgiving, the words of institution, and the invocation of the Holy Spirit, are divided among the Communicants as a Feast upon the Sacrifice. And they did believe, that all who worthily partook of the consecrated Elements, did really and truly, though mystically and spiritually, partake of the Body and Blood of Christ.

In his first address to the clergy, Seabury explains how he came to bring to America the "pure, valid, and free" and "purely ecclesiastical" episcopate. He recapitulates the history of requests for an episcopate made to England, and declines to speculate on the motives behind the mother country's refusal, while making it clear that there must be an accounting to God for their neglect. He then proceeds to make an excuse for the English bishops, at least. "Where the ecclesiastical and civil constitutions are so closely woven together as they are in that country, the first characters in the church for stations and merits, may find their good disposition rendered ineffectual, by the intervention of the civil authority."[82] Perhaps because theirs paralleled the pattern of suffering that loyalists had experienced in this country, he understands the Scots bishops as having been sanctified by their trials, and acting accordingly, to their enduring credit.

> [The bishops] had learned to renounce the pomps and grandeur of the world. . . . As out-casts, they pitied us; as faithful holders of the apostolical commission, what they had *freely received* they *freely gave*. From them we have received a free, valid, and purely ecclesiastical episcopacy. . . . And wherever the American episcopal church shall be mentioned in the world, may this good deed which thy have done for us, be spoken of for a memorial of them![83]

Holy and useful. In a time of warring ecclesiologies and spiritualities, there is about Seabury a down-to-earthness that duplicated the seriousness of the Methodists without leaving the larger community of the Church. Even if he construes it more statically than might be done today, there is a sense of Seabury's being born up by and participating in a living tradition that was not commonplace among those of his contemporaries seeking to understand the identity and function of the church in a new nation.

---

82. SSA, c-7.
83. Ibid., c-5.

– *Chapter Four* –

CHARACTER

The period before Seabury knew a specialized subset of biography in which the writer selected items from a person's history in order to "draw his character." Fuller treatments of Seabury's life than that given here may be found in the works of Steiner, Beardsley, Thoms, and Rowthorn. The present inquiry is not a biography, but its thesis is that the shape of Seabury's character makes the actions attributed to him in matters liturgical enormously improbable.

Samuel Seabury was born in Groton, Connecticut, on November 30, 1729, and died in New London on February 25, 1796. His parents were Samuel and Abigail (Mumford) Seabury. His mother and her family were staunch episcopalians, and her father was churchwarden at St. James, New London. Those ties may have had something to do with the fact that shortly after Seabury's birth, his father resigned his Congregationalist post in North Groton, and went to London for episcopal ordination. Timothy Cutler, precipitator of the Dark Day at Yale, sponsored the elder Seabury's application to the English Church for ordination. Seabury was returned by the SPG to Hempstead, Long Island, where he served as rector and schoolmaster at St. George's Church, and also practiced medicine, until his death in 1764.

The Connecticut Seabury family traced its American roots to Plymouth Rock and America's first melodrama, the story of Priscilla telling John not to speak for Miles but for himself. Priscilla and John Alden's granddaughter Elizabeth married John Seabury, whose family came to America in 1638. Elizabeth and John were the grandparents of our subject.

Little is known of the younger Seabury's childhood and early adult years. His mother died when he was very young, and he was raised by his step-mother, Elizabeth Powell Seabury, who remained very close to him until her own death fifty years later. He is said by all of his biographers to have been rugged and muscular, and possessed of a keen mind. A regrettable portrait at the General Theological Seminary in New York portrays Seabury as obese and distracted. Likenesses at the College of Preachers and in the Diocese of Connecticut show a man of power, and they resemble the descriptions recorded by Seabury's contemporaries. He was graduated from Yale College in 1748. He was subsequently awarded the M.A., not an earned degree in the English system, by both Yale and King's College (Columbia). Two of his Yale classmates also achieved ecclesiastical notoriety. Ezra Stiles became a principal Puritan ideologue and propagandist. John Ogilvie went to England for ordination, and then served as a missionary to the Mohawk tribe. Later Ogilvie became an assistant at Trinity, New York, and helped publish a Mohawk translation of the Book of Common Prayer.

For nearly four years after his Yale graduation, Seabury served under his father's direction as a lay minister in Huntington, Long Island. As he approached the canonical age for ordination, Seabury sailed east. He planned to supplement his clerical income by practicing medicine, and went first to Edinburgh to study "physic" and anatomy, the third generation in his family to practice medicine. It is not known where he attended religious services while in Scotland. His descendents' consistent claim that Seabury worshiped with the Nonjurors is attractive, but he and his consecrators are silent on this subject in their correspondence. Like others who went to England for ordination, Seabury gives no hint as to whether or not he was ever confirmed, or by whom. Given the emphasis Seabury was later to place on this subject, it is not unreasonable to assume that he was confirmed in England prior to being ordered a deacon. In addition, it is known that for more than a hundred years the practice of confirmation and diaconal ordination on the same day was known in England, supporting the idea that confirmation was not widely enjoyed even where it was available.[1]

Seabury was ordained by the Bishop of London in 1753, being made deacon on December 21, and priest on December 23. He returned to the United States, working as an SPG missionary in New Brunswick, New Jersey. In 1756 he married Mary Hicks, incurring the lasting wrath of her prosperous father, against whom he was later to find himself in court.

In 1757 the younger Seabury took charge of Grace Church, Jamaica, Long Island, also serving a congregation in neighboring Flushing. Results

---

1. A book on this subject is forthcoming from Prof. James F. Turrell of the University of the South, to whom I am indebted here.

were mixed at Grace Church, because of government-created power struggles that had become institutionalized long before Seabury's arrival. He was very well received at Flushing, however, and he is remembered for filling the church to standing room when he preached there. In 1766 he went to Saint Peter's Church in Westchester, where in addition to the parish school, he began a private boys' boarding school, which soon boasted twenty students. He also maintained crops and animals on his glebe land, and thus could later write political tracts in his capacity as a "farmer."

Seabury began his public writing career in 1754 by writing to support Samuel Johnson, president of King's College, later Columbia University. Johnson was under attack by Presbyterians for the college's Anglican character, notwithstanding it had been erected and remained almost entirely funded by Anglicans. Seabury was associated with Thomas Bradbury Chandler of New Jersey in this effort.[2]

As chapter 2 reported, from 1765 to 1775, Seabury was a member of the small group of planners, writers, and activists who led Anglican affairs in their region. Their chief concern was the establishment in America of a "primitive" episcopate, equipped with none but spiritual powers. They were not successful in obtaining their desideratum or in convincing the Protestant groups around them that the episcopate they sought would be no threat to the commonweal. It was the hope of his colleagues that he would become more of a literary leader of the group, but Seabury, whose credo was "be useful," can be seen instead to have devoted himself to parish work, teaching, and the practice of medicine, along with his participation in the movement for an American episcopate.

Seabury did exercise his pen in 1773 as revolution loomed larger and larger. His *Letters of a Westchester Farmer* are regarded by many as the finest pieces of Loyalist polemic.[3] The letters were written with the encouragement of Charles Inglis and Thomas Chandler, who, with Seabury, saw rebellion as harmful to church as well as state. His argument in the *Letters* is that the Continental Congress was hardly representative of the population of America (an undeniable truth), and that its proposed ban on imports from and exports to England works for the good of the urban mercantile class and to the detriment of the rest of the population, especially farmers. The sting of his attack was felt. Of the rebuttals that came, those of Alexander Hamilton are the most memorable, marking Hamilton's own

2. Steiner2, 91.
3. The *Letters* have been reprinted many times, most recently in Kenneth Cameron's *Samuel Seabury's Ungathered Imprints* (Hartford, Conn.: Transcendental Books, 1978).

debut in controversial literature.[4] Seabury had made his mark: "Probably no pamphlets more readable, none more witty and brilliant, none argumentatively more effective, were called forth on either side of the question during the whole controversy."[5] Whether or not that assessment is overly generous, it still can be said that, in reading the *Letters,* one encounters a crisp and clear style, a vocabulary accessible to average readers, some wit, and a gift for making careful distinctions. Clarity has its drawbacks, however: The fact that Seabury's words were so easily understood by so many people certainly contributed to his unpopularity with the Sons of Liberty, who, as we saw above, burned his work and later kidnapped him.

Seabury remained at St. Peter's until the hostilities of the Revolution drove him behind British lines, where he served as guide to the army for two months in the autumn of 1776. He then took his family to British-held Manhattan and Staten Island, which remained under British control throughout the war. He secured a chaplaincy to a hospital and to a British regiment, and was also an SPG missionary to Staten Island. These posts, plus his SPG stipend, medical fees, and a small amount that his friends exiled in England raised for him, provided for his family during the war. The fact that he would later receive a pension from the British for his services as a chaplain did not add to his popularity with some members of the emerging Episcopal Church. It was not as widely known that in December 1777 he was awarded *in absentia* the D.D. by Oxford, cited as one who "during the recent violent excesses of fanatical men, has stood with rare fidelity and unshaken fortitude in behalf of the King and the Church against the seditious contrivers of pious frauds."

In October 1780 Mary Seabury died. Samuel Seabury never remarried, and there is no evidence that he considered doing so.[6] He continued his work in New York, taking on the resettlement of refugees in Nova Scotia, where the king was giving each loyalist refugee two hundred acres. At the surrender in Yorktown in October 1781, actual hostilities had ended, but

---

4. Alexander Hamilton, *A Full Vindication of the Measures of Congress* (New York, 1774); *The Farmer Refuted* (New York, 1775). Despite the praises sung of them, Hamilton's stilted replies do not overwhelm the modern reader with their logic or data. The first of them says in essence, "who are you to insult the dignity of the Continental Congress," and never really rises above the level of a supercilious taunt. Hamilton went unanswered, however, for the simple reason that it is impossible to refute a sneer.

5. Moses Coit Tyler, *The Literary History of the American Revolution* (New York: G. P. Putnam, 1898), in Steiner2, 129. C. H. Vance offers even higher praise in the introduction to his edition of *The Letters of a Westchester Farmer* (White Plains, N.Y.: Westchester Country Historical Society, 1930), 12f.

6. "How can a bishop marry? How can he flirt? The most he can say is, 'I will see you in the vestry after service.'" The Rev. Sydney Smith (1771–1845).

it would be two years until the Treaty of Paris was ratified and the British withdrew completely. In this hiatus, while Seabury helped organize the exodus of loyalist refugees, word of his election reached him.[7] At this time that his own transforming journey began.

The Election

It might be asked why Connecticut was the first church to attempt the election of a bishop. The dominance of the SPG outlook and the High Church views represented by Samuel Johnson of Connecticut created a theological climate in the state that included a strong hunger for an episcopate. This can be said, to a lesser extent, of New York and parts of New Jersey as well, but the unanimity of sentiment in Connecticut appears unmatched. As strongly as White and others believed that the episcopate was no more than a preferred form of government, the Connecticut clergy believed it essential and would go to any lengths to get it. We have seen that White's ecclesiology was the last straw for the Connecticut clergy.

Beyond the theological climate, the Church of England in Connecticut enjoyed several other advantages in comparison to the situation in other states. Connecticut was fairly well isolated from the heaviest battles of the Revolution; in terms of both buildings and congregations, the church there was relatively intact. George Washington himself refused, at least once, to burn a Church of England building in Connecticut, remarking that "I am a Churchman myself." The Redcoats were not as respectful of churches in any of the colonies. Much more to the point, there would be a time in the war when the much larger colony of Pennsylvania appears to have had only one or perhaps two active priests, while Connecticut's ranks did not shrink below seventeen, even though some clergy had indeed fled and some would leave after the war. The Connecticut church had also been organized earlier than others, with conventions meeting regularly since 1780. The Church of England in Connecticut had, unlike its southern counterparts, actually grown during the war. Many of the new members

---

7. With uncharacteristic romance, Steiner writes: "It is easy to picture Seabury at work upon the docks, checking details, settling quarrels about passage rights, discussing last-minute emergencies with his fellow agents. Perhaps it was there, on the crowded Manhattan waterfront, that Abraham Jarvis, Secretary of the Convention of Connecticut's clergy, first encountered him with a message which soon altered Seabury's personal plans. At Woodbury on March 25, ten [*sic*] Episcopal ministers had met together in the house of the Reverend John Rutgers Marshall...and elected him, along with Jeremiah Leaming, as candidates for the Connecticut episcopate." Steiner2, 175.

were former Congregationalists who had grown weary of the constant dict of revolutionary politics fed them from the pulpit and who wanted to learn religion in their churches.[8]

In a growing church there is a need for new clergy. While it was thinkable, if inconvenient, that candidates could still cross to England for ordination, the liturgy of the Church of England required that all ordinands take the Oath of the King's Supremacy. It was unlikely that the provisions of the English Ordinal would be repeatedly suspended for numerous American ordinands, but the Connecticut clergy hoped that a way could be found to have the oath deleted on one occasion for the consecration of an American bishop.

In any event, Connecticut clergy had a theological and ecclesiological mission in mind when sending Seabury for consecration. He was later to summarize their point of view succinctly, even if echoing White's fear of strange bishops:

> Before I left America a disposition to run into irregular practices had showed itself; for some had proposed to apply to the Moravian, some to the Swedish Bishops, for ordination; and a pamphlet had been published at Philadelphia urging the appointment of a number of Presbyters and Laymen to ordain Ministers for the Episcopal Church. Necessity was pleaded as the foundation of all these schemes; and this plea could be effectually silenced only by having a resident Bishop in America.[9]

On March 21, 1783, the New York clergy, who had also been part of the movement for an American episcopate, wrote to England with the suggestion that a bishopric be established in Nova Scotia — to which many of their parishioners and not a few of the clergy were already fleeing. Four days later, on the feast of the Annunciation, eleven of the Connecticut clergy met in the glebe house of an SPG missionary, the Rev. John Rutgers Marshall, rector of St. Paul's, Woodbury. The number present is conventionally given as ten, but Cameron demonstrates the presence of eleven: Samuel Andrews, Gideon Bostwick, Richard Clarke, Bela Hubbard, Abraham Jarvis, John Rutgers Marshall, Christopher Newton, James Nichols, James Scovil, Roger Viets, and Richard Mansfield. It is interesting to note

---

8. Ibid., 184.

9. Samuel Seabury to William Morice, February 2, 1785, Hawks & Perry, 2:256–59. Morice, Secretary of the SPG, replied in terms that were just barely civil, discharging Seabury and all SPG missionaries in territories not belonging to Britain.

that the three figures to cause their bishop problems later, Ebenezer Dibblee, James Sayre, and Daniel Fogg, were not present.[10] Eleven is a huge number for the time. William White was chosen bishop at a meeting of four clergy, whose decision was ratified at a later meeting involving laypeople, a meeting at which White presided, as he did at the clergy gathering.[11] We will see Massachusetts convene even fewer clergy, and will note the small size of the first several General Conventions.

The electing clergy met in secret and kept their decision secret because they had no reason to trust the Puritan government. After issuing the pointed reply to White's *Case* noted in the previous chapter, they took steps to ensure that they would not fall victim to White's presbyterian plan, and elected Jeremiah Leaming as their bishop. Leaming was not present at the meeting, so a second choice was elected as well, should Leaming decline, and that person was Seabury, also not present. It seems possible that the election of the elderly and crippled Leaming was a gesture of deepest respect to a senior priest, and that his *nolo episcopari* was assumed from the first.[12] In any case, the refusal came, and Abraham Jarvis traveled to New York to break the news to Seabury.

Why was Seabury a candidate? It is a peculiar fact that the oldest diocese in the Episcopal Church, the Diocese of Connecticut, has always and only elected its diocesan bishops from the ranks of clergy working actively within the diocese. Seabury is the exception to the subsequent pattern. The issue of "one of our own" would certainly play a part in the election of Seabury's successor while suspicion of the southern states lived. It might be argued that he was born and raised in Connecticut and had been educated with a number of its active clergy both at Yale and at the feet of Samuel Johnson. That may well have been partially the case. It is more likely that Seabury was chosen because he was a leading spokesman for a purely ecclesiastical episcopate, and was a well-known leader in the High Church movement in the region. It is also possibly true that he was a candidate

---

10. *Anglican Experience*, 59.

11. Wilson, 116.

12. Leaming expressed second thoughts about his decision to Samuel Peters at least twice when he realized the trouble that Seabury was enduring. "You ask me why I was not Bishop of Connecticut. I was bishop elect, by vote of the clergy here; but fearing the Church might suffer under my poor abilities, caused me to answer *Nolo Episcopari*. Had I known that Dr. Seabury had so many personal enemies, I should not have given the answer I did. This is under the rose; and you force me to say that, which I wish not to be repeated." In 1787 he observed, "Everything ought to be so easy, when it is so easy to be made a Bishop, and so easy to conduct the business when they are made. Had I known this before, I should not have been so diffident as I have been." *Anglican Episcopate*, 17. He was elected coadjutor in 1787, and declined that election also.

because he had ministered to Connecticut effectively in the case of Jonathan Beach, who had caused great disturbance in the diocese with bizarre teachings about the afterlife, apparently occasioned by his grief at the death of this wife.[13]

Consecration

On June 7, 1783, Seabury set sail for England, earning his passage as chaplain on the *Chapham,* a British warship. His SPG stipend for the post on Staten Island, along with gifts and loans from publisher James Rivington, enabled him to support his family while away.

Seabury took with him a general testimonial letter and letters to the Archbishop of York (Canterbury was vacant at the time of writing). The letters repeat the need for an episcopate designed on primitive models, and explain the threat posed of having an American church that would be episcopal in name only. They therefore beg that "you will espouse the cause of our sinking Church" and assist it in obtaining a bishop.[14]

Seabury's treatment at the hands of the English is not a happy story, and it is pointless to dwell on it here.[15] Briefly, the archiepiscopate was sympathetic, and in fact all bishops in the House of Lords had voted for peace and independence at the end of the Revolution. Nonetheless, the Whig government had no intention of allowing the consecration to proceed. They had also been lobbied by some Americans, including New Englanders. It was only after Seabury had jumped through a number of hoops, including demonstrating that the consecration would not offend the laws of Connecticut, that in June 1784, after another meeting with the Archbishop of Canterbury, Seabury concluded that government opposition to the consecration was insuperable. He then wrote to the clergy of Connecticut that, absent any instructions from them to the contrary, he was going to Scotland to seek consecration.[16] There is no surviving reply to this letter, but Seabury had written similarly to Leaming some weeks

---

13. The testimonial of election that Seabury carried with him to England included: "we have been personally and intimately acquainted with the said Doctor Seabury for many years past," Perry, 216.

14. Clergy of Connecticut to the Archbishop of York, April 21, 1783, ibid., 215f. The testimonial of Seabury's election and character is appended to the letter.

15. Seabury's own account may be read in the letters to the Connecticut clergy of July 15, 1783, through June 26, 1784, ibid., 219–35.

16. Samuel Seabury to Abraham Jarvis, June 26, 1784. Perry, ibid., 232ff.

before. Leaming both received and answered the letter after Seabury had in fact been consecrated, but was unaware of this. His answer concluded:

> You may be assured that the Clergy will gladly receive you, in this State, in case you bring Episcopal Authority from a valid line.... You must not come over without the Episcopal Character.[17]

The Connecticut clergy had written earlier that same month, also in ignorance of what had transpired in Aberdeen, but in terms that at the least reinforced Seabury's decision:

> A Bishop in Connecticut must in some degree, be of the primitive style. With patience & a share of primitive zeal, he must rest for support on the church which he serves, as head in her ministrations unornamented with the temporal Dignity, & without the props of secular power. An episcopate of this plain and simple character, amidst the doubts & uncertainty which at present in a measure pervade everything, we hope may pass unenvied & its sacred functions be performed unobstructed.[18]

This letter suggests that the clergy of Connecticut knew and had discussed alternatives. There is nonetheless some mystery attached to Seabury's decision to go to the Nonjurors for consecration. Daniel Fogg wrote to Samuel Parker a month after Seabury had embarked for England:

> I likewise mentioned that the Connecticut clergy had done all in their power respecting the matter you were anxious about, but they keep it a profound secret even from their most intimate Friends of the Laity. The matter is this after consulting the clergy in New-york [*sic*] how to keep up the Succession — They unanimously agreed to send a Person to England to be Consecrated Bishop for America & pitched upon Dr. Seabury as the most proper Person for this purpose, who sailed for England the beginning of last month, highly recommended by all the clergy of New York, Connecticut &c & If he succeeds he is to come out as a missionary for New London or some other vacant Mission & if they will not receive him in Connecticut or any other of *States of America*, he is to go to Nova Scotia. Sir Guy [Carleton]

---

17. Jeremiah Leaming to Samuel Seabury, February 15, 1785, ibid., 103. Seabury never got the letter, which reached Peters in London on April 23, 1785, just before Seabury landed in Halifax.

18. The Clergy of Connecticut to Samuel Seabury, February 5, 1784, *Anglican Episcopate*, 26ff.

highly approves of the plan & has used all his influence in favor of it. — The clergy have even gone so far as to instruct Dr. Seabury, if none of the Regular Bishops of the church in England will ordain him, to go down to Scotland & receive ordination from a non-juring Bishop.[19]

In his next letter to Parker, Fogg added that if political conditions mandated that Seabury must go to Nova Scotia, someone "who was not obnoxious to the *Powers that be*," would be sent to be consecrated by him.[20]

There is some detail in this letter that has the ring of truth to it, such as the recommendation from New York, plans for a rectorship in New London, and an eye toward Nova Scotia. In fact, it would not be too long before Thomas Bradbury Chandler, an associate of Seabury's, was named the first bishop of Nova Scotia. What is tantalizing is the statement that Scotland had always been Plan B in the eyes of the Connecticut clergy, or at least in the minds of an inner core. This would explain both Leaming's response to election and also the relative calm with which Seabury introduces the idea of Scottish ordination in the last paragraph of his letter of June 26, 1784. It also adds ambiguity to that letter's final report:

> I have had opportunities of consulting some very respectable Clergy-men in this matter, and their invariable opinion is, that should I be disappointed here, where the business had been so fairly, candidly and honourably pursued, it would become my duty to obtain Episco-pal consecration wherever it can be had, and that no exception could be taken here at my doing so. The Scotch succession was named.[21]

Seabury is silent concerning the time or place of those conversations, or with whom they had occurred. It is nonetheless difficult to overcome the suspicion that Fogg made a lucky guess, or was repeating gossip in his letters to Parker. Seabury carried credentials addressed to the English hierarchy, and none addressed to the Scots. He waited until the summer of 1784 to approach the Scots. Finally, Fogg himself is not giving data he had firsthand, as he was not present in Woodbury at the election of Leaming and Seabury.

---

19. Daniel Fogg to Samuel Parker, July 14, 1783, *Parker*, 8.
20. Daniel Fogg to Samuel Parker, August 1, 1783, ibid., 10.
21. Samuel Seabury to Abraham Jarvis, June 26, 1784, Perry, 233.

When Berkeley wrote to the Scottish bishops clearing the way for an American bishop, he added presciently that they should move to provide bishops "before general assemblies can be held and covenants taken, for their perpetual exclusion."[22] After the peace establishing the United States was concluded, and after an exchange of correspondence clearing up fine points, the question was put before the Scots bishops. After further inquiry into the character of the American candidate now on the scene, the bishops agreed that they were prepared to proceed, should Seabury apply to them.

In July 1784, Seabury was in London, giving the English every chance to act, waiting for legislation authorizing the consecration to make its way through Parliament. In a letter to the Connecticut clergy, he simply states, "If nothing be done, I shall give up the matter here as unattainable, and apply to the North, unless I should receive contrary directions from the Clergy of Connecticut."[23]

In August, Seabury gave up, and wrote to his friend Myles Cooper (Samuel Johnson's assistant and successor at Kings/Columbia), asking him to forward his testimonials to the Scots bishops.[24] Cooper did so.

Bishop Kilgour spoke for all of the Scots bishops by stating that the amount of time that had passed between expressing their willingness to ordain Seabury and his making application to them left them wondering if he was willing to be associated with them. The problem was resolved for them by Seabury's detailed account of his giving the English every chance to act.[25] Kilgour was not the last person to be irritated by Seabury's rather deliberate pace and his willingness to let situations play themselves out. This strategy would have lasting effect on the Constitution of the Episcopal Church.

On October 14, Seabury wrote to Kilgour, thanking him for communicating, through John Allen

> The consent of the Bishops in Scotland to convey, through me, the blessing of a free, valid and purely ecclesiastical Episcopacy to the Western world. My most hearty thanks are due to you, and to the other Bishops, for the kind and Christian attention which they shew

---

22. Quoting Samuel Wilberforce, *History of the Protestant Episcopal Church* (London, 1846) in Perry, 235ff.
23. Samuel Seabury to the Clergy of Connecticut, July 26, 1784, Perry, 240f.
24. Samuel Seabury to Myles Cooper, August 31, 1784, ibid., 241f.
25. Robert Kilgour to John Allen, October 2, 1784, ibid., 243f.

to the destitute and suffering Church in North America in general, and that of Connecticut in particular. . . . Whatever appearances there may have been of inattention on my part they will, I trust, when I shall have the happiness of a personal conference, be fully, and to a mind so candid and liberal as yours, satisfactorily explained.

Seabury then explained his travel plans and commended himself to the prayers of his consecrators.[26] This should have been the end of the matter.

We will have more to do with the elder William Smith because he was also an enormously productive man of intelligence, learning, and diligence, but he enters here because he and his friends tried to interfere with the plans for Seabury's consecration — in the hopes of increasing his own chances for consecration as bishop of Maryland. Smith, who was ordained deacon and priest at the same time as Seabury, had turned Presbyterian for the sake of getting one job, and having resurfaced as a Church of England clergyman in America to get another, had subsequently switched sides during the Revolution, some say three times. Because Seabury's familiarity with Smith's past might lead him to interfere with Smith's ambitions for consecration, Smith decided that the best course was to put Seabury out of the running to be the bishop in America. Smith and his supporters wrote to the Scots maligning Seabury.[27] The Scots are not usually thought of as inhabiting a culture that encourages gullibility, so it is perhaps not surprising that after Smith had done his worst, Bishop Skinner wrote to Bishop Kilgour that Seabury's reputation was enhanced by his being opposed by someone of the likes of Smith, "a man of no principle, honor, or integrity, and who, by all accounts, would be a disgrace to the Episcopal character."[28] Seabury was not unaware of Smith's activities, and wrote to Skinner, "I expect from him every trouble that he shall be able to give me;

---

26. Samuel Seabury to Robert Kilgour, October 14, 1784, ibid., 244f.

27. This unpleasant episode is summarized and the related correspondence quoted in ibid., 233ff., and Steiner2, 213ff.

28. Steiner2, 215. Nor was this the end of the matter. In the summer of 1785 Bishop Skinner wrote: "The busy, bustling President of Washington College, Maryland, seems to be laying a foundation for much confusion throughout the churches of North America, and it will require all Bishop Seabury's prudence and good management to counteract his preposterous measures. I saw a letter from this man lately to a Clergyman in this country, wherein he proposes to be in London . . . and wishes to know what the bishops in Scotland would do, on an application to them from any foreign country, such as America is now declared to be, for a succession in their ministry, by the consecration of one or more Bishops for them! By this time, I suppose, he knows both what we would do and what we have done; and perhaps is not ignorant, that as our terms would not please him, so his measures would be equally displeasing to us." John Skinner to Rev. Jonathan Boucher, June 25, 1785, Skinner, 50f.

but I shall endeavor to keep straight forward in my duty, and leave the issues to God's good providence."[29]

At long last, twenty months after his election, on November 14, 1784, Seabury was consecrated in Aberdeen at the age of fifty-six by Bishops Robert Kilgour (Primus), Arthur Petrie, and John Skinner. The travel time by coach from London to Edinburgh was fourteen days. The question is seldom, if ever, asked, why Seabury put himself to all of the trouble of going to Scotland, when there were nonjuring bishops in England. The answer appears not only to be that Berkeley had paved the way in Scotland, but Seabury did not consider the remnant of English Nonjurors a living church, as they had no places of worship and had generally retired from active life.[30]

The Concordat

The revisionist position is that Seabury did not honor the liturgical content of the "Concordate" he signed as a condition of his consecration through ignorance, cowardice, or both.[31] Before evaluating his subsequent actions it is important to note what in fact was the agreement between Seabury and the Scots bishops. It was not a condition precedent to Seabury's consecration, but was concluded the day following. It should also be noted that Seabury was also given a copy of the Concordat to deliver to the Connecticut clergy, along with a pastoral letter from his consecrators.

The agreement between Seabury and his consecrators is straightforward. (1) They agree on the "whole doctrine of the Gospel, as revealed and set forth in the holy Scriptures." (2) The church is the creation of Christ, and its bishops are free to represent him, "independent of all Lay powers." (3) Their churches are in full communion with each other, and the Connecticut church will not recognize the English clergy sent into Scotland as an alternative Anglican presence. (4) Both churches will use "prudent Generality" in praying for the secular powers. (5) The liturgical article:

Art. V. As the Celebration of the holy Eucharist, or the Administration of the Sacrament of the Body and Blood of Christ, is the principal

---

29. Samuel Seabury to John Skinner, February 11, 1785, in the *The Historiographer* 1, no. 10 (December 10, 1954): 15.

30. *Parker,* 4.

31. Hatchett1, 110; Hatchett2, 45; Sydnor, 44. Sydnor summarizes: "Neither the minutes nor any of the addresses contain any mention of Seabury's concordat with the Scottish bishops. Moreover, the proposed alterations to the Prayer Book, presented by Seabury himself before the meeting ended completely ignored the concordat."

Bond of Union among Christians, as well as the most Solemn Act of
Worship in the Christian Church, the Bishops aforesaid agree in desiring that there may be as little Variance here as possible. And tho' the
Scottish Bishops are very far from prescribing to their Brethren in this
matter, they cannot help ardently wishing that Bishop Seabury would
endeavour all he can consistently with peace and prudence, to make
the Celebration of this venerable Mystery conformable to the most
primitive Doctrine and practice in that respect: Which is the pattern
the Church of Scotland has copied after in her Communion Office,
and which it has been the Wish of some of the most eminent Divines
of the Church of England that she also had more closely followed,
than she seems to have done since she gave up her first reformed
Liturgy used in the Reign of King Edward VI.; between which, and
the form used in the Church of Scotland, there is no Difference in
any point, which the primitive Church reckoned essential to the right
Ministration of the holy Eucharist. — In this capital Article therefore
of the Eucharistic Service, in which the Scottish Bishops so earnestly
wish for as much Unity as possible, Bishop Seabury also agrees to
take a serious View of the Communion Office recommended by them,
and if found agreeable to the genuine Standards of Antiquity, to give
his Sanction to it, and by gentle Methods of Argument and Persuasion, to endeavour, as they have done, to introduce it by degrees into
practice without the Compulsion of Authority on the one side, or the
prejudice of former Custom on the other.

(6) The two churches will remain in contact via regular correspondence.
(7) They have no motives other than the glory and service of God.[32]

It must noted here that Article V begins by saying that the Eucharist is
the principal bond among Christians, and that therefore the two churches
will worship in as much uniformity as possible. The Scots will not attempt
to prescribe forms of worship for Connecticut, however. They express the
hope that Seabury will do all he can to conform worship in his church to
the primitive model, which the Scots believe themselves to follow. What
Seabury promises is (1) to carefully study carefully the Scottish Communion Office, and, (2) if he finds it to be agreeable to the standards of
Antiquity to give it his official approval, and (3) by "gentle Methods of
Argument and Persuasion" to introduce its use "by degrees...without

---

32. The Concordat may be found in Appendix C-1.

Compulsion." Seabury was to fulfill both the letter and spirit of this agreement, and in fact would publish a version of the Scottish office that is in some respects "higher" than the original, and did so in less than a year after taking up his episcopal duties.[33]

Seabury expressed several times his desire to conclude his business in time to avoid a winter crossing — all New Englanders knew of someone who had been lost at sea, and like it or not, the fledgling bishop had become precious cargo. As it happened, he could not depart before winter, and so stayed in Edinburgh into mid-December and passed the rest of winter primarily in London. Early in December he wrote to Jonathan Boucher:

> The Bishops expect the clergy of Connecticut will form their own Liturgy and Offices; yet they hope the English Liturgy, which is the one they use, will be retained, except the Communion Office, and that they wish should give place to the one in Edward the Sixth's Prayer Book. This matter I have engaged to lay before the clergy of Connecticut, and they will be left to their own judgment which to prefer. Some of the congregations in Scotland use one and some the other Office; but they communicate with each other on every occasion that offers.[34]

Boucher is given explicit permission to make this information public. Unless he had access to a 1549 prayer book or to L'Estrange's *Alliance of Divine Offices*, Seabury possibly was not aware of the several ways in which the eucharistic half of the 1549 book differed in the arrangement of its parts from the order in the Scots office. Even in the worst case, with Seabury not aware of the difference, Seabury is in this letter making public his commitment to study and to lay the liturgy before the clergy and to do so without compulsion. Late in the month after his consecration he was still gathering reading material on the Nonjuror position, so any supposed gaps in his knowledge were likely to be filled before he arrived in Connecticut.[35] This is one of several letters that further demonstrate that Seabury did not hide from the clergy of Connecticut the provisions

---

33. Steiner took a different view, thinking Seabury incautious in accepting Article V, although he admits that it was only a commitment to study and recommend. This may reflect the limited scope Steiner assigns to eucharistic questions.

34. Samuel Seabury to Jonathan Boucher, December 13, 1784, Perry, 252.

35. "Please to draw upon me for...the expense of the Tracts, & any other publications you shall think proper to send me." Samuel Seabury to John Skinner, December 27, 1784, SSECR, 186.

of the Concordat, although conclusive evidence of that fact appears in the discussion of the Middletown convocation.

Seabury did become temporarily reticent about the Concordat while still in England, however. He reported to Skinner in February 1785 that he had received a letter from George Berkeley criticizing some of the terms of the Concordat and had from that time developed some reserve in the matter, "as I was not willing to get into any new embarrassments, till I had got rid of the old ones."[36] Skinner had also received a letter from Berkeley along the same lines, and wrote to Seabury to remind him that the Scots bishop's view was that unity is the main thing, and that no one should suggest that their liturgical concerns are more important than their hope for a united American church.[37]

On June 20, 1785, Seabury arrived in Newport, Rhode Island, and thence moved to New London, which remained his home for the eleven remaining years of his life.

The "Bishop of All America"

Sooner or later, the student of Seabury's life and thought comes across the two-volume "reconstructed Seabury journal" assembled by Kenneth Cameron.[38] Among its treasures are collected specimens of the vehement Congregationalist attacks to which Seabury was subject for calling himself "bishop" or "Bishop of Connecticut and Rhode Island." The reader is therefore startled to read the revisionist claim that Seabury "alienated" church people to the south by signing letters "Bishop of All America."[39] A search of Seabury's correspondence reveals nothing more grand than the modest "Samuel, Bishop Episcopal Church of Connecticut," or variations on that formula, and the authors who have made the claim have been unable to document it upon personal inquiry. Seabury's nemesis in New York is also known to have signed documents with his first name and that of his see.[40]

Where might the mistaken idea have originated? The expression is attested to twice in the body, not the signature, of correspondence with one

---

36. Samuel Seabury to John Skinner, February 11, 1785, in *The Historiographer* 1, no. 10 (December 10, 1954): 14.

37. John Skinner to Samuel Seabury, January 29, 1785, Perry, 254f.

38. ST1, ST2.

39. Hatchett2, 5, followed by three histories of the period.

40. I owe this information about Provoost to the kindness of Professor Charles Henery of Nashotah House.

of his consecrators, Bishop John Skinner, in whose household the joke apparently arose. It is never employed in correspondence with anyone else, never used as a signature, and never appears at all after the euphoria of consecration subsided. The first occurrence is shortly after the consecration. Seabury concludes his letter, after mentioning all members of the Skinner family name, "The Bishop *of all America* also remembers Mr. and Mrs. Mcfarlane."[41] The emphasis is Seabury's, it is only "of all America" that receives it. The other use of the expression is as near to making a joke as Seabury seems to have come (he preferred wit to humor): "The Master [of his ship homeward] is of my particular acquaintance, a friendly and obliging man and a good Churchman and very anxious to have the *honor of carrying over the Bishop of All America*. I pray God he may have a good voyage, not only for his own, but also for the Bishop's sake, for whom you will suppose I have a great regard."[42] It is even possible that Seabury is quoting the captain. Seabury shortly after this concludes the pleasantries and returns to his customary seriousness and several times mentions more his desire to be "useful" in his new ministry.

It is striking to observe how much influence one can have if he or she is not concerned about getting the credit. Seabury never sought an ecclesiastical empire. The most highly evolved ordination promise he ever exacted was that the ordinand would hold himself "subject to the Bishop of Connecticut to whose ecclesiastical authority I do promise all due obedience until there shall be a Bishop regularly settled in the state where I shall preside." In its more common forms, the promise Seabury exacted was not this strong.[43] It is clear, however, that he understood the presbyterate as having its existence in relationship to the episcopate, and tried to keep that model intact.

---

41. Samuel Seabury to John Skinner, December 3, 1784, *The Historiographer* 1, no. 10 (December 1954): 14.

42. Samuel Seabury to John Skinner, December 27, 1784, *Anglican Episcopate,* 37ff. In this letter Seabury also makes it clear that he knows what William Smith the elder is up to, and states his view that Smith will not be well-received in Britain.

The reader unfamiliar with Anglican terminology and/or what passes for the clerical sense of humor may wish to know that in England there are two archbishops. The Archbishop of York is styled "Primate of England," while the Archbishop of Canterbury bears the title "Primate of all England." The same situation applies in Armagh (Primate of All Ireland) and Dublin (Primate of Ireland) in the Church of Ireland. The attempted "joke" arises in Seabury's case because in all of America there would be no other bishops for him to have precedence of, and no province over which he could preside, and none of the handsome emoluments that accompanied metropolitical status in his day. The practice of American bishops and bishops-elect joking about themselves or a colleague as being the "bishop of 'all' X" continues, especially when "X" is small, remote, or pest-ridden.

43. This matter is set out in more detail in Steiner2, 254.

Reaction to the Nonjuror Consecration

News of the consecration reached America before Seabury did. On the negative side, there was something to offend everyone disposed to object. For many a Congregationalist, the mere presence of someone pretending to be in other than presbyter's orders was an outrage. For others, Seabury's zealous loyalism during the late revolution was unforgivable. For those who had in the Revolution renounced their solemn oaths of allegiance to the king, the presence of one who had been ordained by Nonjurors was an irritating reminder that their acts were questionable from at least one theological point of view. Those who were still secretly loyal to George III were of course confronted now by a bishop made by bishops who recognized another dynasty as rightly entitled to the British throne. Those who believed that church governance proceeded from the will of the people were here confronted with a bishop who believed, as his consecrators did, that church order had been established by God, and that the bishops, as successors to the apostles, were the divinely appointed governors of the church.

The nascent Episcopal Church, like the Episcopal Church today, comprehended those who considered episcopacy a perhaps venerable but not strictly necessary institution, along with those who would go to any lengths, including recourse to the Nonjurors, to obtain a valid succession of apostolic governors because they believed it to be necessary. White (at least in *The Case*) and Seabury represented these poles for many people, so their eventual ability to work together became iconic of the viability of the new church.

The hostility of some of the New England press to Seabury was evident before he landed. The *Connecticut Courant* delivered the prophecy that he would support himself by performing ordinations at twenty guineas each.

Among the many that Cameron has collected, this poem from the Boston *Sentinel* for April 12, 1785, is one of the milder examples:

The Bishop and Toad

> A Toad who liv'd in Bishop's gardens,
> Grown *saucy* went to granting *pardons,*
> Or what's the same, *true confirmation,*
> Just as he pleas'd, or had occasion;
> To all rich elves that kept around
> Such sacred spots of *Holy-Ground:*

> And more belike his pomp to dish up,
> Assum'd the title of a Bishop,
> (Though' Bishops Godlike are, *'tis true*
> They've always *filthy things* in view —)
> As S——y strutted on the road,
> *In awful* pomp, he spy'd this toad,
> And drawing nigher to the elf,
> Saw just the image of himself —
> For on the stool, with all his *beauties,*
> He'd just got up to go to *duties...*
> And down below (*Priest-rid*) this station;
> An hundred stood for *confirmation.*
> But when our Bishop saw full wisely,
> *All things,* from toad-stool done so nicely,
> He sneak'd away, 'tis said, full sure,
> To leave behind his *miniature.*[44]

Some of the reaction Seabury found amusing, at least at first. Reporting to Skinner that Connecticut people have generally received him well, he notes that the exceptions are the Congregationalist clergy, who since his arrival "appeared...to be rather alarmed, & have in consequence of my arrival, assumed & give to each other the stile and title of Bishop, which formerly they reprobated as a remnant of Popery. They are a good deal laughed at by their own people."[45]

Much more serious were the efforts of low-church evangelical Granville Sharpe, who wrote to non-Anglicans in America disparaging the Scottish succession as well as Seabury's character.[46] After Seabury's arrival, things grew worse. A letter exists congratulating Ezra Stiles for his famous commencement snub of Seabury at Yale.[47] The *New York Packet* carried the following letter from Boston in 1786:

> I don't recollect any thing else that is new to tell you — O yes, Miss! We have a Bishop in town named Seabury — he dresses in a black shirt with the fore-flap hanging out, that's one suit; at other times he appears in a black satin gown, white satin sleeves, white belly

---

44. ST1, 27.
45. Samuel Seabury to John Skinner, December 23, 1785, *The Historiographer* 1, no. 10 (December 10, 1954): 15.
46. For example, see Perry, 272.
47. No author given. ST2, 15ff.

band, with a scarlet knapsack at his back, and something resembling
a pyramid on his head. — Fine times now! We can have our sins
pardoned without going to Rome — if you have any to repent of, let
know for I guess you may obtain *absolution* by *proxy*.[48]

Religious people of any inclination do not always tolerate differences
well, especially if those differences could be seen to call their own viewpoints into question. Attacks on Seabury's character and "pretensions"
continue to the present day, as we have seen. What had to wound him
more, and he was a man who noticed criticism, were the barbs hurled by
members of his own communion, and of them, those from his own diocese
must have hurt the most. At the August 1785 convocation of the clergy,
at least three did not present themselves to accept Seabury as their bishop,
namely, Messrs. Fogg, Tyler, and Dibblee. None of them had been at the
electing convocation, and it is to be wondered whether they would have
accepted any bishop.

Dibblee, a chronic nonattender of meetings, was nonetheless never at
a loss for opinions about their results. He objected in the strongest terms
to the Scottish consecration "by the Back Door" and "by Climbing over
the Wall," and voiced his underlying concern that the SPG would disown
the American missionaries in the United States. They did. Dibblee had
been a loyalist during the Revolution, so it is interesting to note one of
his complaints: "was there no possible way for Doctor Seabury to obtain
Consecration but in a Method so obnoxious to Revolutional Principles?"[49]

We will come again to Seabury's greatest self-declared enemy, Samuel
Provoost, first bishop of New York, associated with some leading New
York figures in the Revolution. The immaturity of his obsession with
Seabury can be seen in his endlessly repeated misspelling of his name as
"Cebra," which apparently sounded Scottish to him. E. E. Beardsley wrote
of this, quoting a contemporary of Seabury's, that Provoost "didn't care
a picayune for the Non Jurors as Churchmen. He hated them as Jacobites and Tories. It was easy for him to make Jurorism a cover for his
political malignity as a Whig. The *odium politicum* is more remorseless
than the *odium theologicum* — let worldlings say what they will."[50] The

---

48. ST1, 28. Anne Rowthorn seems to mistake the ignorance of a Congregationalist clum-
sily trying to describe the traditional bishop's choir dress (rochet, chimere, hood, and tippet)
with a foppish tendency on the part of Seabury. What *is* remarkable in his dress is his combi-
nation of a mitre with choir habit, but the more traditional accompanying vestments were not
to be seen in Anglicanism for the best part of a century.

49. Dibblee, 63.

50. *Anglican Episcopate*, 53.

observation seems to be born out by Provoost's letter to White in May 1786:

> As the General Convention did not think it proper to acknowledge Dr. Cebra as a Bishop, much less as a Bishop of our Church, it would be highly improper for us, in our private capacities, to give any sanction to his ordination.... For my own part, I ... should be extremely sorry that the conduct of my brethren here should tend to the resurrection of the sect of Nonjurors, (nearly buried in oblivion,) whose slavish and absurd tenets were a disgrace to humanity.[51]

While much of the press was bad, there survives a broader spectrum of positive reaction, beginning with praise from a perhaps unexpected quarter, holy Charles Wesley. Thomas Bradbury Chandler wrote to Seabury in 1786 that Wesley continued to speak of Seabury "in terms of high respect and affection."[52] Wesley had written in 1785 of the plight of Methodists in America, a statement quoted at length above. A key passage bears repeating:

> What will become of those poor sheep in the wilderness, the American Methodists? How have they been betrayed into a separation from the Church of England, which their preachers and they no more intended than the Methodists here? Had they had patience a little longer, they would have seen a *real primitive Bishop* in America, duly *consecrated by three Scotch Bishops,* who had *their* consecration from the English Bishops, and are acknowledged by them as the same as themselves. There is therefore, not the least difference betwixt the members of Bishop Seabury's Church and the members of the Church of England.
>
> You know I had the happiness to converse with that truly apostolical man, who is esteemed by all that know him as much as by you and me.[53]

Jacob Duché wrote to former curate William White twice regarding the new bishop for America. A few weeks after the Aberdeen consecration, he told White:

---

51. Samuel Provoost to William White, May 20, 1786, *SSECR,* 42.
52. Thomas Bradbury Chandler to Samuel Seabury, February 16, 1786, ST1, 25f.
53. Charles Wesley to Thomas Bradbury Chandler, April 28, 1785, Hawks & Perry, 2:261.

Your American Bishop — for so I must now call him — is a *Scholar,*
a *Gentleman,* and I am happy to be able to say (what I verily believe
to be true) *a real Christian* — I hope you will take the earliest opportunity of calling together a Convention, a Synod, or Convocation,
or some General Ecclesiastical Meeting, from the several States —
to receive him, and at the same time, to fix upon an Ecclesiastical
Constitution, for your future Union & Comfort.[54]

That was not the kind of "General Ecclesiastical Meeting" that White
had in mind, and the organizing convention in New York adopted the Fundamental Principles. Duché was shocked by them, and took White to task,
especially for not awaiting Seabury, as "Providence has sent him to accomplish and preserve a compleat Union in your new American Episcopal
Church."[55]

There is ample evidence that the English archbishops publicly disapproved of Seabury's move. There is some evidence that Canterbury secretly
sent his approval to the Scots bishops, knowing that Seabury's Scottish
consecration would help open the way for similar consecrations in England.[56] Samuel Peters certainly thought that way, observing that "Seabury
however has done *right* in acting *wrong,* as our Bishops, Ministers, and
Dissenters never designed to afford America a Bishop."[57]

Samuel Parker, to be second bishop of Massachusetts, only warmed
to the idea of Seabury and of Scottish orders slowly. In July 1783, he
thought that Seabury's Tory past and prospective Nonjuror ordination
would make him unsuitable.[58] Two years later, it occurred to him that "*If*
the succession among the Nonjurors is good, a Bishop from thence will be
better for us than an English one, because there can be no fear of an undue
influence from the British Crown."[59] In 1786 he could say that "we should
never have obtained the Succession from England, had [Seabury] or some
other not have obtained it first from Scotland."[60] Nonetheless, he remained
opposed to Scottish ordination for a bishop in his own Massachusetts.[61]
Parker's journey is recapped here because it shows growing acceptance of
the Seabury episcopate, but also demonstrates Parker's sometimes shifting

---

54. Jacob Duché to William White, December 1, 1784, *CtFirst*, 5.
55. Jacob Duché to William White, February 10, 1785, Perry, 269.
56. Lathbury, 476.
57. Samuel Peters to William Samuel Johnson, February 12, 1786, *Peters2*, 17.
58. Samuel Parker to Daniel Fogg, July 7, 1783, *Parker*, 10.
59. Samuel Parker to Samuel Peters, May 7, 1785, ibid., 15. Emphasis added.
60. Samuel Parker to William White, September 15, 1786, *SAC*, 93.
61. Samuel Parker to Bela Hubbard, June 1, 1787, Perry, 343.

point of view. This pattern will be seen to repeat itself in matters liturgical from Middletown onward.

Later Life

Seabury continued to serve both his parish and his diocese. He also took the time to write, edit, and publish for the church.[62] He occasionally preached to his Masonic brethren, as did bishops White, Bass, Jarvis, and Inglis; the elder Smith was also active as a Mason.[63] On the day of his death, February 25, 1796, Seabury had been making parish calls, "useful" to the end. He was laid to rest in the public cemetery, but is now buried in St. James Church, New London. His epitaph, by Dr. Bowden of Columbia, reads:

Here lieth the body of
SAMUEL SEABURY, D.D.
Bishop of Connecticut and Rhode Island
Who departed from this transitory scene, February 25th, 1796
In the sixty eighth year of his age.
Ingenious without pride, learned without pedantry,
Good without severity,
He was duly qualified to discharge the duties of
the Christian & the Bishop:
In the pulpit he enforced religion:
In his conduct he exemplified it:
The poor he assisted with his charity:
The ignorant he blessed with his instruction:
The friend of man, he ever desired their good:
The enemy of vice, he ever opposed it:
Christian! Dost thou aspire to Happiness?
Seabury has shown the way that leads to it.

---

62. Seabury's printed works are listed in Appendix D-1.

63. Sydney Hayden, *Washington and His Masonic Compeers* (New York, 1867). Seabury dedicated one of his printed sermons to his "Most Worshipful President," from his "brother" Samuel Seabury. Hayden includes other clergy in his study. He also notes the existence of both British and American military lodges following the Revolution. It is tantalizing to consider what the relationship between Samuel Provoost and the Bishop of Connecticut would have been had they shared a Masonic bond. Seabury's published Masonic works include *A Discourse Delivered...Before an Assembly of Free and Accepted Masons, Convened for the Purpose of Installing a Lodge in that City* (1795), and *A Sermon Preached Before the Grand Lodge, and the Other Lodges of Ancient Freemasons, in New York, at St. Paul's Chapel* (1782).

Seabury's biographers all illustrate the epitaph's point with accounts of
Seabury's ministry. Because of its topic, this study shortchanges Seabury
as pastor, preacher, writer, and physician to the poor. Redress and balance can be found by reading the standard biographies, but even more
impressive are the calendar of the events of Seabury's ministry. His Diary
"B" was edited by Anne Rowthorn as *Miles to Go Before I Sleep*,[64] an
exquisitely appropriate title for the record of one who defined himself in
part by the promises he had to keep. What strikes the reader, besides the
estimated nine thousand miles Seabury traveled by horse or coach, is how
often his record of an event culminates in a prayerful reflection or reflec-
tive prayer. Shortly before his death Seabury records the following for All
Souls Day, 1795:

> On Monday the 2nd of November, I went on, accompanied by the
> Rev. Deacon Miles, to Branford. Passing through East Haven, my
> horse fell and threw me, or rather obliged me to jump, out of the
> sulky. But, by the mercy of God, I escaped with only a slight bruise
> on the knee. At Branford I that day preached and confirmed twenty-
> one persons. The next day I set out for New London on Wednesday,
> the 4th of November, after an absence of almost four weeks and
> found my family safe and well.
>
> In this journey I traveled one hundred and thirty-four miles,
> preached ten times, administered the Communion five times and
> confirmed one hundred and ninety-eight persons.
>
> And now, all glory to God for his innumerable benefits. Thou,
> O God, tookest me out of my mother's womb; thou has preserved
> me ever since; thou hast blessed me with health; thou hast provided
> me with the comforts and decencies of life; thou hast vouchsafed me
> the means of grace and the hope of glory; thou hast raised me to an
> honourable station in thy Church; thou hast given me a willing heart
> to do my duty in it. Confirm that ready disposition; let thy Holy
> Spirit ever direct it to thy glory and the good of thy Church. May
> thy goodness lead me to love thee above all things, through Jesus
> Christ. Amen.

Seabury's prayer is an example of an unforced blending of biblical and
liturgical phrase, the result of the kind of spiritual formation that all who

---

64. Hartford, Conn.: Church Missions Publishing Company, 1982. The complete diary is
in the Seabury collection at General Seminary.

set out liturgies hope will take shape in those who pray them. In June 1794, he "set out for New Haven to meet the Convention of the clergy and lay deputies." He prays with simplicity:

> Preserve me, O my God, from all accidents in this journey and keep me in health and spirits to serve thee by consulting the interest of thy Church and promoting the spiritual welfare of thy people. May no bitterness or ill will arise in our deliberations, but only such tempers and disposition as tend to thy glory and the honour of thy Christ.

For the reader more adventurous and patient of detail, Cameron's "reconstructed journal" (ST1, ST2) of Seabury's entire episcopate presents the minutiae of an enormously constructive and useful career.

In addition, it may be helpful for our inquiries to examine Seabury's care of Ebenezer Dibblee. Dibblee was a Yale graduate serving a Congregationalist congregation in Danbury when he converted to Anglicanism. The church people of Stamford committed to support him, and he was ordained deacon and priest in London in 1748. A staunch loyalist, he wrote as early as 1767, "God have mercy upon us, if the provinces here should throw off their connection, dependence, and subjection to the mother country." His fear was that should clergy support the Revolution, all church people would face "terrible calamities."[65]

Dibblee is a specimen of the kind of priest who is a torment to a bishop. Chronically depressed, he almost never attended meetings, but nonetheless did not hesitate to criticize loudly the results of deliberations he had declined to join. When Seabury reported to the SPG at the end of 1776, all the Connecticut clergy were either "carried away from their cures, or confined to their houses, except Mr. Dibblee, who is gone to Sharon to be inoculated for the small-pox — possibly hoping thereby to enjoy a few week's respite from persecution."[66] In fairness, it needs to be added that Dibblee remained steadfastly in his parish on no salary throughout the war, lost a son to banishment, and saw his daughter driven insane by the circumstances that attended the war.

Dibblee was one of the three priests who refused to receive Seabury as bishop in 1785. Although he did not dispute the legality or even the appropriateness of Seabury's election, he was deeply troubled by Seabury's "final triumph over all opposition, by *Climbing over the Wall.*" Dibblee did not

---

65. Dibblee, 57f.
66. Samuel Seabury to SPG, December 29, 1776, Dibblee, 58.

question the reality of Seabury's consecration, but believed that the choice would alienate the Americans from the mother church and leave Connecticut church people open to the charge of Jacobitism. Samuel Provoost was happy to oblige in this latter regard.[67]

In March 1786, Dibblee was still on this track, terming the failure to stay in channels, particularly the SPG's, "the height of ingratitude and unpardonable." Of course, by this time SPG stipends to Americans were cut. Dibblee is grieved that "the innocent should suffer with the guilty." But something is changing in his apprehensions. After he confesses that he did not attend the Middletown reception of the bishop or send him even a congratulatory note, he confesses himself impressed that "the Bishop conducts [himself] with great wisdom and prudence" regarding choice of ordinands and a deliberate pace in liturgical revision. He is heartened that Seabury shares a special interest of his: education.[68]

In 1787 Dibblee writes of Seabury's wisdom and prudence, and shares the general irritation at the conduct of Bishop Provoost toward the Bishop of Connecticut. But his old fearful nature asserts itself. His fear that "the Cement of British Union" with the American church will be broken was heightened by the appearance of Seabury's Communion Office. His back is up to anything he perceives as imposed "by dint of Episcopal supremacy," and he reports that it was "with a noble Spirit rejected" by the clergy.[69] We must take this to mean that it was rejected by Dibblee and perhaps one of the other objectors to Seabury's consecration, as the rest of the evidence we will examine points to widespread and prolonged use of the Office. Any examination of the Communion Office dispels the notion that it was "imposed" at all, with or without Episcopal supremacy.

Seabury's choice not to confront Dibblee, and to join him in the one project they could agree upon, education, coupled with his slow but steady movement in liturgical matters, was not without its fruit. By October 1789, Dibblee would write of "Bishop Seabury, an ornament to the Episcopal character" going to Philadelphia for the adjourned Convention. Despite the claim that Dibblee would have none of Seabury's liturgical work, he can write of the 1789 prayer book as at least being "without any mutilated Service," even though it employed a revised version of the very Scottish eucharistic prayer that was the heart of Seabury's *Office*.[70]

67. Ebenezer Dibblee to Samuel Peters, May 3, 1785, ibid., 63.
68. Ebenezer Dibblee to Samuel Peters, March 20, 1786, ibid., 69
69. Ebenezer Dibblee to Samuel Peters, June 13, 1787, ibid., 72.
70. Ebenezer Dibblee to Samuel Peters, October 22, 1789, ST1, 75.

Seabury's strategy with Dibblee involved no "dint of Episcopal supremacy." When the 1789 book was published, the Connecticut clergy (except
for James Sayre) voted to adopt it. (They were later to decide as a group
to use the Apostles' Creed at the daily office and the Nicene at Holy Communion.) Dibblee was not at the meeting, and made it clear to everyone
that he would never use the new prayer book. The rest of the clergy agreed
to introduce the book in the most pastoral way in their parishes. By 1792,
Seabury considered that the time had come to persuade Dibblee, but his
approach was both gentle and straightforward.

Seabury wrote to him with restraint and with respect for his years:

Rev'd and very dear Sir, — Did I not know to whom I am writing,
I should fear doing hurt and not good by this letter. But when I
consider you, as I have ever esteemed you, as an old, and worthy, and
good friend, who has a regard for me a fellow-minister with me of
the Church of Christ, and equally with me solicitous for her welfare,
and the peace and quiet and Christian lives of all her members, — as
a gentleman whom strong abilities, a candid mind, long experience
in the world, and the long and constant practice of all Christian
virtues, hath deservedly raised to a good and eminent character, —
every apprehension that I shall give you pain, or excite in you any
resentment, or any idea that I wish to interfere needlessly in your
affairs, vanishes and disappears. My earnest desire is that you would
review in your own mind the ground and principles on which you
have hitherto refrained from the use of the Prayer-book of the Church
of the United States — to consider whether you cannot use that book
in divine service with a good conscience, and so as to offer to God
an acceptable service? If you can, whether Christian charity, the love
of peace and unity, and the edification of the body of Christ, do not
require that you should use it, and whether the peace and prosperity
of your own congregations, and consequently your own peace and
quiet, do not also require it? To use particular arguments with you is
unnecessary. They will occur to you, probably, with more force than
I could give them. If you cannot use the book with a good conscience,
I have not a word to say to prevail on you to do so. But if you can,
remember, my dear sir, the peace of the churches in Connecticut,
and your own peace, and the quiet and Christian temper of your
own people, are nearly concerned, and sooner or later will suffer by
your refusal. The question is not which book is the best in itself, but

which will best promote the peace and unity of the Church. Such was
the temper of the people to the southward, that unity could not be
had with the old book. Is not, then, the unity of the whole Church
through the States a price sufficient to justify the alterations which
have been made? supposing (and in this I believe you will join with
me) that there is no alteration made but what is consistent with the
analogy of the Christian faith. Let me, therefore, *entreat you as a
father,* to review this matter, and I have no doubt but that you will
join with your brethren, and *walk by the same rule* in your public
ministrations. This will rejoice their hearts and mine also. May God
be your director in all things, and grant that we may meet together
in his own heavenly kingdom.

I am, Rev'd and dear Sir, your affectionate brother and very humble
serv't.

S, *Bishop. Connect*[71]

The reader may wish to note the modesty of the single-letter signature.
More to the point is the approach taken to Dibblee, who is treated as
a "friend." Seabury invites some thinking out of the liturgical box by
introducing the question of unity: "The question is not which book is
the best in itself, but which will best promote the peace and unity of the
Church." Here Seabury gives a hint of what we shall see was his strategy
at Philadelphia. Dibblee's response reported that he brought it before the
annual meeting of his parish, and that the new book would be used as
soon as copies arrived. He notes that his mind was made up for him both
by the tone of Seabury's letter and his agreement with Seabury that unity
was important; he was frightened by extremist opposition to prayer book
reform. His usual slightly pathetic note is present as well:

> ...I purposely omitted writing till after Easter Monday, and since
> [I am] ill able to Sit & write. On Palm Sunday returning in haste
> from Horseback, Mrs. Dibblee lying dangerously Sick, I met with an
> unhappy fall from my Horse, which hath unfitted me for public Duty
> almost ever since.
> ·...I confess I love the prayer book my Mother gave me, and
> think the Sacrifice great, but nevertheless wise & prudent, under the

---

71. Samuel Seabury to Ebenezer Dibblee, February 22, 1792, Ecclesiastical Letter Book,
Samuel Seabury Papers; Middleton, 409f.

present State of the church if a Coalition, with our brethren in the Southern States could not otherwise be effected. May God prosper and Succeed *all* your pious endeavors to promote the interest of religion, the peace, unity & well-being of the Redeemer's Kingdom, is the Sincere wish & fervent prayer of him, who with every Sentiment of esteem & personal respect, subscribes Your most Obedient and Humble Servant.[72]

No strong-arm approach would have received such an answer.

A kind, generous, and helpful man, a pastoral man who had also shown himself bold and courageous, the survivor of very difficult circumstances — it seems highly unlikely that such a one would dissemble about the Concordat, or could be "paralyzed by fear" because some people were opposed to liturgical revision.[73] With an outlook to be formed by the preponderance of the evidence, rather than a hermeneutic of suspicion, we can begin to assess the liturgical work of Middletown.

---

72. Ebenezer Dibblee to Samuel Seabury, April 30, 1792, ST1, 98.

73. The motto on the Seabury crest is *Supera alta tenere* (Hold to the Highest). The Seabury line is an interesting one. Our subject produced children who were dutiful if not particularly noted in their day. A depressive grandson, Samuel III, is the subject of *Moneygripe's Apprentice*, ed. with commentary Robert Bruce Mullin (New Haven, Conn.: Yale University Press, 1989), and a Samuel Seabury (rector and sometime General Seminary professor) produced the lamentable *American Slavery* (New York: Mason Brothers, 1861, repr. 1969). Seminary teaching (also at General) occupied the son of the proslavery writer, priest-cum-lawyer William Jones Seabury, but it was the great-great-grandson, jurist Samuel Seabury (1873–1958) who would bring the most credit to his lineage and its motto. This Samuel Seabury was willing to stand virtually alone against New York City corruption and, by characteristically never yielding an inch, gave the city meaningful reform. Interestingly, his friend Mayor LaGuardia referred to Judge Seabury as "the Bishop" on account of his rectitude. He is the only Seabury known to have been called Sam. Through his writing, he also continued to have influence on public policy. Herbert Mitgang, *The Man Who Rode the Tiger* (New York: Viking, 1963) is still available secondhand, as is Walter Chambers, *Samuel Seabury: A Challenge* (New York: Century, 1932). Also easy to locate is Judge Seabury's own *The New Federalism* (New York: E. P. Dutton, 1950), which discusses the best way to share power in post–World War II political and economic realities, a scholarly yet accessible work. Harder to find but the most instructive is William and John Northrop, *The Insolence of Office: The Story of the Seabury Investigations* (New York: G. P. Putnam's Sons, 1932). The world is a small place: Bishop Provoost's ghost still hovered over the Seabury family. The young lawyer Seabury's first involvement with a trial was Trinity Church's attempt to evade a law requiring it to provide bathrooms in the tenement slums it owned.

– Chapter Five –

MIDDLETOWN

The Bishop of Ely said: "I once took W. H. Auden out to a meal and introduced discussion by saying he was on the PECUSA Liturgical Commission. He replied: 'I gave it up. I've joined the Orthodox: liturgical revision is a clerical hobby.' "

— News of Liturgy, no. 240, December 1994, 8

It was at my request that the Bishop with his Clergy agreed to make some alterations in the Liturgy and Offices of the church.

—Samuel Parker to William White

The tempest of revisionism that thrust Seabury's name into a new round of controversy in the late twentieth century arose in the teacup of the Convocation at which he presided in Middletown in August 1785. Interest in reconstruction of this first meeting between Seabury and the clergy dates from the nineteenth century. The sketchy minutes that survive in Bishop Jarvis's papers have been seldom reprinted, perhaps because they reveal so little. Although Samuel Farmer Jarvis claims to have seen a list of liturgical proposals among Bishop Jarvis's papers, there is no way to know whether was he speaking of the political adjustments to the prayer book or of the discussion of more adventurous proposals. Bishop Seabury indicated that he kept a list of the points discussed, and believed that freshly ordained Colin Ferguson also had a list. The political adjustments were printed in a broadside "Injunction," but there is no surviving list of other proposals. E. C. Chorley, who had examined the Jarvis papers, leaves the impression that he had seen an "unpublished document" and that "Mr. Parker carried this back to Boston." His description of the contents does not entirely match either the Boston proposals or other reconstructions of Middletown.[1]

---

1. Chorley1, 42. Chorley's usually reliable work has some anachronistic reporting with regard to this period as well.

Revision in the Air

Inability to appreciate the lovely prose of the Bible and Book of Common Prayer seems to have been quite common in the eighteenth century. One of the writers of the time decided to rewrite the parable of the Prodigal Son. He began, "A gentleman of splendid family and opulent fortune had two sons."[2]

H. Boone Porter noted that prayer book history in this country begins in 1607 in Jamestown, yet "It is striking that for the next 170 years, Americans appear to have contributed nothing to the development of Anglican liturgical history, but simply to have used the Prayer Book week after week, or among a more pious minority, day after day. In view of this long and stable tradition, unequaled by other groups in the English colonies, it is remarkable that at the time of independence American Anglicans immediately engaged in rather drastic liturgical revision."[3] Of these revisions, the most startling to the modern eye is probably that wrongly attributed to the vestryman of Christ Church, Philadelphia, Benjamin Franklin, *An Abridgement of the Book of Common Prayer*.[4] The title is a remarkable exercise in understatement, as this prayer book is no less abridged than would be Mr. Jefferson's "Bible" of 1819. For instance, the service of Holy Communion is "abridged" by eliminating the ante-communion and stripping what remained of proper prefaces, the prayer of humble access, the consecration prayer, the postcommunion prayer, Gloria in Excelsis, and Trinitarian blessing. Similarly, the daily office is shorn of Old Testament readings, the usual canticles, the creeds, Kyrie, Collects of the Day and for the Clergy. The Gloria Patri is reduced to the single word, "Amen."

Franklin did have some thoughts of his own on liturgy, and wrote to his daughter about the Book of Common Prayer in 1764. "Go constantly to church, whoever preaches. The act of devotion in the Common Prayer-book is your principal business there; and if properly attended to, will do more towards amending the heart than sermons generally can do; for they

---

2. Peaston, 21f.

3. Porter2, 99.

4. *An Abridgment of the Book of Common Prayer* (London, 1773). See also, Marion J. Hatchett, "Benjamin Franklin's Prayer Book" in *This Sacred History*, ed. Donald S. Armentrout (Cambridge, Mass.: Cowley, 1990). According to Hatchett, Franklin's participation was limited to the Catechism (reduced to duty toward God and neighbor). White liked the layout of the table for finding holy days, and approved of the placement of the exhortation before the eucharistic rite.

were composed by men of greater piety and wisdom than our common composers of sermons can pretend to be."[5]

This 1773 "Franklin" abridgement lays our problem neatly open all the same. Not all revisions were alike. The seventeenth and eighteenth centuries saw many proposed liturgical revisions printed and discussed, and the fascination continued into the next century as well. A. E. Peaston cataloged fifty-four published revisions of the 1662 Book of Common Prayer between 1713 and 1854, the majority of which did not come from dissenters.[6] Thus liturgical revision was of interest to perfectly loyal church people. In the eighteenth century Peaston knows of five revisions of the prayer book and several others not based on it as attempts to produce a liturgy that was traditional in sound but usable by non-Trinitarians. Other revisions of the 1600s and 1700s were attempts to moderate doctrinal emphases and ceremonial expressions that were offensive to those dissenters often lumped together as "Puritans" or, later, "Evangelicals." Of these moderate revisions, the great 1689 proposal usually called *The Liturgy of Comprehension* is most important. The appointment of a commission to revise the prayer book with an eye toward comprehension was one expression of William III's gratitude to nonconformists for their support in the Glorious Revolution of 1688.

The 1689 ideal of modification to minimize offense was very much on the mind of William Smith during the American revision of 1785–86, and he invokes it in his *Preface* to that proposed liturgy. This kind of revision we may call revision for the sake of unity in England. At the same time, it was a revision proposed along lines that would clarify obsolete expressions, such as "impartially" for "indifferently." It also proposed the excision of the *filioque,* hoping for better relations with "the Greek church." A single scheme of revision thus might at the same time contain doctrinal, ecclesial, practical, and ecumenical concerns. It is not always easy for those who come later to sort among the variety of revisions. Revisers of almost any stripe removed the canticles Magnificat and Nunc Dimittis (and the verses of Benedictus beginning "and thou, child") because of a cultural distaste for using canticles that invoked the experience of "particular persons," a concept difficult to grasp in our highly first-person age. The Benedicite was proposed for omission because its source was apocryphal. The 1789 prayer book of the Episcopal Church was to

---

5. John Norton, *Life of Bishop Provoost* (New York, 1859), 36.
6. Peaston, 34.

adopt just this approach by eliminating the traditional evensong canticles and trimming the Benedictus of the personal parts without anyone claiming it was doctrinal sabotage.

The Commonwealth period in England spurred a more creative kind of revision. The Long Parliament had abolished the prayer book in 1641, so bishops and priests mined the scriptures and the ancient liturgical tradition for passages and prayers not technically illegal. Some of their findings were useful at the time, and others spurred later work. The search for substitution evolved into what our age might call "enrichment." Some writers have dismissed this trend as "archaeology," but work of this kind had a role to play in awakening awareness that liturgical development did not begin in the late spring of 1549. As it is with the 1689 proposals, it is a mistake to classify proposals based on ancient material as a single group. Jeremy Taylor's liturgical work allowed for maintenance of traditional structure and action.[7] William Whiston (1667–1752), on the other hand, in some ways prefigured the patristic fundamentalism through which Christian liturgy passed in the twentieth century. His devotion to the recension he knew of the *Apostolic Constitutions* has been exceeded only by more recent commitment to its ancestor, the *Apostolic Tradition* of Hippolytus. Whiston read the ancient liturgical material as requiring Arian Christology and mandating liturgical reform in England in accordance with that Christology. He thus set out, among other liturgical writings, *The Liturgy of the Church of England reduc'd nearer to the Primitive Standard, Humbly Proposed to Publick Consideration* (1713, 1750). In 1747 he left the English Church, which he considered incapable of reform, and became a kind of Baptist. His work was known and discussed by American revisers.[8] His work is sometimes considered "Latitudinarian," because it modified the conventional Trinitarianism of the prayer book. Whiston and Taylor represent "archaeology" used for very different purposes.

The Latitudinarians were those in the English Church of the 1600s who were relatively unconcerned with traditional doctrines or structures.[9]

---

7. Taylor's liturgy is set out in Grisbrooke, 19ff. See also H. Boone Porter, *Jeremy Taylor, Liturgist* (London: SPCK, 1979). It is also interesting to note that Taylor's substitution of the Beatitudes for the Summary of the Law lived on into the early twentieth century and was proposed for inclusion in the 1892 and 1928 books. On Taylor's theology, see H. R. McAdoo, *The Eucharistic Theology of Jeremy Taylor Today* (Norwich, Norfolk: Canterbury Press, 1988).

8. Hatchett2, 20.

9. For detailed discussion, see Martin I. J. Griffen, *Latitudinariansim in the Seventeenth-Century Church of England* (Leiden: E. J. Brill, 1992); W. M. Spellman, *The Latitudinarians and the Church of England, 1600–1700* (Athens: University of Georgia, 1993); and Donald

In liturgy, then, this implied a certain transcendence over strictly orthodox formulations, a kind of proto-ecumenism. The battle over the Trinity
and its place in liturgical prayer was to take on new significance in the
following generations with the gradual rise of what would formally become Unitarianism in 1825 from the tracts of John Biddle in the 1650s.
In fact, by 1719 there was a distinct division among dissenters over
the "Arian blight," with parties formed that would produce the creedal
orthodoxy of English Congregationalism and the "Presbyterian" scripture-
only party that would become the Unitarians. "Latitudinarian," then,
is already an anachronistic term applied to the eighteenth-century proposals, as the Trinitarian battle had been fully joined. One takes it to
mean, however, when used in accounts of American revisions of that
period, revisions that were elastic with regard to doctrinal precision,
particularly regarding the Trinity, and those that lessened reference to
God acting in sacraments. Strictly speaking, it should not be applied to
eighteenth-century reforms undertaken with the lessening or elimination
of Trinitarian teaching in mind.

> A liturgy needs mending; are free thinkers
> The only coppersmiths — the only tinkers?
> Where are the clergy? Doth not reformation
> Purely religious, need a Convocation?[10]

Those who wanted to minimize Trinitarian teaching naturally wanted
excision of the creeds, particularly the Nicene and Athanasian. The Athanasian Creed, awkward as it is, was detested not so much for its tedious
prose, its unliturgical nature, and its constant reference to damnation, but
because it was inescapably Trinitarian, impossible to explain away. The
revisers of 1689 all wanted it gone, but agreed to let it remain for fear of
being considered heretical. When Seabury sees the loss of the Creeds as an
attack on Trinitarian doctrine, history is on his side.[11]

The Philadelphia revisers of 1785 could not have been unaware of a
proposal of a distinctly hybrid type, the semi-Arian John Jones's *Free and
Candid Disquisitions Relating to the Church of England* (1746, 1749).

Greene, "Latitudinarianism Reconsidered," *Anglican and Episcopal History* 62, no. 2 (June
1993): 159–74.

    10. *Gentleman's Magazine* of 1750, quoted in Peaston, 7.

    11. There is an interesting exception. The unnamed but orthodox editor of *A New and
Correct Edition of the Book of Common Prayer* deliberately omitted the Athanasian Creed so
that anti-Trinitarians would not have it to complain about, and thus be forced to confess their
real concern. Peaston, 27.

While its origins were in the nascent Unitarian camp, many of its suggestions merely involved the elimination of whatever was repeated, or the clarification of opaque expressions. It sought one unified service for each Sunday in place of the Morning Prayer, Litany, [Ante-] Communion pattern. There were indeed doctrinal emphases. The proposal favored elimination of those psalms or verses that were not "suitable" for Christian use, and the excision of readings from the Apocrypha and certain parts of the Old Testament. Jones also sought liturgical additions. He wanted a better metrical Psalter, more proper anthems for feast days, and provision for singing hymns, especially at communion time. Jones sought a less condemnatory set of Exhortations at Holy Communion, the addition of family prayers, and prayers for use in prison. Presaging a modern dilemma, he desired prayers appropriate to an evolving understanding of sickness and health, and recognized the need for revision of the Churching of Women who had survived childbirth. Jones sought an invocation of the Holy Spirit in the Eucharist. Like so many streamliners before and since, he had a singular lack of imagination and stunning literalness at points. Thus he wanted "lighten our darkness" removed from Evening Prayer, as it was often said before sunset (this was done in the Proposed Book). The wonderfully poetic realism of "with my body I thee worship" in the marriage rite was similarly disdained. The only thoroughgoing doctrinal change contemplated in the *Disquisitions* is the repair or total elimination of infant baptism and the disuse of sponsors for anyone baptized. There were other sets of suggestions, along with the customary pamphlet wars, helpfully cataloged by Calcote, Peaston, Hatchett, and Grisbrooke.[12]

It is commonplace to observe that whenever liturgical change is discussed there are people who see a plot to corrupt orthodox Christianity. It is not as commonly pointed out that while sometimes such people are too suspicious of their coreligionists, sometimes they are right. Samuel Parker's own conversion from liturgical radical to liturgical conservative would be sparked by just such a liturgical "plot," that of King's Chapel in Boston, to which we shall return. Here we note that the liturgical ancestor of the King's Chapel book was the 1774 publication of Theophilus Lindsey's *The Book of Common Prayer Reformed according to the Plan of the Late Dr. Samuel Clarke*. Lindsey was a member of the "Feathers Tavern Association," which had as its principal purpose the elimination of subscription to the Articles of Religion as a requirement for ordination.

12. See works of these authors in the Key.

Lindsey was a principled person, and when the petition of the association was denied, he left the Church of England in 1773, despite the fact that he was about to be made a bishop. He opened a Unitarian chapel in London, for which he made his revisions. Thus Lindsey's was a doctrinally tendentious reform by any standard.

His source, Samuel Clarke (1675–1729), was a man of no mean intellect, holding his own in conversation with Newton and later in correspondence with Leibnitz.[13] He was chaplain to the Bishop of Norwich and later to Queen Anne. His theology leans toward Deism and certainly toward Unitarianism. His attempt to prove the existence of God by pure mathematics provoked a good deal of comment, including a rebuttal from David Hume. Clarke drew the most fire with his *Scripture Doctrine of the Trinity* (1712), which earned him his reputation as an Arian. He also produced a manuscript revision of the prayer book, which was the basis for Lindsey's work. Lindsey took a few of Clarke's ideas one step further, but is generally faithful to Clarke's intent, although he acknowledges his debt to the *Disquisitions* as well. Thus his version of the Gloria Patri reads, "Glory to God, by Jesus Christ, through the assistance of the Holy Ghost." The words are not felicitous, perhaps, but they are not far from the ancient "Glory to the Father, through the Son, in the Holy Spirit" that the Arians sang so happily that the Catholic party changed the formula to the one now known in the West. Most canticles are deleted from the daily office, which are trimmed as well of other Trinitarian references. Clarke has been characterized as "the father" of prayer book reform, with the Unitarians as "his ultimate heirs."[14]

Lindsey's personal stamp is most clearly seen in the Holy Communion, where the Summary of the Law and the Decalogue are presented in that order. There is no Nicene Creed, no preface for Trinity and Ascension, and no Prayer of Humble Access. The Gloria in Excelsis is revised so as to be entirely addressed to God the Father, and the blessing is replaced with the Grace. Baptism sees parents take the place of sponsors; the creed is

---

13. Only in the light of Clarke's tremendous intellect would this eighteenth-century attempt at theological humor be remotely funny: In 1719 "Caroline of Ansbach, wife of the future George II, a lady with theological tastes, arranged a meeting between Dr. Samuel Clarke and Dr. Edward Hawarden, a celebrated Roman Catholic clergyman. Hawarden asked Clarke for a plain 'Yes' or 'No' to his question, 'Can God the Father annihilate the Son and the Holy Ghost?' Dr. Clarke, it is said, 'continued some time in deep thought, and then said, "It is a question which he had never considered."'" Peaston, 18.

14. Peaston, 23.

not repeated, nor is there the sign of the cross or any mention of original sin or regeneration.

Lindsey also omitted some psalms, communion of the sick, churching of women after childbirth, and the Ash Wednesday Commination service. He adds 131 hymns and metrical psalms, the majority of which were the work of Isaac Watts.

Hymnody was indeed to play an ever-growing importance in defining Protestant worship. The hundreds of hymns produced by Isaac Watts and the thousands by Charles Wesley remind us of the energy put into the project of popular song. The "popular" nature of the worship created with hymn-singing lends credence to Calcote's observation on the failure of so many revision proposals; they were the work of clergy or academics, and had little to do with the religious needs of the mass of believers.[15] It was, after all, Wesley's band of Methodists who were to thrive beside the much more modest growth of the Protestant Episcopal Church, discarding Wesley's liturgy but cherishing the hymns of the two brothers (most come from Charles).

These sketches of only a few of the sentiments around revision of the prayer book show us that most people concerned had both an interest in the past and a zeal to streamline. Virtually everyone was willing to accommodate the times in allowing parents to sponsor their children at baptism, and in omitting the references to the physical aspects of marriage and so on. Where the real divisions would evidence themselves was in language about the godhead, original sin, regeneration, absolution, consecration, and the retention of ancient creeds. When viewing a party advancing or objecting to revisions, it is of paramount importance to notice whether or not those revisions significantly touched doctrine. While Seabury will be seen not to object to streamlining, he had a horror of changes that lowered doctrinal positions in the liturgy.

As the American Revolution wound down and that of France wound up, change hung thickly in the air in both church and state. The civil and ecclesiastical themes met as the elder William Smith led the Maryland convention of August 1783 in drafting "certain fundamental rights and liberties" of the Protestant Episcopal Church mentioned above. Among those enumerated is the right "to revise her Liturgy . . . in order to adapt the same to the late Revolution and other local circumstances in America." What those local circumstances might require is left open, and into that opening

---

15. Calcote, 280.

Smith would later leap headlong. When Smith proposed a formal revision the following year, the Maryland convention disappointed him by limiting change to political matters. The following spring Parker would write to White indicating that the time for revision is here and asking what White contemplates. He was to be disappointed again: White replied that uniformity would be maintained until there can be "a general Communication of Sentiment."[16] The brakes stayed on. The convention of October 6–7, 1784, in New York City, gathered representatives from New York, New Jersey, Pennsylvania, Delaware, and Maryland, with Parker representing Massachusetts and Rhode Island. As the members contemplated a new church, they enumerated "Fundamental Principles," of which the fourth was "That the said church shall maintain the doctrines of the Gospel, as it is now held by the Church of England, and shall adhere to the liturgy of the said church, as far as shall be consistent with the American Revolution, and the constitutions of the respective states." This agreement was to last for twelve months.

Parker still worked to build a constituency for progressive liturgical change. His correspondence with future bishop Edward Bass ended with Bass agreeing that "we might part with the Athanas'n Creed, one or two Lord's prayers, and leave the use of Sponsors to the option of those who have children to christen; which, in my opinion, would be much better than to let it remain a Law of the Church and at the same time unobserved by the greater part of her Members." Also to the point was Bass's supposition that these sentiments were rife "in the Southern Colonies and in Connecticut." However, like Seabury and the Scots, and indeed, White himself, Bass would prefer to see no revision if such forbearance would help to ensure the unity of an American church.[17]

Parker apparently also tested the waters with Daniel Fogg, who was blunt in writing in September 1784 that it would "be time enough to rcvise our Liturgy" when Seabury returned from his consecration.[18] Until the shock of King's Chapel hit him full in the face in 1786, however, nothing and no one would limit Parker's enthusiasm for change. He saved a letter from Joshua Wingate Weeks reminding him that it was important to give dissenters as little to complain of as possible, and that only "the low

---

16. Hatchett1, 94.
17. Edward Bass to Samuel Parker, July 7, 1785, *Parker,* 16.
18. Daniel Fogg to Samuel Parker, September 28, 1784. Courtesy of the Episcopal Divinity School.

state of religion in England has prevented so useful a work from taking place."[19]

Parker's official brief at Middletown was "to collect the Sentiments of the Connecticut Clergy in respect to Dr. Seabury's episcopal Consecration, and Regulations of his Episcopal Jurisdiction, and thoughts on connecting themselves with them, under his Episcopal Charge."[20] That was a large enough responsibility, but Parker had other plans as well. He would write to William White that "It was at my Request that the Bishop with his Clergy agreed to make some alterations in the Liturgy and Offices of the Church."[21] Kind indulgence of a neighbor's request would earn Seabury the title of coward two centuries later.

The Problem of Middletown: The Concordat and the Proposed Revisions

It has not been noted that the Middletown meeting was the first overture from Seabury for church union. The Middletown date was advertised in a letter to none other than William White, who was not moved to act. Attendance was urged "for a Christian Union of all the Churches in the thirteen states." This, the first of two invitations to the South to meet with Connecticut, has been left unnoted by contemporary writers. The temper of the times seemed to require an explanation that "We have no Views of Usurping any Authority over our Brothers and Neighbors, but wish them to unite with us in the friendly manner, that we are ready and willing to do with them."[22] Seabury's first public meeting included work toward the unity that his consecrators hoped he would effect.

Among the reasons that we know so little about liturgical discussions at Middletown is that both chronologically and figuratively, liturgy was the last thing on the minds of most of the participants. The great issues of the constitution of the church and the relationship Connecticut was to have to the Anglicans in the other states dominated the sessions. Internally, Connecticut clergy were concerned to inspect the credentials of their new bishop, and then to receive him properly. Then Seabury presented the clergy with his ordination certificate and the pastoral letter from the Scots

---

19. Joshua Wingate Weeks to Samuel Parker, August 28, 1784, *Parker*, 12.
20. *Anglican Episcopate*, 50.
21. Samuel Parker to William White, September 14, 1785, Hawks & Perry, 2:285.
22. Jeremiah Leaming to William White, July 14, 1785. Courtesy of the Archives of the Episcopal Church.

bishops. The latter discussed the terms of the Concordat and included a copy.[23] The Concordat could not have been kept secret in any case, as Seabury had already shared its terms with George Berkeley, who was free in his criticism of it.

Liturgy was on the back burner for another reason. Both Seabury and his consecrators insisted that liturgy must not hinder unity in the new American church. In response to George Berkeley's letters critical of the liturgical portion of the Concordat, primarily the Eucharist, the Scots wrote to Seabury asking him to remember this primacy of unity. At almost the same time, Seabury responded to a letter from Berkeley on this issue by saying that he would not press the point immediately, "as I was not willing to get into any new embarrassments till I had got rid of the old ones."[24] The overall failure of twentieth-century writers to understand Seabury's actions at Middletown and after comes from a mistaken attempt to isolate and examine his liturgical concerns and words without dealing generally with the principles and demands of his episcopate.

The meeting with the clergy and the presentation of credentials took up August 2, and together with ordinations of new clergy, ran until 5:00 p.m. of August 3. At that time the last of the "conventions" of the clergy of Connecticut was dissolved, and they joined their bishop in their first Convocation. After discussion of the altered condition of the church in the wake of the Revolution, including its undoubted liturgical implications, the morning of August 4 was concluded with prayers and a sermon by Benjamin Moore. Following the service, Seabury delivered his first charge to the clergy.[25]

In the charge, we have seen that Seabury sets his agenda. The episcopate to be initiated is to be "purely ecclesiastical." In the conferral of holy orders, he is looking for men who are both educated and "useful," and goes on to say that he is concerned about the pragmatic issues of "their personal appearance, voice, manner, clearness of expression, and facility of communicating their sentiments," and implies that this is not the normal standard. He is clearly not interested in perpetuating the system of ordaining the less gifted sons of wealthy families. Rather, Seabury thinks himself

23. Robert Kilgour, Arthur Petrie, John Skinner to the Clergy of Connecticut, November 15, 1784. Courtesy of the Archives of the Diocese of Connecticut.

24. John Skinner to Samuel Seabury, January 1, 1785; Samuel Seabury to John Skinner, February 11, 1785. Archives of the Diocese of Connecticut.

25. SSA.

somewhat countercultural in looking for "good temper, prudence, diligence, capacity and aptitude to teach."[26] Seabury's own aptness to teach is evident in his approach to Confirmation, a rite most American church folk had never seen performed. He recognized that he had a great deal of teaching to do before launching a liturgical program: "it is unreasonable to expect that people should comply with a rite before they are convinced of their obligation to do so."[27] This reasonable approach to informed change was to mark his plans with regard to the liturgical article of the Concordat, but already at this first meeting Seabury speaks of the Eucharist as a "feast with their brethren on the sacrifice." To speak of a "feast upon a sacrifice" was to invoke the key sentiments of the Nonjuror eucharistic platform.

It being established that Seabury did not hide the Concordat, this is perhaps the best point to deal with the idea that Seabury did not understand the terms of that agreement. As we saw in the previous chapter, the liturgical article is much more modest than some writers have implied. The Scots bishops are "very far from prescribing" a eucharistic rite for Connecticut. They find themselves "ardently wishing" that Seabury will work "with peace and prudence" to make the celebration of that sacrament "conformable to the most primitive Doctrine and practice." Their belief is that the Scottish church has done this by celebrating a liturgy between which and the 1549 English book there is no important difference. To repeat, Bishop Seabury therefore commits himself to (1) take a careful look at their liturgy, (2) determine whether it conforms to the standard of antiquity, (3) if, and only if, he finds it "agreeable to the genuine Standards of Antiquity, to give it his sanction," and (4) by "gentle Methods and Argument and Persuasion, to endeavour" to introduce it "by degrees" and "without the Compulsion of Authority." This is not the charter for liturgical totalitarianism. In the famous letter to Boucher, Seabury correctly states that with regard to the Eucharist, "This matter I have engaged to lay before the Clergy of Connecticut, & they will be left to their own judgment which to prefer."[28] His faithfulness to this undertaking is what would guide his future work.

On the basis of another passage in the letter to Boucher just quoted, it has been alleged that Seabury did not understand the Concordat with the Scots, and kept its contents from his clergy. This is an untenable position.

---

26. Ibid., C1–8.
27. Ibid., C10.
28. Seabury to Jonathan Boucher, December 3, 1784, Hawks & Perry, 2:253f.

In the first place, the Concordat's liturgical article just reviewed primarily commits Seabury to nothing more than to study liturgy and come to a decision. Only if he found himself to favor the Scots liturgy was he gently to persuade people to adopt it, and then only "by degrees." We know that the study took place, in that Seabury thanked the bishops for sending on what they considered the relevant books.[29] There is no reason to assume that this study was undertaken to compensate for total ignorance of the matter at hand. In the letter he represented his obligations with precision. He wrote to Jonathan Boucher that

> The Bishops expect the clergy of Connecticut will form their own Liturgy and Offices; yet they hope the English Liturgy, which is the one they use, will be retained, except the Communion Office, and that they wish should give place to the one in Edward the Sixth's Prayer Book. *This matter I have engaged to lay before the clergy of Connecticut, and they will be left to their own judgment which to prefer.* Some of the congregations in Scotland use one and some the other Office; but they communicate with each other on every occasion that offers.[30]

Writers have unproductively ignored the collegial and communal commitments expressed in that passage, as it has impaired their understanding of man driven by a sense of duty. They have instead focused on Seabury's apparently mistaken description of the 1764 Scots Communion Office as that of 1549. In a day when almost all Anglican liturgies have been reprinted many times and the principal ones are available online, Seabury's reference to the 1549 book may appear to be ignorance or a slip. It was probably neither ignorance nor lapse (Seabury was a precise man). The eucharistic prayer of 1764 *was* essentially 1549 with the order of some textual units rearranged. As one reads in this period, "Edward VI" seems to be the general code for any rite with a full eucharistic prayer, particularly a prayer containing an invocation of the Holy Spirit. Seabury may have thought that Boucher would not understand a more involved answer — how many clergy today can readily draw fine distinctions between a two-hundred-year-old liturgy they have never seen and a similar

---

29. Samuel Seabury to John Skinner, March 3, 1785, in "The Election and Consecration," *HMPEC* 3, no. 1 (March 1934): 250.

30. Seabury to Jonathan Boucher Edinburgh, December 3, 1784. Seabury adds that the days of nonjuring are rapidly ending; in four years he would be proved right. In Hawks & Perry, 2:253f.; emphasis added.

one used by a small sect in a foreign country? In any case, in 1786 even William Smith the elder would call his Maryland epiclesis "analogous" to the liturgy of Edward VI *and* the Scots liturgy, even though his epiclesis was verbally much closer to 1637, and could hardly be considered consecratory.[31] When writing to White about baptism, Seabury demonstrates detailed familiarity with the 1549 book.[32]

Even if, *arguendo*, we posit that Seabury made an unconscious slip in his letter, it does not follow that he had no knowledge of the liturgy of his consecrators. Surely he would have experienced the Scots' liturgy while he was with them, and certainly he would have been particularly aware of the liturgy celebrated at his own episcopal consecration. Again, as the eucharistic prayer in the 1764 Scottish rite is composed primarily of elements of the 1549 prayer adjusted to the "natural order," the charge of gross liturgical ignorance based on a slightly inaccurate statement here begins to look like a quibble.

Besides the probability that Seabury noticed what was going on when he attended services in Scotland, particularly at his consecration, there is another reason to believe that he was well acquainted with the eucharistic doctrine of the Nonjuror party. In a sermon preached a full thirty years before his episcopate began, this student of Samuel Johnson's wrote that

> The Sacrament of the Lord's Supper was instituted to be the Christian Sacrifice; and an emblem of the Sacrifice our blessed Redeemer made, when he offered himself upon the cross a price and atonement for the sins of the whole world. Bread, the staff of life and emblem of strength, the grand support of the human kind; and Wine, the emblem of joy and thankfulness, are chosen for the materials of this Sacrifice and of commemorating the death and passion of our Redeemer; and of expressing our gratitude to Almighty God for the wonderful work of Man's Redemption. And they mightily express the temper and design of the Christian Religion.... Thus the Sacrament is a continual Sacrifice to God. And our blessed Saviour hath chosen these things to be the materials of this Sacrifice and Symbols of his Body and Blood, which have the greatest analogy to the Graces which we need; and which should shine brightest in the Christian life, namely perseverance in well doing, and the continual increase in the divine likeness; and sincere gratitude, and unfeigned joy and

---

31. William Smith to Samuel Parker, April 17, 1786, Perry, 199f.
32. Samuel Seabury to William White, June 20, 1789. Reprinted in Appendix B-8.

thankfulness to Almighty God, and our adorable Saviour for the in-
numerable benefits which his precious Blood shedding hath obtained
for us. And by the consecrated Elements of Bread and Wine we figure unto God the Father, the Passion of his Son, that according to
the tenor of his Covenant, he may be gracious and propitious to us
miserable sinners.[33]

The last sentence quoted, in particular, contains a doctrine of eucharistic sacrifice that would be considered very high in any age. The centrality
of that doctrine in Nonjuror thought will become evident below. Here
the sermon reminds us that Seabury knew the theology the rite was con-
structed to enact. As that theology had reached its epitome with the second
edition of John Johnson's *The Unbloody Sacrifice,* and as he was a leader
of the group of High Churchmen attempting to complete the orders of the
American Church, for him not to have known about it would be highly
unlikely. Steiner discounts this sermon, relying on his New England "consensus," but does not quote enough of it to have to confront Seabury's use
of the concept of "propitiation," or even of "joy," both of which would
take him out of the alleged consensus.

To return to the bishops' letter to their new American nephews, it is
to be noted that after reporting Seabury's consecration, repeating their ar-
dent desire for full communion between the churches, they conclude by
noting that "according to this standard of primitive practice, a Concordate
has been drawn up and signed by us ... and by Bishop Seabury. *Of this
Concordate a copy is herewith sent for your satisfaction.*"[34] Maintaining
that Seabury hid the Concordat must mean that he withheld this letter as
well, a letter that revisionists do not discuss. It is hard to imagine a man
so thoroughly driven by duty presuming to thwart the will of those from
whom he received his orders. Supposition is not necessary, however. We
can know that the clergy did receive the bishops' letter because we have
their reply to it.[35] Abraham Jarvis wrote for the clergy, acknowledging and
thanking the bishops for the letter, which they had indeed seen at the August convocation.[36] Why had they not replied sooner? "We should much
earlier have made our acknowledgments had not our dispersed situation

---

33. *Memoir,* 14f.
34. Scots Bishops to Connecticut Clergy, November 15, 1784, Hawks & Perry, 251f. Emphasis added.
35. The text of the letter is to be found in Appendix B-2.
36. Jarvis (D.D., Yale, 1796) had been a Tory, and is described by Sprague as orthodox, with a theology like that of the Nonjurors.

made the difficulty of our meeting together so very great, and the multiplicity of business absolutely necessary to be immediately dispatched, so entirely engrossed our time at our first meeting at Middletown as to render it then impracticable." As to the great questions of doctrine and worship addressed in the Concordat, Jarvis adds directly that "Our utmost exertions shall be joined with those of our Bishop to preserve the unity of faith, doctrine, discipline, and uniformity of worship, with the Church from which we derived our Episcopacy, and with which it will be our praise and happiness to keep up the most intimate intercourse and communion." On this basis it is safe to conclude that Seabury had put the clergy into the picture regarding the agreement with the Scots. Perhaps with this secondary corroboration, we may credit Seabury's own claim. Later in 1785, in a catch-up letter covering many matters, Seabury wrote to Skinner:

> I met our Clergy at Middletown on the third of August; & joyful indeed was the meeting. The letter from the good Bps, & the Concordate were laid before them, and were received as I could wish. But with regard to the Article in the Concordate relating to the Celebration of the Eucharist they thought it best to wait a little, till by preaching & conversation the minds of the Communicants were prepared for reception of the Scots office. Another reason of delay was the propensity that had discovered itself to the south of making alterations in the Liturgy, and we were afraid they would plead our example. I have not, at present, the least doubt but that the Scots Communion Office will be adopted, as I have yet heard no objection, & most people are convinced of its superior excellency. I shall first introduce it here, but I believe not till Easter Sunday, as I should choose to have the era marked by one of our great Festivals.[37]

Keeping uniformity in doctrine and liturgy with the Scots according to the terms of the Concordat was a project which, on the doctrinal side, was to dominate Seabury's writing and teaching, as his first two Charges and collected *Discourses* illustrate. Making possible a uniformity in liturgy was the comparably simple task that he would accomplish in less than a year, and do so without violating his principle of the bishop acting with the presbyters, just as he had written.

---

37. Samuel Seabury to John Skinner, December 23, 1785, *CtFirst*, 60f.

Hatchett wrote that "Seabury's resistance to the Proposed Book was not due to his convictions; rather it was an effort to reestablish himself with reactionary Connecticut churchmen, who were very much upset by his first revision proposals."[38] We come now to the great question of what "his" proposals were, and what effect they had on the creation of the Proposed Book.

After lunch on August 4, Samuel Parker brought greetings from Massachusetts, and there may have followed discussion of the possibility of Massachusetts churches and clergy coming under Seabury's oversight. Rhode Island was shortly to do so. Parker's mission at Middletown was "to collect the Sentiments of the Connecticut Clergy in respect of Dr. Seabury's episcopal Consecration, and Regulations of his episcopal Jurisdiction, and their thoughts of connecting themselves with them, under his Episcopal Charge."[39] As we saw, Parker later boasted that "it was at my request" that Seabury appointed a committee to discuss liturgy. Steiner agrees that this was Parker acting on his own but interpreted Parker's request only as his attempt to extend Seabury's authority over Massachusetts and Maine in matters liturgical.[40]

Parker's request for a discussion of nonpolitical liturgical change was taken up. As the Convocation adjourned on August 5, a committee to discuss liturgy was appointed, and their report was to be presented for further discussion at the reconvened Convocation on September 14. Their only authority was to bring suggestions for the entire college of presbyters to consider. With Seabury there were Parker, John Bowden, and Jarvis. We can imagine the bishop sitting with the clergy enjoying the brainstorming about what ideas might be interesting to discuss in September at New Haven. We are also forced to imagine Parker sitting in the same meeting taking notes for what he would present as a done deal in Boston.

By August 12, the list of political changes in the liturgy was in print, as the bishop's "Injunction" to the clergy, and in sending copies of it outside of Connecticut, Seabury echoed Bass's sentiments. Copies were sent to William White and William Smith the elder, although we do not know whether it influenced their thought or not.

---

38. Hatchett2, 2. Hatchett's argument loses appeal as he goes from what was "probably" included at Middletown, to speak of the probability as fact, and finally speaks of changes "proposed by Seabury and adopted by the Middletown committee," as though that were established and as though there was not going to be a September meeting in New Haven. Hatchett1, 111, 116, 117.

39. *Anglican Episcopate*, 50.

40. Steiner2, 241.

Determining what else happened at Middletown is a matter of guess-work, as Hatchett points out. Basic to his reconstruction are documents that give hints but not more, and he makes no attempt to hide this fact. The one undisputed fact is that Parker wrote to Seabury that Boston had "mostly" adopted in principle the items discussed at Middletown, plus a "few others." Parker considers some modifications not adopted to be in-significant, and adds that "the only material ones that we have not agreed to are the omitting the second Lesson in the Morning Service and the Gos-pel and exhortation in the Baptismal Office."[41] We do not know what Parker considered to be "mostly," or immaterial, and we do not know what and how many are the "few others."

Hatchett's approach to detecting Middletown's content was to subtract from the Boston list of changes the two items that Parker specifically men-tioned but leave it essentially intact. He also believes that Middletown had additionally proposed an alternative phrase for the *descensus* in the Apostles' Creed, and retained the Athanasian for Trinity Sunday. This de-cision of Hatchett's is instructive. It is not based on direct documentary evidence, although Chorley almost describes creedal reform, but on what we know about Seabury's strong position on such matters. It seems that taking this approach another step is warranted. If we take seriously what we have seen of Seabury's character and history so far, and his almost punctilious (if occasionally cunctative) adherence to his commitments, it seems reasonable to subtract from the Boston list all of those few items to which Seabury was to object in the Proposed Book as a worst-case list. My attempt to do this is found in Appendix A, table 1. The list is not very different from other reconstructions, but does not include removing the Nicene Creed, the sign of the cross, resurrection emphasis at burial, and priestly absolution. The table directs the reader to Seabury's statements on these issues.

In this view Middletown reforms called for

1. Modernizing the language of the Te Deum.

2. Adjusting the response to "Give peace in our time, O Lord" from a rather ferocious reference to God as warrior to "and make all nations to rejoice in thy loving kindness, O God."

3. Trimming the Daily Office of its second Lord's Prayer, and the lesser litany.

---

41. Samuel Parker to Samuel Seabury, September 12, 1785, Hawks & Perry, 2:284f.

4. Shortening the Great Litany.

5. Omitting the Lord's Prayer at the beginning of the Holy Communion service.

6. Having but one iteration of the Gloria Patri in the Daily Office.

7. Clarifying the language of the Prayer for the Clergy and People.

8. Changing "damnation" to "condemnation" in the "first warning" of the celebration of Holy Communion.

9. Excising the excluding language that followed.

10. Ceasing to refer to clergy as "learned and discreet" in the Exhortation at Holy Communion.

11. Adjusting the language of the Exhortation in the Holy Communion to make it less frightening to potential communicants (Seabury had been doing this as early as his Westchester days).

12. Allowing the distribution formula to be said to a group, rather than the entire formula to each communicant.

13. Allowing parents to be among their child's sponsors at baptism.

14. Lessening the emphasis on original sin in the first part of the baptismal service.

15. Removing the reference to actual sin in the address to the sponsors.

16. Reducing the Apostles' Creed to a question about its contents. (It is certainly arguable that Seabury might have opposed this.)

17. Removing "vulgar tongue" from the final address to the sponsors.

18. Adding "if opportunity presents" to the reference to Confirmation.

19. Omitting the prayer after the Lord's Prayer in the burial service.

20. Lengthening the one that follows.

21. Stripping the Churching of Women of everything except the introduction, which is altered.

22. Revising the collect for the Churching of Women.

23. Trimming the beginning of the Ash Wednesday Commination.

24. Trimming much of the cursing section of the Commination.[42]

---

42. The "Commination" service was the reading of curses out of the Old Testament law on those who broke it, followed by the people's assent and repentance.

25. Trimming the introduction of the marriage service.

26. Changing "plight thee my troth" to "pledge thee my truth" in the marriage service.

27. Eliminating "with my body I thee worship, and with all my worldly good I thee endow" at the giving of the ring.

28. Leaving it to the clergy to decide whether or not to repeat the Collect for the Day at all services.

29. Leaving it to the clergy whether to read the first half of the Holy Communion service "in the Altar" or at the Reading Desk.

30. [Not accepted in Boston: omitting the second lesson (New Testament) from Morning Prayer because the Ante-Communion with its epistle and gospel readings were soon to follow.]

31. [Not accepted in Boston: omitting the gospel reading (Jesus blessing children) at baptismal celebrations; baptism is not really about children, and two lessons have just been read in the Office, with baptism following the second lesson.]

That the last two were not accepted is puzzling, as they fit the mode of streamlining very well. The remaining twenty-nine changes compared with Boston's thirty-six form a list very much like Hatchett's, with an important exception. Middletown in this reconstruction is found to be limited to changes that streamlined (omitting repetitions), explained ("truth" for "troth"), or accommodated the spirit of the times (parents as sponsors). They were, in short, what everybody interested in revision was discussing, and were not radical or "advanced" — and certainly not "Latitudinarian."[43] Nonetheless, shortly after Middletown and before New Haven, Seabury decided that nothing at all be done until people were ready; he also decided to wait until it was clear what the southern states would do at their rapidly approaching Philadelphia convention. As far as Seabury was concerned, Boston was also to delay any changes.

The learning curve for a bishop who begins an episcopate as diocesan bishop, rather than beginning as suffragan or coadjutor, is extremely steep. It was unimaginably steeper when an episcopate was begun in a new nation and in a new church whose members have almost no experience of the episcopate. As one trails William White and Samuel Seabury through

---

43. One might suggest that they were approximately as "radical" as coming out in support of *versus populum* celebration of the Eucharist would have been in 1978 rather than 1878 or even 1928.

the formative years of the Episcopal Church, it is important to recognize that they were trying to follow a vocation that was being defined as they followed it. In any event, where other writers may bring a hermeneutic of suspicion to documents arising out of Parker's visit to Middletown, it may be useful to remember that White and Seabury were both working toward union and unity on the national level, and also overseeing affairs at home, where people were behaving in congregational and diocesan life in all the customary ways. I think this means, first of all, that absent compelling evidence to the contrary, we may begin a reading believing that they meant what they wrote when they wrote it, and then read on prepared to see how their thought developed along with the increasing complexity of the new church's life. In this case, within two weeks Seabury realized that his new colleagues and laypeople were not ready for change beyond those made necessary by the independence of the thirteen colonies.

Everyone agrees that the liturgical think tank at Middletown was merely that. Any suggestions it produced were no more than suggestions for discussion by the whole assembly of clergy to be held the following month in New Haven. The proposals bore no imprimatur beyond that. Nonetheless, Parker, who had gone beyond his brief in requesting a liturgical consultation in the first place, wrote to the wardens of Trinity, Newport (and to how many others is unknown), describing events at Middletown. He apparently decided not to claim any responsibility for the liturgical committee's creation when writing to fellow members of his convention, as that might betray the secret of his *ultra vires* activity. He did report that

> A committee was chosen to attend the Bishop and with him to propose such alterations in the liturgy as should be thought expedient for the present, to be laid before the convention at New Haven next month; which alterations I am requested to propose to the church in this and your State, to see if they will unite with the Churches in Connecticut in promoting a uniformity of worship.[44]

Parker would make this claim again, but there is no confirmation anywhere that he was given such a commission. The position in Connecticut was that a final set of proposals did not exist yet. What Parker missed at Middletown, the bigger picture, was Seabury's repeated emphasis on the clergy acting collegially in all important matters.

---

44. Samuel Parker to Messrs. Bours and Malbone, August 15, 1785, *Journals*, vol. 1, 11f.

On the same day that Parker wrote to Newport, Seabury was writing to the elder William Smith (Appendix B-1). No toadying or punch-pulling is evident in this letter, which is highly critical of the proposed system of church governance.[45] Seabury can bring himself to express his view that the "rights of the Christian Church arise not from nature or compact, but from the institution of Christ, & we ought not to alter them, but to receive & maintain them, as the holy Apostles left them." To our point, Seabury adds at the very end of the letter:

> I send you the alterations which it has been here thought proper to make in the Liturgy, to accommodate it to the civil Constitution of this State. You will observe that there is no collect for the Congress. We have no backwardness in that respect, but thought it our duty to know whether the civil authority in this State has any directions to give in this matter; and that cannot be known till their next meeting in October.
>
> Some other alterations were proposed, of which Mr. Ferguson took a copy, and I would send you a copy had I time to transcribe it. The matter will be resumed at New Haven, the 14th of September. Should we come to any determination the Brethren to the southward shall be informed of it.

The first paragraph addresses a question that was to arise later, why Seabury provided nothing for Congress (and the president).[46] He explains that he wanted a determination from the government of Connecticut on this matter: Was Connecticut indeed a sovereign state, or was it subservient to the national Congress?[47] As soon as he knew, he did issue such prayers.[48] It is interesting to wonder what the *Westchester Farmer* thought of the *Federalist Papers* principally featuring his former opponent, Alexander Hamilton. Having seen the damage the Church endured during one revolution, Seabury was being characteristically cautious and precise before drawing conclusions about the next mutation in his surroundings. The second paragraph puts the matter of nonpolitical revision with clarity and

---

45. The entire letter may be studied in Appendix B-1.

46. Tristram Dalton, for example, was to write to Parker on September 12, 1785, warning him not to use the alterations of the Injunction until there was a prayer for Congress "as this omission, though not designed, will be, by some, deemed criminal.... You can perhaps tell, if any, what particular Reason induced Bishop Seabury to leave Congress unnoticed." *Parker,* 17f. Seabury did write to the governor for instructions on October 14, 1786, *SAC,* 87.

47. Samuel Seabury to William Smith, August 15, 1785. Courtesy of the Archives of the Episcopal Church. For the full text, see Appendix B-1.

48. SUI, 41.

brevity. There are no signs of panic or set-up here. There can, after all, be no attempt to hide the list of alterations in what Seabury writes here, as note-taking Colin Ferguson had been sent for ordination by none other than his theology tutor, the William Smith to whom Seabury is writing, and would be returning to Maryland with the whole story of his adventures among the "Jacobite" Yankees.

On August 18, Seabury writes to Parker that revision must be put on hold at least until after the Philadelphia convention, because he had been told that the nascent national church already had some "jealousy" about its prerogatives in the making of liturgy.[49] There is no reason to doubt this claim, as William Smith was very much preparing to revise. This letter is to be found among Parker's own papers, so it shows the strength of his commitment to revision that despite Seabury's decision, he proceeded incorrectly to inform his convention that he had a warrant to bring this matter up at all.

On August 19, Seabury wrote to William White. He forthrightly informs him that he cannot attend the convention in Philadelphia; the Fundamental Principles contain provisions "which I fear are not right," and denigrate the episcopal office. Seabury's major concerns are the very limited power of bishops (among other things, they were to deliberate as part of a unicameral house at General Convention), and "your subjecting him to be tried before a court of Presbyters and laymen." His logic, repeatedly, is that what one has no power to confer, one has no power to take away. After this forthright declaration, Seabury adds a note about liturgy, just as modest — and clear — as that to Smith. "The enclosed are such alterations as have been thought necessary, to accommodate our Liturgy to the civil Constitution of the State. Should more be done, it must be a work of time and great deliberation."[50] This observation may well have been designed to quiet southern "jealousy" over liturgical proprietorship as well as describe the situation in Connecticut, where Seabury had learned that pastoral work had of necessity to come before liturgical fine-tuning. Seabury adds to White that "it is my wish" that Smith would read the letter he had received from Seabury to the entire convention. Neither White nor Smith did so until the 1786 convention, when the delegates' fury was unleashed on Seabury.

These letters demonstrate that Seabury has clearly made a decision, and has communicated it three times, with increasing exactness, to three

---

49. Samuel Seabury to Samuel Parker, August 18, 1785, STi, 12.
50. Samuel Seabury to William White, August 19, 1785, Hawks & Perry, 2:281f.

key figures in the formation of the Episcopal Church. Parker went ahead, nonetheless, and after bringing the matter before the delegates, reported on September 12 that the Boston convention had "directed him" to forward their proposed alterations for Seabury's "inspection and approbation."[51] The minutes of the convention reveal no such charge to Parker. In fact, the convention, while approving Parker's list of changes on the one hand, had simultaneously voted not to implement them, waiting at least until after the Philadelphia convention. The fact is that they did not return to the subject until the following July, when they decided not to adopt Parker's or Philadelphia's plan. (Given that Parker was one fifth or one fourth of the clergy present, one suspects a certain amount of finely honed politeness in the double-edged decision to "adopt" his proposals but not to implement them.) Regarding Philadelphia, Parker wrote, "I flatter myself that no other alterations will be adopted by them than those we proposed at Middletown." It is perplexing (but not the only occasion) that Parker would say in one breath that he is submitting proposals, some of which Seabury had never seen or heard, for the bishop's "inspection and approbation," and in the next breath say that he was sure that what "we" proposed (for discussion in New Haven) at Middletown would be adopted in Philadelphia.

On September 14, Parker opined to White that Seabury might have gone to Philadelphia if he had been asked to preside. Given Seabury's communication to White of objections to a unicameral house, we must lay this ingratiating opinion aside. This is the letter in which Parker also claimed responsibility for initiating the Middletown liturgical consultation. Boston, he says, adopted the recommendations of Middletown plus "a few others." He claims that he was "directed" to send the enclosed Boston proposals to Philadelphia for their convention. Speaking for himself, he said he would also like to see the Articles of Religion modernized, amended, and limited to what scripture teaches unambiguously. At this time, of course, it was usually the liberal-leaning who made this request, which was a kind of code for not insisting on too high a Christology or too precise a Trinitarian theology. He also wanted to know what Philadelphia did before October 6, when the Massachusetts & Rhode Island convention would reconvene.[52]

---

51. Samuel Parker to Samuel Seabury, September 12, 1785, ibid., 2:284f.
52. Parker to White, September 14, 1785. Courtesy of the Archives of the Episcopal Church.

The minutes from Boston do not show any such commission given to Parker, and take a rather more cautious view of what would happen in the South than did he. What is most interesting is that what he sent off to Seabury for "approval" he sent off to White before getting anything like Seabury's approval. Was Philadelphia to infer that Seabury and his clergy had already assented to these items which Parker sends White, claiming baldly that they "are to be proposed to the Churches in the other States"? If so, Samuel Parker created one of the great debacles in the Episcopal Church's history.

Even if every word of the Boston proposals had flowed directly from Seabury's mouth, and even if Parker had misunderstood Seabury's polite message to halt given in the letter of August 18, Parker had to know that Boston had "proposed" nothing to the other states, and in fact was waiting to see what Philadelphia would do before implementing any reform. What the Boston minutes[53] say is that the proceedings of the convention (including the motion suspending nonpolitical liturgical change) be sent to Connecticut *and* Philadelphia, with the request that Connecticut and Philadelphia provide "a speedy communication of each of their proceedings." The Boston convention proposed nothing for the wider church, but did want to share and gather information. It did determine that its proceedings also go to the churches in its neighborhood of "three States" who were not represented at the convention, and "to those whose members are absent,"[54] requesting them to let Boston know what they thought of the proceedings. It will always be a matter of opinion as to which adaptations, political or nonpolitical, these minutes refer in each case, but it is clear that Parker is once more stretching truth a bit in his report. The convention also decided that it was "neither necessary nor convenient" to be represented at the Philadelphia convention. One can only wonder what the Proposed Book would have been like if Parker had gone to Philadelphia and had taken part in the revision with committee members such as Samuel Provoost, James Duane, William White, William Smith, and Henry Purcell.

---

53. See Appendix A-2 and 3.

54. This convention was a tiny affair, comprising five clergy and nine lay members, representing eleven places: nine in Massachusetts, and one each in Rhode Island and New Hampshire. None of the attendees are known to have had an interest in liturgy except Parker. Of the copies that went out, three went to New Hampshire churches, five to Rhode Island, and eight to Massachusetts. Personal copies were sent to Seabury and Hubbard in Connecticut, Moore in New York, and White in Pennsylvania.

In any event, as a result of these proceedings and correspondence, the Philadelphia convention met with a mixed picture of New England. They had from Parker indications that New England was ready for far-reaching change in the liturgy, but White and Smith each had a letter from Seabury indicating that it would be a long time before Connecticut was stable enough for such changes. Of this Parker was also on notice, but he went ahead, as did Philadelphia.

Important evidence arises from the history of the Proposed Book. William Smith the elder was not a man to disregard anything episcopal. He would write to Parker in 1786 that he worked on the Proposed Book with Parker's alterations beside him. If these alterations were known to be those of Connecticut and its bishop, it is hard to imagine Smith not mentioning that in selling the book to New England.

Seabury did not answer Parker's report of Boston immediately, but Bela Hubbard had written to Parker that Connecticut was far from going where Boston had walked,[55] for which lapse he apologizes. Seabury begins, "It is so long since I received your letter, that I am almost ashamed to write to you. In truth, I have been so little at home, and so exceedingly hurried when I was at home, that what ought to have been done in the letter-writing way was too long put off from day to day." There is nothing here of a man scurrying to put things in the best light. Seabury had in fact been busy with other projects. At the very least, we know that from the New Haven conference of September 14, Seabury traveled to Bridge-port (Stratfield), and back to New London, then to New Haven, thence to Hempstead, Long Island, and back to New London and then to Walling-ford, where he wrote his November letter to Parker. These are the stops of which there is a record, and each involved one or more sermons. Given the transportation system of those days and the distance between his stops, it is not hard to believe that Seabury was indeed very busy, and with much more on his mind than liturgy. In an age when few English clergy, let alone bishops, died of overexertion, Seabury's schedule is very striking. He continues to Parker,

Between the time of our parting at Middletown and the Clerical meeting at New Haven, it was found that the Church people in Connecticut were much alarmed at the thought of any considerable

55. Bela Hubbard to Samuel Parker, September 17, 1785, Hawks & Perry, 2:287. As to Hubbard himself, Sprague, always straining to be kind, says that his sermons were not very good, but were "neatly written," Sprague, 236.

alterations being made in the Prayer Book; and, upon the whole, it was judged best that no alterations should be attempted at present, but to wait till a little time shall have cooled down the tempers and conciliated the affections of people to each other.[56]

There is nothing defensive here, nor does Seabury seem to be scrambling, nor, as charged, is he simultaneously and curiously both "paralyzed" and "in retreat."[57] In fact, he is obeying both the letter and the spirit of the Concordat with the Scots, minding the unity of his church before adjusting its liturgy. He is obeying both the letter and the spirit of Skinner's instructions to him by not moving unilaterally when the presbyters are divided and laypeople frightened. There is no reason to refuse to believe that in a group of Episcopalians tempers could heat over matters liturgical. Seabury is blunt about wanting first to upbuild the community before perfecting its ritual. But there is something else is on his mind.

Since the Convention at Philadelphia, which, as report says, has abrogated two creeds and nineteen Articles, and taken great liberties with the Prayers, &c., we are more apprehensive of proceeding to any alterations.

Seabury continues that when the "eastern states" in New England get bishops, that will provide the opportunity for liturgical consultation. Until that happens,

Our wish and hope then is, that no alterations may at present take place with you, but that you would turn your attention to the procuring another Bishop, to the eastward, in the course of the next Summer. Let me have your sentiments on this matter, as soon as your conveniency shall permit.

It is hard to imagine anything clearer than this request that no alterations take place and that the energy go into finding a bishop. The reasons and reasoning are believable; there is no evidence to contradict the tale Seabury relates. We do not know when he received Parker's letter, and he no doubt wished he could have written sooner. Nonetheless, the very blunt statements in Seabury's letter suggest his disappointment that his letter of

---

56. The full text of the letter is reproduced in Appendix B-3. Courtesy of the Archives of the Episcopal Church.

57. Hatchett1, 120.

August 18 had not been taken to heart by Parker. In the light of the gentleness that pervades the vast Seabury correspondence, this November letter is something like a thunderbolt when one remembers that it came from a man whom Sprague would describe as follows:

> Mild in his deportment, his approval of men or principles was oftener known by his countenance than by his words, and his reproofs were administered with so much kindness and discretion that they usually accomplished their legitimate end without giving offense. His manners, I should think, resembled those of an English gentleman, in the reign of Queen Anne.[58]

This letter left Parker out in the cold indeed, as is charged, but Parker had been following his own path from the beginning. His own convention had declined to put alterations in place, and would in the following summer formally reject the Proposed Book as well. Parker would reprint and use the new book's Psalter with the Boston alterations nonetheless — and be defiant about it when challenged by Seabury in 1788.

Seabury was just as clear and nondefensive in writing to Jonathan Boucher, vicar at Epsom. After repeating his complaints about the alteration of the Articles of Religion and the rejection of the creeds, Seabury returns to his large concern, the downgrading of episcopal government. Then he adds:

> I cannot relish the idea of having...the best Liturgy in the world defaced and spoiled by hasty alterations. Some conversation passed on this subject among the Connecticut Clergy at Middletown, & the alterations of some expressions were proposed; but it was soon found that more would be disgusted than gratified by the Measures. It was therefore laid aside, & they determined to wait & see whether time would not conciliate the affections & soften the asperities of resentment of many persons who now look with rather an unfriendly eye on each other.[59]

Seabury here is opposed to bad revision, but he also believes that revision is inevitable — and that it must wait for the right time, a time when charity would prevail, again reflecting both his concordat with the Scots and his principal ethical commitment, that of charity. Nothing craven or

---

58. Sprague, 157.
59. Samuel Seabury to Jonathan Boucher, December 14, 1785, *CtFirst*, 10f.

sniveling appears here. In fact, like White, Seabury shows his greatest concern for keeping the community whole, and this was the level on which they would finally meet. Tempers would calm down in Connecticut, and in February 1787, the Convocation of Connecticut clergy voted "that the Liturgy of the Church of England be accommodated to the present Situation of the Church," and appointed a committee "to attend to Bishop Seabury to make the necessary arrangements, to be laid before the Convocation."[60] Seabury may have taken more time than younger men would like, but he seldom failed to produce what he undertook to do. Neither paralyzed nor retreating, he is pursuing *all* of his stated goals relentlessly, as we will see when we have the opportunity to examine the published liturgical output in an episcopate of but eleven years.

There is nothing here to support the allegation that in these letters Seabury is "beginning to try to set things up so that he would not have to assume responsibility for changes in the liturgy and can work himself back into the good graces of his constituents."[61] His view of the episcopate did not include such categories.

Parker was to come around to Seabury's view of the relative importance of a unified church and its liturgy, but he did so during and after a most trying encounter with King's Chapel. In the meantime he would try to hold things together with Seabury in a letter in January 1786 (his "earliest conveniency," apparently). Much of it he will spin differently later in the month, when writing to White and Smith.

Parker told Seabury that the Boston convention had not made any alterations other than the political changes contained in Seabury's Injunction. He added that Philadelphia's changes were not as radical as rumor had it. We know from his letter to White later in the month that he had not seen the parts of the book that would offend Seabury most: baptism, burial, and the loss of the true absolution in the ministry to the sick. In the parts he did see, Parker misjudged Seabury if he thought the bishop would think that the replacement of priestly vocabulary with "minister" was of no importance in the communion service. He does allow that the loss of the Nicene Creed occurred, but "the Doctrine of the Trinity stands as full as in our present Liturgy."

Parker concludes with a telling slip: "So far as I have yet examined, it strikes me as a matter of great Indifferency whether I should adopt ours or

---

60. *Jarvis1*, 12.
61. Hatchett1, 114.

their Alterations." He then hastens to correct himself: "Provided I mean that theirs had been made by Episcopal Authority." It is to be noted that he has now been told twice that Seabury did not want the alterations to go forward, and yet maintains that there was episcopal authority to be had for the alterations he had implemented. Seabury would later tell White that Parker had gone ahead and used the nonpolitical revisions as well.

Parker was as committed as anyone to a single church united in worship, discipline, and doctrine, and expresses his belief that this was still a possibility. He adds that he was "very sorry" to see that the convention was applying to England for the ordination of bishops. In fact, he adds, "I can see no Defect in the line of the Scotch Bishops & as we have already the Happiness of an unexceptionable Episcopate from them, I must confess *I never wish to see any in America from a different Quarter.*"[62] To Seabury's urging Boston to focus on getting a bishop, their future second bishop Parker remains quietly defiant, and simply says that they cannot do that at present, and besides that, they have Seabury.

In January, Parker took a very different attitude with William White.[63] He has seen some of the proposed liturgy through packets received from White and by studying the daily office on the sheets sent to Charles Miller of King's Chapel. At the same time he is grateful that White's letter to the King's Chapel people was sent to Parker first: "It was no small Addition to their Mortification, that such a Letter should come to them through me, & that I should be acquainted with its Contents, which would never have been the Case, had it been received by Mr. Miller before I had perused it."

There is a special reason for Parker's pleasure. King's Chapel had been claiming that their homemade revision of the prayer book was like that of the General Convention, a claim that could no longer be made. He then turns to "our own Ecclesiastical Affairs." He now wonders if liturgical reform can be undertaken without bishops. He then says that Boston only took up the question of revising beyond the political prayers because "a Bishop in a neighboring state, whose Authority did not extend to the Churches represented in this Convention," sent them to Boston "for their Approbation." It will be recalled that Parker sent the Boston alterations to Seabury for his "Approbation," the opposite of what is claimed here.

---

62. Samuel Parker to Samuel Seabury, January 9, 1786, in Appendix B-4.
63. Samuel Parker to William White, January 31, 1786. Courtesy of the Archives of the Episcopal Church.

If we take up the revisionist suggestion that we are to look for persons attempting to lessen personal responsibility in this narrative, we might begin with Samuel Parker.

The contradictions between Parker's letter to White and that to Seabury grow when the question of episcopal pedigree arises. Two weeks before, he had written to Seabury that he "never" wished to see in America a line other than the Scots. To White he writes:

> I sincerely wish the Address to the Archbishops and Bishops of England drawn up by your Convention, had been done at the Convention held at New York last year. It might probably have procured Dr. Seabury's Consecration by them, & prevented an Application to the Scotch Bishops. Not that I have any doubts of the Succession through that Line, but I could have wished a Continuance of our Connection with the English Church....I frankly confess, *I should rather have the Succession from the English Church* to which we have always been accustomed to look as children to a Parent.

Parker slightly modifies this view by suggesting that a Scots bishop is probably better for New England, as the bishop would have no connection with the crown, as though sentiments were less republican in the Philadelphia or Richmond of 1786!

As if determined to contradict everything he had written to Seabury, Parker goes on to say that he welcomes all the changes made in the liturgy at Philadelphia, except the omission of the Nicene Creed:

> *not that I am fond of that Creed,* for some Expressions in it are as obscure & unintelligible as many of the Athanasian; the omission of which but very few will regret. My Objection to the omission of the Nicene Creed arises only from the peculiar temper of the times. The Arian Doctrine is making rapid Strides among us, & the rejecting two Creeds at once which were inserted in our Liturgy as Barriers against that Doctrine will be looked upon by People abroad as well as at home, as agreeing in the same Opinions. Perhaps the not having a prospect of another Opportunity will be a sufficient Apology for making the Omission at this time.

It is King's Chapel that is controlling Parker's thinking and turning his gaze to the right in matters of liturgy. He is even concerned that the Proposed Book is not as attractive to the shopper as is the King's Chapel volume.

You will give me leave to observe, that the new Prayerbook printed at Boston exceeds yours in paper, type, & perhaps in binding. Your[s] is printed with too small a type, especially for persons in years who are not fond of appearing in public with Spectacles.

Parker concludes with the wish that none of the Psalms had been dropped, but translated differently, using the future tense rather than the imperative mood in the cursing psalms. It will be some months, he adds, until a convention can decide whether or not to adopt "your prayer book."

If Parker is being more sincere in his letter to White than he was to Seabury, or if something about the King's Chapel had caused an alteration in his thinking, he has become more conservative in every respect. Unless he is being disingenuous in his letter, English bishops and ancient creeds now seem to form a bulwark against heresy in his thinking. Whether a "fondness" for the Nicene Creed would return to him, not even time would tell, for after becoming bishop, he died without having performed a single episcopal act.

The story of King's Chapel is still told by its members through pamphlets and a carefully researched monograph.[64] Building with stone in 1749 was not that common, so the blocks quarried in nearby Quincy gave the chapel the name "the stone church," by which it is called in much of the writing of the time. Even though Peter Harrison had adapted the architecture from an Old World plan, lay reader James Freeman understood its religious charter differently:

The Church of England had expired amidst the flames of the Revolution; but we expected, or at least hoped, that a new and more beautiful Church would arise from its ashes, an American Protestant Episcopal Church, which should be purified from all the puerilities, superstitions, and corruptions of the old establishment.[65]

Among the puerilities and superstitions that Freeman wished to see gone stood the Trinity, and the doctrine of the full divinity and full humanity of Christ. When Freeman took the plunge and preached about his complete break with Trinitarian theology on November 14, 1784, the very day on which Seabury was consecrated bishop, he was overwhelmed by how many in his audience agreed with him. Among the consequences of his

---

64. Margaret Barry Chinkes, *James Freeman and Boston's Religious Revolution* (Glade Valley, N.C.: Glade Valley Books, 1991).

65. In ibid., 7.

forthright sermon was that on February 20, 1785, a committee (obviously all laypeople) was appointed to revise the prayer book. The committee took as its model Lindsey's liturgy, and acknowledged other Unitarian thinkers as well. Forty years later, Freeman viewed the 1785 reform as an opportunity that men such as White and Provoost had missed to make the Episcopal Church the leader. All those years later, he still expressed a willingness to be ordained in the Episcopal Church, "provided I can be admitted on my own terms."[66]

The "proprietors" of the chapel voted twenty to seven to adopt the changes on June 19, 1785. On July 7, Freeman wrote to Lindsey about further needed changes. Whether the Middletown committee could have had, as is claimed, "access" to the King's Chapel book on August 4 is not clear.

The story of Freeman's attempts to be ordained by bishops in the Episcopal Church cannot detain us. What is of importance is the assumption of the King's Chapel congregation that the changes they were making would be echoed to the south. Charles Miller wrote to William White of his hope that the Proposed Book would "expunge all disputable doctrines, and the doctrine of the Trinity is certainly disputable, to say nothing more of it." Miller hoped for a liturgy that would not "wound an Athanasian" but would also not "hurt the conscience of a Unitarian." He writes that the Proposed Book was a good start, and that with "a few omissions, easily be conformable to every Christian mind." He continues by saying that unless this happens, the chapel will become an "independent society."

In pleading with White, Miller adopts the "scripture alone" principle to which Parker himself would appeal — to his regret:

> [Clarke has] omitted every petition to the son [*sic*] and to the Holy Ghost, or converted them into prayers to God. The opinion of the fathers, either before or after the council of Nice[a], is, I humbly conceive, of no consequence in a question of this kind, unless fully authorized by the sacred Scriptures.

He adds that the chapel's liturgy converts the absolution into a prayer, so as not to give the impression that anyone other than God can forgive sins. He admits that the "power of remitting sins" had indeed been "communicated to the apostles," but that it "is not continued down to

---

66. Ibid., 37.

the ministers of the present day."[67] Reading what came from Philadelphia in the introductory sermon and the preface to the Proposed Book, Miller and Freeman can fairly have assumed that this convention would welcome their reforms. White, still putting the finishing touches on the Proposed Book, replied in an undated letter of March 1786, that an individual congregation simply did not have the power to alter liturgy.[68]

The full title of the King's Chapel book is *A Liturgy Collected Principally from the Book of Common Prayer, for the Use of the First Episcopal Church in Boston; Together with the Psalter, or Psalms of David*. Although this society was indeed descended from the first group to worship according to the Church of England in Massachusetts a century earlier, Parker and others were to react strongly to their claim still to be Episcopalian while producing their own liturgy. After they had been turned down by Episcopal bishops and went on to ordain Freeman in a lay ceremony in November 1787 the Episcopalians published a broadside.

Whereas a certain Congregation in Boston, calling themselves the first EPISCOPAL Church in said town, have, in an irregular manner, introduced a Liturgy essentially differing from any used in the Episcopal Churches in this Common wealth, and in the United States, not to mention the protestant Episcopal Church in general; and have also assumed to themselves a power, unprecedented in said Church, of separating to the work of the Ministry, Mr. *James Freeman*, who has for some time past been their Reader, and of themselves have authorized, or pretendedly authorized him, to administer the Sacraments of Baptism and the Lord's Supper; and at the same time, most inconsistently and absurdly take to themselves the name and style of an Episcopal Church.

We the Ministers of the protestant Episcopal Church, whose names are underwritten, do hereby declare the proceedings of said Congregation, usually meeting at the Stone Chapel in Boston, to be irregular, unconstitutional, diametrically opposite to every principle adopted in *any* Episcopal Church; subversive of all order and regularity, and pregnant with Consequences fatal to the Interests of Religion. And we do hereby, and in this public manner, protest against the aforesaid Proceedings, to the end that all those of our Communion,

---

67. Charles Miller to William White, January 8, 1786. Courtesy of the Archives of the Episcopal Church.
68. William White to Charles Miller, March 1786. Courtesy of the Archives of the Episcopal Church.

wherever dispersed, may be cautioned against receiving said Reader
or Preacher (*Mr. James Freeman*) as a Clergyman of our Church,
or holding any Communion with him as such, and may be induced
to look upon his Congregation in the light, in which it ought to be
looked upon, by all true Episcopalians.

> *Edward Bass,* of St. Paul's Church, Newbury-Port.
> *Nathanael Fisher,* St. Peter's Church, Salem.
> *Samuel Parker,* Trinity Church, Boston.
> *Thomas Fitch Oliver,* St. Michael's Church, Marblehead.
> *William Montague,* Christ's Church, Boston.
> *John C. Ogden,* Queen's Chapel, Portsmouth, N. Hampshire.
>   December 1787.

That group of signatures is the entire clericus of Massachusetts, with
an additional name from New Hampshire. Liturgical criticism is not expressed here, but it is the manner of making change and the unprecedented
irregular ordination that are complained of. Parker is learning by experience that questions of church and church order precede those of liturgical
change.

The King's Chapel book went through a number of editions. That original edition of summer 1785 removes all specific reference to the Trinity,
and to the divinity of Christ. Thus in the Litany, for "Son of God, redeemer of the world," there is "O God, who by the Son has redeemed the
world." The Psalter indicates verses of the Psalms to be omitted. There
is no creed at all in the Holy Communion, but rather the Shema ("the
Lord your God is one"), followed by the Summary of the Law. There is
a general lack of rubric throughout, perhaps indicating great flexibility.
Absolution is replaced with a prayer.

Baptism is reduced to a very brief rite, and parents "most properly" act
as sponsors. There is no hint of regeneration, and those baptized are spoken of as "now dedicated to thee." The revised catechism says of baptism:
"The washing of water in baptism properly represents the purity of heart
and life, required from all who become the disciples of Christ."

The Holy Communion does retain the Apostles' Creed (Lindsey was
finally to expunge even that creed in his church in 1789), but with the
descent into hell deleted, a deletion that could not have gone unnoticed in
Connecticut. The catechism dramatically reduces what is understood by
the rite: "By eating bread and drinking wine in remembrance of Christ,
we keep alive the memory of his death and resurrection, we acknowledge

ourselves to be Christians, we cherish a grateful sense of the blessing of the gospel of Christ, and strengthen our resolution to live as becomes his disciples." This is the entire eucharistic teaching in the book.

The marriage service deletes the promise to obey, and "with my body I thee worship" is also removed. The burial service says at the committal: "in sure and certain hope that there shall be a resurrection to eternal life of all those who died in the fear and love of God." At the end of the book, nine non-Trinitarian doxologies are provided in various meters. Of these, none mention the Holy Spirit, and three refer to Christ as "the Lamb."

For Seabury, Bass, and, at last, Parker, to criticize the Proposed Book because of what it omitted was entirely reasonable in the New England setting. Strategic omission was the tool of Socinians, Arians, and semi-Arians. The same may be said of the position taken by the English Archbishops in their objections to the Proposed Book. Parker's experience with King's Chapel explains his increasingly hard line about irregularly made revisions. It was not the Episcopal way. Six months before the broadside occasioned by Freeman's ordination, Parker wrote to White that "I cannot myself consent to any further alterations till a uniform Liturgy is agreed upon by the whole Church in these States, and to effect this I shall be willing to give up anything but the essential doctrines of our Church, and to adopt anything not repugnant thereto."[69] He goes on to say that he is not sure that New England and the southern states can be united in discipline at this point, but he is sure that the bishops of Connecticut, New York, and Pennsylvania can agree on a uniform liturgy. White wrote a general reply but committed to no action.[70]

Even given the strong stand taken with White and the much stronger stand taken against King's Chapel, both in 1787, Parker was in an uncertain position with Seabury. The Boston convention of 1786 had declined to adopt any set of nonpolitical changes as official. Parker nonetheless produced a hybrid liturgy for Trinity Church, using the Boston list of 1785 and the revised Psalter of the Proposed Book.

In November 1785 Seabury had specifically asked that Parker not make any changes other than the political alterations. Despite his professed loyalty to Seabury, Parker made and kept the (hybrid) changes anyway. Seabury apparently declined an invitation to participate in a service using the changes, although a letter to that effect does not survive. In a long

---

69. Samuel Parker to William White, July 19, 1787. Courtesy of the Archives of the Episcopal Church.

70. William White to Samuel Parker, August 6, 1787, Perry, 358.

and defensive letter of January 28, 1788, Parker ignores Seabury's letters to him of August and November 1785 and repeats at length the story of Middletown.[71] This time nothing liturgical is represented as being his request or at the request of his Massachusetts colleagues. Parker makes no distinctions between political and nonpolitical changes, and implies that all changes were officially sent to Boston at Seabury's "express desire."

Parker feigns surprise (despite Seabury's two letters and that of Hubbard in August, September, and November) to have learned in July 1786 that Connecticut had not gone forward either with the Middletown/Boston changes or those of Philadelphia. He reports that Philadelphia had "acceded to" some of "our alterations," but had "gone much further" with regard to state prayers and other matters.

The difficult paragraph reads, in just three sentences:

> When our Convention met in July, by adjournment, we found that we were left by our brethren in Connecticut — that they thought it not advisable to make any alterations. The convention at the Southward, though they acceded to some of our alterations, had gone much further, and did not adopt the substitute for the state prayers; and the Churches in this and the neighbouring states had readily come into our proposed alterations, as they had signified to the Convention, only one excepted: what was there, in the power of the convention, then left to do, to preserve a uniformity? For my own part I was nonplused — we found we missed our object, and the only thing left to our choice was, to leave it to the option of the several Churches to adopt the new alterations, or continue the old Liturgy as should be most agreeable.

At this point one remembers Seabury's instruction to do nothing, and the option the other three or four priests at the Boston convention had to do nothing until there was a bishop or a consultation of a bishop, as Parker had advised White six months before.

Parker would not take personal responsibility, in this letter at least, even for the changes adopted at Trinity: "My Church chose the alterations." They were put in place on the first Sunday of August 1786, "and have been strictly adhered to ever since." Again the third person, "it was judged best" to add the abbreviated Psalter from the Proposed Book. Parker goes on to justify that change, completely forgetting the issue of governance. Edward

---

71. The letter is reproduced in Appendix B-6.

(later Bishop) Bass also wrote in 1786 that he was using the alterations, but took responsibility for the decision — and also reporting its popularity in Newbury Port.[72]

Parker concludes by saying that he would give up everything if Seabury insisted, except the omission of the Athanasian creed and the multiple recitations of the Lord's Prayer. He immediately qualifies this offer by adding that reversion to 1662 would cause a "convulsion" in the church of such magnitude "as would go near to its total destruction." His final argument is that if they returned to the old ways, people would think them afflicted with "an instability and fondness for change." "I will venture to assert," he adds, that when the "Bishops in America have agreed upon a uniform Liturgy, that it will be adopted by the Churches in this state." This last statement, of course, implies the possibility that the state might not adopt the bishops' liturgy, and we are once again wondering what Parker thought about the role of bishops in the church in practice.

Seabury's reply is lost, except for a fragment of a draft in his letter book. He would not quibble with Parker about the details of his narrative, but simply says in response to the letter that "Notwithstanding the statement of matters in it, I cannot help thinking you have been too hasty in adopting the alterations you have done — that it has rendered a union among the churches the more difficult, and clouded the small prospect of uniformity, which gave any encouragement to aim at it."[73]

By way of consolation, Seabury adds an observation directed to Parker's impatience regarding revision. "That some of our clergy have been too backward in accommodating the service of the church to the state, or rather the temper of the country, I will not deny; I have more than once told them so. But errors may be committed through haste, as well as by delay. I am far from ascribing ill designs to you, or to any one who acted with you: but you must forgive me if I repeat it — such alterations as have been made are unprecedented in the Episcopal Church, without the concurrence of your proper Bishop."

Seabury adds that this is not personal, but about the office of bishop and the unity of the church: "Forgive me, too, if I say, I did not flatter myself with having any steps taken in returning to the old service for my sake. I have been too long acquainted with my own unimportance, to expect it. But I did and do wish to have as great a uniformity as possible among

---

72. Edward Bass to Samuel Parker, January 3, 1786, Hawks & Perry, 2:288.
73. Samuel Seabury to Samuel Parker, February 13, 1789, ibid.,

our Churches; and I was grieved at a measure which I thought impeded so good a work. I never thought there was any heterodoxy in the Southern Prayer Book: but I do think the true doctrine is left too unguarded, and that the offices are, some of them, lowered to such a degree, that they will, in a great measure, lose their influence." I shall argue below that Seabury was more than correct in this assessment.

From this point, we hear no more of Parker on liturgy except in support of revision undertaken by the church as a whole, with the leadership of its bishops. There is no evidence, however, that before 1790 he ever ceased to use an altered liturgy at Trinity, even though it most emphatically had no "episcopal approbation."

– Chapter Six –

THE SOUTHERN
PRAYER BOOK

The Sermon and the Preface

In the preface to the Proposed Book, William Smith advises readers who are interested in identifying particular changes to compare the book with that of 1662. The readers of the present work will find in Appendices A-2 and A-3 that this task has been done for them, with the 1662 book, Boston proposals, and 1789 present for comparison. The shaded area represents what the committee was authorized to do. The unshaded portion indicates much of what it did on its own authority. The changes are generally the streamlining that the age called for, also some word changes, and a few points concerning doctrine. To these last we will return. Appendix C-4 contains White's "Hints at a Preface." The reader of White's list will find a detailed apologia for the changes, but an overwhelming defensiveness draws one's attention most of all. This list will also assist those interested in more complete knowledge of the book.[1] Because, as Hatchett rightly points out, the Proposed Book evoked such strong reaction across the entire church, we tend to be blind to its moderation and occasional brilliance.

If we are to catch the spirit of the book, William Smith's sermon at its Philadelphia premiere and his preface to the completed book the following spring must have our attention. They also pinpoint some of the areas of Seabury's discomfort with the book. The entire sermon, with the footnotes Smith added for the press, can be found in Appendix C-3.

---

1. Hatchett1 and Hatchett2 are also good guides. The reader may see the entire service laid out for comparison with the English 1662 and American 1789, 1892, 1928, and 1979 in *Parallels*, vol. 1. For the purpose of comparison with 1662, McGarvey's *Liturgia Americana* will also serve, and he also compares through 1892, although his columns read from right to left chronologically.

Smith takes Luke 14:23 as the text for his fifty-three-hundred-word sermon, "And the Lord said unto the servant, Go out into the highways and hedges, and compel them to come in, that my house may be filled." He explains the text as meaning first the gathering into Christ's church from the diaspora of Israel, and finally the whole Gentile world. Nowhere in the sermon does he connect the coming Feast with the Eucharist that prefigures it, but in this he is a person of his time.

The mission of the church, he maintains, has been and always will be to compel "them" to come in. He is quick to point out that "compel" here means to constrain, draw, or attract, and gives biblical examples. This is important to his theme, so he is explicit in saying that "compel them" can involve no physical or mental coercion. Invoking the familiar language of the Te Deum, he goes one step more. "Witness, ye noble army of Saints and Martyrs of every age, that no man's judgment was ever convicted by stripes, by imprisonments, by racks or by flames." Living memory is then invoked: "Nay, witness, even ye unenlightened tribes of Mexico and Peru, that the murder of millions for the pretense of religion but served for nothing more than to rivet the unhappy survivors still deeper in their tenets."

After discarding "internal compulsion," which includes watering down the message so that people "may become Christians on easier terms than Christ hath appointed," Smith gets to his point, the "more joyous and important subject." There are three ways in which the church can legitimately compel others to come in. "1st. By special instruction and exhortation; 2dly. By living example; and 3dly. By the decency, devotion, fervency and solemnity of our forms of public worship, and by embracing every opportunity for their further improvement." The Proposed Book might have fared better if its preface and other promotion had made the point Smith makes here: Liturgy is to be examined in terms of mission strategy. John Henry Hobart and William Augustus Muhlenberg would try to make this point in the next century, but it would not be heard until the preparation of the 1892 revision.

Interestingly, Smith locates the teaching and exhortation exclusively in the arena of clerical activity. He believes that preaching emerges from the preacher's being fully aware of "the whole counsel of God — the terrors and judgments of the law, as well as the marvelous grace and rich mercies of the gospel — the duties of love and evangelical obedience, as well as the divine virtues of faith and heavenly hope!" When theology is interiorized, results cannot but follow:

A preacher of the gospel, truly animated with these exalted subjects, impressed with the weight of eternal truth, glowing for the good of his fellow-creatures, and convinced of the immense value of their immortal souls, has noble opportunities of touching the hearts of men, and even of constraining, or compelling them to the love of God.

The clergy are to give people a "ravishing view of God's goodness." Smith expects the result to be rhapsody:

O love unspeakable, which astonishes even angels, and hath broken the kingdom of devils! Think you that if a servant of God, really inflamed with this love, were proposing its rich overtures, even to the most unenlightened Gentile, *in a language and sense intelligible to him* — he would not cry out — O the heights and the depth thereof! O blessed Saviour! I desire to taste of this love of thine — I am ready to follow thy divine call, and the calls of thy faithful servants, who speak in thy name — Draw me, I beseech thee, more and more by this constraining love — Draw me and I will follow, nay I will run, after thee! [emphasis added]

The second kind of compulsion belongs to all Christians, and that is the duty to live lives that make Christianity attractive. He believes that this will occur only when the truth of the gospel reaches the depths of the personality.

Finally Smith reaches his objective. The third point is "compelling men to come in ... by the decency, devotion, fervency and solemnity of our forms of public worship, using every endeavour in our power for their further improvement."

Speaking then of the revision, he devotes ink to protesting how reluctant the committee was to alter the heritage of the church's worship:

Arduous was the work that lay before us. When we took up our liturgy with a view to certain necessary alterations, we were struck with the utmost diffidence. We contemplated our church service as an august and beautiful fabric — venerable for its antiquity — venerable from the memory of those glorious and now glorified luminaries, saints and martyrs, who laid the foundations of our church on the rock of ages. We stood arrested, as it were, at an awful distance — It appeared almost sacrilege to approach the porch, or lift a hand to touch a single part, to polish a single corner, or to clear it from its rust of years!

Some of the luster and effect of this passage is lost for moderns who know that Smith did not mean a word of it, that at least since 1784 he had been waiting for the opportunity to alter the prayer book. As a rhetorical device, however, it works, setting the changes in the context of the greatest reluctance to touch the monument.

Smith then recounts how they took courage from remembering the work of the reformers, and how "those pious worthies broke down the enormous pile of rubbish and error" which infected the life of the church. Then he plays his big card, invoking all that his hearers believe to be noble — about themselves.

> Blessed be God, we live in a liberal and enlightened age, when religion, if not so generally practiced as it ought, is nevertheless generally better understood; and when nothing can be considered as deserving the name of religion, which is not rational, solid, serious, charitable, and worthy of the nature and perfections of God to receive, and of free and reasonable creatures to perform.

With a nod to the late Revolution, he immediately adds:

> Nor had we to contend against, or suffer from, the rulers of this world. Blessed be God again, they yield us that best protection and assistance which religion can receive from earthly powers — perfect and equal liberty to worship God according to that sense of holy scripture which our reason and conscience approve.

Implying that no liberal and enlightened people would disagree, Smith quickly covers the political changes in the prayer book. Then he says that having the political freedom, the knowledge, and of course the support of the liberal and enlightened members of the church, the committee undertook to complete the work begun in 1689. He claims that "all those proposed alterations and amendments were in our hands." However, Nichols and Calamy had produced inaccurate versions of the 1689 provisions, and the actual work of the commissioners was not to be published until 1854.[2]

---

2. See Timothy J. Fawcett, *The Liturgy of Comprehension, 1689* (Southend-on-Sea, U.K.: Mayhew-McCrimmon, 1973). Relevant documents were reproduced in Edward Cardwell, *A History of Conferences and other Proceedings connect with the revision of the Book of Common Prayer* (Oxford: University Press, 1840). It strains credibility beyond the breaking point to assume that a missing manuscript copy of the 1689 plan was in the 1786 revisers' hands without their mentioning it, and simply sank back into oblivion when the revision was completed.

Smith continues with the observation that people in general, but religious people in particular, and of them Anglicans most particularly, feel more accepting of something new when it can be demonstrated to be old. Thus the length of Smith's observations on the 1689 project is for a purpose: Establish the precedent. His points are the familiar ones. "Language itself is fluctuating," which lily he gilds with "and receiving frequent improvement." His entire description is taken up with the changes desired in 1689. He then notes the tragedy of that project's failure, so as to emphasize that now is the acceptable time. But he has yet another carrot:

> What glories will shine upon the heads of our clergy whom God hath made instrumental in this good work! How much shall our laity be venerated for the candor, liberality, and abilities, which they have manifested on this great occasion.

There is more for the laity, too, and here the words of a known Tory must have evoked the odd chuckle. Smith expresses the gratitude of the Church that the laypeople present "after all their illustrious toils for the civil happiness of their country" were giving attention to the welfare of their church. Not content to leave it there, Smith goes on to explain this virtuous behavior not in terms of pleasing God, but in the practical terms of building a stronger, better nation on the foundation of morality and religion. He adds that it would be basest ingratitude of God to let the opportunity to revise pass ungrasped.

Many would consider this an ideal place to end the sermon, but Smith has one more arrow in his quiver. He tells the audience that many of them are used to hearing him preach at Christ Church, but he is aging, and this may be his last sermon (he would live another sixteen years). So his dying wish, so to speak, "exhort[s] you again to receive and examine with a meek, candid, teachable, and charitable temper of mind, what is proposed to you on this occasion." He asks them to save any objections for the next revision, and to use this liturgy, and observe that the people will be compelled to come in. This is not language designed to introduce a mere proposal.

Smith understands this liturgy to be bound up with the destiny of the new country and invites the hearer to

> look for a time, when there shall be an universal diffusion of the gospel throughout this land — when they who dwell in the wilderness

shall come and bow down before the Lord; then among the highways and hedges to the remotest parts of this continent, decent places of worship will probably be erected — villages, towns, and great cities arise — and the service and worship of our church *(as we have this day introduced it)* be not only adopted, but through the blessing of God become happily instrumental in compelling fullness of the Gentile world to come in!

The preacher says that if Christ were here, "he would not narrow the terms of communion." Thus the revisers felt a duty "to make the consciences of those easy who believe in the true principles of Christianity in general" but who cannot accept certain relatively inessential teachings. This would be the kind of "lowering of doctrine" to which Seabury would point.

Smith's is not a style of rhetoric one would employ today, but one can still imagine the congregation hanging on his words. No "trial" liturgy before or since has claimed this much for itself. It would be White's view that precisely in its claims lay one of the reasons for its downfall. Smith's capital error was that he did not say anything clearly about the tentativeness of this book, about its being merely a proposal. Smith's sermon does not leave people with many options, particularly as it ends with a kind of deathbed request.

Smith's sermon was florid and diverting, but his preface covers the ground very differently. Half the length of the sermon, it gives more information of the kind not easily molded into preaching. The writing is clear and sharp, and the sentences are a little shorter. A preface had been authorized by Convention and was to set "forth the reasons and expediency of the alterations."

The first paragraph touches political, biblical, and traditional bases. "It is a most invaluable part of the blessed 'liberty wherewith Christ hath made us free'" invokes the temper of republican times while coopting scripture (Gal. 5:1) and concluding with a quotation from the preface to the English book of 1662. He continues in the next paragraphs to demonstrate that the church has a right to liturgical revision, as protestants and even the Council of Trent agree. Borrowing from the English book, he defines the goal of revision as the peace and unity of the church, increased reverence and piety, and prevention of disputes. As secondary reasons he adduces once more "the fluctuation of our language," the clarifying of instructions to the clergy, and better translations. He adds at the end "the addition of some Offices, Prayers, and Thanksgivings" for special occasions.

Then Smith gets down to business. The Church of England had between 1549 and 1662 at least five major liturgical revisions. Between 1662 and 1689 pressure had built for revision as well. So considering that 1662 to 1786 is a longer time, the reader is left to conclude how long overdue is a review. He reminds the reader that the Commissioners of 1689 were the brightest and the best, in fact "the Church of England was never, at any one time, blessed with either wiser or better since it was a church." Then he lists the matters for review, which are the familiar list.

It is noteworthy that the familiar list is presented with much greater emphasis on music, which Smith tells us elsewhere he supported because of competition from the Methodists.[3] A future bishop of Maryland, Thomas Claggett, also complained to the attractiveness of "Methodist hymns and tunes."[4] Whatever his motive, Smith overcame White's opposition and with significant help from Charles Wharton, the third member of the editorial team, gave Anglicanism its first official hymnal in any place.[5] It would be almost fifty years before hymnody was welcomed as legal in the Church of England, and that church has never had an official hymnal. The most unusual thing about this first collection of fifty-one hymns is that it had never been discussed in the 1785 convention. White would work, right through 1826, to keep the number of hymns as small as possible. Francis Hopkins, who had published *A Collection of Psalm Tunes, with a Few Anthems and Hymns* for Christ Church in 1763, produced in 1786 *Tunes Suited to the Psalms and Hymns of the Book of Common Prayer*. Done in great haste, it is a poor successor to the 1763 collection in terms of both content and appearance.

Another oddity that strikes a reader of the preface is that only the Athanasian Creed is discussed under missing creeds. White had asked Smith to

---

3. Perry, 151.

4. Thomas Claggett to William West, August 23, 1788, *CtFirst*, 17.

5. On Wharton in general and on his liturgical work, Christopher M. Agnew, "The Reverend Charles Wharton, Bishop William White, and the Proposed Book of Common Prayer, 1785," *Anglican and Episcopal History* 58 (December 1989): 510–25. Despite White's assignment of the July Fourth service to Smith's authorship, Agnew credits Wharton, but does not tell us why. Similarly, he assigns the Psalter to Wharton rather than White. Wharton was a Roman Catholic priest until 1784, when he decided to marry. He has more significance for the history of the Episcopal Church than even Agnew suggests. It was from him that a way was found to receive priests from Rome into the ordained ministry of the Episcopal Church. He served as a priest of the Episcopal Church for forty-nine years.

explain the loss of the creeds, which he did in the case of the Athanasian, but did not in the case of the Nicene, because he already knew that its return would be discussed at his state convention and probably at others: "I would say nothing concerning [the Nicene Creed] because I believe some whole States will agree with the three New England States, in having it inserted."[6]

After sending to White what is essentially the preface we have received, Smith wanted to draw some blood (Seabury's and the younger Smith's) with a note explaining how Nonjurors and other conservatives aborted the salutary 1689 plan.[7] White prevailed upon him not to do this.

As in the sermon, Smith tells the reader that the freedom of the church in a republic was a gift not to be ignored, and that the opportunity to revise was grasped gladly. Gone is the pious cant about unwillingness to alter a sacred object, approach its porch, and so on. Some particular changes are mentioned, and the readers of the preface are once again directed by Smith to do their own comparison with 1662 to discover the changes in detail. The situation was not really this harsh, however, as there was eventually reproduced a pamphlet listing the changes approved by Convention, but of course not identifying those changes that the editorial committee was making on its own.

Smith describes the rite but does not cite the Church of Ireland as source for the service for Visitation of Prisoners, despite White's request. He then explains the elimination of the *descensus* from the Apostles' Creed, and mentions the revision of the Articles of Religion. He concludes as artfully as he began, and as in the sermon, does not leave much room for dissent:

> And now, this important work being brought to a conclusion, it is hoped the whole will be received and examined by every true member of our church, and every sincere christian with a meek, candid, and charitable frame of mind; without prejudice or prepossessions; seriously considering what *christianity* is, and what the truths of the gospel are; and earnestly beseeching Almighty God to accompany with his blessing every endeavor for promulgating them to mankind in the clearest, plainest, most affecting and majestic manner, for the sake of Jesus Christ, our blessed Lord and Saviour.

---

6. William Smith to William White, March 17, 1786. *L&C Smith,* 183ff. He reports Maryland's decision in a letter to William White, April 9, 1786, *L&C Smith,* 197f.

7. I have reproduced the note *in situ* in the Preface, Appendix C-5.

It is not always clear as to why the Proposed Book reads as it does. The convention journal tells us almost nothing about the work of the committee during the convention. In fact, Perry's summary of the convention data is that "a more guarded and less communicative record could hardly be found."[8] Slightly more information comes to us through the correspondence of the editorial committee composed of Smith, White, and Wharton. The reader who consults the lengthy table in Appendix A-3 will, again, notice that the changes the editors made on their own authority are largely inconsequential. There are some exceptions. Under the twenty-ninth alteration, the address to the sponsors at baptism has been changed: The child is not doing the promising through the sponsors, and the description of the Christian life is changed, with the curious omission of raising the child "to believe in God," although the "Fear of God" is introduced. Purcell will later insist that the gospel canticles were to have been omitted, and this does not appear in the editorial correspondence, perhaps yielding to the new book an accidental conservativism. Likewise, the committee did not replace every absolution with a prayer, did not delete "as generally necessary to salvation" from the Catechism, and did not remove saints' days from the Kalendar.

On the matter of the Kalendar and lectionary, White wrote to Smith that

> It is not within our Appointment; and yet I believe we shall be thanked for so dividing the Lessons as to serve the triple Purpose of shortening the Service, expunging the Apocryphal Chapters, and getting rid of some of the public Readings which may seem immodest. I fear we must let the New Test't Lessons stand at present: and yet the Gospels and Acts might be very well worded so as to be read twice instead of thrice in the year. As to the Table of proper Lessons, I have taken great Pains with it and hope it will meet your Approbation.[9]

To sum up the two public pieces promoting the book, we find considerable energy spent on establishing the right of the church to revise its liturgy, and also on the role of liturgy in the church's mission. It is to attract people by its style and grace; its celebrations are to contain sermons by preachers enflamed with passion for the souls of hearers; it is to make

---

8. Perry, 109.
9. William White to William Smith, February 10, 1786, Perry, 167.

room for as many shades of believer as possible. Smith's idea that compelling people by a "ravishing view of God's goodness" still has the power to move the reader. The book is held out as consonant with an enlightened and reasonable age, and therefore naturally must adjust itself to the time. This means first the political changes, and then the completion of the agenda of 1689, and the making of further "Latitudinarian" revisions that would make the book attractive to those who stood on the periphery of the church, wanting to commit to "Christian principles," if not to Christ. They also celebrated the American Revolution as part of the divine will, and saw their book as helping to build national character.

White's hints were, as Smith notes on the last page of White's letter communicating them, suggestive of several topics he addressed in his preface, but there are no instances where White's words are taken up into it.

More than one contemporary cleric surmised that the Proposed Book was written with *Free and Candid Disquisitions* at Smith's side. White is explicit in telling us that Smith had a source for revision of the Articles of Religion. Writers agree that this must have been the anonymous *Reasons Humbly Offered for Composing a New Set of Articles of Religion* (1751). It repeated the old refrain and suggested reducing the Articles to only that which could be proved from the scriptures. There was, of course, no agreement about what that meant.

In the new Articles, the five articles on the Trinity are reduced to one. Missing entirely is the article on the descent of Christ into hell. In general, all technical or conciliar language is removed. The resulting text is not Unitarian, but it would not much discomfort a subordinationist.[10]

The listing of the creeds is, of course, trimmed back to the Apostles' Creed only. The articles concerning works before justification and supererogation are deleted. Reference to the sin against the Holy Ghost is removed, as is the entire article regarding purgatory. Article Twenty "Of the Authority of the Church" is blended into a general article on the church. Interestingly, "The Church hath power to decree Rites or Ceremonies, etc." becomes "Every Church hath power...."

The article against speaking in tongues is omitted, as is that against Donatism. The article "Of the Sacraments" is trimmed of the famous passage against lifting up, gazing upon, and so on, but is also trimmed of the warning against unworthy reception. One feels hackles rising on the necks

---

10. The texts of the Articles can be found in *Parallels*, 2:166ff.

of many who read the article "Of Baptism," to discover that the affirmation of infant baptism is completely removed. Articles on the manducation of unbelievers, both kinds in the sacrament, the marriage of priests, excommunication, and "of the Traditions of the Church" are all deleted. Naturally, the homilies are gone, as they have not been set forth by any authority. No attempt is made to adjust "of the civil Magistrates" to the new civil state, and most surprisingly, given Smith's hard-fought battle for riches, Article XXXVIII, "Of Christian Men's Goods, which are not common," is also omitted entirely.

The resulting articles would not have offended anyone seeing them as their first exposure to articles of religion. For those at all familiar with the Articles of Religion as they had existed in previous prayer books, loss and confusion must have been the dominant experience.

In his 1784 liturgy, John Wesley reduced the thirty-nine to twenty-four articles, retaining that which supports the right to private property. He left the articles about the godhead intact, except for the omission of the descent into hell. He eliminated entirely the article on creeds, shortened the article on Original Sin, and trimmed the article on justification to exactly the wording Smith would use — this may be happenstance, as both simply lopped off the reference to the Homily on Justification.

Wesley's major surgery is on the last section of articles. He changes "sin after Baptism" to "sin after Justification," skips predestination, the uniqueness of Christ, and goes directly to the church. Here his abbreviation is much more radical than Smith's, with the two articles on church and authority reduced to a short statement about the church and nothing about authority:

> The visible Church of Christ is a Congregation of faithful men, in which the pure Word of God is preached, and the Sacraments duly administered according to Christ's Ordinance, in all those things that of necessity are requisite to the same.[11]

Wesley leaves unchanged the articles on purgatory through "Of the Sacraments." In the article on baptism, he retains the baptism of infants, but deletes the benefits of baptism. The article on the Lord's Supper is unchanged. The article regarding the manducation of unbelievers is omitted, and the marriage of priests becomes the marriage of ministers. The article

---

11. James F. White, ed., *John Wesley's Prayer Book: The Sunday Service of the Methodists in North America* (Akron, Ohio: OSL Publications, 1991), 310.

regarding traditions is changed to "rites and ceremonies," and reference to national churches is made congregational — Smith had simply eliminated this article. The article regarding oaths is left unchanged, whereas Smith had trimmed it of reference to the teaching of Jesus.

Wesley's text has been discussed here because it was a widely known variation used in a living church community. When one compares the work of Wesley and Smith on the Articles of Religion, we see Wesley leaning more to the Puritans and their ancient "exceptions" to the prayer book, and Smith trolling the waters of Deism and various heresies having to do with the godhead. To oversimplify, Wesley's articles are revised with an eye toward a church community that will use them, while Smith's seem much more oriented to how people hovering on the edge of the church will think about the topics covered. Consequently, although Wesley makes more actual change in the text, he is in some ways more orthodox from the perspective of 1662.

If we pursue the comparison with Wesley, we continue to see that he is more likely to keep traditional wording of texts that do not interrupt his theological agenda. Thus the Te Deum is unaltered, as is the Confession, complete with the phrase omitted in the Proposed Book, "and there is no health in us."[12] The confession is not followed with an absolution, but with a prayer for forgiveness, not unlike what King's Chapel would insert. There is only one Lord's Prayer. There is no effort to cut down on iterations of the Gloria Patri, but the Venite is gone, although it survived in Wesley's shortened Psalter. Benedicite is removed in Morning Prayer, as is the Benedictus. The traditional canticles are also omitted in Evening Prayer, but the "lighten our darkness" collect is present, unchanged. The Litany is less altered than in the Proposed Book. At the Holy Communion the minister presiding is termed "The Elder." Absolution is a prayer again, and "meekly kneeling" is gone, but the rest is 1662, although there would be a later version with no manual acts prescribed.

The sign of the cross is retained in baptism, but all mention of regeneration is gone. The marriage service is much less trimmed than in the Proposed Book, with more of the purposes of marriage in the opening address retained. There is no ring at all, and consequently no reference to bodily worship or the endowment of goods. Communion of the sick is

---

12. This phrase has troubled many revisers well into the twentieth century. Writers tend to replay Calvinist-Arminian disagreements, rather than translate "health" properly, with a result something like "and we cannot save ourselves," a sentiment with which both sides would agree then and now.

stripped to the bone, with no confession or absolution at all. There is no committal formula at the burial, with a cento of biblical verses being read "when the corpse is laid in the earth."

The question presents itself, then, was the Proposed Book really a conservative reform when compared to its competitors? Clearly, the King's Chapel book was a deliberate move away from orthodox Christianity, which leaves 1785 and Wesley as candidates for more conservative of the choices available in the United States at the time. The question becomes one of nuance or emphasis. There are fewer alterations of familiar texts in Wesley — that is, of those that survive, for there are more outright excisions or replacements. The familiar language of ecclesiastical offices is replaced with "minister," "elder," and "superintendent" in Wesley, but the Proposed Book also replaced the word "Priest" with "minister." Both revisions "mutilated," as Seabury was to put it, the Psalter.

If one's question is which book retained clearest affirmation of Trinitarian doctrine, Wesley is certainly the more conservative. If the question is about the replacement of texts, the "trembling hands" of the 1785 revisers are the more conservative. Wesley is the more honest about the life of his community, removing "daily throughout the year" from the Morning and Evening Prayer liturgies.

From the point of view of the former SPG missionaries in New England, it would probably be the case that Wesley's protection of traditional doctrines about the godhead from the predations of their Unitarian neighbors would be preferred. As for the rest, however, they would find the Proposed Book less offensive; more of what they knew was retained, and expressions concerning the church and its ministry were the more commonly known. One has to agree with Hatchett that, compared with the two other revisions of the prayer book on the market in 1786 America, the Proposed Book was the conservative choice. The real conservatives, of course, did not wish to make the choice.

July Fourth

William White was candid in his estimate of the reasons for the failure of the Proposed Book. The two "capital errors" were the printing of such a large edition (five thousand), "which did not well consist with the principle of a mere proposal," and using it, together with Smith's sermon at the conclusion of Convention, which "helped to confirm the opinion of its being introduced with a high hand."[13] However, he kept a special place in his list of errors for the Independence Day liturgy, "the most injudicious step taken by the convention...was it not the dictate of moderation, to avoid the introducing of extraneous matter of difference of opinion, in a Church that was to be built up? Especially, when there was in contemplation the moderating of religious tests, was it consistent to introduce a political one?"[14]

White thought it "a little extraordinary" that Smith, whom he knew to be a Tory, "who had written and acted against the declaration of independence; and was unfavorably looked on by supporters of it," had the nerve to serve as author of this service. The modern reader at all familiar with Smith will see it as his customary going with the trend, and also as something of an attempted political rehabilitation. If we remember that Holmes, cited above, found about 150 clergy who supported the king to 123 who supported the Revolution, this liturgy was more likely to bring laughter than anything else in most churches of 1786. White's point about a political test is telling. It is not Seabury who is "showing little respect" for the revolutionists, but the former loyalists who are having words forced on them. Jeremiah Leaming believed that this service was "an insuperable difficulty."[15]

The liturgy in question, along with that for the harvest, is meant to replace the special services in the 1662 book. The old book contained services for the sovereign's accession to the throne, the execution of Charles I, and the Gunpowder Plot, among those appointed. While the American Church continues to have a Society of King Charles the Martyr, the other state services were of no use to the new church, and a gap was perceived, as the preface points out.

The title of the service is "A Form of Prayer and Thanksgiving to Almighty God, For the inestimable Blessings of Religious and Civil Liberty; to be used yearly Fourth Day of July, unless it happen to be on *Sunday...,*" and then on the day following, one of the few services to have a rubric built into the title.[16]

Provided are sentences for Morning Prayer including "Happy art thou, O Israel: who is like unto thee, O people favoured by the Lord, the shield of thy help, and who is the sword of thy Excellency." The Venite was

---

13. White1; Perry, 205f.
14. White1, 117.
15. Hatchett1, 211.
16. Service to be found in *Parallels,* 1:222ff.

replaced with a cento of Psalm verses. After the Psalter and Lessons, all specially appointed, there was a thanksgiving for the day, which would stick in the throats of many who simply wanted to forget the bad years and get on with life in a situation they would not have invented. The faint echo of the Whitsunday collect in the 1662 book ("who as on this day didst inspire") could not have made things easier, in equating the Declaration of Independence with Pentecost, or at least with works the church views as inspired:

> O God, whose Name is excellent in all the earth, and thy glory above the heavens, who as on this day didst inspire and direct the hearts of our delegates in Congress, to lay the perpetual foundations of peace, liberty, and safety; we bless and adore thy glorious Majesty, for this thy loving kindness and providence. And we humbly pray that the devout sense of this signal mercy may renew and increase in us a spirit of love and thankfulness to thee its only author, a spirit of peaceable submission to the laws and government of our country, and a spirit of fervent zeal for our holy religion, which thou hast preserved and secured to us and our posterity. May we improve these inestimable blessings for the advancement of religion, liberty, and science throughout this land, till the wilderness and solitary place be glad through us, and the desert rejoice and blossom as the rose. This we beg through the merits of Jesus Christ our Saviour. *Amen.*

In the Holy Communion, the collect for the day does not display the economy of diction that characterizes this form of prayer. It runs:

> Almighty God, who hast in all ages shewed forth thy power and mercy in the wonderful preservation of thy church, and in the protection of every nation and people professing thy holy and eternal Truth, and putting their sure trust in thee; We yield thee our unfeigned thanks and praise for all thy public mercies, and more especially for that signal and wonderful manifestation of thy providence which we commemorate this day; Wherefore not unto us, O Lord, not unto us, but unto thy Name be ascribed all honor and glory, in all churches of the Saints, from generation to generation, through Jesus Christ our Lord. *Amen.*

The gospel concluded with the words of Jesus in John, tortured by their new context in this service: "If the Son therefore shall make you free, ye shall be free indeed." We may count ourselves fortunate that Smith did not essay a proper preface for July Fourth in the Holy Communion service, or live to write liturgies for the period of Reconstruction, when the Episcopal Church healed divisions much more satisfactorily than it did in the 1780s. This little service, to which few in the United States would take exception today, was in its own day bound to alienate, belittle, and embarrass many of the clergy, and uncounted laypeople. History is admittedly written by the winners, but great liturgy can often to be shown to come from those untainted by triumphalism, those who have tasted not victory but oppression. The existence of this service, together with the absence of a single unkind word from Seabury, should settle the question of who was showing disrespect for the integrity of the other side in the nascent church.

Promotion, Sales, and Improvements

The Proposed Book was advertised in the *Pennsylvania Gazette* during the late spring and summer of 1786, but Hall and Sellers never listed a price, and some of the correspondence involves the question of what to charge for the book now that it was available.

On April 17, 1786, Smith wrote to Parker, pitching the Proposed Book and his Maryland convention's alterations. Smith gently chides Parker for not being present to take part in the revision, but assures him that he had the Boston proposals with him and believes the Proposed Book addresses all of their concerns, except the Nicene Creed, which it had suppressed. He does not discuss the changes that go beyond Boston. Here is a telling point about the assignment of the Boston changes to Seabury. If Smith believed that Seabury was behind the revisions or that they bore his stamp in any way, he would have said that to Seabury and certainly would have mentioned it in this letter to Parker, but he does not. Indeed, White will later acknowledge Seabury's 1785 letter stating flatly that he endorsed nothing beyond political change.[17] Smith hopes that Massachusetts will give a "serious and candid Consideration" to the Book, and adopt it. If there are problems, "we can in future Editions come to an easy Agreement." He then describes the Maryland additions to the Proposed Book. He proceeds to the other revisions and "other matters which ['I' lightly crossed out and 'we' disingenuously inserted] we have set forth in the Preface. We can only

---

17. The acknowledgment is in White's wonted oblique style: "I have been informed that you, Sir, and our Brethren in Connecticut think a review expedient, although you wish not to be in haste in the matter." William White to Samuel Seabury, May 21, 1787, Perry, 346.

in the different States receive the book for temporary use, till our churches are organized, and the book comes again under review of the Conventions having their Bishops &c., as the primitive rules of Episcopacy require." What Smith does not add, but what he did include in a letter to White, was that this tentativeness should comfort Seabury and his camp, partially into which he places Parker. Smith also does not address the service for the Fourth of July, even though Parker had been a "nominal patriot."

White's former curate, Joseph Bend, seems to have given him moral support if not actual advice. He opposed the unaltered Psalter for the same reasons that White did: They are "unfit for the general use of a congregation." He went beyond this and said that they were "a blemish in our public worship for a considerable time."[18] Bend, who supported the Proposed Book, gives us evidence that it was "coldly received by a great part of the Church."[19]

Although there is not one instance of a verbal parallel, Smith claims that he had Boston on his mind from the first, and that the Proposed Book agrees with Boston completely, except for the Nicene Creed. He does not discuss the changes made in the Proposed Book that go beyond what Boston envisioned. He is quick to add that his convention has restored the missing creed as well as an invocation in the Holy Communion, "something analogous to the Liturgy of Edward VI and the Scots liturgy." He adds his criticism that present Scottish liturgy favored the doctrine of transubstantiation by using the words "that they may become the body and blood." Although his own invocation is based on 1637, he confuses them in his letter and is here quoting 1764! Smith was not an ignorant man, and here illustrates the relative vagueness employed when discussing liturgies most people had only heard of. He cannot have failed to know of Seabury's attachment to the 1764 prayer, if not from his own Colin Ferguson (who was at Middletown in 1785), then certainly from the younger Smith, and by writing this way to Parker, he is landing his punch.[20] Parker would eventually correct him. It is useful to note here the identity of 1549 and 1764 in Smith's mind (despite their very different structure). As mentioned above, this is how most Anglicans thought of complete eucharistic prayers: They were like 1549. If Smith knew the Roman Canon, he would have recognized that his formula was more "papist" than the 1764 liturgy, as it came before the institution narrative. Chapters 7 and 8 will return us to

---

18. Middleton, 62.
19. Ibid., 61.
20. The text is in Appendix B-5.

this topic. The following table illustrates the Maryland changes compared with other invocations and their location in the eucharistic prayer.

1549	1637	1764	1785
before Institution Narrative	before Institution Narrative	following Memorial and Oblation	before Institution Narrative
Hear us (O merciful father) we beseech thee:	Hear us, O merciful Father, we most humbly beseech thee,	And we most humbly beseech thee O merciful Father, to hear us,	Hear us, O merciful Father, we most humbly beseech thee,
and with thy holy spirit and word vouchsafe to ble✝ss and sanc✝tify these thy gifts, and creatures of bread and wine,	and of thy Almighty goodness vouchsafe so to bless and sanctify with thy word and Holy Spirit these thy gifts and creatures of bread and wine,	and of thy almighty goodness vouchsafe to bless and sanctify, with thy word and holy Spirit, these thy gifts and creatures of bread and wine,	[MD and PA proposed adding here: and of thy Almighty goodness vouchsafe so to bless and sanctify these thy creatures of bread and wine]
that they may be unto us the body and blood of thy most dearly beloved son Jesus Christ.	That they may be unto us the body and blood of thy most dearly beloved Son;	that they may become the body and blood of thy most dearly beloved Son	
	so that we, receiving them according to thy Son our Saviour Jesus Christ's holy institution, in remembrance of his death and passion, may be partakers of the same his most precious body and blood:		and grant that we, receiving them according to thy Son our Saviour Jesus Christ's holy institution, in remembrance of his death and passion, may be partakers of his most precious body and blood:

   Thus, of those available, the proposed Maryland formula is the weakest, and least consecratory. It is not clear how Smith thought this would please everyone. It is probably the most that White would put up with, a concern that would also affect the book of 1789.

   How well the Proposed Book sold is disputed. There has also been disagreement about how large the edition was. The printers Hall and Sellers (Christ Church communicants) did not leave records for 1786. The usual number given is 4,000. Hannah French, basing her estimate on the accounting for the twenty "tokens" (250 pulls through a hand press) that were let out to subcontractors, calculates that the edition was of 5,000, and there is no reason to disagree. She has also identified 22 surviving copies. White, in charge of production, engaged one Caleb Buglass of Philadelphia to produce a hand-tooled special leather binding of two dozen of the books, including those sent to the English bishops.[21]

The use of the book seems to have been centralized in the Philadelphia vicinity. In New York, 150 may have been sold. Other places were not that well saturated. White writes to Parker that he has had to buy them where he could find them for use in Philadelphia, and fourteen months after publication believes the actual sales to be "between the half and two-thirds, I believe nearer the latter." Elsewhere he reports that the Philadelphia-area clergy feel that they are alone in giving the book a real trial.[22] White was a Philadelphia cleric, and given his preference for expressing himself indirectly, he may well have been including himself in the sentiment.

Reaction of the States

"The failure of the book was not just a sectional one, however, for it was rejected in varying degrees by almost all state conventions following the Philadelphia meeting in 1785."[23] This fact makes it easier to assess Seabury's opposition, and to compare his objections with those of others, for each state convention took its own approach.

The first response was in Maryland. Before the ink was dry on the complete Proposed Book, and certainly before it was distributed throughout the nation, Smith's convention met in Annapolis on April 4, 1786. Smith's hand is on the tiller, but Claggett's resentments about Smith's (and White's) influence are given voice in the beginning of the report to the convention, noting that "they could have wished that the book had been published in time enough for every member to have had a deliberate consideration and perusal of it." They would "nevertheless" approve of it "as far as their powers extend," but with some alterations: the Nicene Creed is to be restored, the Trinity is to be more fully represented in the Articles, the baptismal rite smoothed out for occasions when large numbers are to be baptized, and the Consecration Prayer at the Holy Communion be changed as already noted.[24]

---

21. Hannah D. French, "Caleb Buglass, Binder of the Proposed Book of Common Prayer, Philadelphia, 1786," offprint from Winterthur Portfolio 6. Published for the H. F. duPont Winterthur Museum by the University Press of Virginia, Charlottesville, 1970.

22. White, 120f.

23. Calcote, 289.

24. *Parallels*, 2:516f.

The Maryland version of the invocation in the eucharistic prayer eliminates both the "word and holy Spirit," and any transformation or transignification of the elements. Smith felt justified in writing to White, reporting on the Maryland convention, that "In the Scots and Edw'd 1st's Liturgy the Prayer was exceptionable and leaning much to *Transubstantiation* in these words — 'Vouchsafe to bless and sanctify these thy Creatures of Bread and Wine, that they *may* BE unto us the *Body* and *Blood*,' The Alteration as we propose it is thus, beginning at the words in the Consecration Prayer, 'Hear us O merciful Father, we most humbly beseech Thee, and vouchsafe so to *bless* and *sanctify* these thy Creatures of Bread and Wine that we receiving them according to thy Son our Saviour J. C. holy Institution, in Remembrance' &c. as it now stands. This reads as well as before, pleases all sides, and is certainly an Improvement, as there was before no Invocation of a Blessing on the sacred Elements."[25] Again, there is no way to tell how he thought this addition pleased all sides or what sides they were.

New Jersey met later in that month, on the nineteenth, and adopted the political changes made in the liturgy by the Proposed Book. It was their view that the liturgy proposed could not but hurt the chances for English consecration of bishops for America. They stated that making alterations was beyond the powers of a convention acting without bishops, and that publishing them without the concurrence of the episcopate was simply wrong. Then addressing only the merits of the revisions, they declare that they could not accept the book because it did not square with antiquity and its improvements were erratic and inconsistent. They saw the existence of the Proposed Book as a major obstacle to union of the churches in the various states into a national body, and in fact expected it to produce "dissentions and schisms."[26]

Pennsylvania met on May 27, and perhaps unsurprisingly, White's convention did what Smith's did, and more. The Nicene Creed was to be restored (and made mandatory on great feasts). The Maryland invocation was added to the Holy Communion. The actual recitation of the creed was to be restored to baptism, and some of the burial service restored. The Articles of Religion were to be essentially restored, with a bit of tinkering and the creation of a new article on relation to civil rulers requested.[27]

---

25. William Smith to William White, April 9, 1786, Perry, 190.
26. *Parallels,* 2:517f.
27. Ibid., 2:519f.

On May 29, Virginia met. It had no comments about liturgy for the record, and accepted the new book in the main, but had some alterations to make in the revised Articles of Religion. The Virginia convention called for the elimination of all reference to the Apocrypha and in Article VII curiously wanted "justified by faith alone" changed to "justified by faith." The instructions to their General Convention deputies include this memorable charge:

> We consider the Protestant Episcopal Church in America as an incorporate Society, and therefore unity in doctrine and worship its characteristic: Conformable to this, you will not carp at expression, nor carry your objections to unessential points; guarding against schism by all possible means, and giving our Church every benefit and strength it can acquire from union.[28]

South Carolina was the only other state to join with Virginia in accepting the liturgy as published, but with the concern that "the punctuation throughout be critically attended to." This is understandable: both Smith's and White's copies of the Proposed Book survive, and they are riddled through with punctuation and other language corrections. While adopting the liturgy, in addition to improved punctuation, South Carolina wished to have a further deletion from the Apostles' Creed (eliminate the "again" from "he rose again"), the removal of introductory (nonpenitential) sentences from the office, and a host of minor changes. Major changes requested were the omission of the Magnificat and Nunc Dimittis (Purcell was sure the 1785 convention committee had already eliminated them, which may well be true, as he was a member), and phrases relative to the clergy be "lowered" as Seabury would put it. The convention members offered further adjustments to the catechism, confirmation, and matrimony. Regarding the burial service, they tactfully suggested that reference to our hope that our deceased brother or sister was a partaker in the kingdom was an accident. They suggested minor changes to the Fourth of July service, Prayers at Sea, and the Articles.[29]

New York met, and as Provoost had foretold, did not adopt the book, tabling it "out of respect to the English Bishops, and because the minds of the people are not yet sufficiently informed."[30]

---

28. Ibid.
29. Ibid., 2:521f.
30. Ibid., 2:522.

Massachusetts, despite the apparent harmony between Parker and Smith, on July 20, 1786, declined to accept either the proposed liturgy or Parker's "Middletown/Boston" proposals. The delegates postponed all revision until there were bishops — just as Seabury had asked them to do, and as Parker had declined to do.

Delaware never took the matter up at all.

If nothing else, these broadly scattered criticisms put White, Smith, and for that matter, General Convention, on notice that they really were not in England anymore: The liturgy of the new church could not be adopted if it were perceived as being imposed. The method of revision adopted in 1789 would involve many more voices in the revision process.

The English Bishops

The copies of the Proposed Book prepared for the English bishops were not back from the binder until June 17, 1786,[31] but the pamphlet describing the changes must have reached them, because they gave their analysis sometime in June as well. They acknowledge receipt of the convention journal and the Articles in late April, so White may have been sending them individual parts as they came off the press. In any event, their rebuke is rather as Seabury's was to be:

> it was impossible not to observe with concern, that if the essential doctrines of our common faith were retained, less respect, however, was paid to our Liturgy than its own excellence, [and] your declared attachment to it, had led us to expect; not to mention a variety of verbal alterations, of the necessity or propriety or which we are by no means satisfied.

The bishops were just warming to their task, however. They go on to notice "with grief" that two creeds were missing, and the *descensus* removed from the Apostles' Creed. They continue to add that "trusting that [the list of their corrections] will have their desired effect," they are nonetheless preparing legislation to make consecration of American bishops possible. They are as critical as New England was of the subjection of clergy to trial and deposition by laity in Article VIII of the proposed Constitution.[32] The convention at Wilmington would address the bishops' concerns.

---

31. French, "Caleb Buglass," 18.
32. *Parallels*, 1:523–25.

After the Wilmington convention, Charles Wharton wrote to White, apparently a rubrical solution like that which would be put in place in the 1789 book.

> I see no difficulty in complying with the Archbishops' requisition, except the making our past Conventions appear rather ridiculous. However if Hell must all events be retained, I think a rubrick should be inserted to explain its meaning in that place. If the use of the Creeds be discretional, no harm can arise from giving them a place in an Appendix.[33]

Individual Responses

The post was busy with letters about the new liturgy and constitution in 1786. In January the future bishop of Massachusetts wrote to Parker. Like Parker, Edward Bass had been using the alterations proposed to the Boston convention immediately from September, not waiting for even state convention approval. He believes the southern states to have engaged in "unepiscopal conduct" with regard to Seabury. In reporting this to Parker he reflected a wedding of the issues of liturgy with regional sentiment. His comment was occasioned by his reading of Smith's October sermon.

> Dr. Smith observes somewhere in his Sermon, that the convention at Philadelphia touched, or were disposed to touch the Liturgy, in the way of revisal and amendment, with trembling hands. If that were really the case, I fancy their hands were paralytic during their whole session; for, by Dr. White's letter, they seem to have touched abundance of the Service, and to have made many and weighty alterations. I have always been of opinion, that we never should coalesce with these gentry, and that it was much more natural for us to endeavor to come to a uniformity in these four Northern States.[34]

Bass concludes, "For my part, I wish to have little to do with them." His position illustrates what Parker and Seabury had to contend with in the search for an ecclesiastical union: Those who did not think it was worth the bother to unite with Steiner's "non-theological" Episcopalians to the south.

---

33. Charles Wharton to William White, September 18, 1786, Perry, 327
34. Edward Bass to Samuel Parker, January 3, 1786, *Parker*, 19; Hawks & Perry, 2:288.

In December of the previous year, Thomas Bradbury Chandler had written to Jonathan Boucher a letter that gives us some idea of the books that everyone knew or knew about. "On the subject of Liturgy, the *Free &* *Candid Disquisitions*, was the Oracle they consulted. The amendment proposed in that book they have generally adopted, & added farther one of their own. They have knocked off, at a Stroke, the Nicene & Athanasian Creeds, & a Clause of that one called the Apostles; they have corrected the Lord's Prayer and Te Deum; & it would be well for them if they could alter the Commandments."[35]

In February, William White wrote to Seabury apologizing for not getting copies of the proposed liturgy to the bishop, and enclosed some of the parts then in print. He adds that the question of who may try bishops is not yet settled, although for himself, there is no objection to laypersons participating in the verdict, as long as a bishop would pronounce sentence.[36] In April White would send the entire book to Seabury.

Samuel Peters's comment from abroad addressed both the constitution and liturgy produced in Philadelphia, noting that its "comprehensive system...offends no people except Christians," and that "their new prayer Book would make Baxter blush...because they have mended the Lord's Prayer and the Apostles' Creed...and have much improved on Lindsey's and on Arius' System."[37]

In March, White's former employer acknowledges that the Proposed Book is mostly harmless in its alterations, but that the ecclesiological question remains. He makes the point very directly: "The Necessity of the Case, & our particular Circumstances may justify in some Measure your adopting a Republican Form of church Discipline — But surely there could have been no Necessity for a few Clergymen & Laymen undertaking to leave out a single Article in a Creed, which is received & adopted by every Christian Communion — even by the Socinians, I believe."[38]

The July Fourth service was a sticking point in New York, in Provoost's opinion. "Such a strong party has been raised against the Alterations, that I am afraid we should not be able to adopt the Book at present, without danger of a Schism. The ostensible object is that they were made without the sanction of a Bishop, but the Thanksgiving for the Fourth of July, in

35. Thomas Bradbury Chandler to Jonathan Boucher, December 5, 1785, *CtFirst*, 89f. Chandler also reports that Benjamin Franklin told some at Philadelphia that there had been a break in the Scottish succession.

36. William White to Samuel Seabury. February 1, 1786, ST1, 24.

37. Samuel Peter to Arthur Petrie, February 20, 1786, *Peters2*, 10.

38. Jacob Duché to William White, March 25, 1786, *CtFirst*, 11f.

all probability, is one principal cause of the opposition. The sale of the Books has been very dull — only thirteen have been disposed of."[39] By the end of the month he would report that the first hundred were sold, and acknowledges receipt of fifty more.[40]

Parker wrote on May 15 to White liking the book, especially the Psalter, and proposing some minor adjustments. Perhaps not minor is his suggestion that the church rather than the United States be prayed for in the litany, arguing that in England the king was prayed for as head of the church. King's Chapel has left its mark: Parker unequivocally expresses a wish to see the Nicene Creed return. Seabury had by this time debuted the Scottish Communion Office. Parker is one of the few characters in this study who understands the Scots prayer, and responds to Smith's news about the epiclesis that he could "only wish that they had moved also for the Oblation in the prayer as it stands in the Scots communion Service."[41] William Smith the elder seems not to have understood this point until the 1790s, and White remained in denial.

Future bishops Provoost and Parker are joined by Thomas Claggett (to be bishop of Maryland in place of Smith), who is aware of the amount of control Smith and White have in general, and their working beyond their brief on the prayer book. Claggett writes:

> It is now pretty clear that I shall not go to Philadelphia this Summer. I'm tired, my dear Sir, of being hurried about, merely to give a little Sanction to measures which generally have received the *Royal Assent* before I hear of them. . . .

He adds that the "Church's real Friends, the Communicants" universally disapprove of the new Book

> I have written to Dr. West not to send me any of them at present, for I am persuaded it can not be introduced here, without giving great uneasiness and perhaps it would be attended with worse Consequence. Their Objections are such as these, viz. That our new Reformers have altered too much, & have Presbyterianized in many instances, particularly they have virtually denied the Doctrine of Regeneration in Baptism taught by the Church of England which Tenet they think is sufficiently founded on John 3, 5 Acts 2, 38 & 22, 16, & several

39. Samuel Provoost to William White, May 4, 1786, Perry, 297.
40. Samuel Provoost to William White, May 20, 1786, ibid., 300.
41. Samuel Parker to William White, May 15, 1786. ST1, 30; Seabury correspondence, 112.

other parts of sacred writ, they contend that the primitive Church always held this Doctrine, & as a proof of it, they instance the Nicene Creed and the Evidence it affords of this Truth they think is the true Cause of its being displaced; among several other Things they oppose themselves warmly to the mutilating and leaving out a great part of the Psalms of David, they contend that this Procedure may serve as a precedent for the Clergy's depriving them of any part of the whole of the sacred Canon, whenever they choose to introduce them to the halcyon Times of monkish Superstition: at any rate they think that such a practice has a tendency to weaken the authority of sacred Scripture & is flatly reprobated by the Scripture itself.... [42]

One marvels at the theological sophistication of Claggett's communicants, but also notes that here the loss of the Nicene Creed is connected to the loss of baptismal regeneration in the rite. The creed speaks of "one baptism for the remission of sins." The revision of the Psalter is seen as the clergy depriving the laity of the entire canon of scripture. As much as Parker liked the revised Psalter, Claggett seems to have disliked it to at least the same extent. The red flag remains Romanism, however. Just as Smith would argue that the Scots' eucharistic prayer smacked of transubstantiation, Claggett argues that the trimming of the Psalter can bring back the days of "monkish Superstition."

A Wintry Blast from the North

Unusual in the history of the early liturgical revisions of the Episcopal Church is a pamphlet that appeared in Boston in 1786, *Remarks on the Proceedings of the Episcopal Conventions for Forming an American Constitution*. The author is identified only as "a layman." Anonymous authorship was still quite common — especially when everyone knew who wrote a work, as was the case of much of William Smith's writing. This screed is important not because of any great insights (there are none), but here is a writer who sees the questions of bishop, constitution, and liturgy as one. The author agrees with the revisers that time had indeed come to accommodate the Church of England to the new world, both in structure and liturgical form. He wonders, as would Muhlenberg in the next century, why all Christians were not invited, so that instead of an imitation

---

42. Thomas Claggett to William Duke, June 19, 1786, Hatchett1, 200.

of the Church of England, an inclusive American church could have been formed. This was the thinking of Freeman and his flock.

The writer knows of the Boston alterations, and has heard of Philadelphia's decisions, but still has not been able to get the pamphlet describing the changes. He says that he can neither understand nor forgive the disrespect shown Seabury in the 1785 convention; however, he puts forth principles that would have troubled the bishop very much. He thinks liturgical reform should be the right of every parish minister, in consultation with the laity. He begins to tip his hand, and one increasingly sees the likelihood that *Remarks* is the work of a member of King's Chapel, especially when he discusses the work of Clarke, and then adds

> I have always hoped that we, as an independent people, might be favored with an American Church, more free from a bigoted attachment to ancient creeds, doctrines, and tests of orthodoxy, than could be allowed by the Clergy in England; but I fear that some of our Clergy here are in favor of the like hierarchical powers.

Was this an attack on Parker, the leading opponent of King's Chapel? This cannot be proved, but seems likely, as the writer goes on to defend ordination by the laity. He understands the clergy to derive their "office and powers" from the laity. The pamphlet is a liturgical Trojan Horse, and King's Chapel seems likely to have been its source.

Seabury's Response

Compared to some of what was being said, and the petty comments arising in some of the state conventions, Seabury's three known occasions to comment on the Proposed Book seem to be models of restraint and depth and in no way resemble Guelzo's alleged "muttering."

His theme is set out most clearly in his response to Parker's long, angry letter of January 28, 1788, where he does not yield to Parker's confabulation. After noting that he has pointed out to the Connecticut clergy the need for revision at a quicker pace than they prefer, he adds:

> Errors may be committed thro' haste, as well as by delay. I am far from describing ill designs to you, or to any who acted with you. *But you must forgive me if I repeat it* — such alterations as have been made, are unprecedented in the Episcopal Church, without the concurrence of your proper Bishop. . . . I never thought there was any

heterodoxy in the southern Prayer book. But I do think the true doctrine is left too unguarded, & that the Offices are, some of them, lowered to such a degree, that they will, in a great measure, loose their influence.[43]

We do not have a reply from Parker, but can see here that the very elasticity that Smith thought would invite those who hesitate to join the church, Seabury sees as elimination of the liturgical expressions that helped maintain the identity and orthodoxy of the church. It is hard to disagree with him at the time and place where he lived. The people at King's Chapel had shown how much of the skeleton of the prayer book could be maintained while abandoning Trinitarian faith. Perhaps to the south this was not as strongly felt, unless perhaps Smith wanted ultimately to embrace the Deists who held pews at Christ Church, Franklin among them. Again, referring to the Proposed Book as conservative is an accurate claim only when the book is compared to the alternatives, such as the King's Chapel book or John Wesley's revision. But Seabury was very much aware of what doors innocent-looking omissions and expansions could and did open to the heresies of the day.

The other two recorded occasions of his criticism of the Proposed Book are Seabury's second charge to the clergy, and his letter to White before the 1789 convention. In the second charge he begins by saying that it is a disagreeable task to have to criticize, and given the length of the charge, he does spend very little ink on the matters in contention. His first comment is a constitutional one: Nowhere in the early Christian tradition is there precedent for what has been done in Philadelphia. After discussing the questions of authority, the importance of using the consensus of the patristic writers rather than picking a favorite, and how the Bible is to be the basis of belief, he returns to the Proposed Book. He notes that there are "some" who are "depressing the Offices, corrupting the Government, and degrading the Priesthood of Christ's Church" by lessening emphasis on Christ's divinity, dropping two creeds and the descent into hell, and by removing baptismal regeneration.

Degrading the priesthood seems to mean two things. The proposed liturgy changed all the 1662 rubrics regarding "priest" to "minister." Seabury also thought the removal of a clear expression of priestly absolution

---

43. Samuel Seabury to Samuel Parker, February 13, 1788, Hawks & Perry 2:321. Emphasis added.

was unwarranted, and would fight this battle again when the ordination rites were considered in 1792.

Seabury addresses the whole constellation of issues (and like the "layman" of the *Remarks,* he sees them as connected) in a long letter to White on June 20, 1789.[44] He has clearly waited for this moment. The southern states are increasingly eager to bring Connecticut into the ecclesiastical union. Correspondence has passed between him and White, and Parker, Leaming, and others are trying to generate momentum for a union. Provoost is viewed as rather a lost cause even by his own clergy, so the Bishop of Connecticut believes he has White's ear. He has in April indicated that Connecticut will send two priests to the upcoming convention. Replying to the important letter from White, discussed in chapter 8, he thanks White for his expressions of charity and for his desire for union.

Seabury reports that he called a convention of lay delegates to raise money for his salary, build a college, and ask if they wished to send lay deputies to General Convention. (He held this meeting on May 13 in the portentous venue of Middletown.) The circumstances are very important here. Seabury is asking them for money and wants to know about convention representation as well; he is certainly not going to try to railroad a clergy-only deputation through a group whose cooperation and cash he needs. Having been trained by conservative SPG clergy for three or four generations, the lay delegates from Connecticut parishes were not minded to go to General Convention. They also determined to go forward with the Episcopal Academy and to accept a tax to pay the bishop.

Returning to Seabury's letter to White: after reporting that the laity did not wish to participate in convention, but very much did want unity and uniformity, Seabury asks the question. May the clergy deputies attend if there are no lay representatives? Here Bishop Provoost's image looms in Seabury's mind, as Provoost was thoroughly opposed to seating any defective deputation:

> The Clergy supposed that, in your Constitution, any representation from them would be inadmissible without Lay delegates, nor could they submit to offer themselves to make a part of any meeting where the authority of their Bishop had been disputed by one Bishop, and probably by his influence, by a number of others who were to

---

44. Samuel Seabury to William White, June 20, 1789, Hawks & Perry, 2:328ff.; Perry, 384ff. The whole letter is reproduced in Appendix B-8.

compose that meeting. They therefore, must consider themselves excluded, till that point shall be settled to their satisfaction, which they hope will be done by your Convention.

For my own part, gladly would I contribute to the union and uniformity of all our Churches; but while Bishop Provoost disputes the validity of my consecration, I can take no step toward the accomplishment of so great and desirable an object.

Seabury adds, ominously, that if the convention cannot solve this problem it must be resolved "by an appeal to the good sense of the Christian world." If this means by a pamphlet war of the kind he knows how to win, this passage makes sense. Otherwise, it is not obvious what is intended. He immediately adds, "But as this is a subject in which I am personally concerned, I shall refrain from any remarks upon it, hoping that the candour and good sense of the Convention will render the further mention of it altogether unnecessary."

Seabury next mentions White's insistence on a complete battery of English-made bishops, and wishes it were not so, notwithstanding any engagements White had made with the archbishops. Seabury had either forgotten the complete rejection of non-English bishops that White had expressed in the *Case*,[45] or dared to hope that White had broadened his outlook.

After more discussion of constitutional issues, Seabury acknowledges that Parker has on his own adopted a revised liturgy, including the Psalter from the Proposed Book, and goes on to discuss the prayer book. He cannot be complete, he says, because "it would run this letter to an unreasonable length." He is listing the specific ills he hopes to see redressed in Convention.

Seabury's concern about the editing down of the Psalms has to do with the church's need to encounter the scriptures as they are. Furthermore, "by discarding the word Absolution, and making no mention of Regeneration in Baptism, you appear to give up those points, and to open the door to error and delusion." As to the creeds, his concerns are Trinitarian and in particular christological — "If the doctrine of those Creeds be offensive to some, we are sorry for it and shall hold ourselves so much more bound to

---

45. Moderns seldom consider the degree to which the eighteenth-century English considered the Scots thoroughly foreign and utterly contemptible. See Linda Colley, *Britons* (New Haven, Conn.: Yale University Press, 1994), esp. 12–16.

retain them." He explains the necessity of professing the descent into hell because it relates to Christ's full humanity.

Seabury adds that given the state of the baptismal rite in the Proposed Book, the confirmation service makes no sense: "In the latter there is a renewal of a vow, which in the former does not appear to have been explicitly made." Something of the same discordance appears in the Catechism. Out of "regard for primitive practice" Seabury finds himself "exceedingly grieved" that the sign of the cross is not mandatory in baptismal liturgy. After discussing some ancient history, he observes about recent history: "If the humour be pursued of giving up points on every demand, in fifty years we shall scarce have the name of Christianity left."

At this point Seabury interjects, "For God's sake, my dear Sir, let us remember that it is the particular business of the Bishops of Christ's Church to preserve it pure and undefiled, in faith and practice."

He finds the alterations in the Articles of Religion pointless — but at this time Seabury did not think the Articles were necessary. He would change his mind.

Then Seabury comes to the Eucharist. Here we see what it is that Smith and others did not have, an appreciation for the whole eucharistic prayer as process and event more than a means of manufacturing a sacrament:

> The grand fault [in 1662] is the deficiency of a more formal oblation of the elements, and of the invocation of the Holy Ghost to sanctify and bless them.

The Maryland/Pennsylvania epiclesis simply asked for God's blessing, not the operation of the Holy Spirit. Seabury then picks up Smith's ill-informed charge of transubstantiation, and hurls it back, politely:

> [In 1662/1785] the Consecration is made to consist merely in the Priest's laying his hands on the elements and pronouncing "This is my body, &c," which words are not consecration at all, nor were they addressed by Christ to the Father, but were declarative to the Apostles. This is so exactly symbolizing with the Church of Rome in an error; an error, to, on which the absurdity of Transubstantiation is built, that nothing but having fallen in the same error themselves, could have prevented the enemies of the Church from casting it in her teeth.

Seabury adds the positive part of his disagreement: "The efficacy of Baptism, of Confirmation, of Orders, is ascribed to the Holy Ghost, and his energy is implored for that purpose; and why [the Holy Ghost] should not be invoked in the consecration of the Eucharist, especially as all the old Liturgies are full to the point, I cannot conceive." Seabury then notes that White's own convention had opened this door, and modestly hopes that "some worthy and able advocate" for a complete eucharistic prayer will arise.

There is an enticement added, although Seabury may be forgetting White's youth, and concomitantly lesser concern about his place in history. "It would do you more honour in the world, and contribute more to the union of the Churches than any other alterations you can make, and would restore the Holy Eucharist to its ancient dignity and efficacy." Understanding how Seabury meant those words is our task in the next chapter. Here it is important to note that none of Seabury's complaints are about streamlining of Morning Prayer; none criticize changes on the order of "our Father, which/who"; none share the English bishops' concern about familiar patterns of words, and certainly none address punctuation. They are about the church's need to be faithful to its calling and its identifying tradition, and the opportunity it has to reclaim its eucharistic heritage.

– Chapter Seven –

THE COMMUNION OFFICE
OF 1786

I show you a better way.

— 1 Corinthians 12:31

In Seabury's eyes the Proposed Book "lowered" the Holy Communion service by changing its "priest" to a "minister," removing its creed, and deliberately removing from it the word "absolution."[1] Worse still, from his perspective, it also left unchanged a eucharistic prayer which, as Bishop White tells it, Seabury found irredeemably defective. On the first Sunday of the reconvened 1789 General Convention, White hospitably "wished him to consecrate the elements. This he declined. On the offer being again made at the time when the service was to begin, he still declined, and, smiling, added — To confess the truth, I hardly consider the form to be used, as strictly amounting to a consecration."[2] Even those who argue that Seabury did not understand the agreement with his consecrators would agree that he followed a strict "Usager" view of the Eucharist in his Communion Office of 1786. Again in this incident, as White recalls it, Seabury adheres to his principles firmly — but with a smile as well.

Seabury and White might illustrate Buxton's suggestion that by the middle of the eighteenth century, there were generally two schools of eucharistic thought in Anglicanism.[3] One, which he calls the 1662 tradition,

---

1. The editorial committee removed the word, but in this place allowed the text to stand. That this may have been an oversight is an intriguing possibility, especially as we have seen Purcell's evidence that the Magnificat and Nunc Dimittis were to be left out of the daily office.

2. White1, 178.

3. Dugmore, in his painstaking and unparalleled work, distributes approaches among three types, adding the category of "central," which Buxton would include in the 1662 camp. Its chief exponent was John Bramhall, as far as presence is concerned (Dugmore, 71ff.), and his view of sacrifice is in the vein that the Nonjurors would follow, but he would not share an understanding of Calvary as creating salvation that was "conditional" on our use of the Eucharist to cover our sins.

arose from the existence of that rite, "and thus a consequence of the balance of ecclesiastical and political forces that produced the 1662 rite." In other words, it was an attempt to make sense of what simply *was*. The other, which he terms the 1718 and 1764 tradition "were composed to give liturgical expression to a previously developed theological tradition of some sophistication and refinement." Of course, he adds, with what certainly must be tongue-in-cheek, "the 1662 tradition cannot be stated with the same degree of precision as the 1718–1764 tradition."[4]

Nonjurors and the Eucharist

Steiner's suggested "New England Consensus" on the Eucharist is impossible to accept because it asks the wrong question. All parties were clear in saying that Christ was not present in the elements in any corporal or even consubstantial way. They might even come close to agreeing that Christ's presence was virtual "in power and effect." Where they would have parted company dramatically was on the question of what *transpires* in the celebration. To the High Churchman (a term dating to Queen Anne's day — just right for our subjects), *doing* the commanded memorial was at least as important as *receiving* the gifts of consecrated bread and wine, and the fact is they thought Calvin quite wrong in his well-known concept of the Spirit lifting our souls to heaven at communion time. We have seen that Samuel Johnson taught the High Church view; it is present in the early Seabury sermon on the Eucharist, and it is the essence of the Nonjuror reconstructions of Anglican rite. The question for them was always how best to obey the dominical command to "do this for my memorial." Jeremy Taylor, even in what Dugmore would consider his later and more moderate period, says that "What Christ does in heaven, he hath commanded us to do on earth... represent his death... keep it before the eyes of our heavenly Father."[5]

To understand what Seabury did with the Nonjurors' liturgy some explanation is in order, although an epoch (1689–1805) and a school of thought cannot be reduced to a few paragraphs.[6] Very generally,

---

4. Buxton, 191.
5. Dugmore, 102.
6. The classics are Lathbury and Overton, as given in the Key. Indispensable for liturgical study is Grisbrooke, along with Dugmore and Brett. Where Hall's *Fragmenta Liturgiae* can be found, they can provide documents as well. A self-identified revisionist view of the Usages controversy is J. D. Smith, *The Eucharistic Doctrine of the Later Nonjurors* (Bramcote, U.K.:

Episcopacy was abolished in the Scottish established church in 1560, appropriated again in 1610, only to be disestablished in 1638, restored in 1660, and discarded again in 1688. An episcopally led community of Nonjurors continued in spite of the presence of a parallel communion staffed by Church of England clergy sent up from the South, but that community survived under increasing disabilities. The Stuarts were Scots, and most of the Episcopalians in Scotland found their loyalty to that house bringing them into sympathy with the English Nonjurors. Their rejection by the state Kirk and the legal penalties they incurred from their Nonjuror status left them in an unhappy condition. Perhaps the easiest way for moderns to sympathize with the Nonjuror political question in England and Scotland is to ask, what does a group do when that which the state requires is a violation of conscience, integrity, and honor?

What most people did and do is find a rationale, a way to get over a bump in their life's road and keep moving despite paradox or contradiction.[7] This would certainly be the case for religious folk in newly independent America in the 1770s and 1780s. In the United Kingdom, most of the clergy found a way to swear allegiance to the new king and queen after the Glorious Revolution of 1688 put William and Mary on the throne. It is the eternal trap of the contemporary to patronize seemingly ignorant forbears, so it is important to note that the Nonjurors, who were to include Thomas Ken, Thomas Brett, and William Law, were very far from being unintelligent, unlearned, or imperceptive. The Nonjurors' consciences had been formed in a way that did not permit them to do that thing no more complicated than dropping a little incense on a coal burning before Caesar's bust in ancient Rome, and they indeed spoke of the state prayers as "immoral." Less romantically put, they were willing to lose their careers for the sake of conscience. At least to that extent they must be taken seriously, incredible as the application of their conscience

---

Grove, 2000). A retelling of the eighteenth-century portion of the tale is interspersed throughout J. C. D. Clark, *Samuel Johnson: Literature, Religion, and English Cultural Politics from the Restoration to Romanticism* (Cambridge: Cambridge University Press, 1994). On the intersection of religion and politics, see Robert D. Cornwall, "Divine Right Monarchy: Henry Dodwell's Critique of the Reformation and Defense of the Nonjuror Bishops," *Anglican and Episcopal History* 68 (1999): 37–66, and Robert D. Cornwall, *Visible and Apostolic: The Constitution of the Church in High Church Anglican and Non-Juror Thought* (Newark: University of Delaware Press, 1993). Cornwall's sensitivities are those of the historian rather than the historian of doctrine.

7. A convenient introduction and meditation on this situation is J. W. C. Wand, *The High Church Schism* (London: Faith Press, 1951). Bishop Wand explains the crisis in part as the birth pangs of modern notions of government, with particular reference to the limited allegiance given to a constitutional monarch.

may seem in the present day. As in any group that defines itself in terms of what it negates, there were some among the Nonjurors who were stubborn and contentious, but that cannot be said of their leading theological and spiritual lights. For all of them, their commitment to a vision of the integrity *in* as well as *of* the church was a principle that would make them attractive to young John Wesley as well as to early Tractarians.

Having been dispossessed of the rights and privileges of their ordination, some of them perceived themselves to be equally free of the obligations of holy orders as far as liturgical conformity was concerned. Our focus here is on what they did with their unsought freedom from the liturgy of 1662.

As students beginning the study of liturgy soon learn, the English rite of 1549 has never ceased to fascinate Anglicans. There are many reasons for this attraction, but items such as the retention of introits and singing the Gloria in Excelsis at the right end of the service are entirely minor in comparison to 1549's place as the only classic English liturgy to maintain a complete (albeit medieval Western) eucharistic prayer. Comparing the parts of the prayer that follow the Sanctus next to the same section of the Roman Canon (*Te igitur* and following), one discovers that Cranmer echoes most of the thoughts of the Roman prayer, and does so in the same order. What later became a freestanding "Prayer for the Whole State of Christ's Church" was originally Cranmer's post-Sanctus supplication. The post-Sanctus structure of prolonged intercession, petition for the blessing of the eucharistic elements, the institution narrative, the memorial and oblation, further supplication, and doxology was indeed the classic tradition of the West, as Cranmer's critics of the left pointedly observed and his critics on the right unwisely agreed.

The Nonjurors, like others before them, found much to admire in ancient eastern prayers, particularly those of Book Eight of the Apostolic Constitutions and the Liturgy of St. James. We have already seen that even those who had profound doubts about Trinitarian Christianity shared the wide fascination with the Apostolic Constitutions as well. In it many believed that they heard the voices of the Apostles or at least the voices of the generation the Apostles spiritually begat.

In Book Eight's eucharistic prayer, the pattern was (1) extended praise and thanks for creation and all of the Old Covenant, concluding with the Sanctus; (2) praise and thanks for salvation under the New Covenant, concluding with institution narrative and the memorial-and-oblation; and (3) supplication (including above all an invocation of the Holy Spirit along with other petitions) and final doxology. The memorial, oblation, and invocation read thus:

> [immediately after the institution narrative] Therefore remembering his passion and his death, and his resurrection from the dead, as also his return into the heavens, and his second appearing to come, when he will come with glory and power to judge the living and the dead, and to render to each according to his works, we offer to you, our King and our God, according to his command, this bread and this cup, giving you thanks through him for counting us worthy to stand before you, and to sacrifice to you.
>
> And we entreat you that you will mercifully look down upon these gifts which are here set before you, O God who stands in the need of none [of our offerings], and will be well-pleased to accept them to the honor of your Christ, and so send down upon this sacrifice your Holy Spirit, the witness of the sufferings of the Lord Jesus, that he may make this bread the body of your Christ, and this cup the blood of your Christ.... [8]

It is difficult to imagine today the impact of this prayer on Anglicans in an age of reason and religious reticence. The culture did not prepare them for a prayer in which the assembly so vividly "recalls" the future with as much certainty as it remembers the past, so the impact must have been profound. Study of Eastern prayers, especially Apostolic Constitutions VIII (and the Liturgy of St. James), seemed to solve problems for the High Church party, who were to no small degree still children of the Reformation, even though they had been delivered from the fixation on eucharistic presence. That fixation to this day somewhat binds the thought of Lutherans and Calvinists, whose thought must describe epicycles around all otherwise-foundational patristic evidence to enjoy rich liturgy without the concept of sacrifice. The first of the problems that the Antiochene prayers solved was transubstantiation; the second was sacrifice. For those who followed the East, locating a consecratory invocation of the Holy Spirit after the institution narrative, memorial, and oblation, made it clear that the priest did not exercise a power to change the elements by saying

---

8. This translation is slightly altered from W. Jardine Grisbrooke, *The Liturgical Portions of the Apostolic Constitutions: A Text for Students,* Grove Liturgical Study 61 (Bramcote, U.K.: Grove Books, 1990). The verb "to make" in the epiclesis can be made to bear the sense of "manifest" or "show," but Grisbrooke demonstrates that the Constitutions always use the word in the sense given: to make.

the words of institution. Because the bread and cup were not seen to be fully consecrated until the invocation, that is, after the words of institution had been spoken and the elements offered to God, there was for them no question of offering anew Christ's actual body and blood. For them there was only one sacrifice, perpetually represented and pled before God the Father.

Put another way, in this view consecration was perfected after the church offered its memorial sacrifice of praise and thanksgiving with the "symbols" that were the bread and cup, reciting the institution narrative as its warrant. Consecration was the result of sacrifice, not the means for obtaining a victim.[9] Thus the Spirit was besought to work in the Eucharist just as in baptism, confirmation, and ordination. With this understanding, the seventeenth- and eighteenth-century advocates of what have become known as West Syrian eucharistic prayers could make the oblation of the gifts as explicit as they liked; they could make the epiclesis of the Spirit as consecratory and realistic as they liked because it followed the oblation.[10] Both offering and presence could be spoken of unblushingly because they occurred in what the early aficionados of Eastern texts came to call "the natural order." This natural order included putting the supplicatory sections (the prayer for the whole state) after the invocation.

Among the varied attempts at liturgical reform along the lines just described there emerged two distinct styles within the High tradition. One camp took into its rite as much of the actual Eastern texts as possible: the best example is the English Nonjuror rite of 1718. Others took chunks of traditional prayer book text, notably from 1549, and rearranged them in "natural order," with a few emendations and supplements. Of this variety the most carefully crafted before Seabury is the Scottish eucharistic prayer of 1764.[11]

The theological tradition that accompanied these rites, the tradition that Seabury and Smith the younger brought to America, was most memorably

---

9. I owe this wonderful aphorism to Dr. Thomas Julian Talley.

10. It is interesting to note that the prayers in the post-1928 rites of the Episcopal Church that vary from the West Syrian pattern become cautious about both invocation and oblation when they come in the Roman order, their language trapped by the implications of their structure. In Prayer C and its parallels in the Order for Celebrating the Holy Eucharist ("Rite 3") and some of the supplemental liturgical materials authorized by General Convention in the 1990s, a consecratory epiclesis before the memorial and oblation vitiates all three units, apparently to prevent the assembly's finding itself offering Christ's body and blood anew.

11. The 1718 text is available on the World Wide Web in a number of places, most conveniently at www.justus.anglican.org/resources/bcp/, and also in Grisbrooke. The 1764 text is reproduced in Grisbrooke, 71ff. It may also be seen in comparison with other rites in Appendix A-4.

articulated by John Johnson of Cranbrook in Kent. Johnson was never a Nonjuror and held a comfortable living.[12] Despite his views, he also managed to use the 1662 prayer book, although with what private prayers at the altar no one knows to this day. Johnson marks the high-water mark in the shift away from studying ancient texts as liturgical "resources" to contemplation of the theology implicit in their textual content and in the sequence of action within their structure.

In *The Unbloody Sacrifice* (1714–18),[13] Johnson appears, like his contemporary J. S. Bach, as both the recapitulation and ultimate expression of a tradition, although his prose has not the genius of Bach's music. This failing is perhaps understandable if Archdeacon Hutton was correct in his observation:

> Admirably straightforward though much of the writing of English divines in the early eighteenth century was, it had fewer of the elements of permanence than any of the systems that had preceded it; to appropriate words of [Dr. Samuel] Johnson, it had not sufficient vitality to preserve it from putrefaction.[14]

The second edition is enlarged in the light of criticism, and just as it was going to press none other than Samuel Clarke preached against Johnson's eucharistic interpretation of John 6. To this Johnson addresses himself as well; following sixty pages of preface, it is daunting reading.

When he reverts to the book's original plan, Johnson makes three chief points that would influence Nonjuror liturgy and theology. The first is that each celebration of the Eucharist occasions a real *and effective* pleading of Christ's offering before God the Father. The second is that there is an objective presence of Christ in the elements that is virtually that of his body and blood "in power and effect." The third is that consecration is the result

---

12. At the same time it must be noted that High Churchmen were routinely excluded from major appointments. Cornwall, *Visible and Apostolic*, 106.

13. The full title is both daunting and instructive: *The Unbloody Sacrifice, and Altar, Unvailed and Supported, in which the nature of the Eucharist is explained according to the sentiments of the Christian Church in the four first centuries; proving, That the Eucharist is a proper material Sacrifice, That it is both eucharistic, and propitiatory, That it is to be offered by proper officers, That the Oblation is to be made on a proper Altar, That it is properly consumed by manducation: To which is added, A Proof, that what our Saviour speaks concerning eating His Flesh, and drinking His Blood, in the vith Chapter of St. John's Gospel, is principally meant of the Eucharist, With a Prefatory Epistle to the Lord Bishop of Norwich; Animadversions on the Reverend Dr. Wise's Book, which he calls The Christian Eucharist rightly stated: And some reflections on a stitched book, entitled, An Answer to the exceptions made against the Lord Bishop of Oxford's Charge.*

14. *Cambridge History of English and American Literature* (New York: G. P. Putnam, 1918–1921), vol. 10, 15, Divines, §9.

of the narrative-memorial-oblation-invocation pattern we have discussed above, and that the Holy Spirit acts in this pattern to effect consecration. Adding a Maryland-style weak epiclesis to 1662's bifurcated remnant of a eucharistic prayer would not meet these euchological requirements, of course.

Johnson's interpretation of a proper sacrifice is that it offers something to God as an act of worship or in order to receive a blessing (especially forgiveness of sin); it is to be offered upon a "proper altar" by a "proper Officer" using a correct rite, and it is to be consumed or disposed of in the way prescribed by God.[15] In his view the Eucharist is both an act of thanksgiving and a propitiatory sacrifice in that "none but the rankest Antinomians will say that Sins are forgiven, before they are committed."[16] The Eucharist is the sacrifice we are to perform to comply with the "conditions" laid down in the New Covenant.

To tighten the band of sacrifice around the Last Supper, Johnson introduces what would perhaps become the most difficult point in Nonjuror theology: He believed that Christ began "the one only Oblation of his Body and Blood" at the Last Supper, "which he finished on the cross."[17] His logic is not uncompelling. He reads "the great high priestly prayer" in John 17 as just that, Christ's declaration of the "intention" for which he was offering himself. In John this prayer is offered immediately before the small band goes across the brook to the garden of betrayal. Johnson understands John 17 to be telling us the theological meaning of what is described in the synoptic gospels when they recount the institution narrative. Johnson observes that in the Old Covenant, the victim was identified and dedicated before it was slain, and understands that to be the burden of both the great prayer and the institution narrative. Several times Johnson refers to Jesus executing his "Melchisedechian Priesthood" in consecrating himself "for their sake" at the Last Supper. The sacrifice was "not finished 'till our Saviour expired on the Cross, nay till he entered into the Holy of Holies, even Heav'n itself."[18]

Rejecting the views of Rome, Luther, and Calvin, Johnson explains consecration as providing, in words that would be repeated many times, "the true spiritual Body and Blood of Christ, tho' not in the substance, yet

---

15. Johnson, 1:4f.
16. Ibid., 1:394.
17. Ibid.
18. Ibid., 1:87f.

in power and effect."[19] This presence is objective, however, and the unworthy communicant receives the sacramental body, but not its benefit. Consecration is, again, the result of the pattern of thanksgiving through the institution narrative, the "oblation of the Symbols," and the invocation of the Holy Spirit: "All these three did, in the Ancient Liturgies, immediately follow each other, in the order that I have mentioned them; and each of them was believed to contribute toward the Consecration." He adds that "The Church of *Rome* attributes the Consecration wholly to the Words of Institution; the *Greek* Church, wholly to the Prayer of Invocation; but I conceive the Ancients did not attribute the Consecration to any one of these Actions, in such a manner as to exclude the other."[20]

Johnson considered certain liturgical usages appropriate but not necessary, the mixed chalice among them. His reading of ancient euchology led him to believe that six elements were necessary in a valid and efficacious Eucharist. (1) Bread and wine were to be placed on the altar, and praise and thanks to be given for God's glory, for creation, and for redemption.[21] (2) The institution narrative is rehearsed as "commission" or warrant. (3) The bread is to be broken and the wine poured out (it is not clear when he thinks this should occur). (4) The priest is to offer the gifts after the institution narrative "in Commemoration of Christ's Death, Resurrection and Ascension." (5) The Holy Spirit is to be invoked. (6) Following Christ's example in the high priestly prayer, supplication is to be made for all of the church. Although Johnson does not explicitly say so here, he should be taken to include the departed when mentioning the entire church.

Those who took Johnson's account seriously insisted on certain additions to the prayer book rite: the usage of the mixed chalice, the oblation of the gifts, the invocation of the Holy Spirit, and prayers for the dead. They became known as the Usagers. Those content to use the English or Scottish tradition as it stood in 1549 or 1637 or even 1662 were the non-Usagers, who would not agree to the alteration of the texts they used. In the style of the times, pamphlet warfare began, and Smith counts over forty pamphlets on the topic of the Usages between 1717 and 1725. While it could be claimed (with a small stretch in the matter of oblation) that the Usages were all present in 1549, in that liturgy they were not in the order in which the Usagers believed they should occur.

---

19. Ibid., 1:146.
20. Ibid., 1:239ff.
21. Johnson here also demonstrates his knowledge of Jewish table prayers.

The Usages were laid down in the Injunction of 1717, which was a stopgap "until a fuller Form can be Fram'd." The injunction replaced the Decalogue with the Summary of the Law, mixed water into the wine "openly," omitted "militant" from the prayer for the whole state, required prayer for the departed, and inserted an oblation and epiclesis after the institution narrative.[22]

The fuller form was framed in the next year, when Usagers produced the liturgy of 1718, officially approved by eight English and six Scottish representatives. This rite seems to have influenced Seabury in a few places, although he followed the 1764 tradition in the main. What made and makes the 1718 rite compelling is its attempt to bring texts from the Apostolic Constitutions directly into a liturgy largely comprising Cranmerian modules.

The rite was published together with those for Confirmation and Visitation of the Sick.[23] It prefaces the usual 1662 disciplinary rubrics with a grim reminder of schismatic times, a warning that "every priest shall take particular care not to admit any to the Holy Sacrament of the Eucharist, but those whom he knows to be in the Communion of the [Nonjuror] Church." There is a rubric which follows Johnson in calling for an "Altar" set up in the east end of the church, which altar priest and people are to face when so directed.

The Eucharist begins as in 1549, with an introit; the entrance rite continues with Kyrie, Our Father, Collect for Purity, Summary of the Law, Collect for the (unnamed) King, and Collect of the Day.

The liturgy of the word is fairly unremarkable. The epistle is read, and the gospel follows without intervenient chant. The Gloria Tibi is said as usual, but the Laus Tibi is replaced with "Thanks be to thee, O Lord." The Nicene Creed is followed by the announcements, with all the restrictions on what may be announced, and the sermon.

The exhortations (omitted on weekdays) are followed by the offertory. The offertory verses are from both 1549 and 1637, making for a very full set. The offertory rubric provides for a privacy veil, so that no one will see what anyone else contributes. The offerings of money are spoken of as oblations, not alms, a point that has eluded a number of commentators, to their perplexity. The rubrics provide for a mixed chalice. A prayer concludes the offertory:

---

22. The text may be seen in Grisbrooke, 94ff.

23. *A Communion Office, Taken Partly from Primitive Liturgies, and partly from the First English Reformed Common-Prayer-Book: together with Offices for Confirmation and the Visitation of the Sick* (London, 1718).

O Almighty God, who has created us, and placed us in this ministry by the power of thy Holy Spirit; may it please thee, O Lord, as we are ministers of the New Testament, and dispensers of thy holy mysteries, to receive us who are approaching thy Holy Altar, according to the multitude of thy mercies, that we may be worthy to offer unto thee this reasonably and unbloody Sacrifice for our Sins and the Sins of the People. Receive it, O God, as a sweet smelling savour, and send down the grace of thy Holy Spirit upon us. And as thou didst accept this worship and service from thy Holy Apostles: so of thy goodness, O Lord, vouchsafe to receive these Offerings from the hands of us sinners, that being made worthy to minister at thy Holy Altar without blame, we may have the reward of good and faithful servants at that great and terrible day of account and just retribution; through our Lord....

The "we" in the prayer refers unmistakably to the president of the assembly ("dispensers of thy holy mysteries"), as is often the case with the "we" in the Roman Canon. It will be important to recall this point when we examine Seabury's work.

The eucharistic prayer begins with the dialog (including the salutation and response), preface, and Sanctus; the Sanctus is complete with Benedictus, but following Cranmer's form, which in turn followed Hermann's *Einfaltiges Bedencken*, translates the second Hosanna in excelsis as "Glory be to thee, O Lord most high."

The eucharistic prayer's post-Sanctus thanksgiving for creation and redemption is an extremely compressed reminder of Apostolic Constitutions VIII, through the institution narrative. Then follows the anamnesis/oblation and epiclesis as given above.

Where the anaphora in the Apostolic Constitutions VIII goes on to pray for all those "for whom we offer," the 1718 rite slips into the prayer for the whole state — with no bidding or identifying rubric, a third fact to remember when looking at 1764 and Seabury. The fourth point to note is that the "Oblations" of money are here offered to God, there being nothing identified as alms.

This set of supplications for the whole state is in the 1549 form, and thus satisfies the requirement of the fourth Usage, prayer for the dead. The Lord's Prayer, Peace, and Pascha Nostrum follow. Then, as in 1549, the Invitation, Confession, Absolution, and Comfortable words from Cranmer's *Order of the Communion* follow. The distribution formula is the 1549 form, "the Body...unto everlasting life," with no "take this in remembrance...." The liturgy ends as does 1637, not 1549, with the Gloria in Excelsis sung as a postcommunion hymn rather than as part of the entrance rite.

Concluding rubrics direct that the celebration of the Eucharist take place on every Sunday and holy day, and provide for reservation of the sacrament for those who are kept from attending, especially the sick. The priest is also directed to urge the people to frequent communion, reminding them that their offering, no matter how small, is acceptable to God "if it be given according to their abilities with a cheerful and devout heart."

The adoption of this liturgy by the Usagers created a schism in the ranks of Nonjurors. Among the writings that were fired back and forth there most notably came Thomas Brett's great work, *A Collection of the Principal Liturgies Used by the Christian Church* (1720) to which he added *A Dissertation Upon Them* of 426 pages. Although it was presented as a general summation of the themes present in ancient texts, Brett's work was primarily focused on the Usages controversy, and was in particular a response to criticism of the rite of 1718, and he frequently acknowledges his debt to Johnson. Brett's field of study is nothing less than the Eucharist from Justin Martyr through 1549 and 1718, and the book drew the interest of readers not concerned with the Usages. It is for the modern reader to judge how much, in style and content, Brett was to influence Gregory Dix's reawakening of rank-and-file Anglican interest in structure as theological key to the study of the Eucharist. At the very least, from the work of Herbert Thorndike (1598–1672) on ancient texts and Hamon L'Estrange (1605–1660) on the prayer book tradition, seventeenth- and eighteenth-century scholars were on notice that liturgical "shape" conveys at least as much as text, and that liturgical shape and liturgical theology were intimately and essentially interconnected.[24]

Brett handsomely illustrates the contention that the key to the Usages problem lies in hermeneutics more than historical liturgiology.[25] Brett asserts against the non-Usagers that tradition is to be consulted in all matters, and that it is the authoritative guide to interpretation of the scriptures and

24. I have discussed Thorndike more fully and L'Estrange extensively in *The Voice of a Stranger* (New York: Church Publishing Incorporated, 1993), chap. 6. Usually dutiful Dugmore nods when Thorndike appears in his work. Dugmore focuses so closely on eucharistic presence in Thorndike's work that he does not give adequate appreciation of Thorndike's understanding of eucharistic action.

25. The hermeneutical crunch in the Usages controversy is pithily dealt with in a monograph by James Smith, *The Eucharistic Doctrine of the Later Nonjurors,* Joint Liturgical Studies 46 (Cambridge: Grove Books, 2000).

source of apostolic information from which it is not safe to deviate.[26] He agrees with Johnson that there was a *disciplina arcani,* a secret teaching that was not present in the scriptures, was only gradually recorded, and the contents of which may be inferred from the early liturgical texts.

Regarding the Usages, Brett supplies every instance he can find of testimony to the mixed cup. As to the oblation, the invocation, and the prayers for the faithful departed, the ancient texts provide him with an abundance of material.

As to the Usages concerning oblation and invocation, Brett is clear on where they occur in the "natural order" of euchology. Brett insisted that unlike what he considered the corruptions of the Roman Canon, a eucharistic prayer should always include praise and thanks for the creation and redemption, and he scores 1549 and 1637 heavily on this point.[27] When discussing the movement of the prayer, Brett's understanding of the institution narrative would give those influenced by the continental reforms serious pause, as the narrative is not understood as consecratory, and perhaps not strictly necessary. Here Brett's conclusion almost directly presages what is taken for granted by most modern scholarship: The institution narrative appears in the prayer to provide warrant for and bridge to the thanksgiving's climax in memorial and oblation. "Thus the Thanksgiving form is continued to the End of the Oblation, which plainly renders the whole an Eucharistical Sacrifice, or a sacrifice of Praise and Thanksgiving."[28] He sees the Roman Canon and the prayer book of 1549 as equally mistaken, as in those texts the institution narrative occurs in a post-Sanctus that is supplicatory, not eucharistic.[29] Again taking on most of the Reformation churches, which saw the narrative as evangelical proclamation, he asserts that "consecration consists in the Oblation or Dedication of something to God, and therefore must be performed by some Address made to him, and not by Words directed and applied to men."[30] Thus, following Johnson, he says that consecration requires [the thanksgiving through] the narrative, "oblation of the symbols," and the invocation of the Holy Spirit.[31]

---

26. BrettDis, vff.

27. Ibid., 59f.

28. Ibid., 18, and quoting 64. Brett is quite willing to say that Romans, Lutherans, and Calvinists all have it wrong, a sentiment that Seabury echoes.

29. Ibid., 67, 558.

30. Ibid., 70.

31. Ibid., 74.

Like most of the Nonjurors, Brett dislikes "supplemental consecration" in general, and certainly would not permit it by mere recitation of the institution narrative. In fact, the 1718 rite contains provision for reservation but not for supplemental consecration. This reflects Brett's belief that even Christ effected consecration "by blessing and prayer," and so must we.[32]

Seabury's later criticism that the 1662 rite "hardly amounted to a consecration" is mild compared to Brett's judgment. Brett assumes a willful disobedience: "The Church of England has *willingly and designedly omitted to make the Oblation of the Sacramental Body and Blood of Christ which he himself made and commanded us to make,* and therefore according to what Mr. Johnson says, she is *without Excuse* as to this Matter."[33] As to the absence of invocation of the Spirit, in a prayer "without such a Petition, the Consecration is lame and defective, and not performed according to our Saviour's institution."[34] Note that Brett says "lame and defective," not invalid or inefficacious.

How John Johnson made peace with the 1662 liturgy is not known, but Brett gives important evidence of liturgical practice, and perhaps even Johnson's, when he notes that many English clergy quietly supplemented the 1662 Holy Communion service with remedial private prayers. He can cite at least one bishop among them, Overall of Norwich, and we have already seen that Wilson also did this. A third bishop appears on the screen when Brett quotes approvingly a one-line supplementary prayer drawn from the work of Jeremy Taylor: "We humbly present to Thee, O Lord, this present Sacrifice of Remembrance and Thanksgiving."[35] His own practice in the time before he "left the publick communion" included leaving out of the prayer for "The Whole State of Christ's Church" the expression "Militant here in Earth," which he thought by virtue of that omission then included the departed. It was also his practice to insert the oblation and epiclesis of Apostolic Constitutions VIII. When Brett joined the Nonjurors, Bishop Hickes permitted him to continue these practices.[36]

Brett concludes his work with a summary of his findings that the Usages were in invariable employ in the primitive church, and the hope that his arguments would silence the criticisms of Romans and protestants alike.

---

32. Ibid., 76, 84.
33. Ibid., 120; emphasis in original.
34. Ibid., 134.
35. Ibid., 120f.
36. Ibid., 359.

The schism of which Brett's work was an important part was not overcome until 1732, when an agreement was signed leaving behind the liturgy
of 1718, but authoritatively and officially interpreting the received prayer
books to intend what the Usagers believed, with the specific addition of
permission to add water to the wine, but privately. The apparent victory
was a defeat for the Usagers, and Brett can only have signed the agreement for unity's sake. It was Overton's view that regarding the English
Nonjurors, their great emphasis on the details of liturgy led to their "de-
cay and downfall; for a small community at variance with the spirit of the
age cannot afford to have disputes among its own members."[37]

Denying one's principles seldom adds stability to a situation. A generation ago Grisbrooke wrote of the Nonjuror liturgical compromise that "It
need cause little surprise that unity was not to be bought by the sacrifice of
intellectual integrity," and adds cryptically (it was 1958), "although there
are many to-day who do not appear to have learnt the lesson of the past in
this respect."[38] The result of the 1732 attempt at union without unity was
further division among the Nonjurors. Thus Usager Bishop Thomas Deacon issued yet another liturgy in 1734. Its rite was that of 1718, except that
the enormously lengthy anaphora of Apostolic Constitutions Book VIII is
reproduced completely.[39]

Bishop Thomas Rattray moves this tale directly to Scotland, where he
was bishop of Brechin and ultimately Primus (1739–1743). In 1722 only
two Scottish bishops had favored the Usages (Campbell and Gadderar),
but that was changing, and Rattray's work helped. Beginning in the 1720s,
Bishop Gadderar brought the concerns of the Usagers to the popular level,
where they appear to have been well enough received that by 1745 the Usages were firmly in place in Scotland.[40] Rattray's scholarship led him to
believe, rightly, that the liturgy presented in the Apostolic Constitutions
was late and full of accretions. The leaner form of the 1718 eucharistic prayer appealed to him accordingly, and he used it regularly. Rattray,
whom seminarians tend to remember because he was accustomed to wear
scarlet gloves in the liturgy, published a revision of the liturgy of St. James,
which provided texts only for the liturgy of the meal. It was never given

---

37. Overton, 280.
38. Grisbrooke, 115.
39. Deacon also included a rite for the ordination of deaconesses, very much like that for
the ordination of deacons. Deacon, whom Campbell consecrated *solus*, produced a number of
liturgical books, a commentary, and a catechism, and receives detailed treatment in Grisbrooke,
115–35.
40. Lathbury, 472.

much use, being almost entirely foreign to clergy and people alike, but it does testify to how ancient texts were being studied and appropriated, sometimes without cultural translation.

Both the Usagers and non-Usagers in England appealed to the Scottish bishops for support. In Scotland the bishops determined in 1731 to authorize the 1637 rite with its epiclesis of the Spirit and its memorial made "with these thy holy gifts." They provided for the addition of a *privately* mixed chalice, although no other textual additions were to be made. They had good reason to suspect textual changes made by committee: The 1616 Scottish assembly appointed a committee to revise liturgy, and their clumsy prayer was "Send down O Lord thy blessing upon this Sacrament, that it may be unto us the effectual exhibitive instrument of the Lord Jesus." In any event, three of the Usages were now explicitly sanctioned in Scotland, and the departed were at least mentioned in the prayer for the whole state, even though that prayer stood outside of the eucharistic action in the 1637 rite.

The meal liturgy of the 1637 prayer book had been reprinted in 1722 and 1724, the first of the "wee bookies" that every discussion of the topic must mention by that name to prove the writer's bona fides. Grisbrooke observes that in Scottish practice, parts of the 1637 rite were freely moved about and sometimes altered, making the oblation more pronounced.[41] The wee bookie of 1735 printed the parts of the service in the order in which they were being used, that is, "the natural order" of the Eastern rites. The words "militant here in earth" were removed from the prayer for the whole state, satisfying the Usager need to include the dead. The most striking thing about the 1735 booklet is the insertion of the words "which we now offer unto thee" into the memorial at the mention of "these thy holy gifts." This book was printed as a commercial venture by two printers; they would hardly have emended a central text in such a marked way had this version not reflected actual use. More bookies appeared in 1752, 1759, and 1764. In 1764 came the rite by Falconar and Forbes which was handed to Samuel Seabury.

The Communion Offices of 1764 and 1786

The 1764 rite may be examined in comparison with others in Appendix A-4. It is chiefly the work of Bishop Forbes. Buxton has cataloged the

---

41. Grisbrooke, 153.

sources of 1764 as 1549, 1552, 1637, 1718, and ancient Eastern texts.[42] The first thing to strike the eye is that, as in 1637, the word "priest" is replaced with "presbyter" in 1764. The rite preserved the customary prayer book language through the Sanctus (with no Benedictus). The post-Sanctus is that of 1637, with the epiclesis of the Spirit strengthened and moved so as to follow the anamnesis/oblation. The oblation contains the additional words "which we now offer unto thee" and also shows them in block capital letters. Whether this capitalization is an error or not, it is matched for bluntness by the result sought in the epiclesis, which asks that the elements "become the body and blood," an expression perhaps more realistic than the "virtualist" theology of John Johnson required. It was objected that this epiclesis and that of 1718 lean toward transubstantiation (the elder Smith would agree) because the elements are not prayed to become "unto us" the body and blood of Christ. This conclusion is by no means inescapable. It could be argued in turn that "unto us" occurs in 1549, but it also does in the *Quam oblationem* section of the Roman Canon![43] The real defense of these words came from the observation that no ancient Eastern text felt the need to add "unto us" or other blurring language.

A number of writers, including sympathizers such as Buxton and Dean Hart, have considered the inclusion of "oblations" in the intercession a problem, thinking that they had already been offered in the anaphora. They are, however, reading those words in an evolved and anachronistic sense where "alms and oblations" are two different things, and the oblations of bread and wine could not be offered again in a post-epiclesis supplication. Such a sensibility is not that of the framers of Nonjuror liturgies. In 1718, the people's "oblations" are gifts of money — not unimportant in a disestablished church. This is also the case in 1764. Seabury completes the progress when he refers to all gifts of the people in his rubric as the "devotions of the people," a 1662 expression that can cover almsgiving as well the tithe and other gifts given in token of the sacrifice of one's life. For 1718, 1764, and Seabury, "alms and oblations" refer to one thing: gifts of money. These words are only "a piece of unintelligent copying"[44] if one ignores the historical and liturgical context.

---

42. Buxton, 188.

43. It can also be said that the prayers of the Roman Canon do not require a Lateran or Tridentine view of the sacrament. It is a sobering thought that it took the reforms of the Second Vatican Council to give Roman Catholics a prayer that said clearly "we offer you his Body and Blood." See the Roman Missal, Eucharistic Prayer IV, where we also see the Alexandrian text of Basil distorted by the insertion of a consecratory epiclesis before the institution narrative.

44. Buxton, 190.

After the doxology and its Amen there comes the supplication for the whole state. The invitation, "let us pray for the whole state of Christ's church," is printed in italics and with the paragraph sign [¶] that marks rubrics in American prayer books through that of 1928. Although later generations would "correct" this error, it is probable that reducing the invitation to a "rubric" was quite intentional, both here and in Seabury's edition. If we assume that the Scots were as intelligent as we, and went over their rite with Seabury to the point that he could reproduce it, is there an explanation possible other than repeated error? The earlier Nonjuror liturgy suggests one. In the 1718 rite there is no invitation at all before the supplications, and they flow smoothly out of the epiclesis and doxology. By printing the invitation as a rubric, the familiar words are visible, but because they are now a rubric, they do not interrupt the flow of prayer. This knits the supplication closer to the heart of the eucharistic action and recalls more directly the "for whom we offer" petitions of Apostolic Constitutions VIII. We are left then with the possibility that succeeding generations with less appreciation for the liturgical sensibilities of the framers of the rite would not intuit what was done and incorrectly decide that the elders were mistaken.

The Lord's Prayer follows the supplication, and then follows the penitential section from Cranmer's *Order for the Communion* including the Prayer of Humble Access. That prayer now reads, "to come to this thy holy table," but no source has been identified for the insertion of "holy." It may reflect Johnson's belief that sacrifice must take place upon "a proper altar."

The distribution formula remains the short 1549 version. The post-communion thanksgiving prayer is introduced at length, however:

> Having now received the precious body and blood of Christ, let us give thanks to our Lord God, who hath graciously vouchsafed to admit us to the participation of his holy mysteries; and let us beg of him grace to perform our vows, and to persevere in our good resolutions; and that being made holy, we may obtain everlasting life, through the merits of the all-sufficient sacrifice of our Lord and Saviour Jesus Christ. Almighty and everliving God. . . .

The collect that follows is enriched by a single word, "now." The prayer reads "We now most humbly beseech thee," but it is difficult to explain why, unless the added adverb serves to connect the latter third of the prayer to what has preceded it, or else was added for the sake of euphony. Both this addition to the prayer and the new introduction were to be retained in Connecticut.

In June 1786 Seabury published *The Communion-Office, or order for the administration of the Holy Eucharist or Supper of the Lord. With private devotions. Recommended to the Episcopal Congregations in Connecticut, by the Right Reverend Bishop Seabury*. Even the use of the word "recommended" in the title shows his understanding of the Concordat's requirement that the Scots liturgy be introduced gently. Despite Dibblee's complaint, there is no "dint of episcopal supremacy" here.

A close reading of the text reveals the level of subtlety Seabury's liturgical thought had reached. Almost without exception, the alterations he makes in the 1764 text are significant of Seabury's grappling with the liturgical issues of his day. We also gather from his edition some evidence that the Middletown trimming of the exhortation to communion of parts that frightened tender consciences was agreeable to Seabury, or came from him.

The Nonjuror emphasis on sacerdotal ministry is reflected in Seabury's replacing "presbyter" with "priest" throughout his rite. Seabury's commitment to the Usages is also expressed in his rubric, not found in the offertory section of the 1764 office, directing the addition of water to the chalice. Significantly, Seabury bases his own direction on the 1549 rubric, not that of 1718, demonstrating that he could make fine distinctions between the two rites when necessary.

Seabury does not follow the 1764 rite in the question of the Last Supper and the Cross. We have seen how it was John Johnson's view that the consecration and oblation of himself as sacrifice was made by Christ at the Last Supper. This stood in direct contradiction, so it seemed to many, of the prayer book passage about Christ on the cross "who made there, by his one oblation of himself once offered," and so on. Some Nonjurors altered this text to read, "by his *own* oblation of himself once offered," as did the Scots in 1764. They thought that this alteration left enough space for the view that the oblation had been previously offered at the Last Supper; they also removed "there" from "he made there," but such deletions really do not refer us back to the Lord's Supper, and from that point of view are useless — not a category for which Seabury had any patience, especially as it meant that members of the assembly were to be subjected to pointless change. In the excisions *one* and *there*, the Nonjurors were giving themselves room, they thought, to hold a doctrine without stating it.[45] The extreme of the High view was stated neatly in Thomas Deacon's 1749 catechism: "Our Lord instituted the Sacrifice of the Eucharist when He began to offer Himself for the sins of all ... immediately after eating. ... He did not offer the Sacrifice upon the cross; it was slain there but was offered at the Institution of the Eucharist."[46] The same Wilson, bishop of Sodor and Mann, who provided the epiclesis found in Seabury's notebook but was not a Nonjuror, also believed that "Christ offered Himself as a sacrifice to God, as a priest, under the symbols of bread and wine in the Last Supper, before he was apprehended." "His own" oblation was not entirely unprecedented, however; it appears in some editions of the 1604 prayer book and in the *Durham Book*.

Again, in the 1786 office, Seabury does not alter the text at this point. Some, including Steiner, have suggested that he perhaps did not yet understand the Nonjurors on this point and later changed his mind. In fact, Steiner says that Seabury does not speak of the Lord's Supper as Christ's self-oblation until 1793.[47] It might be suggested that Seabury was still gently introducing a theology which could be more fully expressed in the liturgical revision that Connecticut would authorize in 1785. Perhaps he did not wish to make a change that did not really change anything. Perhaps this was a copying or editorial error. We do know that Seabury introduced other liturgical ideas, such as confirmation, gently and by degrees, so a progression in his thought without contradiction of previous statements might provide us with an answer to why this one word differed in the 1786 office and its parent of 1764. None of these solutions seems correct, and the answer does seem to come from Seabury's writing of 1793, to which we will come in the next section of this chapter.

Beardsley, Hart, and Echlin all tell us that the Communion Office was well received, and it is Beardsley who had evidence of its use as late as 1835 at St. Peter's Church in Cheshire, where the younger William Smith served for a time, and where the Episcopal Academy made its home. The

---

45. Kenneth Stevenson praises this approach in "Eucharistic Sacrifice — An Insoluble Liturgical Problem?" *Scottish Journal of Theology* 42, no. 4 (1984): 469–92. He urges that by its nature, liturgical language should not be overly precise. Besides the "rich ambiguity" that liturgical language requires he summarizes his advice on the subject of offering: "To be too precise about how the Eucharist is a sacrifice is to court the same kind of theological and ecumenical disasters as the corresponding approach to eucharistic presence." He admires the American books through 1979 along with the Scottish counterparts for finding the way through the difficulties of sacrificial language.

46. Dugmore, 148.

47. Thus Steiner2, 349ff.

rector there, the Rev. Reuben Ives, had been ordained by Seabury and had been his assistant in New London.[48] Bishop Brownell reported that when he came into Connecticut in 1819 he found it in use, and that later he had "considerable difficulty" persuading clergy to abandon it. On the other hand, Dibblee reports that it was rejected, but there is no evidence that anyone joined him in this rejection. In the realm of guesses, perhaps James Sayre, who would cast the lone vote against adopting the 1789 book, also rejected the Communion Office of 1786, but we do not have evidence that he even took notice of it.

Regarding Seabury's following the 1764 rite in casting "let us pray for the whole state of Christ's church" as a rubric so that no announcement would break up the flow of the anaphora, we see the influence of 1718, where no such invitation occurs, just as we observed regarding 1764.

There are smaller changes that also tell us something of Seabury. He clips unnecessary words from rubrics. For example, regarding the offertory sentences the Scots do not want them extended unduly, and to give the presbyter permission have optional shortening "by his discretion, according to the length or shortness of the time that the people are offering." Seabury (who has a priest, not a presbyter) simply has, "by his discretion," again leaning toward 1662. Similarly at the conclusion of the offertory the Scots have "bring the said bason with the oblations [note the term] therein, and deliver it upon the Lord's Table." Seabury has "bring and deliver it upon the Lord's table."

As had the Proposed Book, Seabury updates "indifferently" to "impartially" when praying for those who administer justice. Another change Seabury made has been difficult for some to interpret. In examining the tabular presentation of the rites in Appendix A-4, one can see in the section of the Scottish anaphora that prays for fruitful communion that it does so "beseeching thee, that whosoever shall be partakers...." Seabury again raises the level of churchmanship in language. We have already noted in the 1718 prayer at the offering and in the Roman tradition as well, Seabury refers to the celebrant as the modest "we," leaving "and all others" for the congregation (*circumadstantes*). Seabury consistently refers to the Eucharist sacrifice as being offered "by God's Priest" here on earth, so the sacerdotalism of the expression is consistent with his teaching, and so we read, "that we and all other who shall...." Seabury's conclusion of the thought with

---

48. Eben Edwards Beardsley, *History of the Episcopal Church in Connecticut*, 3rd ed. (New York: Hurd and Houghton, 1868), 1:388; Hart.

"them" is not actually dictated by grammar (a very fluid subject in English at the time), but by style, a sense of the antecedent of "them." This usage perplexed William Jones Seabury and Dean Hart. If we posit that "we" is the celebrant, which is clearly the case for the Nonjuror theology, the use of "us" would be presumptuous and too narrowly focused; "them" agrees with "all others" and has a more general and pastoral focus. If "them" is merely an error, 1789 repeats it, despite the sharp eyes of White and Smith.

Seabury did something in the Communion Office that was and remains unique in official Anglican liturgy. He provides what he calls "private ejaculations," javelin- or arrow-prayers, during the liturgy, and a set of longer "Private Devotions for the Altar," for clergy and laity alike. There is no source known for these prayers other than Seabury's pen.[49] Like the Scots, Seabury uses the Alexandrian form of the Gloria in Excelsis to conclude his rite.

In his second charge to the clergy, September 1786, after the publication of the Communion Office, Seabury observed, "It would be a good rule, in altering anything in our sacred liturgy that might be thought to need it, to go back to early Christianity ... and conform our own as nearly to it as the state of the Church will permit." We have no way to second-guess him in how he followed that path, and whether or not he gauged the pastoral realities (the state of the church) correctly. With that dictum as his guiding principle, the small liturgical concessions he was to make in Philadelphia may make sense to us.

Seabury on the Eucharist

Steiner quotes favorably White's assertion that Seabury got his beliefs about the Eucharist from his consecrators, and believes that he did not fully grow into them until 1793. Inasmuch as White still did not understand Seabury's beliefs twenty years after the making of the prayer book, his evidence is not to be taken seriously. It becomes even more dubious when we recall the teaching in Seabury's sermon of 1754, his tutelage under Samuel Johnson, and the sheer difficulty of internalizing a new tradition and spirituality well enough to edit it so quickly, given everything else that made a claim on his time and attention. Because it is claimed that he did not adopt Nonjuror views until 1793, we must examine sequentially his moments of teaching.

---

49. *Parallels*, 2:494f.

Seabury expressed himself at length on the Eucharist in the sermon already quoted, in a sermon of 1788, in two charges to the clergy, in a pamphlet for the laity, in the publication of a catechism, and in a "discourse" of 1793.

The sermon of 1754 we have seen before, and it will be recalled as terming the Eucharist "the Christian sacrifice" and "a continual Sacrifice." The elements are regarded as "symbols of his Body and Blood," and when we "figure unto God the Father, the Passion of his Son," God will be "gracious and propitious to us." The language of propitiation simply was not used of the sacraments in the protestant circles of the suggested New England consensus.

In the First Charge to the Clergy at Middletown in 1785 Seabury has much ground to cover. Nonetheless the gradualist gets in a bit of Cranbrook theology when he speaks of the Eucharist as the opportunity for those confirmed "to feast with their brethren on the sacrifice of the Holy Eucharist, the memorials of Christ's death."[50] Only the highest of churchmen used the concept of "a feast upon a sacrifice."

The Second Charge, delivered at Derby in 1786, after the publication of the Communion Office and the appearance of the Proposed Book, has more to say. As we saw above, in the best Nonjuror tradition Seabury emphasizes the essential role of tradition, and the present-day obligation to model church belief and behavior on the consensus of apostolic testimony.[51] Drawing a boundary between Anglican and Congregationalist teaching, he notes that the Eucharist should be seen "not as the renewal of the Christian Covenant, but a privilege to which the Christian Covenant...entitles us...the appointed means to keep up that spiritual life that we received in our New-birth."[52]

A master of the nutshell explanation, Seabury shares his understanding that the early Christians "called and esteemed it to be the Christian Sacrifice, commemorative of the great sacrifice of atonement which Christ had made for the sins of the whole world; wherein, under the symbols of bread and this cup, the body and blood of Christ which he offered up" — note the sequence — "and which were broken and shed upon the cross are figured forth." So as early as September 1786 we hear Seabury easily speaking of the Nonjuror scenario of offering at the Last Supper and

---

50. SSA, 14.
51. SSB, 14.
52. SSA, 18.

slaying on the cross several years before it is said that he understood this point. What is figured forth is "presented to God our heavenly Father by his Priest here on earth, the merits of Christ for the remission of sins, are pleaded by him, and we trust, by our great High Priest himself in heaven." After all this the elements "being sanctified by prayer, thanksgiving, the words of institution, and the invocation of the Holy Spirit, are divided among the Communicants as a Feast upon the Sacrifice."[53]

John Johnson taught that the eucharistic elements had the function of the showbread in Israel.[54] In his sermon on Christmas Day 1788 in New London, consideration of the presence of Emmanuel, God with us, leads Seabury to observe that "the bread of God," like the showbread of the Old Covenant, should not be wanting, "For this is the true and real Christian sacrifice, and succeeds in the Christian Church in the room of the daily sacrifice in the Jewish." He then announces his "wish and design" that the Eucharist be henceforth celebrated each Sunday, and if possible, every day in the octaves of Easter and Pentecost.

This sermon was expanded in 1789, and published as *An Earnest Persuasive to Frequent Communion: Addressed to those Professors of the Church of England, in Connecticut, Who Neglect That Holy Ordinance.* His first appeal, rather naturally for him, is to duty: the Eucharist is the one liturgical command we have from Christ (excepting baptism in a general way). The "power of administration" has been left to the Apostles and their successors in the episcopate together with their colleagues in the presbyterate. As in the Second Charge, but even more clearly, in explaining the institution as the beginning of Christ's offering, Seabury does not wait until 1793, but here teaches that the Eucharist is the "memorial or representative of that body which Christ *in the institution* willingly offered up and devoted to God."[55] He goes on to say that "in consequence of his offering, was soon after slain upon the cross for our redemption."

In this document we see Seabury using the language of his Congregationalist neighbors, language that might give the impression of consensus until it is looked at carefully. Seabury will agree that the Eucharist involves "covenanting," but draws a distinction. Anticipating twentieth-century emphasis, Seabury teaches that the primary covenant is that of baptism. "And when it is our unhappiness to break our baptismal covenant . . . how

53. SSB, 18.
54. SSC, 7.
55. Ibid., 5.

gracious God is to permit us, upon our repentance, again to renew it at his Holy table!"[56]

As to what is received in the sacrament, it is the "life-giving body and blood of Christ, i.e., all of the benefits of his passion, death, and resurrection."[57] At the same time, he insists his teaching "is not to be understood as though the elements became upon Consecration, that natural Body and Blood of Christ.... But they become his representative or sacramental Body and Blood."[58] Seabury, like his teacher Samuel Johnson, sees reception of the Eucharist as part of the lifelong process of sanctification: "The Holy Communion is, at least, as great an instrument of holy living as prayer, and the efficacy of both, on our part, rests on the same circumstances — penitence and faith."[59] However, Seabury also ventures the opinion that "Prayers offered up at the altar have more efficacy with God than other prayers have," adding that this is "saying no more than the Catholic Church has always said and taught."[60] This is true for him, in part, because he holds that the Eucharist is "a memorial or representation of [Christ's] sufferings before the Almighty Father, to put him in mind of the meritorious sacrifice of his blessed Son on our behalf."[61] We make this memorial "not that God will forget, unless we refresh his memory, but because in so doing, we use the means that Christ has appointed to convey to us the benefits of that sacrifice which he offered for sin."[62]

We hear John Johnson's list of requisites in Seabury's description of the Eucharist: "when God's priest offers up the elements of bread and wine upon the Holy altar, they are thereby made God's property, and being blessed and sanctified by prayer and thanksgiving, they become through the operation of the Holy Ghost, the body and blood of Christ in power and effect."[63]

Seabury concludes the *Earnest Persuasive* by encouraging frequent celebrations; in fact, he thinks one should occur whenever an epistle and gospel are appointed.

In 1791 Seabury reprinted Scottish Bishop Innes's catechism with a preface of his own. This document is a succinct treasury of High Church

---

56. Ibid., 17.
57. Ibid., 6.
58. Ibid., 17.
59. Ibid., 14.
60. Ibid.
61. Ibid., 16.
62. Ibid.
63. Ibid., 18.

thought on all the areas of church life. The catechetical answers include that Christ began to offer himself "immediately after eating his last Passover." Christ's sacrifice "was slain upon the Cross; but it was offered at the Institution of the Eucharist." There is a description, in question-and-answer form, of a normative eucharistic prayer: "The Priest, first of all, gives God Thanks for all his Benefits and Mercies, especially those of Creation and Redemption." Then "he recites how Jesus Christ instituted this Sacrament.... To shew the Authority by which he acts, and in order to perform Christ's Command." The oblation "in behalf of the whole Church and all the Members of it" is described as well as the work of the Holy Spirit. After describing what the elements are not and are, Seabury gets to the fruits of this "Feast upon this Sacrifice." They are "The Pardon of their past Sins; fresh Supplies of the Holy Spirit, and a Principle of immortality, Life to their Bodies as well as to their souls."[64]

The 1793 publication of *Discourses on Several Subjects* contained a twenty-one-page discourse, "Of the Holy Eucharist." In addition to repeating the sentiments expressed in earlier work about the offering of Christ at the Last Supper, the feast on the sacrifice that had been offered by the proper priest, and so on, Seabury does a bit of battle. He rejects explicitly and by name Roman, Lutheran, and Calvinist teaching about the nature of the sacramental presence of Christ.[65] Seabury's treatment of the Last Supper and Cross does not separate them as sharply as some Nonjurors would have liked: "[Christ] began to fulfill the divine decrees by *offering up* himself for the sins of the whole world" at the Last Supper. He does not treat the cross here as the almost incidental slaying of the victim, but says that the "offering was fully completed and rendered effectual, when he yielded up his life on the cross."[66] And it is precisely this document, one that some believe demonstrated Seabury's late apprehension of what John Johnson was teaching, that ironically shows where he maintained some liturgical and theological independence of it. Seabury's *liturgical* emphasis on the cross is then seen to square with this *theological* understanding. The result is a teaching that balances the Nonjuror thought with the great weight of Western tradition.

---

64. *A Catechism, or the Principles of the Christian Religion Explained in a familiar and easy Manner, adapted to the lowest Capacities by the late Bp. Innes, Brechin Diocese, Aberdeen* (New Haven, Conn., 1791), 48ff.

65. SSE, 163f.

66. Ibid., 172.

– Chapter Eight –

DIFFICULT PEOPLE

Samuel Provoost (1742–1815)

It has been said that "animosities between loyalists and patriots in the Episcopal Church died with remarkable swiftness."[1] That may well be true, but Benjamin Moore could still write of New York ten years after the Declaration of Independence that "A few people in this state, from old grudges on the score of politics, have determined to circumscribe, as far as they possibly can, the authority of Bishop Seabury."[2]

Those "few" would certainly include two figures important in New York history of the period, John Jay and Mayor James Duane, sometime wardens of Trinity Church, along with Samuel Provoost, who was to some extent their creature. In 1776 New York adopted a measure condemning to death anyone who supported the king. In September of that year Jay and Duane were members of the New York Committee for Safety, and voted to send an expedition to arrest Seabury, who was on Long Island assisting General Howe. That they were to serve as deputies to several General Conventions, their patriotism uncontaminated by theology, is partially responsible for the delay in forming a unified Episcopal Church.[3]

---

1. Holmes, 286.

2. Benjamin Moore to Samuel Parker, November 4, 1786, Hawks & Perry, 2:305. Moore continues by saying that south of New York, Seabury's authority is increasingly accepted, and that he does not share Parker's fears that unity is impossible.

3. In 1862 William Stevens Perry printed one hundred copies of "Bishop Seabury and Bishop Provoost," one of which I have managed to obtain only after completing this chapter. Perry adds no documentary evidence to that examined here, but his homiletical conclusion is interesting. "Death soon after translated the first Mitred American to Paradise. His unworthy brother in the Episcopate lived long enough to be a troubler of Israel, by a strange opposition to Hobart's Consecration, and, by a subsequent course of laxity in morals and belief, proved, most incontrovertibly, that political opinions are hardly the best grounds to influence us in the choice of a Bishop for the Church of God!" 20. Perry's "Bishop Seabury and the 'Episcopal Recorder': A Vindication," of 1863, is unknown to most library catalogs. It is reproduced in Cameron's *Samuel Seabury among His Contemporaries* (Hartford, Conn.: Transcendental Books, 1980), 70–94. The *Recorder* went out of its way to discredit Seabury personally and professionally. Perry, as always, answers from documents, providing a mass of evidence of Seabury's good faith and proper behavior. Cameron reproduces other examples, also from the South, of Low

In recounting this tale, it will be possible to explode further the myth that Seabury had "little respect" for the victorious revolutionists.[4] There is no record of Seabury being anything but cordial and conciliatory to those who had, after all, won the war and would write the history. On quite the other hand, it was Samuel Provoost who was Seabury's most relentless and unyielding foe. This may seem unlikely at first, as the two men never met until after ecclesiastical union had been effected, and as it cannot be shown that Seabury ever said or wrote an unkind word about Provoost. Without overly psychologizing Provoost, it seems fair to say with Anne Rowthorn that for him Seabury became the focus of all his anger over his own troubles during the 1770s.[5] Psychology aside, he was also, like a majority of New York and Pennsylvania legislators of the time, convinced that the rights hard-won in the Revolution did not belong to citizens who had been Tories. William Smith would learn this political reality to his cost in Pennsylvania.

Samuel Provoost is unfortunately remembered by most writers for his opposition to Seabury, his attempt to resign his episcopate, and his later attempt to displace Hobart as bishop of New York. Provoost's two principal biographers were John Norton and Morgan Dix. Each contends with the fact that Provoost's ministry was not adorned with accomplishment.[6] Norton's 183 pages are three-quarters a description of the times and the notable events going on around Provoost; at two points he apologizes for writing about him at all. Norton's overall approach to Provoost was that although he did not do much, he did live in interesting times. Dix's parish history simply tells us that the parish records do not provide evidence of a busy rectorate or episcopate.

Provoost's misfortune was not that he did not do great things; few bishops in Christian history are remembered at all. Provoost had the misfortune to live in a time that has remained in the historical spotlight; it was a time that called for prodigies, and he was in his best moments merely adequate for a cleric. (The first bishop of Virginia seems not to have put much energy into *episcope* at all, and devoted himself to work as a college

---

Church partisans attempting to demolish the reputation of the person whose history challenged their own myth of the protestant origins of the American church's worship.

4. Thus Hatchett2, 5.

5. Rowthorn, 69–72.

6. John Norton, *Bishop Provoost* (New York, 1859); Morgan Dix, *The Parish of Trinity Church in the City of New York,* vol. 2 (New York: Putnam, 1901), 1–119. Seven hundred and fifty copies of Dix's seven-volume work were printed. A nineteenth-century encyclopedia refers to a biography, *Samuel Provoost,* by J. G. Wilson, but the Library of Congress, the New York Public Library, and several seminary and university libraries have no record of such a book.

president.) Provoost lived in a time when unity was the main concern, but his sentiments made him an agent of discord.

Provoost was the son of wealthy Huguenots, and was raised in the Dutch Reformed tradition. We have no information as to the circumstances or motivation attending his conversion to the Church of England. It has been suggested that his conversion took place in his days as a student at King's College (Columbia), under the tutelage of Samuel Johnson. This is creditable, as he would not have been Johnson's first convert. While a student at Cambridge, Provoost sought ordination in the Church of England. Norton claims to have seen a letter to Provoost's father explaining his decision.[7] He was ordained deacon in February and priest in March 1766. In June he married Maria Bousfield, daughter of a wealthy banker and the sister of a classmate. The fact that his wife's family and assets were in Ireland and England was to prove a great difficulty during the Revolution.

Provoost came to Trinity in New York, and served until 1769, when he traveled with his wife to visit family and friends in Ireland and tour the continent. Back in New York, he was soon pressured to resign (in 1771), as the vestry had made his salary subject to voluntary subscription. Parishes will put up with bad preaching, and even Provoost's friends considered him a bad preacher, but they do expect their ethos to be honored. Provoost's termination seems to have been based on two factors related to ethos. First, he strongly opposed revivalists, particularly Asbury, who had just been through the city and had quite a following. Second, he used the pulpit to attack the English government at length.[8] It is important to understand that in his political principles he was perfectly sincere and quite well informed. His later attacks on Seabury and the Connecticut church certainly suppurate personal animus, but some attacks also appeal to political or constitutional principles, albeit not religious ones. It may have been the very sincerity of Provoost's political views that kept him from recognizing the nature of his obsession with Seabury. What survives from his pen certainly demonstrates much more of an interest in politics than religion. At the same time, it cannot have been at all easy for Provoost to have been the only priest in New York who actively supported the Revolution.[9] Whether priests were right in endorsing bloodshed is a question

---

7. Norton, *Bishop Provoost,* 30.
8. Chorley2, 4f.
9. See Holmes, 266, for an overview of the Church of England clergy during the war.

that would haunt White in the writings of his later life, but Provoost never expressed any doubts.

Following Provoost's Trinity termination, he retired to a country estate for fourteen years, and despite his claims of relative poverty (he apparently did go into some debt), he turned down opportunities to earn a living as rector, including appointment at King's Chapel in Boston in 1782. His reason for not accepting any appointments is difficult to credit, as he had retired to the country five years before independence was declared:

> In the beginning of the present war, when each province was endeavouring to unite the more effectually to oppose the tyranny of the British court, I remarked with great concern, that all the Church clergy in these northern States, who received salaries from the society, or emoluments from England, were unanimous in opposing the salutary measure of a vast majority of their countrymen; so great a harmony among the people in their particular circumstances pretty clearly convinced me that some, at least, were biased by interested motives. As I entertained political opinions diametrically opposite to those of my brethren, I was apprehensive that a profession of these opinions might be imputed to mercenary views, and an ungenerous desire of rising on their ruin. To obviate any suspicions of this kind, I formed a resolution never to accept of any preferment during the present contest.[10]

This excuse was also given when he was nominated to the Provincial Congress. He repeated it, almost verbatim, in declining a post in Charleston, South Carolina, in 1777, and King's Chapel in 1782. What strikes one when reading the lengthy letters is that nowhere is there any reference to God, let alone the spiritual issues involved in considering a call to serve a parish. Everything is reduced to the political question. Even in a time when many educated people exhibited a marked reluctance to talk about God, Provoost's lack of interest in the subject is remarkable. Whether or not the reason he gave for declining these calls accurately reflected his beliefs, he passed the fourteen years by devoting himself to botany, reading, and translation (he knew at least six languages well). He was to be found sometimes preaching and also on at least two occasions

---

10. In E. Charles Chorley, "Samuel Provoost, First Bishop of New York," *HMPEC* 2, no. 2 (June 1933): 8f.

performing pastoral offices. In a few instances he wrote prayers for revolutionary gatherings, and at least once took up his musket against the British. Fortunately for the little band of ad hoc soldiers, they were spared contact with the enemy.

At the conclusion of the war he regained access to his and his wife's resources, and resumed life in Manhattan. His rustication had earned him something like martyr status among many of those who called themselves "Whig Episcopalians" and who would shortly hijack the rectorship of Trinity Church on Provoost's behalf.

That Provoost was not an effective priest in either tenure at Trinity is not as interesting here as is the evidence of his theological leanings.[11] His Cambridge tutor held advanced views on theology, and it is known that in university days he was an associate of Lindsey's brother-in-law, and was given a copy of Lindsey's liturgy when he returned to England for consecration.[12] His theological leanings are further indicated by the call to King's Chapel, and confirmed by a 1786 letter to William White. There Provoost insists that "The doctrine of the Trinity has been a bone of contention since the first ages of Christianity, and will be to the end of the world. It is an abstruse point, upon which great charity is due to different opinions, and the only way of securing *ourselves* from error, is to adhere to Scripture expressions, without turning into definitions."[13] Again, limiting liturgy to "scriptural" expressions was at this time the cry of Arians, Socinians, and others of like mind. Asking for charity and toleration for the camel's nose in the tent remains the first step in ecclesiastical revolutions of any kind.

Trinity's vestry lawfully elected parish assistant Benjamin Moore as rector as 1783 drew to a close. By this time, however, the Whig Episcopalians had returned in strength sufficient to exert their will effectively. After half-hearted attempts at negotiation in which neither side distinguished itself, the Whigs petitioned the regional council with more than a hundred signatures, although only twelve of the petitioners were actually Trinity communicants. The council was a relic of the war and had

---

11. More detail is given in Sprague 241ff., and Chorley2. Chorley quotes a friend of Provoost, struggling to be kind, who observes, "He read the noble Liturgy of his Church with critical accuracy without impairing the devotional spirit it is so well calculated to excite. As a preacher he was not so happy. Although his enunciation was distinct as well as forcible, yet his sermons were delivered so emphatically — *ore rotundo*, that the exertion this induced, together with his plethoric habit, rendered the public services of the Church tedious and labourious to himself and to his hearers. But it is by no means certain that these circumstances did not tend to the improvement of his Sermons by rendering them shorter."

12. Winter, 147.

13. Samuel Provoost to William White, June 10, 1786, Hawks & Perry, 2:288f.

nearly unlimited power. It appointed the Whig leaders "trustees" for all of the temporalities of the parish, thus giving them control of personnel matters. These trustees, including Jay and Duane, engaged Provoost, and with a letter coolly advised Moore that he was no longer rector. Moore remained an assistant at Trinity until 1800, when he was again elected rector. Chorley reports that "despite bad preaching and frequent invalid status, [Provoost's return] was understood and celebrated as a political event." Chorley quotes a contemporary witness: "It was a glorious occasion, and many friends of their country met that day for the first time in years. There were no rascally Tories present that morning."[14] That much is certainly true, as eighty thousand had fled the country, twelve thousand from the New York area.

Provoost conducted a service for the inauguration of George Washington and was for a time Senate chaplain. Provoost is remembered as being about six feet in height, a little corpulent with a flushed face, and as a most gracious and generous host. After the demise of Bishop Edward Bass of Massachusetts, Provoost alone of American bishops retained use of a powdered wig. "Frequent invalid status" refers at least to his migraines, depression, and in later life the "apoplectic fits" to which he was finally to succumb. He was awarded the D.D. from the University of Pennsylvania (Smith's College of Philadelphia) in 1786. He is remembered as being very generous, disposing of much of his own money in charitable causes. His very large library and all of his papers were last known to be in his daughter's possession, but have been mysteriously lost. Provoost was not ungenerous with the unseated Moore, and asked him to preach at the first ordination he presided over, on July 15, 1787.

Provoost created the first constitutional crisis of the nineteenth-century Protestant Episcopal Church. In England, as readers of Trollope will recall, there was no expectation that Lords Spiritual would retire. It was assumed that they would not relinquish their generous livings until respiration ceased. It was thus not unnatural that the new American church had given no consideration to the issue of retirement. The House of Bishops was accordingly nonplussed when Provoost attempted to resign his episcopate in 1801. He had not recovered from Maria Provoost's death and their son's suicide (Provoost would not permit him Christian burial). The House ultimately refused to accept the resignation, but instead authorized the election of an assistant (we would say coadjutor) bishop in New York,

---

14. Chorley2, 10f.

Benjamin Moore. If Provoost could not retire from office, he retired from sight, making but one public appearance between his resignation in 1801 and his death in 1815.

As long as Provoost was in office the Diocese of New York never recognized Christ Church, Ann Street, because its priest had been ordained by Samuel Seabury. Seabury never had a chance with Provoost: Seabury had been a loyalist, was higher than High Church, had a different social background, and had been connected with the allegedly "Jacobite" bishops in Scotland. All of the major aspects of Seabury's biography were abhorrent to Provoost. Most writers emphasize the political aspect of Provoost's position, and the weight of an anachronistic charge of Jacobitism is perhaps understandable. A country that had just rejected all allegiance to a king crowned and anointed by the Church of England did not need the company of those whose view of monarchy was stronger than that of mere Loyalists.

It is the view of Perry, Steiner, and others that "Had Provoost, Duane and Jay had their way, Connecticut would never have been brought into a general ecclesiastical union."[15] Documents from the bishop's pen support that conclusion. Provoost began his attack in 1785, shortly after Seabury's return. He circulated the wildly inaccurate letter by Granville Sharpe to the point that the Scottish succession of bishops was defective.[16] Sharpe also alleged that the Scottish bishops were all rabid Jacobites, a charge that was simply untrue. (In any case, the entire Nonjuror situation would soon change permanently.) Provoost made the mistake of showing the letter to Henry Purcell, a close friend of publisher James Rivington (he of the "southern bastards" remark wrongly attributed to Seabury), who urged him to speak to Benjamin Moore. Moore pointed out the errors in the letter, and Provoost stopped circulating it openly, but the damage had been already done in many quarters. To this day some Connecticut churches have on display in a library or meeting room a yellowing chart entitled

---

15. Steiner2, 250f.

16. Actually and intriguingly, given the dates, the purity of Scottish line, and the liturgical forms used in the Reformation and post-Reformation era, Scottish succession alone may be at least partially immune to the condemnation of *Apostolicae Curae*. It can be further argued that some Nonjuror lines were excluded from those to be condemned in the bull because they were already recognized as "Catholic" by Rome. When James II arrived in France with Bishop John Gordon of the Scottish Episcopal Church he was then received without reconsecration into the Roman church by the Bishop of Meaux at the request of the pope. As to Granville Sharpe, we have caught him at a bad moment; his more noble accomplishments include his efforts for the abolition of slavery long before it was a majority opinion.

"Apostolic Succession," showing the descent of their bishops through an unbroken and ancient line.

In October 1785, Provoost wrote to White about attempts to loosen the British government's stranglehold on consecration and his desire to see the Proposed Book in print. He adds, "I have been told that another Gentleman has just passed through this City in his way to Connecticut for Ordination with recommendations from some Clergymen in Virginia. If private persons continue these recommendations to Dr. Cebra, the Validity of whose Consecration as a Bishop has neither been acknowledged nor Discussed in Convention — I foresee that the Bands which united us together in Philadelphia will be converted into a Rope of Sand."[17]

John Jay had been a deputy at the 1785 General Convention, and wrote to John Adams that "the convention are not inclined to acknowledge or have any thing to do with Mr. Seabury. His own high church principles, and the high church principles of those who ordained him, do not quadrate either with the political principles of our Episcopalians in general, or with those on which our revolution and constitution are founded."[18] Note that for him, the civil and ecclesiastical governments were to share a philosophy.

Later that month, Provoost writes of his suspicion that the purpose of Seabury's recent visit to New York on the way to an engagement in Long Island had been to scheme against the acquisition of English consecration. Provoost cannot see the courage in Seabury's risking arrest and prosecution in coming to minister in New York.[19] The next month he writes to White:

> If we may judge from appearances, Dr. Cebra and his friends are using every art to prevent the success of our application to the English Prelates. A close correspondence is kept up between him, Chandler, &c., and a few days ago two large packets were seen at Rivington's [in New York] addressed to the Archbishop of Canterbury, one of which it was imagined came from Dr. Chandler. Governor Clinton assures me that Dr. Cebra is in the Bill of Attainder, a circumstance which I did not know when I mentioned him in a late letter. He certainly

---

17. Samuel Provoost to William White, October 25, 1785. Archives of the Episcopal Church, RG 117–1–73.

18. John Jay to John Adams, November 1, 1785, *The Works of John Adams* (Boston, 1850–56), VIII, 355.

19. Samuel Provoost to William White, November 7, 1785. Perry, 283.

would not have run the risk he did by coming to New York, unless some political ends of consequence were to be answered by it.[20]

Ultimately, the United States would ban bills of attainder. Needless to say, there is no evidence of any plot against English consecration, and the likelihood of the Whig government giving much heed to Samuel Seabury or his companions is so slight as to be risible.

Provoost's last salvo of the season came on May 20, and gives us a picture of his political feelings and his reading of the convention.

> But I really think our Line of Conduct is plain before us. As the General Convention did not think proper to acknowledge Dr. Cebra as a Bishop, much less as Bishop of our Church, it would be highly improper for us in our own private Capacities to give any sanction to his Ordinations. It would also be an insult upon the Church and to the truly venerable prelates to whom we are now making Applications for the Succession. For my own part, I carry the matter still further, and as a friend to the liberties of mankind, should be extremely sorry that the conduct of my brethren here should tend to the resurrection of the sect of Nonjurors, (nearly buried in oblivion), whose slavish and absurd tenets were a disgrace to humanity; and God grant that they may never be cherished in America, which, as my native country, I wish may always be sacred to Liberty, both civil and religious.[21]

Readying for the General Convention of June 1786 the church in New York instructed its deputies "not to consent to any acts that may imply the validity of Dr. Seabury's Ordinations." At the convention, Provoost himself moved that "This Convention will resolve to do no act that shall imply the validity of Ordinations made by Dr. Seabury." This was seconded by Robert Smith of South Carolina, a Revolutionary War veteran. Smith had been both chaplain and common soldier, and suffered banishment after the British capture of Charleston. This motion was lost, but its clear implication is that a real bishop's ordinations may be *irregular* for any number of reasons, but, assuming proper form, matter, and subject, if they are all in and of themselves *invalid,* he is no bishop. When that resolution failed, William White offered a resolution, adopted unanimously, that injected the same venom while seeming to diminish the sting:

---

20. Samuel Provoost to William White, December 23, 1785, *SSECR*, 43f.
21. May 20, 1786, Perry, 300.

That it be recommended to this Church, in the States here represented, not to receive to the Pastoral Charge, within their respective
limits, Clergymen professing Canonical subjection to any Bishop, in
any State or country, other than those Bishops who may be duly
settled in the States represented in this Convention.

What the evening conversations produced was a tighter and more
reasonable-sounding resolution to add to the fire, a resolution that Smith
of South Carolina put on the floor first thing in the morning. It was also
adopted unanimously.

That it be recommended to the Conventions of the Churches, represented in this General Convention, not to admit any person as a
Minister within their respective limits, who shall receive ordination
from any Bishop residing in America, during the application now
pending to the English Bishops for Episcopal consecration.[22]

While a plausible *rationale* had been found in the last resolution, the
reason appeared in the earlier attempts, and it had nothing to do with
the application to England. The English archbishops had objected to the
southern prayer book, not to the presence of Seabury as bishop. In fact,
they could not even take note of his existence. As the thirteen states were
not teeming with bishops in 1786, it would be difficult for Seabury not
to conclude that the resolutions were directed at him. The penchant for
taking an action while leaving the reasons undefined was to become a
hallmark of General Convention legislation on difficult points.

Samuel Parker was certainly not deceived, and in September he wrote
to White:

I am very sorry to see with what coolness and Indifference some
of the Gentlemen in your Convention speak of Bishop Seabury. . . . I
am firmly of the opinion that we should never have obtained the
Succession from England, had he or some other not have Obtained
it first from Scotland.

When the Convention discouraged the settling of more Clergymen
in your States under Bishop Seabury's Ordination, if they meant to
limit it, during the pending of your application to England, and were
actuated herein from a principle of not doing any thing that might
possibly give Umbrage to the English Bishops, it may be a prudent

---

22. *Journals,* Thursday, June 22, 1786; Friday June 23, 1786.

Step; but if it was not from this motive, it seems to be a declaring war against him at a very early period and forebodes a settled and perpetual Enmity.[23]

The resolution must have made some members of the convention blush. Those of a religious bent may even have felt a pang of conscience. After all, Seabury ordained a total of seventeen people in 1785–1786, and a good number of them were sent to him by none other than future bishops William White, James Madison, Thomas Claggett, and William Smith (elected but not consecrated) — but the resolution was adopted unanimously by the very men who sent candidates to Seabury. It is well to address another charge against Seabury here. Repeating mere gossip from an anti-Anglican newspaper (*The Courant*) in New England, writers ancient and modern have alleged that Seabury took money for ordinations, twenty guineas being the amount reported. No writer has ever produced even a hint of proof that he did. In the context of what we know of Seabury's giving nature from his diaries and letters, such a suggestion seems to be much less than improbable and suggests insufficient knowledge of the context. An ordination does involve the ordinand's making promises to and sharing in the ministry of *some* bishop. The only "submission" Seabury ever received in its strictest form was that the ordinand would use the received liturgy except for changes by "competent ecclesiastical authority," and that he promised obedience to Seabury temporarily, until "there shall be a Bishop regularly settled in the state where I shall reside."[24]

It is hard to imagine what the clergy in Connecticut thought when the journal of the convention was published. It was, after all, their conservative theology that had sought out Leaming and Seabury. They and their laity had instituted a form of government by clergy alone long before they had a bishop. In numbers of clergy, New England had a quite respectable population, twenty-eight, and most of those were in Connecticut. Were they and their thousands of laypeople really not wanted? Seabury had several opportunities to address the 1786 resolutions as they affected him, but chose to speak of the acts of General Convention only in terms of the issues of church order and doctrine.

In the letter of May 5, 1786, quoted above, Provoost also wrote to White in a way that suggests that Pennsylvania would no longer recognize

---

23. Samuel Parker to William White, September 15, 1786, Perry, 324ff.

24. Steiner2, 254. Seabury also discusses his policy in a letter to John Skinner, December 23, 1785. From a transcript made in Scotland, Archives of the Diocese of Connecticut.

those whom Seabury ordained. There is no corroboration of Provoost's statement, but if it is accurate, the letter suggests that White was something other than a mere facilitator of union:

> Your best friends in this City approve of your conduct in not admitting persons ordained by Dr. Cebra to your pulpit. The Clergy in N. Jersey act with the same precaution. Mr. Sprague and Mr. Rowe were not to be received as members of their Convention.

Samuel Parker expressed enough despair over New England's apparent exclusion that Benjamin Moore could conclude his letter cited above, confident that in time "Truth and Justice will...get the better of Prejudice and Partiality." In 1789 Moore would abandon the wishes of Provoost, his own rector and bishop, to ensure that what he considered to be truth and justice did prevail.

What Provoost promised the English prelates while he and White were in England for consecration is not known from their lips or pens. Charles Inglis wrote to Seabury that both White and Provoost promised that they would meet with Seabury, and that Provoost assured the archbishops that he would give his best efforts to get the New York laws against former Loyalists repealed.[25] Whether Inglis had heard correctly or not, Provoost acted in neither arena.

The two new bishops returned on Easter Day, April 8, 1787. Seabury wrote to each with congratulations, and of *his* desire that the bishops get together as soon as possible to work out unity and uniformity of worship (he suggests 1662 as the basis).[26] He invited them to meet with him in Stamford on the Thursday after Pentecost. Provoost did not acknowledge the letter, let alone reply. White did reply and wrote to Provoost about the letter and his response. Unlike Provoost, White referred to "Bishop" Seabury:

> About a fortnight or three weeks ago, I received a letter from Bishop Seabury, in which he mentions that he had also written to you on the subject of it. He proposes a meeting of us three, before any thing be finally done in our Ecclesiastical system. My answer was to this effect: That I shall cheerfully take a journey for any purpose which shall appear to have a tendency to the uniting of our Church over the

---

25. Charles Inglis to Samuel Seabury, April 3, 1781, ST1, 40f.
26. Samuel Seabury to Samuel Provoost, May 1, 1787, Steiner2, 266. Samuel Seabury to William White, May 1, 1787. Courtesy of the Archives of the Episcopal Church.

continent — an object very near my heart; that, however, I thought such a meeting could have no use, if the intentions of our brethren in Connecticut were previously known to be different from the plan adopted in the other States; that we understood this to be the case in relation to the model we have adopted of an Ecclesiastical representative — the general outlines of which had been too maturely adopted to be receded from — at the same time that we have reason to believe that it is thought essentially wrong in Connecticut. As to the Common-Prayer (in regard to which Dr. Seabury has observed that he wished the old to be retained, except the political prayers), I answered, that although I held a review to be desirable, yet that if the retaining of the old should be found the most likely to keep us together, I should cheerfully vote for it: that, however, I very much doubted of this, and was persuaded that the general sense of our Church throughout the continent was for a review.[27]

Upon examination of the letter he actually did send Seabury, White's reply was even cooler than he recalls it. He never did address the Stamford invitation directly. He added that before any meeting could take place, he preferred that the bishops "understand one another, as to the views of the Churches in which we respectively preside." Seabury is sometimes accused of being absolutist. White's response to his suggestion that the bishops have some conversation about unity is not particularly flexible. It is to be noted that White is very tentative about taking a principled stand of his own, and writes of the emerging shape of the church as though it had been attained without leadership:

We have been informed (but perhaps it is a mistake) that the Bishop and Clergy of Connecticut think our proposed Ecclesiastical Constitution essentially wrong, in the leading parts of it. As the general principles on which it is founded were maturely considered and compared with the Maxims which prevail in the ecclesiastical system of England, as they have received the approbation of all the Conventions southward of you, and of one to the northward; as they were not objected to by the Archbishops and Bishops of the English Church, and as they are generally thought among us essential to the giving of effect to future ecclesiastical measures, I do not expect to find the Churches in many of the States willing to associate on any

---

27. William White to Samuel Provoost, June 7, 1787, in Norton, *Provoost,* 134ff.

plan materially different from this. If our Brethren in Connecticut should be of opinion that the giving of any share of the Legislative power of the Church to others than those of the Episcopal order is inconsistent with Episcopal Government, and that the requiring of the consent of the Laity to ecclesiastical Laws is an invasion of Clerical rights, in this case, I see no prospect of doing good in any other way than contributing all in my power to promote a spirit of love.... [28]

Seabury already knew that White had proposed some of the legislation against him, and had joined in the unanimous resolution that followed. From this letter he had sufficient reason to think that White shared a measure of Provoost's malevolence. Certainly White's letter to Provoost indicates at least a temporary solidarity of opinion with the other fledgling bishop.

In the next month, as news of the situation grew, Jeremiah Leaming wrote to White, begging him to get Provoost to come to the table with White and Seabury, adding that Provoost was far out of touch with his own clergy, some of whose colleague Seabury had once been.[29] The tide would turn, even if it did so at a Seabury-like pace of gentle inevitability. Time would need to pass before White would move from his June letter and become ready to compromise.[30]

A year and a half later, in December 1788, when the tide had well begun to turn, Seabury wrote to Parker that he had "several times proposed and urged a union. It is been received and treated, I think, coldly." He continues by expressing surprise at the letters he is getting that imply that he is the one who is unwilling to discuss union.[31] The month before he had written to Bishop Skinner, requesting the Scots to ordain a coadjutor for Connecticut:

---

28. William White to Samuel Seabury, as quoted in a letter from Seabury to Samuel Parker, May 21, 1787, Perry, 346f. Seabury continues to Parker: "The above, my dear Sir, is the whole of a letter from Bishop White, that relates to the subject. It is in answer to one from me to him, in which I proposed a personal interview with him and Bishop Provoost previously to any decided steps being taken respecting the Liturgy and Government of the Church, and mentioned the old Liturgy as the most likely bond of union."

29. Jeremiah Leaming to William White, July 30, 1787. Courtesy of the Archives of the Episcopal Church.

30. It is a peculiarity of Anglican stereotyping that William White is always spoken of as "gentle," "genial," "conciliatory," and the like.

31. Samuel Seabury to Samuel Parker, December 16, 1788, ibid., 377. Steiner thinks there is some, but not conclusive, evidence that Seabury wrote to White repeating his original points and also about a joint consecration (Steiner2, 272). If such a letter existed, it did not reach White.

I really knew not what to write to you, such has been & is the uncertain state of Eccl matters here. The Bps White & Provoost, especially the latter, seem to value themselves so much on their English Consecration that I fear no great cordiality is to be expected from them. I have proposed a union of all the Churches, at least so far as to admit each others Clergy & Communicants.

Believing that White still held the hard line he took in June 1787, Seabury continued to Skinner:

I fear it will scarcely take place unless we adopt their book & lay delegates. The People here dislike their book, & the Clergy will have nothing to do with laymen in Chch Government...Bp P—t goes so far as to affect to doubt the validity of my consecration....[32]

We will probably never know exactly how many letters Seabury wrote White and Provoost urging talks for union, but by December 1788 White believed that his answer to the June 7, 1787, letter had not been received. We know that it was received, as Seabury quoted it to Parker. This leaves us with two possibilities. The first is that Seabury believes his specific invitation to Stamford was not acted upon, and he would be right. The second, as Steiner thinks, is that a different letter from Seabury to White went astray.

In any event, in a tone entirely unlike that of his previous letter, White alleges surprise that he had not answered a letter from the Bishop of Connecticut on the subject of unity, and writes to Seabury that compromise is possible on all of the areas of concern to New England. States could be permitted to decide the nature of their own deputation. He now says that "there are Things in the proposed Book which some of us were far from approving of at the Time: and to those we were for, I believe there are none we should not be disposed to give up, if they appear to give Offence in any considerable Extent." He assures Seabury that his ordinands receive the same treatment from White as that he accords to those ordained by a proper bishop in the English line, but he is obliged to get a third English bishop before any consecrations may take place in America.[33] He closes by saying that his letter to Seabury being lost, so must one to Mr. Leaming be

---

32. Samuel Seabury to John Skinner, November 7, 1788, STi, 63.
33. William White to Samuel Seabury, December 9, 1788, ibid., 65.

also, and would Seabury please mention to Leaming Bishop White's "punc-
tual Acknowledgement of his Favor," as he apparently was not about to
do it personally.

By this time the Proposed Book had seen its day, with most states
declining to adopt it, but the rest were major concessions to Seabury's
platform and were certainly pronounced departures from White's earlier
views. There were more to come in 1789.

Provoost, however, would not give in. In February 1789 he wrote to
White that an invitation to Convention addressed to Connecticut

> I conceive to be neither necessary nor proper — not necessary, be-
> cause I am informed that they have already appointed two persons
> to attend the next General Convention, without our invitation — nor
> proper, because it is so publicly known that they have adopted a form
> of church government which renders them inadmissible as members
> of the Convention or union.[34]

In the first convention of 1789, with Provoost absent, the convention heard correspondence that led it to adopt, unanimously, "That it is
the opinion of this Convention, that the consecration of the Right Rev.
Dr. Seabury to the episcopal office is valid."[35]

"Unanimously" meant including New York's deputation. To this turn
of events Provoost reacted with something very like rage, and frankly
threatened to take his diocese and go home:

> How far I shall be able in future to act in concert with the General
> Convention of the PEC will depend upon the proceedings at their
> next meeting. The delegates from New York have grossly deviated
> from their instructions, which were worded with their consent, *and
> at my particular request*, in a manner that was intended to prevent
> their accession to any scheme of union, which might be purchased
> at the expense of the general constitution.[36]

Provoost wrote two more letters, both very long — perseverative in
fact — in a last-ditch effort to keep Connecticut out of the new church.[37]

---

34. Samuel Provoost to William White, February 24, 1789, Hawks & Perry, 2:326.
35. *Journals,* 51.
36. Samuel Provoost to William White, August 26, 1789, Perry, 408.
37. See Hawks & Perry, 2:351ff. The perseveration theme is bolstered by Provoost's beginning the last of the three by saying, "When I wrote last, it was with so violent a disorder in my
head, that it is not surprising that I did not express myself so fully as to prevent a possibility
of misconstruction," when the previous letter had been quite clear. Perry, 352.

In none of Provoost's letters on the subject is the question one of seeking the divine will, or acting according to a certain theology. Particularly in these three letters the arguments are about a commitment he believed that all have made to the Fundamental Principles and to the English succession, and does not think it fair to alter the constitution, particularly if that means admitting Connecticut. Provoost had chaired the 1785 committee on the constitution.

Provoost's reference above to naughty behavior on the part of deputies brings up an important issue. The early conventions were almost entirely composed of supporters of the late Revolution. The ultimate victory for Seabury's principles owes some "credit" to the fact that deputations to General Convention were changing.[38] One may also wonder whether the fact that in 1788 the Scottish bishops had ceased to be Nonjurors had effect in America. More importantly, some of the later deputies were Seabury's ordinands. Some had in fact been loyalists. Others were simply more moderate. The base of the convention was growing wider; it was becoming more representative. Of this there is no better example than Provoost's New York. His own parish, Trinity, refused to elect Jay as a deputy to the state convention to ratify the 1789 convention, and did elect Duane, but required him to vote for union with Connecticut. He did not attend. Virginia's deputation was all new in 1789. Pennsylvania had three clergy who attended all conventions, but among the laity, there was complete turnover by 1789. Maryland was all new in 1789, except for Dr. William Smith, and he always went with the tide. Delaware and New Jersey had no deputy attend all conventions. South Carolina by 1789 had only one deputy who had been to the 1786 convention, and none from 1785. Appendix A-5 shows all the deputations. The distribution of deputies becomes more even over the years, but Pennsylvania always had the largest deputation. The New York deputation evolved as shown in the table on the following page.

Harrison had already drawn Provoost's particular ire for his pacific tendencies on the state level.[39] Moore was a Seabury supporter, and Beach was also a friend. Thus Provoost's hold on the General Convention deputation had deteriorated to such an extent that he would absent himself again in September on the grounds of a headache.

---

38. See the chart in Appendix A-5.
39. Samuel Provoost to William White (n.d., but after September 15, 1789), Perry, 410.

Sept. 27–Oct. 7, 1785	June 20–26, 1786	Oct. 10–11, 1786	July 28–Aug. 8, 1789	Sept. 29–Oct. 16 1789
Philadelphia	Philadelphia	Wilmington	Philadelphia	Philadelphia
Rev. Samuel Provoost	Rev. Samuel Provoost	Rev. Dr. Samuel Provoost		
	Rev. Joshua Bloomer			Rev. Joshua Bloomer
			Rev. Abraham Beach, D.D.	Abraham Beach, D.D.
			Rev. Benj. Moore, D.D.	Benjamin Moore, D.D.
The Hon. James Duane		Hon. James Duane		
	The Hon. John Jay			
		John Rutherford, Esq.		
			Mr. Moses Rogers	
				Richard Harrison

The strongest defense, if that is the correct term, and one of the few Seabury ever made against Provoost's attacks is a firm yet not combative letter to William Smith.

> The ground on which Bishop P. disputes the validity of the Scotch Episcopal succession can best be explained by himself: I know not what it is. And the ground on which the Letters of Orders were called for from every Clergyman, in a former Convention at Philadelphia — if I have been rightly informed — in order to make a distinction between English and Scotch ordinations, they can best explain who were concerned in it. As I know not precisely how this matter ended, I shall say no more about it. But while this matter stands as it does, and there is a Resolve on the minutes of the New York Convention strongly reflecting on Bishop Seabury's Episcopal character — while by your own Constitution no representation of Clergymen can be admitted without Lay delegates; and no Church can be taken into your union without adopting your whole plan, I leave to you to

say whether it would be right for me, or for my Clergy, to offer ourselves at a Convention where we could be admitted only in courtesy? Should we feel ourselves at home? or, as being on an equal footing with the other ministers?

The necessity of a union of all the Churches, and the disadvantages of the present disunion, we feel and lament equally with you: and I agree with you, that there may be a strong and efficacious union between Churches where the usages are different. I see not why it may not be so in this case, as soon as you have removed those obstructions which, while they remain, must prevent all possibility of uniting.

My joining with Bishops W. and P. in consecrating a fourth Bishop was some time ago proposed to Bishop W., and by him declined. His noncompliance has had a bad effect here. It has raised a jealousy of attempting an undue superiority over the Church of Connecticut, which, as it at present consists of nineteen Clergymen, in full orders, and more than 20,000 people, they suppose as respectable as the Church in any state in the Union.

As the resumption of convention approached, it appeared that things would go smoothly. Provoost or someone very near to him had one more card to play. Here is Bishop White's account, also illustrative of his fondness for the periodic sentence:

But a danger arose from an unexpected question, on the very eve of the arrival of these gentlemen. The danger was on the score of politics. Some lay members of the convention — two of them we know, and perhaps there were more, having obtained information that Bishop Seabury, who had been chaplain to a British regiment during the war, was now in the receipt of half-pay, entertained scruples in regard to the propriety of admitting him as a member of the convention. One of the gentlemen took the author aside, at a gentleman's house where several of the convention were dining, and stated to him this difficulty. His opinion — it is hoped the right one — was, that an ecclesiastical body needed not to be over righteous, or more so than civil bodies, on such a point — that he knew of no law of the land, which the circumstance relative to a former chaplaincy contradicted — that indeed there was an article in the confederation, then the bond of union of the states, providing that no citizen of theirs should receive any title of nobility from a foreign power; a provision not extending to the receipt of money; which seemed impliedly allowed, indeed, in the guard provided against the other — that Bishop Seabury's half-pay was a compensation for former services, and not for any now expected of him — that it did not prevent his being a citizen, with all the rights attached to the character, in Connecticut — and that should he or any person in the like circumstances be returned a member of Congress from that state, he must necessarily be admitted of their body. The gentleman to whom the reasoning was addressed, seemed satisfied, and either from this or from some other cause, the objection was not brought forward. The author very much apprehended, that the contrary would happen, not because of the prejudices of the gentleman who addressed him on the subject, but because of those of another, who had started the difficulty.[40]

When the union was effected and the small House of Bishops met, it was determined that the senior bishop should preside. Provoost was still unreconciled when the triennial meeting was next held in 1792. Sensing Provoost's discomfort at sitting under his presidency, Seabury suggested a rotating scheme that would put Provoost in the chair. As those who have read Seabury's diaries know, he commonly wrote prayers after recording particular incidents. Here he comes close to that.

> I had no inclination to contend who should be greatest in the Kingdom of heaven, & therefore readily consented to relinquish the Presidency into the hands of Bp. Provoost. I thank God for his grace on this occasion, & beseech him that no self-exaltation or envy of others may ever lead me into debate & contention, but that I may ever be willing to be the least, when the peace of his Church requires it.[41]

No similar sentiments from the other bishops survive.

After Rhode Island had placed itself under Seabury's oversight, Provoost's ill will was expressed in the ordination of a cleric for that State. Morgan Dix thinks this is fair play, given Seabury's visit to Hempstead to ordain, shortly after his return from Scotland.[42] Dix's eagerness to excuse Provoost seems to have prevented him from making any distinctions here.

---

40. White, 167ff.

41. Journal B, September 20, 1792. Samuel Seabury, *Miles to Go before I Sleep: Samuel Seabury's Journal from 1791–1795*, ed. Anne W. Rowthorn (Hartford, Conn.: Church Missions Publishing, 1982).

42. Dix, 2:105ff.

When Seabury ordained in Hempstead, he was the only bishop on the continent, and perceived himself as performing a service. When Provoost interfered, it was a deliberate political maneuver against the peace of a state that already had episcopal oversight.

On the matter of joining with Seabury to consecrate a fourth bishop, both Provoost and White stood firm, of course, and it is well-known that he was permitted to participate in an episcopal consecration only after Virginia had an English bishop to make three of that sort, rather on the theory that the worst thing Seabury's hands or presence would contribute was nothing. Nonetheless, and this would not please Bishop Provoost, very soon it would be the case that every bishop consecrated in the American church stands in a succession which in part descends from the Scottish Nonjurors.[43] The preacher on the grand occasion of Thomas Claggett's consecration in the blended succession was Dr. William Smith.[44]

Provost William Smith (1727–1803)

> I made that man my enemy by doing him too much good. Tis the honestest Way of acquiring an enemy, and since 'tis convenient to have at least one Enemy, who by his Readiness to revile one on all Occasions may make one careful of one's Conduct, I shall keep him an Enemy for that purpose.   —Benjamin Franklin of William Smith

Gore Vidal once said that it is not enough to succeed; others must fail. William Smith was very much of that opinion, as his pointless rivalry with Benjamin Franklin illustrates. Like Franklin, he was self-made, brilliant, and energetic. Unlike Franklin, he had a tragic craving for eminence, a craving that by its persistent visibility prevented his achieving his desire. Smith was born in Scotland of an impoverished Episcopalian family, but seems to have become a Presbyterian for employment's sake, and it is not entirely clear why he left the Kirk for Anglican orders, although the answer suggested by his contemporaries, Seabury among them, has also to do with employment. In any event, he was ordained in England in a group that included young Samuel Seabury.

---

43. The table of the American succession is to be found in any edition of *The Episcopal Church Annual*.

44. The sermon is a bravura performance, even for orator Smith, wherein he notes the joy of many in seeing the successions of "the English and the Scots happily united." If held next to Smith's sermon at the inauguration of the Proposed Book, it seems remarkably conservative. *L&C Smith*, 2:352ff.

It may seem odd that a Scot would be ordained in England. All Church of England clergy in Scotland (the parallel church with which Seabury was asked to have nothing to do by his consecrators) of necessity had English ordination. Additionally, those going to America would have to be licensed by the Bishop of London, who would not accept ordinations by the Nonjurors. This explains why even people of High Church sentiment went down to England for ordination.

When the elder Smith reached America he lied about having a degree, and invented an M.A. to go with it; eventually he had his connections get him a pair of honorary doctoral degrees, one of them from Oxford. According to the Vidal rule, he also prevented Franklin from receiving an Oxford doctorate (this was eventually remedied). Franklin was not without revenge, and Smith ultimately found his college taken away from him.[45] Along the way, Franklin interfered with Smith's fund-raising activities, and Smith then revealed the illegitimacy of Franklin's son William in an effort to destroy William's chances to become governor of New Jersey. As irony would have it, Smith and Franklin often attended services in the same parish, White's Christ Church.

Already in the 1760s, Smith's desire for the episcopate ("a pair of lawn sleeves") was something of a standing joke in Philadelphia. The Quakers, whom he actively disliked, returned the favor by referring to Smith as "The Pope." However, he did not waste time because of unrealized ambition; his written output would be amazing even in a day of word processing, faxes, and e-mail. Twice in his life he would build a sturdy educational institution out of almost nothing. He may well have been the leading astronomer in the New World in his day, and wrote prodigiously in a number of fields. He founded a philosophical society and a literary magazine, and his verse was more than respectable. His command of academic theology is strong. Throughout his life he was in great demand as a public speaker for important occasions, particularly Masonic events, and incongruously delivered the oration at the funeral of Benjamin Franklin![46] From the 1760s

---

45. Buxbaum; Bruce R. Lively, "William Smith, the College and Academy of Philadelphia and Pennsylvania Politics, 1753–1758," *HMPEC* 38, no. 3 (1969): 273ff.

46. "*Citizens of Pennsylvania! Luminaries of science! Assembled fathers of America!* Heard you that solemn interrogatory? Who is *he* that now recedes from his labors among you? What citizen, super-eminent in council, do you now deplore? What luminary, what splendid sun of science, from the hallowed walks of philosophy, now withdraws his beams? What father of his country, what hero, what statesman, what law-giver, is now extinguished from your political hemisphere, and invites the mournful obsequies? It is *he* — your Franklin? It cannot be!" *L&C Smith,* 2:329ff. There were those in high places who found this match of speaker and subject more than incongruous and were offended.

onward, Smith was the most prominent voice in the possible union of Church of England and Lutheran congregations. He also served a small church in North Philadelphia with faithfulness, and was the preacher at White's Christ Church with some regularity. He was a very successful land speculator, at one time holding seventy thousand acres from Philadelphia north to Easton, northwest to Lackawanna County (Wilkes-Barre), and west to Juniata Falls. He was a tenderly devoted husband of many years and apparently a satisfactory parent to six children.

There are very few untortured geniuses. Despite his enormous intellectual output and considerable wealth, Smith needed power and absolutely craved the notice and society of his social betters. He aimed high, but the more Smith tried to establish intimacy with George Washington, the further Washington withdrew from him. This became something of an obsession with Smith: He kept inventing new honors for Washington to accept at his hand, but by them he never achieved anything like friendship with Washington.

According to contemporary reports, notwithstanding his abilities and accomplishments, Smith was somewhat coarse, not careful about his dress and hygiene, and a very heavy drinker, although his most recent biographer has opined unhelpfully (especially for use in a book about Seabury) that in all these apparent failings Smith was merely being a Scot.[47] Curmudgeonly Ezra Stiles had long before perfected the habit of disliking people, especially Anglicans, but he saved a special measure of contempt for Smith which is not worthy of quotation. It is enough to note that Smith's friend and physician, Benjamin Rush, recalled him falling down drunk in the streets of Philadelphia.[48]

Granting that he had unattractive aspects, Smith remains a marvel. He had the rare gift of making students love him, and presided over a small

---

47. Thomas Firth Jones, *A Pair of Lawn Sleeves: A Biography of William Smith (1727–1803)* (Philadelphia: Chilton, 1972). Jones is the world's authority on the informal history (gossip) of Philadelphia during the last three centuries, but has remained an innocent in the fields of letters and religion, making his book something of a bumpy read. A more balanced, if less entertaining, and occasionally excruciatingly exculpatory work is Albert Frank Gegenheim, *William Smith, Educator and Churchman, 1727–1803*, Pennsylvania Lives VII (Philadelphia: University of Pennsylvania, 1943). The largest store of information and easiest access to important sermons and letters is in the two quarto volumes of *The Life and Correspondence of William Smith*, ed. Horace Wemyss Smith (Philadelphia, 1880). The reader is warned that this work also contains much information of interest only to a grandson. Some of Smith's works were collected in the early nineteenth century (1803), but many more permanently escaped the editors. H. Wemyss Smith lists many of them in an appendix.

48. Gegenheim, *William Smith*, 198.

circle of very bright young men. Although White would block his consecration as bishop of Maryland because of Smith's problem with drunkenness, the two seemed to work well together, despite what White termed their "frequent collisions." Scholars agree, however, that Smith's was always the upper hand in the making of the Proposed Book. When one compares William White's pedestrian and interminable "hints at a Preface" for the Proposed Book with Smith's crackling preface, whether or not one agrees with him, it is clear that no small mind or unpracticed pen has been at work. Smith helped found what became the wonderfully munificent Widows Corporation for the clergy families of Pennsylvania, and may well be the father of the modern college and university "development" officer, canvassing much of Britain for support of his college. There were occasions when he took highly principled stands on behalf of people in no position to return the favor. His name still appears in historical magazines because of his involvement with the growth of Philadelphia and his having a role even in the design of the first great municipal water supply.[49]

While the church did not believe him to be called to the episcopate, his talents were not underutilized. His gifts as presiding officer were significant enough for Smith to be elected president of the House of Deputies at every convention from 1789 onward until ill health forced him to decline in 1801, in his seventy-fourth year. He was the preacher at the first three consecrations of bishops held on American soil, an honor that may have seemed an irony to Smith and to those in the assembly who knew his history.

As the Revolution began, Smith was a Tory who thought that a little saber-rattling in the colonies would win concessions from the mother country. He was equivocal in his writing and speaking during the war, and at its end found himself without allies, subject with others to repressive acts by the Pennsylvania Assembly. He went into a kind of exile in Maryland for some years, although he never lost touch with the Philadelphia world. His work on the Proposed Book was done from Maryland. He did return to Philadelphia for his final years.

It is this polymath's ambition and his need for others to fail that concern us here as they touched Seabury. Reporting them is not an exercise in ancient gossip. Rather, Smith's manipulations and marked flexibility

---

49. Most recently in an unsigned article relating to a Smithsonian Institution exhibit, "Franklin and His Friends and Their Machines," *Science and Technology* 15, no. 3 (1999): 28–34. The anonymous author is underinformed concerning Smith's astronomical activities.

in matters of principle are adduced to show that claims about his "inclinations" in favor of the Scottish consecration prayer are both unfounded
(the data) and improbable (the man). Smith's inclinations in politics and in
church politics were to go with the dominant party, as all who have studied him agree. Bishop White found it almost incredible that Smith should
have been the author of the service for the Fourth of July, as we have seen.
In the long run, Smith's many contributions to American life outweigh the
perhaps understandable failings of a person who had to invent himself
each day.

Along with friendship with George Washington, what Smith wanted
most in the world was episcopal consecration, and he would tolerate no
competitors. As early as 1766 he is found writing to the Archbishop of
Canterbury, apologizing for and disassociating himself from the appeal of
New York and Connecticut for a bishop because he was afraid it would
be offensive. The archbishop wrote back encouraging him not to be so
concerned, as there was nothing wrong with New York and Connecticut
asking for a bishop or in how they asked for one.[50]

The need to block the attempts of others to be consecrated would focus
on Seabury. Wilberforce writes that when the Scots bishops had agreed to
consecrate Seabury, "an earnest appeal was sent to them from an American
clergyman, whose own views, as it afterwards appeared, would be in some
measure thwarted by the consecration of Dr. Seabury." Smith wrote to the
Scots that the English archbishops did not consecrate Seabury because
of their

> not thinking him a fit person, especially as he was actively and deeply
> engaged against congress; that he would by this forward step render
> Episcopacy suspected there.[51]

Smith goes on to say that there would soon be a much better candidate
who also had the backing of the state. He concludes by warning them
"if you value your own peace and advantage as a Christian society, let
your bishops meddle not in this consecration."[52] Smith's friends joined
the effort. Among them was Alexander Murray, who had been a rival
of Seabury's for an appointment in 1767. In addition to repeating the
aspersions on Seabury's character, Murray even added that if one of the
Scots bishops should himself set up shop in America he would "find the

---

50. Archbishop of Canterbury to William Smith, August 2, 1766, *L&C Smith*, 396f.
51. Beardsley, 142f.
52. Perry, 233.

candidates for Holy Orders abundantly liberal, making him donations from 10 to 20 guineas each at least, and in the course of the first year he would have no fewer than 200 to order for the 13 States."[53] It was Seabury's opponents who thought of selling ordination.

Seabury's response to the charges was not one of surprise, and later he wrote to Bishop Skinner that Smith would probably not be consecrated because Smith "has set the Clerical Character so low [in setting up the new church's government] & subjected the Clergy to such restraints from the Laity, that his scheme, whatever may be his personal qualifications, certainly deserves no encouragement. I expect from him every trouble that he shall be able to give me; but I shall endeavour to keep straight forward in my duty, & leave the issues to God's good providence."[54]

Later in 1785 Skinner wrote to Seabury's friend Jonathan Boucher:

The busy, bustling President of Washington College, Maryland, seems to be laying a foundation for much confusion throughout the churches of North America, and it will require all Bishop Seabury's prudence and good management to counteract his preposterous measures. I saw a letter from this man lately to a Clergyman in this country, wherein he proposes to be in London as last month, and wishes to know what the bishops in Scotland would do, on an application to them from any foreign country, such as America is now declared to be, for a succession in their ministry, by the consecration of one or more Bishops for them! By this time, I suppose, he knows both what we would do and what we have done; and perhaps is not ignorant, that as our terms would not please him, so his measures would be equally displeasing to us.[55]

Hard as it may be to believe, after all of this Smith sent feelers to learn whether Seabury would act alone to consecrate him. Boucher's report also indicates how Smith was esteemed by his colleagues in the presbyterate.

You may perhaps have heard, as I have, that he [Smith] affected to be much pleased with Dr. Seabury's having returned to America, invested with the Episcopal character, all which will be abundantly explained to you when I further inform you of his having found out

---

53. Alexander Murray to William Seller, October 28, 1784, Steiner2, 213.
54. Samuel Seabury to John Skinner, February 11, 1785, in *The Historiographer* 1, no. 10 (December 10, 1954): 15.
55. John Skinner to Jonathan Boucher, June 25, 1785, Skinner, 50f.

that one Bishop alone may, in certain cases, consecrate another. The English of this is plain, and may account for your not having seen him in Scotland! The case is a ticklish one, and will require poor Seabury's uttermost skill to manage. He knows S—th well, and, of course, thinks of him as we all do. Yet, if S—th is thus properly consecrated, such is his influence, it may be the means of preventing that sad state of things in Virginia and Maryland which I hinted at above. Yet it is dreadful to think of having such a man in such a station! I daily expect further and fuller accounts.[56]

When we arrive at the question of Smith's inclinations regarding the Scottish eucharistic prayer, all the evidence is that he disapproved of it very strongly. The younger William Smith wrote to Seabury on November 5, 1785, for guidance and moral support. He had been using the 1764 Scots prayer in his Maryland parish without any complaints. The elder Smith wrote him asking him to return to the English form. The younger replied to the elder regarding the Scottish prayer:

as that prayer symbolized in all points with the primitive practice, of repeating 1st the words of our B. Lord's Institution, 2d. The Oblation & 3d. The Invocation — & the other does not, I could not so far depart from the Apostolic practice, as to adopt the use of a prayer which manifestly is abridged & mutilated.[57]

Seabury's answer was that young Smith should keep using the prayer as long as he can peaceably do so. Smith the elder remained focused on the epiclesis, and not the theology of the prayer as a whole. Thus he could write to Seabury that "you are said of your own authority, to be making very great alterations from the English Liturgy, especially in the administration of the blessed Sacrament of the Lord's Supper, striving, as Archbishop Laud did, to introduce again some of those superstitions of which it had been cleared at the Reformation."[58] Besides being wrong about Laud,[59] Smith repeatedly observed that the Scottish prayer "favored

56. Jonathan Boucher to John Skinner, December 6, 1785, ibid., 52f.
57. William Smith the younger to Samuel Seabury, November 5, 1785, Hatchett1, 218f.
58. William Smith to Samuel Seabury, July 12, 1786, Hawks & Perry, 2:301.
59. There are several retellings of the history of the 1637 book, which was the Scots bishops' plan, not Laud's. A convenient and compact account is Echlin, 103–38.

the doctrine of transubstantiation,"[60] betraying a misunderstanding of the Nonjuror theology and the structure of the prayer.

Where Smith got the idea that this arrangement of the epiclesis in relation to the rest of the prayer "pleases all sides" is unknown. The younger Smith was not pleased, and Samuel Parker could write from a knowledge of the Nonjuror rite to chide Smith. Three years later, the younger Smith would have to remind the elder (as Seabury had written to White) that it is the removal of a postoblation consecratory epiclesis that makes way for transubstantiation, and the oblation of the gifts before any epiclesis is also a key element of the prayer.

> A person of your extensive reading cannot but know that such a prayer did universally obtain in every Church in Christendom 'till that universal practice & doctrine was first interrupted in the 5th Century in the Pontificate of Gelasius, when both the Invocation of the Holy Ghost to bless the Elements & the Oblation of them were ejected by the Romish Church only, as long incompatible with their scheme of Transubstantiation then under dispute; but even for near a century that Church fluctuated in her judgment concerning this prayer in proportion as the Votaries of that Novel Doctrine increased or diminished, 'till finally Transubstantiation gaining general admission into every Church of the Romish Communion, the Original & primitive prayer was extruded from their Missal & the Consecratory influence made to lie in pronouncing the words of Institution in general, but the words "hoc est corpus meum &c" in particular — contrary to the faith & practice of all other Churches throughout the whole world.[61]

Parker wrote to White regarding this change that "I like very well also the addition to the Consecration prayer at the Communion, & only wish they had moved also for the Oblation in the prayer as it stands in the Scots communion Service" and added that he would prefer the shorter distribution formula of the Scots office.[62] As this is the first and only time we hear of Parker on this subject, it seems fair to conclude that he had seen the proof sheets of the Communion Office that Seabury had introduced at Easter and which was being printed and bound as he wrote.

---

60. William Smith to William White, April 9, 1786, Perry, 190; William Smith to Samuel Parker, April 17, 1786, Hawks & Perry, 2:291.
61. William Smith the younger to William Smith the elder, September 26, 1789, *SAC*, 26.
62. Samuel Parker to William White, May 15, 1786, ST1, 30.

Later, in defending the 1790 book, Seabury explains why that epiclesis was weaker than his, and deftly outlines the Scottish view of the eucharistic prayer.

It must be a strange conscience that cannot communicate under its use. The alteration which you advert to, and which you call a material one, I must suppose is agreeable to you. It was made for those Church people who were too weak to digest strong meat, but must be fed with milk. I think the alteration for the worse, but not be an essential one, as All glory is ascribed to God — the Elements are blessed with thanks-giving — there is an oblation of them made to the Almighty Father — the descent of the Holy Ghost is involved to sanctify them — And all is concluded in the name, and through the merit of Jesus Christ — all of which are wanting in the English Office. Indeed, the present Consecration prayer in the English book is not the original prayer of that Church.[63]

A final note on Smith's inclinations. By 1798 he was writing eucharistic theology that might well have come from Seabury or the younger Smith.[64] The wind had shifted, and he was one to pay attention to his weather cock. One would prefer to think that Smith had been overcome by the historical-theological arguments of John Johnson and those who followed him. For that to be true, the writer of the preface to the Proposed Book and the preacher of the October 7, 1785, convention sermon would have had to change his mind considerably.

For one who did not know of Smith's fluidity of position, it is difficult to account for the change from his earlier attempt to block Seabury's consecration, to his badgering him about ordination and liturgy, to writing nearly seductive letters to the bishop in the summer of 1789 when a new body of convention deputies wanted Connecticut included. Smith tried always to back winners, and by 1789, Seabury's agenda had begun to prevail.

Smith and Franklin are both depicted in the somewhat ambitiously entitled painting *The Apotheosis of Pennsylvania,* in the state's capitol. Franklin occupies a place at the highest level in this intentionally hierarchical painting, with Smith three removes from him. Gore Vidal also once complained of being "Always a godfather, never a god."

---

63. Samuel Seabury to Benjamin Gardiner, April 13, 1789, SAC, 34.
64. See Echlin, 228ff.

– Chapter Nine –

SLOUCHING TOWARD UNITY

*For God's sake, my dear Sir, let us remember that it is the partic-
ular business of the Bishops of Christ's Church to preserve it pure
and undefiled, in faith and practice, according to the model left by
apostolic practice. And may God give you grace and courage to act
accordingly!*   —Seabury to White, June 1789

Early in 1786 the king of Denmark informed John Adams that he would
gladly provide ordinations for America without anyone swearing loyalty
to himself or any other ruler. He was also willing to establish a bishop
in the West Indies, so that candidates for ordination would not have to
cross the Atlantic.[1] This offer, in addition to what the Scots had done and
might do again with American bishops-elect, moved the Whig government to change its policy. Parliament made provision for the omission of
the political portions of the Ordinal when candidates for ordination were

---

1. January 10, 1786, *Anglican Experience*, 145ff: Inglis's "Journal of Occurrences" reports
a strange episode of archiepiscopal double-talk. "Col. Bayard called on me, and asked me to
dine with him in company with several gentlemen. At 11 o'clock I carried the children to the
Asylum to see Mr. Duché's family — left them there, and waited on His Grace of Canterbury
at Lambeth, where I met Dr. Parker, who asked me to dine with him at the Chaplain's table,
St. James' tomorrow. Saw the Arch-Bishop. His Grace told me of his having received a packet
from the Convention of Episcopal Clergy who met at Philadelphia last October — desiring
to know whether persons sent over from America would be consecrated Bishops here by the
English Bishops. The packet was presented to him by Mr. Adams, the American ambassador,
His Grace asked Mr. Adams whether in this he acted officially; as an Ambassador and by
Order of Congress? Adams replied in the negative — said that Congress had no right, as such,
to interfere in matters of religion; but added that he was desired by Mr. Lee, President of
Congress, and by others, to promote the measure mentioned in the packet, as a thing much
desired by the American Church people, who are a numerous and respectable body — that
application had been made in Denmark to know whether Bishops might be consecrated there
for America; and assurances were received that they would. But the Americans chose rather
to have them consecrated in England. His Grace in his conversation with me, adverted to the
step taken by Dr. Seabury, how hasty and ill-judged it was; and told me that from the letters
produced by Mr. Adams, it appeared that if Dr. Seabury had been consecrated by English
Bishops when he went to Scotland for consecration, he would have met with opposition in
America, people there not being yet prepared for the measure, and that he, (the A'p) was
apprehensive a schism in America would be the consequence."

citizens of foreign lands. The next February, White and Provoost would be ordained to the episcopate at Lambeth Palace.[2]

General Conventions of 1786 and 1789

The English bishops, it will be recalled, disapproved of the loss of two creeds, and the removal of the *descensus* from the Apostles' Creed. They disapproved of provision for laypeople to be the court for trial and deposition of clergy. They made it clear that they expected their wishes (identical with those expressed by Seabury and others in New England) would be carried out, although there actually was discussion at convention about whether they expected compliance or not.

White, aware of what was being said about the status of that doctrine in the Proposed Book, preached on the centrality of the Trinity on June 21, as General Convention opened in Philadelphia. It was at this June convention that the already-discussed legislation attacking Seabury and his ordinands was taken up.

Smith drafted a deferential reply to the concerns stated by the English bishops. Less conciliatory was John Jay. On June 26 he arrived from New York and with Francis Hopkinson was appointed to the committee for answering the concerns of the English archbishops. The letter had been presented to Convention and was now recommitted to the enlarged committee. Jay was much more assertive than White, Smith, and the rest of the group had been in earlier drafts. The original essentially assured the English that the Proposed Book was just that, "only a proposal," and should not be paid much mind. With Jay's stiffening, the response now read in part:

> We are unanimous and explicit in assuring your Lordships, that we neither have departed nor propose to depart from the doctrines of your Church. We have retained the same discipline and forms of worship, as far as was consistent with our civil constitutions; and we have made no alterations or omissions in the Book of Common Prayer, but such as that consideration prescribed, and such as were calculated to remove objections, which it appeared to us more conducive to union and general content to obviate, than to dispute. It is

---

2. According to Jarvis, the Connecticut clergy saw Pitt's reversal of position as an attempt to "overthrow" Seabury through a rival episcopate to the south. *Jarvis2,* 73.

well known, that many great and pious men of the Church of England have long wished for a revision of the Liturgy, which it was deemed imprudent to hazard, lest it might become a precedent for repeated and improper alterations. This is with us the proper season for such a revision.[3]

The June convention also made constitutional concessions, and added bishops to the trial court of a bishop, and provided that only a bishop might pronounce sentence on any member of the clergy. The constitution limited the use of the Proposed Book; it could be used only until there was a convention assembled with "sufficient power" to set out a book, a somewhat oblique submission to the English demands that laity and presbyters not create liturgy on their own. As these changes were closer to the New England position on liturgy and discipline, the convention was in effect solving two problems at once. If Connecticut had forced the hand of the English to consecrate bishops unawares, the English, also without knowing it, returned the favor by pushing the southern church to a more conventional position on liturgy and governance.

Shortly after the June convention, a second letter arrived from the English bishops. They had now seen the entire Proposed Book and wished to see the Apostles' Creed restored to its full text, and the other two creeds returned, even if only as options.

The brief General Convention that met in Wilmington on October 10, 1786, lasted only two days. Its goal was "to give every satisfaction to their Lordships" and demonstrate its unity of faith with the English Church. Accordingly, the *descensus* was restored to the Apostles' Creed by a slim majority; the Nicene Creed was restored unanimously; restoration of the Athanasian Creed was voted down, however, seventeen to three. White's Pennsylvania deputies all voted against that creed. This is the convention that recommended White, Provoost, and Griffith to the English for consecration. Then was drafted a letter to the archbishops informing them that their wishes regarding the liturgy had been carried out to the fullest extent possible. The preface and Articles of Religion were amended to include reference to the Nicene Creed.

Maryland did not send a deputation to the Wilmington convention, although Smith was present. A week later it met as a state convention and produced testimonials for the consecration of William Smith. He would not be accredited to the English bishops by the General Convention.

---

3. *Journals,* Monday, June 26, 1786, 27.

New York, Pennsylvania, Virginia, and Maryland were not the only states concerned with new bishops between 1786 and 1789. The Connecticut clergy began to worry that with what was happening to the south, should Seabury die, they would be at the mercy of a system they did not accept. Seabury met with them in March 1787 and reported their concerns to Skinner. He reports that the clergy are frightened that "innovation in the Government and Liturgy of the Church" would be thrust upon them. He explains this in part with reference to the spirit of the time and place: "The people, you know, especially in this country, are fond of exercising power, when they have opportunity."[4] We have already seen White's comments on the Proposed Book, particularly the July Fourth service, that it was an example of overgoverning. Parker was to seethe on this point:

> You seem to inveigh very bitterly against Royal Bishops & to suppose that the primitive ones were the mere Creatures of the Saints which, as I take it, is the People — A principle that is spreading very far among our Independent States who all suppose that all power spiritual as well as temporal originates from the Majesty of the People, & has gone so far as to invest Mr. Freeman with Episcopal power, & a more recent Instance in this neighbourhood of a Mr. Murray at Cape Ann, in which acts, the People give grant & convey, constitute ordain & appoint these Persons to be their Ministers, Pastors, ruling elders & Teachers & give all powers & authority with which Gospel Ministers are invested. This is a Doctrine which before 1775 would have sounded strange even in American Ears, but having found out that all civil power is derived from the People, it was an easy matter to go a step farther & believe that there was not other source for ecclesiastical power.[5]

Skinner replied to Seabury that his hopes that the southern states would become more catholic and apostolic were "sadly disappointed." But the Scots were also aware of their own political position. Soon the last Stuart to whom they could be expected to be loyal would be gone, and they were, with the Psalmist, desirous of seeing better times. Seabury and the clergy of Connecticut were to be let down gently. Skinner wrote that despite their unfortunate theology, liturgy, and constitution, he was sure that the bishops of the South would not "refuse their brotherly assistance" in

---

4. Samuel Seabury to John Skinner, March 2, 1787, Skinner, 65.
5. Samuel Parker to Samuel Peters, December 15, 1788. Unpublished manuscript courtesy of the Archives of the Episcopal Church.

consecrating a coadjutor for Connecticut. Only if the other bishops required a violation of the consciences of Connecticut's bishop and clergy would they proceed to consecrate another bishop for them. Their hope was similar to the one they stated in 1785 and 1786, "that there will be no occasion for two separate communions among the Episcopalians of the United States."[6]

Others were watching. Massachusetts was not sure how to proceed in the matter of finding a bishop. There were six clergy in the state. Two thought that a bishop might be gotten via Seabury, two thought to get one from the southern states, and two were undecided. Thus Parker wrote to White that summer that "nothing will be determined in this state respecting a Bishop till we see how matters are settled between you and the Bishop of Connecticut." He adds that no further liturgical revision will be contemplated until there is a bishop.[7]

Seabury replied to Skinner that what had been proposed by the Scots could not happen without capitulation to the terms of the South.[8] Seabury had no way of knowing that those terms would begin to change in one year. His invitations to freshly consecrated White and Provoost to come to Stamford had been ignored. By this time the clergy committee appointed to assist him in the general review of the prayer book had been formed. He thus made inquiries in Edinburgh about having an edition of the prayer book printed with Connecticut's liturgical and canonical needs addressed. It very much looked to Seabury at this point that he might have to go it alone, or perhaps in union with only the New England states. He was prepared to endure the pain that principle would bring, and although he was preparing for every eventuality, he remained in contact with White and the elder Smith.

As we have seen, White was not prepared to let the Proposed Book prevent union. Once again we note White's important admission when writing Seabury in December 1788 assuring him that "There are Things in the proposed Book which some of us were far from approving at the Time: And as to those we were for, I believe there are none we should not be disposed to give up, if they appear to give Offense to any considerable Extent."[9]

---

6. John Skinner to Samuel Seabury, June 20, 1787, Skinner, 69f.
7. Samuel Parker to William White, July 19, 1787, *SSECR*, 52–53.
8. Samuel Seabury to John Skinner, November 7, 1787, Skinner, 72.
9. William White to Samuel Seabury, December 9, 1788, Hatchett1, 228.

In his most manipulative (and slightly disloyal) moment, Parker's anxiety for union brings him to write to White that a way can still be found to work this out, and that as the laity hold the purse strings, they must be granted a place in the government of the church:

> This, however, in my mind, is the greatest obstacle to a union with our brethren in Connecticut. It is in vain to dispute which form comes nearest to the primitive practice. *The question is, which is most expedient under our present circumstances?* They are doubtless too rigid in their sentiments, at least for the latitude of America, and must finally be obliged to relax a little. They think, on the other hand, that your Constitution is too democratical for Episcopal government, and especially in permitting the Laity to sit as judges at the trial of a Bishop, and to have a voice in deposing him.

Then Parker quotes one of Seabury's letters to him asking nothing more than coming to union on even terms, with no one asked to surrender their beliefs or liturgical practice. Parker concludes: "Here certainly appears a disposition to unity; where, then, is the impediment?"[10] A great deal of pain would have entered a lifelong friendship with Parker had Seabury seen this letter and the others that took a variety of positions on the Scottish episcopacy and Connecticut's "stiffness."

Leaming would write to White, also suggesting union without uniformity, and it seems that by the spring of 1789 White came to the belief that with everything else in the nascent church so fragile, 1662 would provide the only basis on which to build something acceptable to nearly everyone.[11]

As the year moved on, Seabury responded to the clergy's acceptance of a revision process with the creation of propers for Ash Wednesday and a collect to be used throughout Lent.[12] Seabury also determined to make one more large effort at union, and wrote to Parker, "I believe we shall send two Clergymen to the Philadelphia Convention, to see whether a union can be affected. If it fail, the point here will be altogether given up."[13]

---

10. Samuel Parker to William White, January 20, 1789. Courtesy of the Archives of the Episcopal Church. Emphasis added

11. William White to William West, February 24, 1789, William McGarvey, *Liturgiae Americanae* (Philadelphia: Church Publishing Company, 1907), xxviii.

12. This undated text appears in SUI, 76. Cameron dates it 1793, but that seems unlikely, given its sequence in the manuscripts. It is also possible that the form was used privately and printed later.

13. Samuel Seabury to Samuel Parker, April 10, 1789, Perry, 383.

No doubt Seabury meant what he said. He cannot but have known that Parker's inclination was to fix things. Whether or not he wrote this letter and a similar one in May to Parker in the hope of Parker's taking action cannot be known. He does speak of "patience" and "variety in public liturgy" as the two thoughts on his mind.[14]

On May 13, as we have seen, the lay convention held in Connecticut declined, as noted above, to go to General Convention.

In June the convention of New Jersey met, and instructed deputies to oppose unnecessary revision in the liturgy and to work for the restoration of the Articles of Religion, the Psalter, and the metrical psalms.

The tide had definitely turned. Smith wrote on June 13, to the effect that even though there is no agreement about the articles and the liturgy and the government of the church, there is no reason to remain apart. Smith then threw bait to Seabury with words he had to know White would never accept:

> And my Wish has long been that we may have the English and Scots Episcopacy united in transmitting our American Episcopacy to future Time, which my be done by your making a *third* Bishop in our next Consecrations.[15]

On June 20, Seabury wrote, perhaps energized by Smith's correspondence, the long letter to White (Appendix B-8) inviting union with diversity, considering an appeal to "the Christian world" about the validity of his consecration, and laying out his relatively modest complaints about the Proposed Book.

Whatever the triggering events, enormous concessions were made to Seabury between June and September 1789. The July convention amended Article VIII of the constitution so that no commitment to the Proposed Book would be required. Article II was revised to read that each state shall be "entitled to" lay deputies, but if they were not present, the deputation would still be entitled to seat, voice, and vote. But closest to Seabury's heart had to be the new Article XXXIII:

> The Bishops of this church, when there shall be three or more, shall, whenever general conventions are held, form a house of revision,

---

14. Samuel Seabury to Samuel Parker, May 27, 1789, manuscript at Boston Public Library; draft at General Theological Seminary.

15. William Smith to Samuel Seabury, June 13, 1789, Hatchett1, 231.

and when any proposed act shall have passed in the general convention, the same shall be transmitted to the house of revision, for their concurrence.

This was not all that he could desire, but it was a step, and the next step would soon be taken in September, when the convention gave bishops the right to initiate legislation, and almost full power to veto (their nonconcurrence could be overridden by four-fifths of the deputies).

In the July session of the 1789 convention, more concessions came to Seabury. There was unanimously adopted a resolution affirming the validity of his consecration. This was in response to Smith's and White's communicating the contents of Seabury's letters to them.

At that July session, it was Smith who drafted the principal resolution of those meant to conciliate Seabury. There were five resolves:

1st. *Resolved,* That a complete order of Bishops, derived as well under the English as the Scots line of Episcopacy, doth now subsist within the United States of America . . . [in White, Provoost, and Seabury, in that order, the exact reverse of their order of consecration]

2d. [They are competent of consecrating others]

3d. [The Convention ought to help Massachusetts and New Hampshire, who have elected Bass]

4th. [The three bishops are asked to consecrate Bass, but] that before the said Bishops comply with the request aforesaid, it be proposed to the churches of the New England states to meet the churches of these states with the said three Bishops, in an adjourned Convention, to settle certain articles of union and discipline among all the churches previous to such consecration.

5th. *Resolved,* That if any difficulty or delicacy, in respect to the Archbishops and Bishops of England, shall remain with the Right Rev. Doctors White and Provoost, or either of them, concerning their compliance with the above request, this Convention will address the Archbishops and Bishops, and hope thereby to remove the difficulty.

How the invitation became demand was that the resolution called for Seabury to join the consecration *after* the union of the church was settled. Consciously or not, this resolution was a subterfuge. The drafter, Smith,

had to know White's determination not to include Seabury as a third consecrator; White had even written of it to Parker. How much Seabury was
taken in by this, if at all, is hard to determine. It may be that he considered
any movement toward him as good news. For whatever reason, the tide
had turned, and the body that barely acknowledged his existence from
1785 on was now very much desirous to have Connecticut and its bishop
among them.

On August 16, 1789, two letters were written to Seabury. One came
from the elder Smith, mentioning that White was unaware of a letter
from Seabury asking him to join in consecrating a bishop, and more than
that, White had seconded the motion regarding the validity of Seabury's
consecration.[16] The correspondence committee of the convention wrote
with five major points. (1) They desire union as much as Seabury does
[an explicit recognition of his efforts for union]. (2) They are enclosing
their proceedings so that he can survey the concessions the convention has
made to Seabury's position. (3) The constitution has been revised to permit
deputations without lay members. (4) His consecration was unanimously
affirmed. (5) The Convention is adjourning until September 29 in order
that Seabury and his state's deputation may join it.[17]

On August 12, White wrote to reinforce the invitation. White and Smith
were then faced with a dilemma: What to do if both Seabury and Provoost appeared? It was decided that White would entertain Provoost, if
he appeared, while Smith would house Seabury and Parker. It was further
decided to award the D.D. to Bass, Parker, and Leaming (if he came).

By the end of the month, Seabury announced a determination to go
to Philadelphia, and southern New England prepared itself accordingly,
rather as it prepares for a nor'easter, tying down and boarding up everything it can. Parker was sent with binding instructions to ensure minimum
alteration of the liturgy (vacating any Middletown/Boston proposals), and
to "Procure the junction of the Church in Connecticut upon just and honorable terms."[18] Connecticut held a special convention. It decided that the
constitution was not a matter for great concern, as Christ and the apostles
gave them all the constitution they needed, and as long as that were not
contradicted they could live with anything else. On a more delicate subject, the deputies were permitted to participate in prayer book revision,
but the ratification of any changes was left to the bishop and clergy in

---

16. William Smith to Samuel Seabury, August 16, 1789, Hawks & Perry, 2:345ff.
17. Committee of General Convention to Samuel Seabury, August 16, 1789, Perry, 405ff.
18. Steiner2, 290f.

convocation. Thus Seabury did not need an artificial reason to abandon any new book made in Philadelphia, as has been suggested; he had a formal right to do so before the revision began. Finally, Bela Hubbard and Abraham Jarvis were elected to represent Connecticut. Like Parker, they would be present when the communion service was generated in the House of Deputies, and like him, would not be the ones to suggest the inclusion of the Scots eucharistic prayer. Although preparations had been carefully made, Parker expected very little to come of the convention, even when it was known that Provoost would not be present.[19]

Other preparations were being made as well, which brings us to examine one of the reasons that have been given to minimize Seabury's role in adopting the eucharistic prayer of 1789. When one confronts the mass of documents that come to us from this period of the church's life, and which are dispersed in at least six collections, one of which is in Scotland, it is inevitable that some confusion may enter one's recollection of what has been examined. This appears to be the case regarding the assertion that the younger William Smith wrote "a circular letter" that he sent to "an unknown number of deputies" advocating the use of the Scottish eucharistic prayer.[20] No source is given for the letter in either place, a fact that complicates the student's task. The passages quoted by Hatchett occur in a very long letter from the younger Smith to Smith the elder now in the Archives of the Episcopal Church. It is reproduced in full form in Appendix B-7. What may have appeared to be a "circular letter" comes next in the documents of the archive's collection. It is a page of extracts from Smith's letter (but not those passages that address the eucharistic prayer *per se*), in the elder Smith's handwriting. The parts the older man copied are indicated in the larger text in the appendix with an underscore. Those familiar with Smith's correspondence know that he frequently quoted other people's words, often to embarrass them. He is famous for quoting Samuel Johnson's words about episcopal ordination in a way that terribly embarrassed Johnson with the Presbyterians who wanted control of King's/Columbia. He had already referred to private mail from the younger Smith once before in this way.[21]

---

19. ST1, 74.
20. Hatchett1, 233f.; Hatchett2, 107f.
21. See also Smith to William White, March 17, 1786, *L&C Smith*, 2:183ff.; Smith to the Archbishop of Canterbury, November 27, 1759, *L&C Smith*, 1:219ff.; and Smith to the Bishop of London, May 6, 1768, *L&C Smith*, 1:414f.

In any event, there is no circular letter from the younger Smith, although one can perhaps understand how the two documents could have been confused and their content switched. This is unfortunate, as those who read the complete text will find that what have been quoted to us are small samples of a letter highly critical of the presence of laypeople in convention, of the ability of the elder Smith and others to create liturgical prose, and of the unhelpful attitudes of the "Southern Brethren." It is, in short, an indictment of incompetence and a repudiation of every major decision Smith and White had taken. The fact that it dwells at length on the inappropriateness of lay participation in the councils of the church lessens to zero the likelihood that it was written to any lay deputies seeking their votes for an exotic liturgical text. Whether one agrees with young Smith's position or not, he does demonstrate the intimate connection of liturgy and the constitution of the church, and what a priest in the tradition of the Nonjurors would expect to find in a valid eucharistic prayer, which was specifically *not* the epiclesis Smith believed would satisfy his "little High Church friend." As much as the younger Smith shared Seabury's views and assisted him in other ways, we must nonetheless resist the attempt to give him credit for circularizing convention deputies on behalf of the 1764 Communion Office. Many deputies would have found the contents of his letter highly offensive. The best one can say is that the letter may have prepared the elder Smith for what would be presented to him by the bishops working quietly in the small room off the gallery in Christ Church.

Upon arrival in Philadelphia, Seabury was not treated as a leper, perhaps to his surprise. He was invited by White to preach in Christ Church to the Widow's Corporation. On October 2, he and the deputies from Connecticut, Massachusetts, and New Hampshire (both of the latter states were represented by Parker) signed the famous single sheet of paper accepting the Constitution of the Protestant Episcopal Church. Union had been achieved, and so the convention went on to the task of unity, to be expressed in the creation and adoption of an American prayer book.

Bishop White's Memory and the 1789 Anaphora

Billy White was born a bishop. I never could persuade him to play any thing but church. He would tie his own or my apron round his neck, for a gown, and stand behind a low chair, which he called his pulpit; I, seated before him on a little bench, was the congregation; and he always preached to me about being good. One day, I heard him crying, and saw him running into the street, and the nurse-maid after him, calling to him to come back and be dressed. He refused, saying, I do not want to go to dancing-school, and I won't be dressed, for I don't think it is good to learn to dance. And that was the only time I ever knew Billy White to be a naughty boy.

—The former Miss Pascal[22]

Following the death of Seabury, Bishop White was the most learned man in the Church.   —Walter H. Stowe

We tend to think of Bishop William White in terms of the visual images left to us: the silhouette of a very old man in top hat, slightly bent over and walking with a cane; or else the wizened and asthenic figure seated in a large chair, not quite filling his rochet and chimere, his legs too short to reach the floor. But the William White with whom this inquiry has to do was a youngish church politician, an ecclesiastical statesman learning on the job, not a venerable old gentleman swimming in his lawn sleeves and convoluted prose. This is not at all to deny that White deservedly became the venerated patriarch of the Episcopal Church. There is a sense in which the elder White is incomparable simply because there is no basis of comparison. As the pious parlance of the time would have put it, "an all-wise Providence did not permit us" to see how Seabury or Madison might have turned out in a fifty-year episcopate, and Provoost's old age contained horrible and destructive moments.

Few would argue with White's (carefully qualified) reflection on the process of union with Connecticut, "that forbearance and mutual toleration are at least sometimes a shorter way to unity than severity and stiffness."[23] He was speaking to Connecticut's inclusion of laypeople in its deputation to the 1792 General Convention, but the same might be said of the larger transactions of 1783–89 as well.

At the same time, an authority on White, Robert Prichard, describes the period of the church's formation as a cluster of mistakes from which White would continue to learn.[24] He assigns even more of the responsibility for

---

22. A septuagenarian Quaker recalling her childhood with White. White added, while confirming the story, that "I am by no means opposed to others learning, if they like to dance." Wilson, 21. But Prichard disagrees with White's recall, pointing out that White disapproved of dancing and a number of other amusements. Prichard, 101.

23. Wilson, 125.

24. Robert W. Prichard, *The Nature of Salvation: Theological Consensus in the Episcopal Church, 1801–73* (Urbana: University of Illinois Press, 1997), 10ff.

the Proposed Book and proposed Articles of Religion to White than the reader will find here.

Prichard's position seems reasonable. White was all of thirty-nine years old when consecrated, and forty-two when the constitution of the American church was settled and its prayer book published. He had upset friends and created foes with the presbyterianism and unremitting congregationalism of *The Case,* as well as with his function as drafter of the 1785 constitution. His work on *The Case* and the constitution along with the proposed liturgy prompted the inquiry from the Lords Spiritual in England as to whether the new establishment in America was "of the Church of England or no." Like other persons who have held a proprietary attitude toward the Episcopal Church over the years, he was not particularly consultative with clergy on anything of real importance, in sharp contrast to Seabury's consistently collegial practice. White's perhaps unconscious preference for the back room may be seen in the liberties taken in composing the Proposed Book and in White's own election, decided in a group of four clergy (at which he presided), with a later rubber stamp applied by a larger meeting of clergy and lay representatives, at which he also presided. Even admiring biographers admit that his low interest in the world beyond urban Philadelphia seriously held back the work of the Episcopal Church in western Pennsylvania.[25]

Despite the manner in which the Episcopal Church came to express itself in liturgy, canon, and constitution, White in later years reaffirmed the views taken in *The Case.* His letters to Hobart and his twice-amplified *Memoirs* of the church betray the entirely natural desire in an important person reviewing his life to present it as a seamless garment, giving the impression that he has always believed, spoken, and acted for precisely the same reasons and in pursuit of precisely the same goals. In such a setting, innocent and unconscious confabulation inevitably occurs. Very few minds are capable of writing with as much candor and self-awareness as Augustine displayed in his *Retractions.* For example, White's own resolution of 1786 that wounded Seabury so deeply he later dismissed as being offered merely to quiet the fears of some members of the convention, as though it had no other effect.[26] Prichard's work on White's syllabus for theological education leads one to conclude that his survival as the only bridge to the church's origins, as much as his own attainments, gave White's

---

25. E.g., Stowe, 377. Stowe also recognizes that White's preaching and written communication were marginal as well.

26. Wilson, 115f.

reminiscences the status of oracle rather than resource. It is helpful here respectfully to suspend that status for a short time.

Prichard demonstrates the extent to which there was, in the first seventy-five years of the nineteenth century, consensus proceeding from White's theological syllabus and the studied ambiguity of his own writing. In White's recollections we may also find his essential difference from the eighteenth-century High Church school, particularly as it was represented in Connecticut. The second chapter of *The Case* concludes that as Parliament must approve what Convocation does in England, it is clear that the laity are to have the last word in church government. He does not seriously argue tradition here, where the High Churchmen will always go beyond the English situation with an eye to the "primitive church," and the origins of what came to be called the monarchical episcopate. When White considered that early period, he concluded without nuance that in primitive days "the bishop was not more than a president." White's view of episcopacy in *The Case,* limited to England and current views of government, might be called American Erastianism, in sharp contrast to the somewhat romantic quest for apostolic order in Connecticut. Both White and Seabury recognized that the conventional wisdom of their day followed Locke in asserting that the will of the people is supreme. White agreed with the spirit of the times, and Seabury did not. White's real failing, from Seabury's point of view, would be that in emphasizing episcopate as presidency, White did not identify the bishop's defining task as being the primary pastor and evangelist of a diocese.[27]

We are concerned with White's views here because he comprised half of the House of Bishops that worked in the General Convention of 1789 to produce the first American Book of Common Prayer. When pressed about the rather High Church eucharistic rite produced in those sessions, his answers tended to be either words to the effect that "Seabury got that from the Scots," or, "the words do not mean what they say." The task is complicated by the fact, as Prichard has demonstrated, that when White really did become the living ancestor for the nineteenth-century church, and because he learned from the 1785–89 debacle not to take extreme positions, both the High and Low/Evangelical schools could appeal to one or the other of the (only modestly separated) poles of his thought to support their positions.[28]

---

27. See, per contra, Temple, 24f.
28. Prichard, *The Nature of Salvation,* 7 and *passim.*

Despite the fact that in 1783 the bishopless clergy of Connecticut quite on their own had written to him strongly about the uncatholic position taken in *The Case*, White would years later still maintain that the Connecticut arrangement was explicable as "the arrangement of the Church in which Bishop Seabury received his Episcopacy."[29] Again, somewhat gratuitously, in the account of Seabury's declining the invitation "to consecrate the elements," on the ground of 1662's defects, White asserts that "These sentiments he had adopted, in his visit to the bishops from whom he received his Episcopacy."[30] In either case, it must have been easier to dismiss these views as yet more foreignness than to admit the presence of such thought among thoroughly American clergy in the church he had crafted. That assertion is not conjecture. In his "Dissertation," on the Eucharist, White is explicit that with respect to Johnsonian views of sacrifice, altar, and priest, "The author would lament an approach to the opposite theory, among the clergy and other members of this Church; as having a threatening aspect on its peace."[31] He wrote to Hobart specifically rejecting the views of Johnson and Hickes.[32]

The greatest part of White's dissertation is given to disproving the theory of transubstantiation, although it is not known that there was a resurgence of that doctrine in the early Episcopal Church. Moving on, White does know that "sacrifice" in English represents several Hebrew terms, but he does not seem to know that some of these rites did not require the death of a victim.[33] He told Hobart that he preferred to "distinguish between sacrifice and oblation," and for that reason cannot understand the difficulties Low critics were making about 1789 being too High.[34]

The High Church view was that scripture is amplified and interpreted by tradition, but White represents a very different approach. The fact that the New Testament does not speak of the Eucharist sacrificially or of any earthly president in sacerdotal terms settled the matter for him. His hermeneutic is not consistent: White once preached on Romans 13, reversing the sense, so that civil powers need not be obeyed.[35] This was part of his recollection of not promoting the Revolution, but at the same time supporting it.

---

29. White1, 113.
30. Ibid., 155.
31. White2, 420f.
32. Temple, 44.
33. White2, 390f.
34. Wilson, 373.
35. Ibid., 52ff.

Perhaps, had the issue depended on my determination, it would have been for submission, with the determined and steady continuance of rightful claim.

It is striking that in the passage so far, White agrees entirely with the *Westchester Farmer*. He continues, however:

> But when my countrymen in general had chosen the dreadful measure of forcible resistance — for certainly the spirit was almost universal at the time of arming — it was the dictate of conscience, to take what seemed the right side.... I continued, as did all of us, to prayer for the king, until Sunday (inclusively) before [sic] the 4th of July, 1776. Within a short time after, I took the oath of allegiance to the United States, and have remained faithful to it. My intentions were upright, and most seriously weighed. I hope they were not in contrariety to my duty.[36]

Applying scripture to liturgy, White will permit the use of "sacrifice" and "altar" in "an accommodated sense."[37] He is aware that the English word "priest" comes from *prester,* itself a shortening of *presbyter,* or elder. He permits its use as long as it is not understood to stand for *sacerdos* or *hiereus.* In the 1806 letter to Hobart, in direct opposition to Seabury's High view of sacerdotal function, White maintains the ministers are special intercessors only in that "the minister is the mouth of the congregation."[38] This may help us to understand the tension that would develop over the ordination formula in 1792.

Illustrative of Prichard's contention that the very Low may find comfort in White, Temple's summary of the bishop on the Eucharist is "It is the means instituted by Christ by which God may know man, man may know God, and through God men may be united with each other."[39] White reduces the benefit of the sacrament to what happens "in the act of communicating."[40] This description is a bit more substantial than it seems, for White understands "the general tenor of Christ's religion [as that] which aims at the influencing of the conduct, through the medium of the affections."[41] For White, the outward manifestation of the Christian's ongoing

---

36. Ibid., 49ff.
37. White2, 397.
38. Wilson, 373.
39. Temple, 45.
40. Ibid., 46.
41. Ibid., 108.

conversion of life (he would say, renewal), is expressed in living the life Christ calls for.

On the question of sacrifice, Temple quotes White's rather singular charge to the clergy in 1807:

> The Lord's Supper in the correspondency apparent with the sacrifices under the law, had for its most distinguishing property, its being a spiritual sacrifice, wherein, as in the former sacrifices the worshippers became one body, in an enjoyment of the benefits of which those ordinances are respectively the celebration.[42]

White would insist as late as 1820 that sacrifice and oblation were different concepts, adding that an oblation is not a sacrifice.[43] He wrote critically of contemporaries who had any more lively view of sacrifice, but tactfully omits comment on Seabury's *Discourses*. He specifically rejects in several places the idea of the Eucharist as a "feast upon a sacrifice," a major tenet of the High tradition, and one repeated in all known utterances of Samuel Seabury on the Eucharist. White considers the idea of feast upon a sacrifice "a remnant of the contemplating of the ordinance as answering to the expiatory sacrifices of the law. We make a memorial of the expiatory sacrifice of Christ: but then feed on the emblems of his person," all of which led him to believe that if there is any Old Testament type for the Eucharist, it is the Peace Offering.[44]

Temple understands him to believe that the Eucharist conveys forgiveness of sins no more than any other announcement of the gospel.[45] That announcement works through creating fellowship and "excitements to charity."[46]

Despite the claim that White was "inclined toward" the Scottish prayer, he comments on it in a way that shows no understanding of its development and purpose:

> The offering to God of the bread and wine, as representative of the body and blood of Christ, but under the proper name of elements, is no more a Sacrifice, than the offering either of alms or praise. It is an edifying act, and ought not to be objected to, merely on account of

---

42. Ibid., 47.
43. Ibid., 142.
44. Ibid., 139.
45. Ibid., 138.
46. Ibid., 141f.

its being sometime associated with errors which spring from another root.[47]

We must ask ourselves if the passage just quoted means that White understood Seabury and did not wish to object, or that he never read or comprehended Seabury's interpretation of the prayer that White identifies with him and his Scottish consecrators. White's report of the 1789 prayer is that "it lay very near to the heart of Bishop Seabury," and that he himself "always thought there was beauty in those ancient forms, and can discover no superstitions in them" although his parishioner Dr. Rush had. White goes on to say:

> If indeed they could have been reasonably thought to imply that a Christian minister is a priest, in the sense of an offerer of sacrifice, and that the table is an altar and the elements a sacrifice, in any other than figurative sense, he would have zealously opposed the admission of such unevangelical sentiments.[48]

How White could have sat in a room with Seabury and not understood what the Bishop of Connecticut was proposing, or how he could have ignored all of Seabury's writings to the extent that twenty years later he would express himself in a way that implies complete ignorance of what the Scottish liturgy was about, is difficult to explain.

The only possibility that reading White's *Memoirs* and the notes he later added to it suggests is a cultivated diffidence he confesses to on more than one occasion. After describing, at length, all the damage and calamity he saw coming with the adoption of Smith's Fourth of July liturgy, White says he raised a caution at one point, but as he was in the chair, did not press the point and let the matter go through, even though he says he foresaw disaster. Having puzzled his reader, he then completely mystifies when he adds that he was one of the very few who actually used this dangerous service.[49]

We are left with the possibility that White did not understand the 1764/1786 prayer, or that he simply caved in, or that in old age his memory was not as clear as he might have wished it to be. It must be concluded that in 1789 he and perhaps Smith compromised in allowing a prayer that Smith had at least twice written against, but if so, they certainly could

---

47. Ibid., 147.
48. White1, 178ff.
49. Ibid., 104f.

not and did not cave in on the very realistic epiclesis in Seabury's prayer. Recall that Seabury's prayer read,

> And we most humbly beseech thee, O merciful Father to hear us, and of thy almighty goodness vouchsafe to bless and sanctify, with thy word and Holy Spirit, these thy gifts and creatures of bread and wine, that they may become the body and blood of thy most dearly beloved Son.

What was adopted in 1789 was somewhat like that from Maryland and Pennsylvania, but the Holy Spirit and God's word are invoked in the manner of 1549 and 1637:[50]

> And we most humbly beseech thee O merciful Father, to hear us, and of thy almighty goodness vouchsafe to bless and sanctify, with thy word and Holy Spirit, these thy gifts and creatures of bread and wine; that we, receiving them according to thy Son our Saviour Jesus Christ's holy institution, in remembrance of his death and passion, may be partakers of his most blessed Body and Blood.

Seabury came down a little, and White and Smith came up a great deal in this text. The emphasis in the text moves from what the elements become (1764) to what the communicant receives (1549, 1637), but the text leaves more than enough room for a stronger sense of consecration to be present. John Johnson managed to use 1662, and uncounted other clergy had inserted quiet prayers of one kind or another into its celebration. Seabury would need to defend the rite in regard to its modification the following year. Nonetheless, the text as modified in 1789 clearly invoked blessing on the elements and allowed room for varieties of "intention." This was certainly on the whole more satisfactory to Seabury than would have been anything John Johnson of Cranbrook had to use. Americans were now possessed of a eucharistic prayer that preserved the shape and action of the prayers Seabury believed to be the determinative deposit of the primitive church.

Again, the Holy Communion service originated in the House of Deputies, where Parker, now "Dr. Parker" in White's account, had insisted that

---

50. 1549 has "holy Spirit and word," while 1637 establishes the familiar pattern of "word and holy Spirit." On the intriguing question of a word-epiclesis, see John H. McKenna, *Eucharist and Holy Spirit,* Alcuin Club Collections 57 (Great Wakering, U.K.: Mayhew-McCrimmon, 1975).

1662 be the basis of all revision, creating no little excitement.[51] None of the deputies alleged to have been inclined toward the use of the Scottish prayer suggested it. After the work put in by the bishops, Smith was summoned to their meeting, where it is likely that any negotiation on the epiclesis took place. We have White's word that Smith as president, quelled opposition from a few deputies with some "pointed" words. There is also the report that Smith made critics hold their tongues while he eloquently declaimed the prayer. While there is not much evidence to support this story, Smith was indeed a famous orator, and despite all his conflicted personal motives certainly did want to advance the unity of the church. There are bits of lore that someone out of sympathy with Smith might prefer not to be true, but there is no reason to doubt this one.

There are other Nonjuror influences, via Seabury, on the 1789 Holy Communion liturgy. The summary of the law comes into the rite. The prayer for grace to keep the commandments comes from the Scottish use; in the English book it is found at the end of the Holy Communion service, and was also used in the confirmation service in both 1662 and the American book. "Glory be to thee, O Lord" was restored. Of principal theological importance is how allowance is made for supplementary consecration: The entire prayer is to be said through the invocation of the Holy Spirit. A Scottish and Connecticut voice sounded in the typography of WHICH WE NOW OFFER UNTO THEE, but this was almost immediately altered.[52]

The Proposed Book was not without its voice in the 1789 revision, and it was an important voice. The Collects, epistles, and gospels are those of 1785, with additional modernizations. The proper preface for Trinity is optional, a gesture of pronounced latitude, although one would also argue that the traditional preface and its alternative fail to be engaging specimens of liturgical language.

The Rest of the Prayer Book

The details of the revision can be studied in Appendices A-2 and A-3 and in Hatchett's detailed recounting.[53] Here the interest is in the alterations that would have impact on Seabury and his Connecticut colleagues.

---

51. White1, 147.
52. White would still feel some embarrassment over this apparent slip in his *Memoirs*. See ibid., 178f.
53. Hatchett1, 249ff.

They would have rejoiced to see the stunning preface improved by the excision of its tendentious passages. Welcome would be the restoration of the complete Psalter (with alternatives). The Sunday lessons followed the trend of the Proposed Book, giving the prophets more voice on Sundays. It is hard to know how welcome the Ash Wednesday propers were, inasmuch as they were a substitution of the Commination service proposed by the bishops and declined by the deputies. The observance of Thanksgiving Day is retained, and the Fourth of July service departs (propers were later added for that day).

The modernization of language had been in both the Middletown and Boston proposals, and the Proposed Book's modernizations are advanced upon. "Publick" and "rubrick" become "public" and "rubric." "Priest" replaces "minister" in those places where a deacon may not preside.

In the daily office, the word "Absolution" returns, as does permission to repeat the Gloria Patri. The Benedicite is restored, in altered form, as an alternative to Te Deum. The Benedictus, however, is shorn of the verses beginning "And thou, child." While the *descensus* reappears, in the 1790 printed version of the book it does so with a permissive rubric allowing omission or the substitution of "He went to the place of departed spirits," to the horror of Seabury, who knew that his clergy had not given carte blanche to revision, and to the embarrassment of White, who knew well what the bishops thought they had agreed to. Despite that troubling occurrence, the Nicene Creed was welcomed back, and printed as an alternative to the Apostles' Creed. Even in the Eucharist, however, the Apostles' Creed could be substituted for it, except on Christmas, Easter, Ascension, and Trinity.

Following Middletown and a host of other proposals, the Kyrie and second Lord's Prayer are deleted from the office, and the suffrages that follow are trimmed. The High Churchman would have mourned the loss of the Magnificat and Nunc Dimittis, which were not to be restored until 1892.

Those from Connecticut studying the book for the first time may have noted that prayers "for a sick person," "for a sick child," "in great sickness and mortality," and "for a person or persons going to sea" had a familiar ring, and that "For a person under Necessity" was somewhat familiar. They were from Seabury's notebook, and would be published again in his office book and Psalter of 1795. Like the few physician-clergy left today, Seabury sometimes found himself practicing two professions at once, so it is not surprising that most of the occasional prayers he offered to those already in store from 1785 should relate to health. In his notebook they bear the titles, "Prayer . . . used at New London during the prevalence of The Dysentery in the year 1787," "For a sick child," "For a person bound to Sea," "For a sick person who desires the prayers of the Church," and "For a person under Affliction." They reflect existing English prayers, and went into 1789 almost unedited from the version Seabury carried. A phrase was clipped from the prayer for a sick child, and only the prayer for a person bound to sea suffered two excisions and one small change. This last prayer had its basis in the Prayers at Sea from 1662, and that for a sick child was modified from petitions in the Visitation of the Sick in 1662 as well. "For a person under Affliction" was the most modified.

Thanksgivings were added for recovery from sickness and for a safe return from a sea voyage. The desideratum shared by the liturgical right and left in the century before, that there be a greater variety of prayers, thus began to be met.

High Church folk were no doubt pleased to see the return of the language of regeneration to the baptismal rite. At the same time there was still considerable fluidity when compared with 1662. Consignation is optional, prayers can be omitted, and gone is the informational rubric to the effect that unbaptized infants who die are "undoubtedly saved." The catechism is repaired to reflect regeneration and the promises made for the baptized. As proposed at Middletown, but not Boston, there is permission to omit the gospel (and the addressing and prayer following).

The marriage service is slightly restored, but largely remains a very thin rite. To it, however, are added the joining of the couple together, and the Lord's Prayer after the giving of the ring. Lost entirely is the Cranmerian intention that this service should lead into the Eucharist.

Visitation of the sick goes beyond the Proposed Book, and omits entirely the opportunity for confession and absolution, which would be a disappointment in the North. The burial service would not appear much improved from the Proposed Book, although the collect "with whom do live the souls" was restored as in 1662. A modified form of the Churching of Women reappeared, but with the additional rubric that the customary offerings be applied to assist needy women in childbirth, a rubric that would be interpreted in a variety ways, sometimes being used to help support institutions for the care of mothers and/or children in difficult situations. Prisoners were still to be visited according the 1711 Irish form, which is the one spot where 1789 retained provision for private confession.

Tate and Brady's "new version" of the entire metrical Psalter was supplied, but the number of hymns was trimmed drastically. This need not be, although it has been, attributed to White's dislike of hymns. Many of those removed were replaced when the entire metrical Psalter was included.

Seabury's Notebook and Liturgical Supplements

Begun no earlier than 1787 (according to the date in the communicant list), Seabury's liturgical notebook has been discussed several times in accounts of the 1789 book. It begins with the list of communicants at St. James in New London. Then follow "Occasional Prayers to be used in Churches," dating from the 1787 dysentery epidemic, prayers that were taken up into the 1789 prayer book. Next is "A Form for Consecrating Churches, Chapels, and Church Yards, or places of Burial," following the 1712 order of the English Convocation and anticipating the American order of 1799. The service was transcribed for use at the dedication of the new St. James in New London in September 1787.

The deed follows. After the deed there is the Lenten prayer Seabury set forth to be used beginning with Ash Wednesday in 1789. This gives us a clear earliest date of 1789 for what comes next. The next item is Seabury's version of the Scottish prayer, entitled "Consecration of the Holy Eucharist." It is not evidence that Seabury's 1786 rite was being ignored, but a prayer copied out for reference at the General Convention, where all the prayers in the book were offered to the new liturgy. Apparently there was no time or interest in establishing an order for consecrating churches, but that would follow in a few conventions.

The next section invites speculation. Except for the communicants' list, all the contents of the book so far appear to have been copied out at one time, probably in preparation for General Convention. After this liturgical section there are copied out in a weak and shaky hand some passages of works by Thomas Wilson, deceased bishop of Sodor and Man. The first is an epiclesis of the Spirit, very much in the style of the Eastern prayers, adding phrase to phrase by way of intensification. From another of Wilson's books come a more modest epiclesis and a supplication for the entire church, the living and the dead. The rest are prayers in preparation for death. Together with the weak hand, they suggest that this part of the notebook was produced during a time of illness or stress. The two epicleses suggest that Seabury considered the 1789 Eucharist as needing supplementation. Beyond that we know nothing. Two sets of prayers and readings follow for the opening of courts, the second in 1795. After Seabury's death the following year, the book may have fallen into Bishop Jarvis's hands, for there follow a list of churches consecrated by the two bishops.

That is the end of the first part of the book. The second begins from the back of the (inverted) book. It is a collection of music in Seabury's (stronger) hand. The first section is a selection of hymn tunes in two parts. For each Seabury gives a melody and a bass line. No notation for realizing the bass is included. The tunes are, as Seabury cites them, THE 100TH PSALM, WELLS, BRAY, PLYMOUTH, BANGOR, MEAR, S. MARTINS, WANTAGE, NEWBURY, FIRST PSALM, 102 PSALM, PARINGDON, PORTSMOUTH, WIRKSWORTH, NEWCASTLE, LITTLE MARLBOROUGH, 46TH PSALM, S. HELENS, 149TH PSALM or HANOVER, and 136TH PSALM or BETHESDA. The liturgical music includes both text and music, called "Chaunts," and given with Seabury's titles, including an abbreviation of Venite Exultemus, and also including the banished Magnificat. No composers are indicated for the hymns or chants. The Venite is abbreviated — something of a common practice, as the Proposed Book and 1789 each abbreviate Psalm 95 in their own way. Much more startling is the inclusion of Magnificat and a restored Benedictus. Combined with the alternative epicleses, we have evidence that there were spots in the 1789 book where Seabury felt he must go his own way. The other possibility is that the Magnificat was copied into the book before 1789, when those canticles were still used. No one actually knows what this musical collection was for, or whether it had any connection to public worship.

What inclines one to the possibility that he was supplementing 1789 is Seabury's publication at New London in 1795 of *The Psalter or Psalms of David, Pointed as They are to be Sung or Said in Churches, With the Order for Morning and Evening Prayer Daily throughout the Year.*[54] "Samuel, Bishop of Connecticut and Rhode Island," signs the prefatory "Advertisement" (in the sense of "information"). In it Seabury explains the reasons for changing the curses into the future tense (putting the onus on God), and indicating that modernization of obscure English has also taken place. Morning and Evening Prayer in this book follow the 1789 edition with some changes. The Apostles' Creed is intact and not footnoted or variable in any way, and the Athanasian Creed is printed at the end of Evening Prayer, but with no indication of how or when it is to be used. The collects, prayers, and thanksgiving are reproduced, as is the Catechism of 1789.

---

54. The book is reproduced in its entirety in SUI, 87ff.

Then comes the Psalter with the language altered as Seabury described and with the insertion of "musical colons" into each verse.

That office book was not Seabury's only liturgical publication. In 1793 Seabury published daily office propers and a lengthy prayer to be used on October 9, apparently a day of prayer called for by the state, in response to a yellow fever outbreak.[55]

Whether or not there should be a separate burial office for children is a question that has been with the Episcopal Church for many years. The little correspondence remaining from the work preparing for the 1928 revision illustrates how difficult a topic this was. The prayer book of 1979 included no such rite, just as it had only one baptismal rite. General Convention in 2000 approved as an authorized supplement a service for the burial of a child. The absence of such a service in the 1789 prayer book was felt. Seabury published in 1795 (according to Cameron, as the pamphlet is undated) a booklet of prayers. The surviving copy may have been part of a larger work, as there are given incipits of other prayers at certain points, indicating use within a larger liturgical structure or context. The contents were "A Prayer for the Courts of Justice," the incipit of the prayer for All Conditions of Men, the incipit of the General Thanksgiving, a "Prayer for the General Assembly," and "A Burial for Infants who depart this life before they have polluted their baptism by actual sin, by Bishop Seabury."[56] The committal has none of the tentative language of burial rites that were proposed, but commits the body "in sure and certain hope of its resurrection to eternal life through our Lord Jesus Christ, who is the resurrection and the life...." After the last prayer and before the Grace comes a section that is both an allocution and a prayer:

> Our deceased Infants who have been baptized into the death of Jesus Christ, shall all be delivered from the hand of the enemy — the great destroyer death, and shall return to their own border [Jer. 31:16, 17], thy heavenly kingdom, O God; for this is the will of the Father, that of all he hath given to the Son, he should lose nothing, but should raise it up again at the last day.

What all these supplements suggest is that just as we know that in parts of the church, sections of the official liturgy were dropped (most notoriously the ante-communion), in other places clergy would make additions.

---

55. Ibid., 78.
56. Text in *Parallels*, 2:496f.; SUI, 84ff.

In the nineteenth-century church this condition would change, and protest would arise mid-century against rigid uniformity.

The General Convention had profited from the 1785–86 experience: The editorial committee was given no leave to alter the texts adopted. Seabury went home thinking there was a book that he and his clergy could use without offense to their consciences. We have already noted Seabury's justifiable anger and White's embarrassment at the errors made over the carefully negotiated return of the *descensus*. In terms of the stand his clergy had taken preconvention, he was well within his rights to abandon the book there and then, as the *descensus* was not a small thing, but one of the key issues in revision. Instead of denouncing it, Seabury tried to promote the book, and the clergy adopted it at their convocation in the autumn of 1790. In addition to the approach taken successfully with Ebenezer Dibblee's resistance to the book, there are two other examples worth recounting.

Fraternal and sweet reason were the proper key with Dibblee. With Benjamin Gardiner, who was deeply troubled by the new epiclesis, Seabury takes the approach of scholar and teacher in a passage we have already seen:

> It must be a strange conscience that cannot communicate under its use. The alteration which you advert to... was made for those Church people who were too weak to digest strong meat, but must be fed with milk. I think the alteration for the worse, but not an essential one, All glory is ascribed to God — the Elements are blessed with thanks-giving — there is an oblation of them made to the Almighty Father — the descent of the Holy Ghost is involved to sanctify them — And all is concluded in the name, and through the merit of Jesus Christ — all of which are wanting in the English Office.[57]

When the Convocation adopted the 1789 book, one priest rose to speak against it, James Sayre, who also had opposed Seabury's election, and who saw the new liturgy as a destructive plot against orthodoxy. One of those people whose personality flaws fasten themselves onto external issues, he was a terribly destructive force, and his story could fill a monograph. He was a man whom Seabury trusted and recommended, but is remembered solely for what and whom he opposed, and he convinced many in his parish to join him in a slough of negativity. In his case, Seabury had to remain

---

57. Samuel Seabury to Benjamin Gardiner, April 13, 1790, *SAC*, 34.

firm. In 1792 he felt obliged to write to Sayre's Stratford parish, informing
them of how Sayre had misled them. Seabury involved the clergy in these
proceedings from the first. Despite the work of bishop and colleagues,
Sayre was obdurate, and his destructiveness grew. The parish was recon-
ciled to the church, but Sayre was not, even after leaving his rectorship.
It was Seabury's duty to depose him, and he did so through a broadside
distributed to the clergy of Connecticut and Rhode Island. It would not
be the last time in the history of the Episcopal Church that such charges
would arise.

> Whereas the Rev. Mr. James Sayre, formerly Rector of Trinity Church
> in Newport in Rhode-Island, having removed into Connecticut, hath
> behaved himself in a very undutiful and unchristian manner, in de-
> praving the Liturgy, contravening the government, and despising
> the discipline of the Protestant Episcopal Church in America — in
> traducing, reviling, and misrepresenting the Bishop and Clergy of
> Connecticut, thereby endeavouring to excite schism, and divisions,
> and to destroy the peace and unity of the Church; and hath also
> withdrawn himself from her Communion. . . . [58]

In three different ways, Seabury did what he had to do to honor both the
commitments he made in Philadelphia and at the signing of the Concordat.

Seabury is revealed in the post-1789 years as consistent with the image
we have of him up until that time, not afraid of change in general, but
enormously conservative when there was suggested any change that "lowered" the doctrine borne by liturgy. There is no clearer example of his
clinging to what he believed in than the 1792 adoption of an Ordinal. He
alone in the House of Bishops wished to keep the English formula:

> Receive the Holy Ghost for the Office and Work of a Priest in the
> Church of God, now committed unto thee by the Imposition of our
> hands. Whose sins thou dost forgive, they are forgiven; and whose
> sins thou dost retain they are retained. And be thou a faithful Dis-
> penser of the Word of God, and of his holy Sacraments; In the Name
> of the Father, and of the Son, and of the Holy Ghost. Amen.

What was proposed was as follows:

> Take thou Authority to execute the Office of a Priest in the Church
> of God, now committed to thee by the Imposition of our hands. And

---

58. Complete text in SUI, 77.

be thou a faithful Dispenser of the Word of God, and of his holy Sacraments; In the Name of the Father, and of the Son, and of the Holy Ghost. Amen.

To modern eyes, both forms are disappointing; modern Episcopalians are used to ordination conferred within a prayer modeled on ancient texts. This situation must have seemed to Seabury as though it were 1786 again. The proposed formula did not link the laying-on of hands with the Holy Spirit, and did not mention the authority to absolve. Because of Seabury's tenacity the traditional vocabulary was retained at least as an option. His journal records the following prayer on this occasion:

All glory be ascribed to God for all his goodness to his Church in the American States. In his goodness I confide for the continuance of that holy episcopate which is now begun to be communicated in this country. May it rebound to his glory, and the good of his Church, though Jesus Christ. Amen.

In October 1789, the Episcopal Church had become one, "as far as its state would allow," because to Seabury's satisfaction it also chose to show itself to be catholic and apostolic. In terms of its liturgical heritage and constitution, Seabury had been more useful to the church than he imagined.

CONCLUSION

To the extent that the foregoing work is accurate, the very first thing that we can revise in the revisionist account of Bishop Seabury is the question of character. Hatchett's notion of Seabury in a "panic" cannot be demonstrated. Wrong he may well have been on many things from today's point of view, but he said what he meant to say, and kept his word, sometimes at considerable cost — and did so calmly. Seabury's integrity is the most attractive thing about him.

We see a man whose devotion to duty and willingness to *work* is unparalleled among the first bishops of the Episcopal Church. There can be no doubt that the people of early Connecticut knew their bishop, as did many he served temporarily in New York and Rhode Island. Reading his addresses to the clergy and his *Discourses*, we encounter a clear writer and apt teacher.

We have seen a man willing to risk lasting opprobrium (which he did receive in some circles) for his connection to the Scottish bishops, pariahs that they were at the time. The duty laid on him of bringing the episcopate to Connecticut was uppermost in his awareness during his sojourn in the British Isles in 1784. As an individual, he was very sensitive to criticism, but we see him engaging in conduct that he knew would subject himself to hostile comment because of his commitment.

Seabury's view of ordained ministry in the days of the sporting parson is very high and very demanding. His insistence on usefulness as the hallmark of the clerical estate remains challenging. Similarly, his willingness to take the presbyterate into his confidence and operate collegially with them challenges some modern models of episcopal ministry. Seabury's kindness to cranky but faithful old Ebenezer Dibblee is instructive. Seabury converted Dibblee by actually loving him. With James Sayre, on the other hand, we have seen that Seabury knew where the boundary was, and with genuine regret observed it. He had lived with real terrorists during the war, and was not about to tolerate them in the church.

In the great matter of Middletown, we have seen a bishop with a sense of proportion. He calmly assessed the fact that there were more issues in the new church than liturgy, and put matters in perspective, suspending liturgical discussion until the fellowship was solid; one must keep the Church together as a community in communion before one can meaningfully ask liturgical questions of it. What Seabury's critics do not note is that his promise to resume liturgical revision when "tempers have cooled" was a promise he kept fully. It sometimes seems that those with a passion for liturgical reform are quite willing to have a perfect liturgy for a church with no remaining members. Seabury's example is instructive in this regard.

Considering the concessions Seabury gained in the summer and fall of 1789, we must reassess his virtues as a strategist. He wanted both union and unity, but not at the cost of his beliefs about the nature and constitution of the church. Only when those were assured and his own orders unquestionably acknowledged, would he go to General Convention. His ability to wait this out, rather than cave into the anxious need for closure, shows us a man confident enough to endure the tension. His letters have shown us a man who felt frustration, and also a man who would not accept just any solution that would alleviate that frustration.

There is a distinct debt owed to Seabury. Over twenty-five years ago in Philadelphia women deacons were ordained priests, validly but irregularly. Their willingness to endure questionable status and the willingness of the ordaining bishops to endure censure moved the Episcopal Church to begin ordaining women to the presbyterate. Similarly, without Seabury's unusual consecration in Scotland, there is no reason to believe that the Whigs would ever have permitted the episcopate to be transmitted to the United States. As with the Philadelphia ordinations, once Seabury appeared in the episcopal character, a way was very quickly found to initiate change. It is not too much of a stretch to say that without Seabury's risk-taking, for many years, if not for many decades, the nearest Anglican bishop may well have been in Canada.

When I prepare to lecture on them, as I have for more than twenty years, I must review in detail the variations in structure and content of various Anglican eucharistic rites, and I have the benefit of Brightman's *The English Rite* and other analytical tools. (*Prayer Book Parallels* was born as a study tool for myself.) Seabury's reference to the liturgy of 1549 when he wrote about the Eucharist after his consecration squares with then-common use for any full anaphora. If it was an error, it is at worst a slip that anyone who must explain Anglican liturgy could make. Nonetheless, there is no reason to suppose that the bishop-physician was a liturgical dunce who plunged himself into a crash course and somehow came up with the Communion Office. The importance of Samuel Johnson as his teacher, the Nonjuror phenomenon as recent history, and his early sermon on the Eucharist all indicate a man on top of his subject. We do see him studying further the unnamed books he got from the Scots. The editing of the Communion Office demonstrates subtleties of phrase or nuance that one can only admire.

Living as we do in a period when ecclesiastical disputes are seldom marked by kindness or forbearance, Seabury strikingly represent a model of vigorous disagreement that stops short of breaking charity.

We have thus seen a man who had a stamina of personality that allowed great risks to be taken on the one hand, and great patience to be exercised on the other. He was a pastor and colleague to his presbyters, a teacher to them and to the laity, and a liturgical editor with an amazingly deft touch. Above all, as the version of the Nicene Creed as used by Episcopalians until 1979 read, he gave himself to the vision of a church that was one, catholic, and apostolic. It is perhaps true that each of those words bears different freight today, but Seabury's devotion to them requires more than a passing nod in an indifferent collect.

BIBLIOGRAPHY

Adams, John. *The Works of John Adams.* 10 vols. Boston, 1850–56.

Address of the Episcopal Clergy of Connecticut, to the Right Reverend Bishop Seabury, with the Bishop's Answer and, a Sermon, Before the Convention at Middletown, August 3d, 1785.... Also Bishop Seabury's First Charge, to the Clergy of His Diocess, [sic] Delivered at Middletown, August 4th, 1785. With a List of the Succession of Scot's Bishops, from the Revolution 1688, to the Present Time. New Haven, Conn.: Thomas and Samuel Green, 1785.

Agnew, Christopher M. "The Reverend Charles Wharton, Bishop William White, and the Proposed Book of Common Prayer, 1785." *Anglican and Episcopal History* 58 (December 1989): 510–25.

Baxter, Simeon. *Tyrannicide Proved Lawful, from the Practice and Writings of Jews, Heathens, and Christians. A Discourse Delivered in the Mines at Symsbury. In the Colony of Connecticut, to the Loyalists Confined There.* London, 1782.

Beardsley, Eben Edwards. *Life and Correspondence of the Right Reverend Samuel Seabury, D.D., First Bishop of Connecticut, and of the Episcopal Church in the United States of America.* Boston: Houghton, Mifflin, 1881.

Beardsley, William A. *The History of the Episcopal Church in Connecticut, from the Settlement of the Colony to the Death of Bishop Seabury.* New York: Hurd and Houghton, 1868.

———. "The Episcopate of Bishop Seabury." *Historical Magazine of the Protestant Episcopal Church* 3 (1934): 224ff.

Berens, John F. "'A God of Order and Not of Confusion': The American Loyalists and Divine Providence, 1774–1783." *Historical Magazine of the Protestant Episcopal Church* 47 (1978): 197–219.

Bowman, Larry G. *Captive Americans.* Athens: Ohio University Press, 1976.

Brett, Thomas. *A Collection of the Principal Liturgies, Used by the Christian Church ... With a Dissertation upon them....* London, 1720.

Bridenbaugh, Carl. *Mitre and Sceptre: Transatlantic Faiths, Ideas, Personalities, and Politics.* New York: Oxford University Press, 1962.

Buxbaum, Melvin H. "Benjamin Franklin and William Smith, Their School and Their Dispute." *Historical Magazine of the Protestant Episcopal Church* 39 (1970): 361–82.

Buxton, Richard F. *Eucharist and Institution Narrative: A Study in the Roman and Anglican Traditions of the Consecration of the Eucharist from the Eighth to the Twentieth Centuries.* Alcuin Club Collections 58. Great Wakering, U.K.: Mayhew-McCrimmon, 1976.

Calcote, A. Dean. "The Proposed Prayer Book of 1785." *Historical Magazine of the Protestant Episcopal Church* 46 (1977): 275–95.

Cameron, Kenneth Walter. *Connecticut's First Diocesan.* Hartford, Conn.: Transcendental Books, 1985.

———. "Two Bishops and Their Mitres," *The Historiographer* 122 (December 1982): 43–47.

Cameron, Kenneth Walter, ed. *Abraham Jarvis, Connecticut's Second Episcopal Bishop: Materials for a Biography.* Hartford, Conn.: Transcendental Books, 1983.

———. *The Anglican Episcopate in Connecticut 1784–1899.* Hartford, Conn.: Transcendental Books, 1970.

———. *The Church of England in Pre-Revolutionary Connecticut.* Hartford, Conn.: Transcendental Books, 1976.

———. *Colonial Anglicanism in New England.* Hartford, Conn.: Transcendental Books, 1981.

———. *The Correspondence of Loyalist Samuel Peters: An Inventory of Additions.* Hartford, Conn.: Transcendental Books, 1985.

———. *Early Anglicanism in Connecticut.* Hartford, Conn.: Transcendental Books, 1962.

———. *The Episcopal Church in Connecticut and New England.* Hartford, Conn.: Transcendental Books, 1981.

———. *The Ethos of Anglicanism in Colonial New England and New York.* Hartford, Conn.: Transcendental Books, 1981.

———. *The Papers of Loyalist Samuel Peters.* Hartford, Conn.: Transcendental Books, 1978.

———. *Samuel Seabury, 1729–1796: His Election, Consecration and Reception. The Documentary History of Francis L. Hawks and William Stevens Perry, reedited with an Index.* Hartford, Conn.: Transcendental Books, 1978.

———. *Samuel Seabury among His Contemporaries.* Hartford, Conn.: Transcendental Books, 1980.

———. *Seabury Traditions: The Reconstructed Journal of Connecticut's First Diocesan.* 2 vols. Hartford, Conn.: Transcendental Books, 1983.

Cardwell, Edward. *A History of Conferences and Other Proceedings Connected with the revision of the Book of Common Prayer.* Oxford: University Press, 1840.

Chambers, Walter. *Samuel Seabury: A Challenge.* New York: Century, 1932.

Chorley E. Clowes. *The New American Prayer Book.* New York: Macmillan, 1930.

———. "Samuel Provoost, First Bishop of New York." *Historical Magazine of the Protestant Episcopal Church* 2, no. 2 (June 1933): 1–25.

Clark, J. C. D. *The Language of Liberty 1660–1832: Political Discourse and Social Dynamics in the Anglo-American World.* Cambridge: Cambridge University Press, 1994.

———. *Samuel Johnson: Literature, Religion and English Cultural Politics from the Restoration to Romanticism.* Cambridge: Cambridge University Press, 1994.

Colley, Linda. *Britons.* New Haven, Conn.: Yale University Press, 1994.

Cornwall, Robert D. "Divine Right Monarchy: Henry Dodwell's Critique of the Reformation and Defense of the Nonjuror Bishops." *Anglican and Episcopal History* 68 (1999): 37–66.

———. *Visible and Apostolic: The Constitution of the Church in High Church Anglican and Non-Juror Thought.* Newark: University of Delaware Press, 1993.

Cross, Arthur L. *The Anglican Episcopate and the American Colonies.* New York and London: Longmans, Green, 1902.

Davidson, Elizabeth. *The Establishment of the English Church in the Continental American Colonies.* Durham, N.C.: Duke University Press, 1936.

Davies, Horton. *The Worship of the American Puritans, 1629–1730.* New York: Peter Lang, 1990.

Dearn, Lloyd F. *Samuel Johnson (1696–1772).* Hartford, Conn.: Transcendental Books, 1980.

DeMille, George E. "One-Man Seminary." *Historical Magazine of the Protestant Episcopal Church* 37 (1969): 373–79.

Dibblee, Ebenezer. "Letters of the Reverend Doctor Ebenezer Dibblee, of Stamford, to the Reverend Doctor Samuel Peters, Loyalist Refugee in London, 1784–1793." *Historical Magazine of the Protestant Episcopal Church* 1, no. 1 (March 1932): 51–85.

Dix, Morgan. *The Parish of Trinity Church in the City of New York.* Vol. 2. New York: Putnam, 1901.

Doll, Peter M. *Revolution, Religion and National Identity.* Madison, N.J.: Farleigh Dickinson University Press, 2000.

Dugmore, C. W. *Eucharistic Doctrine in England from Hooker to Waterland.* London: SPCK, 1942.

Dzielska, Maria. *Hypatia of Alexandria.* Cambridge: Harvard University Press, 1995.

Echlin, Edward P. *The Anglican Eucharist in Ecumenical Perspective.* New York: Seabury, 1968.

Fawcett, Timothy J. *The Liturgy of Comprehension, 1689.* Southend-on-Sea, U.K.: Mayhew-McCrimmon, 1973.

"Franklin and His Friends and Their Machines." *Science and Technology* 15, no. 3 (1999): 28–34.

French, Hannah D. "Caleb Buglass, Binder of the Proposed Book of Common Prayer, Philadelphia, 1786," offprint from Winterthur Portfolio 6. Published for the H. F. duPont Winterthur Museum by the University Press of Virginia, Charlottesville, 1970.

Gable, Martin Dewey, Jr. "The Hymnody of the Church, 1789-1832." *Historical Magazine of the Protestant Episcopal Church* 36 (1967): 249–70.

Gegenheim, Albert Frank. *William Smith, Educator and Churchman, 1727–1803.* Pennsylvania Lives 7. Philadelphia: University of Pennsylvania Press, 1943.

Gerardi, Donald F. M. "Samuel Johnson and the Yale 'Apostasy' of 1722: The Challenge of Anglican Sacramentalism to the New England Way." *Historical Magazine of the Protestant Episcopal Church* 47 (1968): 153–75.

Greene, Donald. "Latitudinarianism Reconsidered." *Anglican and Episcopal History* 62, no. 2 (June 1993): 159–74.

Gregory, Jeremy. *Restoration, Reformation and Reform, 1660–1828.* Oxford: Clarendon Press, 2000.

Griffen, Martin I. J. *Latitudinariansim in the Seventeenth-Century Church of England.* Leiden: E. J. Brill, 1992.

Grisbroke, W. Jardine. *Anglican Liturgies of the Seventeenth and Eighteenth Centuries.* London: SPCK, 1958.

Guelzo, Allen C. *For the Union of Evangelical Christendom: The Irony of the Reformed Episcopalians.* University Park: Pennsylvania State University Press, 1994.

Gunderson, Joan. "The Search for Good Men: Recruiting Ministers in Colonial Virginia." *Historical Magazine of the Protestant Episcopal Church* 48 (1979): 453–64.

Hamilton, Alexander. *The Farmer Refuted.* New York, 1775.

———. *A Full Vindication of the Measures of Congress.* New York, 1774.

Hatchett, Marion J. "Benjamin Franklin's Prayer Book." In *This Sacred History.* Ed. Donald S. Armentrout. Cambridge, Mass.: Cowley, 1990.

———. *The Making of the First American Book of Common Prayer, 1776–1789.* New York: Seabury Press, 1982.

———. "The Making of the First American Prayer Book" Th.D. thesis, General Theological Seminary (New York), 1972.

———. "A Sunday Service of 1776 or Thereabouts." *Historical Magazine of the Protestant Episcopal Church* 45 (December 1976): 369–85.

Hawks, Francis L., and William Stevens Perry. *Documentary History of the Protestant Episcopal Church in the United States of America. Connecticut.* 2 vols. New York: J. Pott, 1863, 1864.

Hayden, Sydney. *Washington and His Masonic Compeers.* New York, 1867.

Hill, Harvey. "Worship in the Ecclesiology of William White." *Anglican and Episcopal History* 62, no. 3 (September 1993): 317–42.

Hogue, William. "The Religious Conspiracy Theory of the American Revolution: Anglican Motive." *Church History* 45, no. 3 (September 1976): 277–92.

Holifield, E. Brooks. "Peace, Conflict, and Ritual in Puritan Congregations." *Journal of Interdisciplinary History* 23, no. 3 (Winter 1993): 551–70.

Holmes, David L. "The Episcopal Church and the American Revolution." *Historical Magazine of the Protestant Episcopal Church* 47 (1978): 261–91.

Jarvis, Samuel Farmar. "Historical Reminiscences of Bishop Jarvis," Addresses Delivered at Trinity Church, New Haven, 1898, pp. 7–24. Reprinted in Kenneth Walter Cameron, *The Anglican Episcopate in Connecticut (1784–1899).* Hartford, Conn.: Transcendental Books, 1970.

———. "Memoir of Bishop Jarvis," *The Evergreen* 3, no. 4 (April 1846): 97–99; no. 5 (May 1846): 147–53; no. 6 (June 1846): 173–79. Reprinted in Kenneth Walter Cameron, *The Anglican Episcopate in Connecticut (1784–1899).* Hartford, Conn.: Transcendental Books, 1970.

Johnson, John. *The Unbloody Sacrifice, and Altar Unveiled and Supported.* 2d ed. London, 1724.

Johnson, Samuel. *Samuel Johnson, President of King's College: His Career and Writings.* Edited by Herbert and Carol Schneider. 4 vols. New York: Columbia University Press, 1929.

Jones, Thomas Firth. *A Pair of Lawn Sleeves: A Biography of William Smith (1727–1803).* Philadelphia: Chilton, 1972.

Journals of the General Conventions of the Protestant Episcopal Church in the United States of America, from the Year 1784, to the Year 1814. Philadelphia: John Bieren, 1817.

King's Chapel. *A Liturgy Collected Principally from the Book of Common Prayer, for the Use of the First Episcopal Church in Boston; Together with the Psalter, or Psalms of David.* Boston, 1785.

Kirkpatrick, Frank G. "Samuel Seabury: Virtue and Christian Community in Late Eighteenth Century America." *Anglican Theological Review* 74, no. 3 (1992): 317–33.

Lathbury, Thomas. *A History of the Nonjurors: The Controversies and Writings; With Remarks on Some of the Rubrics in the Book of Common Prayer.* London, 1845.

Lively, Bruce R. "William Smith, the College and Academy of Philadelphia and Pennsylvania Politics, 1753–1758." *Historical Magazine of the Protestant Episcopal Church* 38, no. 3 (1969): 269ff.

Loveland, Clara. *The Critical Years: The Reconstruction of the Anglican Church in the United States of America, 1780–1789.* Greenwich, Conn.: Seabury, 1956.

Mampoteng, Charles. "The New England Clergy in the American Revolution." *Historical Magazine of the Protestant Episcopal Church* 9 (1940)" 267–303.

Marshall, Paul V. *Prayer Book Parallels.* 2 vols. New York: Church Publishing Incorporated, 1989, 1990.

———. *The Voice of a Stranger.* New York: Church Publishing Incorporated, 1994.

McAdoo, H. R. *The Eucharistic Theology of Jeremy Taylor Today.* Norwich, Norfolk: Canterbury Press, 1988.

McEnerney, John I., trans. *St. Cyril of Alexandria, Letters.* The Fathers of the Church. Washington, D.C.: Catholic University of America, 1987.

McGarvey, William. *Liturgiae Americanae.* Philadelphia: Church Publishing Company, 1895, 1907.

McKenna, John H. *Eucharist and Holy Spirit.* Alcuin Club Collections 57. Great Wakering, U.K.: Alcuin Club, 1965.

Meyers, Ruth. *Re-Visioning Baptism in the Episcopal Church.* New York: Church Publishing Incorporated, 1997.

Middleton, Arthur Pierce. "Prayer Book Revision Explained: Sermons on the Liturgy by Joseph Bend, Rector of St. Paul's, Baltimore, 1791–1812." *Anglican and Episcopal History* 60 (March 1991): 57–74.

Miller, Glenn T. "Fear God and Honour the King: The Failure of Loyalist Civil Theology in the Revolutionary Crisis." *Historical Magazine of the Protestant Episcopal Church* 47 (1978): 221–42.

Mills, Frederick V., Sr., *Bishops by Ballot: An Eighteenth-Century Ecclesiastical Revolution.* New York: Oxford University Press, 1978.

Mitgang, Herbert. *The Man Who Rode the Tiger.* New York: Viking, 1963.

Morgan, John H. *Seabury in Memoriam.* South Bend, Ind.: Parish Life Institute, University of Notre Dame, 1983.

Moriarty, Michael. *The Liturgical Revolution.* New York: Church Publishing Incorporated, 1997.

Nissenbaum, Stephen. *The Battle for Christmas.* New York: Vintage, 1997.

Northrop, William and John. *The Insolence of Office: The Story of the Seabury Investigations.* New York: G. P. Putnam's Sons, 1932.

Northup, Lesley A. *The 1892 Book of Common Prayer.* Lewiston, N.Y.: E. Mellen Press, 1993.

Norton, John N. *Life of Bishop Provoost.* New York, 1859.

————. *The Life of the Rt. Rev. Samuel Seabury,* D.D. New York, 1860.

O'Neil, Maud. "A Struggle for Religious Liberty: An Analysis of the Work of the S.P.G. in Connecticut." *Historical Magazine of the Protestant Episcopal Church* 20 (June 1951), 173–89.

Overton, J. H. *The Nonjurors: Their Lives, Principles, and Writings.* London: Smith, Elder & Co., 1902.

Peaston, A. Elliott. *The Prayer Book Reform Movement in the XVIIIth Century.* Oxford: Blackwell, 1940.

Perry, William Stevens. *Journals of the General Convention of the Protestant Episcopal Church in the United States of America.* Vol. 3: *Historical Notes and Documents Illustrating the Organization of the Protestant Episcopal Church in the United States of America.* Claremont, N.H.: Claremont Manufacturing Company, 1874.

Phelps, Noah. *History of Simsbury, Granby, and Canton.* Hartford, Conn.: Case, Tiffany & Burnham, 1845.

Phelps, Richard H. *Newgate of Connecticut and Other Antiquities.* Copper Hill, Conn.: S. D. Viets, 1895.

Porter, Harry Boone. *Jeremy Taylor, Liturgist.* London: SPCK, 1979.

————. *Samuel Seabury: Bishop in a New Nation.* New York: National Council of the Protestant Episcopal Church in the United States of America, 1962.

————. "Toward an Unofficial History of Episcopal Worship," in *Worship Points the Way,* ed. Malcom C. Burson. New York: Seabury, 1981.

Prichard, Robert W. *The Nature of Salvation: Theological Consensus in the Episcopal Church, 1801–73.* Urbana: University of Illinois Press, 1997.

Reardon, John J. "Religious and Other Factors in the Defeat of the 'Standing Order' in Connecticut, 1800–1818." *Historical Magazine of the Protestant Episcopal Church* 30 (June 1961), 93–110.

Remarks on the Proceedings of the Episcopal Conventions for Forming and American Constitution. By a Layman. Boston, 1786.

Rowthorn, Anne W. *Samuel Seabury: A Bicentennial Biography.* New York: Seabury Press, 1983.

St. Peter's Exhortation to Fear God and Honor the King, Explained and Inculcated: in a Discourse Addressed to His Majesty's Provincial Troops, in Camp at King's-Bridge, on Sunday the 28th Sept. 1777. Published at the desire of His Excellency Major General Tryon. New York: Printed by H. Gaine, at the Bible and Crown in Hanover-Square, 1777.

Schnitker, Thaddäus. *The Church's Worship: The 1979 American Book of Common Prayer in a Historical Perspective.* New York: Peter Lang, 1989.

Seabury, Samuel. *Bishop Seabury's Second Charge, to the Clergy of his Diocess, [sic] Delivered at Derby, in the State of Connecticut, On the 22d of September, 1786.* Published at the earnest desire of the Convocation. New Haven, 1786.

————. *An Earnest Persuasive to Frequent Communion; Addressed to those Professors of the Church of England, in Connecticut, Who Neglect That Holy Ordinance.* By the Right Reverend Father in God, Samuel, their Diocesan Bishop. New Haven, 1789.

————. "Discourse delivered in St. John's Church, in Portsmouth, New Hampshire, At the conferring the Order of Priesthood on The Rev. Robert Fowle, A.M.

of Holderness. On the Festival of St. Peter, 1791. By the Right Rev. Samuel Seabury, D.D. Bishop of Connecticut." Boston, 1791

———. *Discourses on Several Subjects. By Samuel Seabury, D.D., Bishop of Connecticut and Rhode-Island.* New York, 1793.

———. *The Letters of a Westchester Farmer.* Edited by C. H. Vance. White Plains: Westchester County Historical Society, 1930.

———. *Miles to Go before I Sleep: Samuel Seabury's Journal from 1791–1795.* Ed. Anne W. Rowthorn. Hartford, Conn.: Church Missions Publishing, 1982.

———. *The New Federalism.* New York: E. P. Dutton, 1950.

———. *Samuel Seabury's Ungathered Imprints.* Edited by Kenneth Walter Cameron. Hartford, Conn.: Transcendental Books, 1978.

Seabury, William Jones. *Memoir of Bishop Seabury.* New York: Edwin S. Gorham, 1908.

Sears, Edmund. *Visible Saints.* New York: New York University Press, 1963.

Skaggs, David C., and Gerald E. Hardagen. "Sinners and Saints: Anglican Clerical Conduct in Colonial Maryland." *Historical Magazine of the Protestant Episcopal Church* 47 (1978): 177–95.

Skinner, John. *Annals of the Scottish Episcopacy, from the Year 1788 to the Year 1816, Inclusive; Being the Period during Which the Late Right Rev. John Skinner, of Aberdeen, Held the Office of Senior Bishop and Primus: of Whom a Biographical Memoir Is Prefixed.* Edinburgh, 1818.

Smith, Horace Wemyss. *Life and Correspondence of the Rev. William Smith.* 2 vols. Philadelphia, 1880.

Smith, James. *The Eucharistic Doctrine of the Later Nonjurors.* Joint Liturgical Studies 46. Cambridge: Grove Books, 2000.

Spaeth, Donald. *The Church in an Age of Danger.* Cambridge: Cambridge University Press, 2000.

Spaulding, James C. "Loyalist as Royalist, Patriot as Puritan: The American Revolution as Repetition of the English Civil Wars." *Church History* 45, no. 3 (September 1976), 329–40.

Spellman, W. M. *The Latitudinarians and the Church of England, 1600-1700.* Athens: University of Georgia Press, 1993.

Spurr, John. *The Restoration Church of England, 1646–1689.* New Haven, Conn.: Yale University Press, 1991.

Steiner, Bruce E. "Anglican Officeholding in Pre-Revolutionary Connecticut: The Parameters of New England Community." *William and Mary Quarterly* 31 (1974): 369–74.

———. "New England Anglicanism: A Genteel Faith?" *William and Mary Quarterly* 28 (1970): 122–35.

———. *Samuel Seabury, 1729–1796: A Study in the High Church Tradition.* Athens: Ohio University Press, 1971.

Stevenson, Kenneth W. "Eucharistic Sacrifice — An Insoluble Liturgical Problem?" *Scottish Journal of Theology* 42, no. 4 (1984): 469–92.

Stow, Charles E. *Simsbury's Part in the War of the American Revolution.* Hartford, Conn.: Lockwood and Brainard, 1896.

Stowe, Walter H. "William White: Ecclesiastical Statesman." *Historical Magazine of the Protestant Episcopal Church* 22 (1953): 372–79.

Sydnor, William. *The Story of the Real Prayer Book, 1549–1979.* Revised edition. Wilton, Conn.: Morehouse Publishing, 1989.

Thoms, Herbert. *Samuel Seabury: Priest and Physician.* Hamden, Conn.: Shoestring Press, 1963.

Vickers, John. "Episcopal Overtures to Coke and Asbury during the Christmas Conference, 1784." *Methodist History* 14, no. 3 (1976): 203–12.

Wand, J. W. C. *The High Church Schism.* London: Faith Press, 1951.

Warnock, James. "Thomas Bradbury Chandler and William Smith: Diversity within Colonial Anglicanism." *Anglican and Episcopal History* 57 (September 1988), 272–97.

Weaver, Glenn. "Anglican-Congregationalist Tensions in Pre-Revolutionary Connecticut." *Historical Magazine of the Protestant Episcopal Church* 26 (1957): 269–85.

Weil, Louis. "Worship and Sacraments in the Teaching of Samuel Johnson of Connecticut: A Study of the Sources and Development of the High Church Tradition in America, 1722–1789." Th.D. thesis, Institute Catholique de Paris, 1972.

White, James F., ed. *John Wesley's Prayer Book: The Sunday Service of the Methodists in North America.* Akron, Ohio: OSL Publications, 1991.

White, William. *The Case of the Episcopal Church in the United States Considered (1782).* Edited, with introduction and appendices, by Richard G. Salomon, *Historical Magazine of the Protestant Episcopal Church* 22 (1953): 435–506.

———. " 'Copy of a Letter to Bishop Hobart, Sept. 1, 1819: Relating at His Request, the Incidents of the Early Part of My Life,' Together with Twenty-One 'Notes Connected with My Letter Bp. Hobart,' Added 'Dec. 21, 1830,' " edited, with introduction and notes by Walter H. Stowe, *Historical Magazine of the Protestant Episcopal Church* 22 (1953): 380–434.

———. *Lectures on the Catechism . . . and Dissertations on Select Subjects in the Lectures.* Philadelphia, 1813.

———. *Memoirs of the Protestant Episcopal Church in the United States of America.* New York: E. P. Dutton & Company, 1880.

Wilberforce, Samuel. *History of the Protestant Episcopal Church in America.* London, 1846.

Wilson, Bird. *Memoir of the Life of the Right Reverend William White, D.D., Bishop of the Protestant Episcopal Church in the State of Pennsylvania.* Philadelphia: James Kay, 1839.

Winslow, O. E. *Jonathan Edwards, 1703–1758: A Biography.* New York: Macmillan, 1940.

Winter, Robert M. "American Churches and the Holy Communion: A Comparative Study in Sacramental Theology, Practice, and Piety in the Episcopal, Presbyterian, Methodist, and German Reformed Traditions, 1607–1875." Ph.D. dissertation, Union Theological Seminary in Virginia, 1988.

Wood, Gordon S. *The Radicalism of the American Revolution.* New York: Alfred A. Knopf, 1992.

INDEX